SEVEN SEAS ENTERTAINMENT PRESENTS

Re:Monster vol. 4

story by **KOGITSUNE KANEKIRU**   art by **HARUYOSHI KOBAYAKAWA**

TRANSLATION
Wesley Bridges

ADAPTATION
Rebecca Spinner

LETTERING AND RETOUCH
Meaghan Tucker

ENGLISH COVER DESIGN
KC Fabellon

PROOFREADER
Janet Houck

EDITOR
Peter Adrian Behravesh

PREPRESS TECHNICIAN
Rhiannon Rasmussen-Silverstein

PRODUCTION MANAGER
Lissa Pattillo

MANAGING EDITOR
Julie Davis

ASSOCIATE PUBLISHER
Adam Arnold

PUBLISHER
Jason DeAngelis

RE:MONSTER VOL. 4
© KOGITSUNE KANEKIRU, HARUYOSHI KOBAYAKAWA 2018.
First published in Japan in 2018 by KOGITSUNE KANEKIRU and
HARUYOSHI KOBAYAKAWA.
English translation rights arranged with AlphaPolis.
Original book design: ansyyqdesign.

Seven Seas press and purchase enquiries can be sent to Marketing Manager
Lianne Sentar at press@gomanga.com. Information regarding the distribution
and purchase of digital editions is available from Digital Manager CK Russell
at digital@gomanga.com.

Seven Seas and the Seven Seas logo are trademarks of
Seven Seas Entertainment. All rights reserved.

ISBN: 978-1-626927-10-0

Printed in Canada

First Printing: April 2020

10 9 8 7 6 5 4 3 2

FOLLOW US ONLINE: *www.sevenseasentertainment.com*

READING DIRECTIONS

This book reads from *right to left*, Japanese style.
If this is your first time reading manga, you start
reading from the top right panel on each page and
take it from there. If you get lost, just follow the
numbered diagram here. It may seem backwards at
first, but you'll get the hang of it! Have fun!!

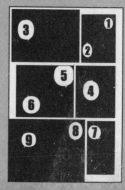

Parabellum's Winning Streak! The mercenary group's leader, Ogre-Rou, has three secrets...

1 Gobbling Up Strong Foes with Absorption

Ogre-Rou's special Absorption ability allows him to gain new skills by eating foreign bodies and objects. After defeating a stronger opponent, Ogre-Rou can eat it and acquire its abilities, allowing him to face even tougher foes. That's Ogre-Rou's dog-eat-dog strategy!

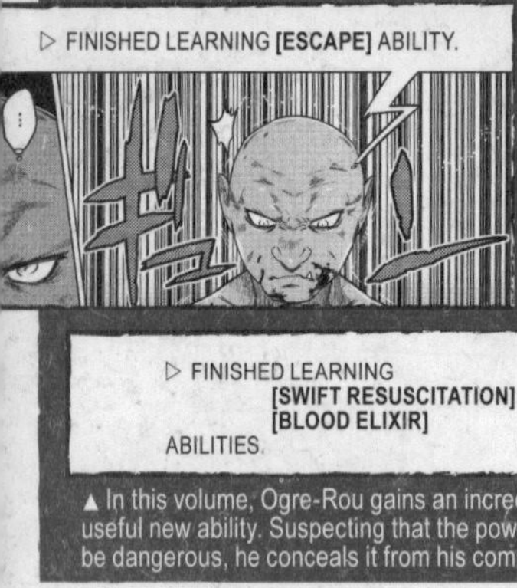
▷ FINISHED LEARNING [ESCAPE] ABILITY.

◀ After being reincarnated, Gob-Rou tests out his Absorption ability.

▷ FINISHED LEARNING
[SWIFT RESUSCITATION]
[BLOOD ELIXIR]
ABILITIES.

▲ In this volume, Ogre-Rou gains an incredibly useful new ability. Suspecting that the power might be dangerous, he conceals it from his companions.

2 Gaining Power Through Rank-Ups

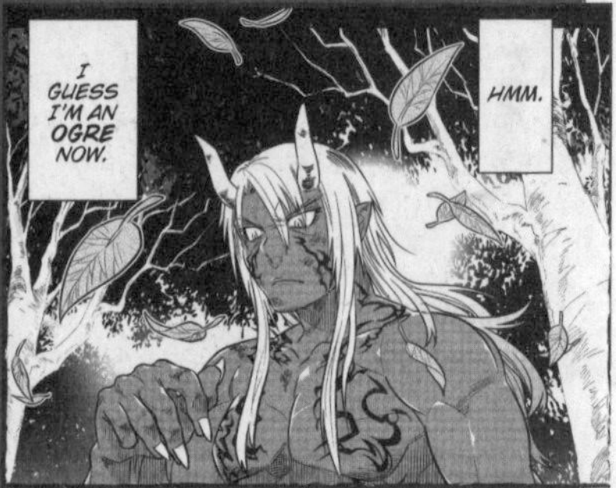
HMM.
I GUESS I'M AN OGRE NOW.

As monsters like Ogre-Rou and his companions fight, they gain experience, raising their levels. Most are capable of ranking up into different species entirely. Their "ranked-up" form varies based on their individual merits. Ogre-Rou's Absorption ability, however, makes him a special case. Rather than ranking up into a normal ogre, he's become a much more powerful ogre variant.

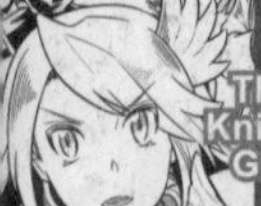
The Knight Girl

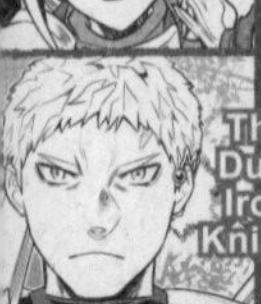
The Dull-Iron Knight

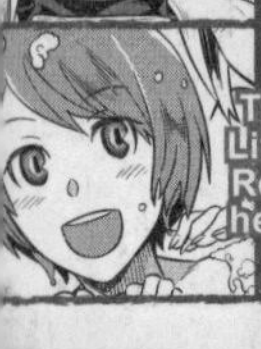
The Little Red-head

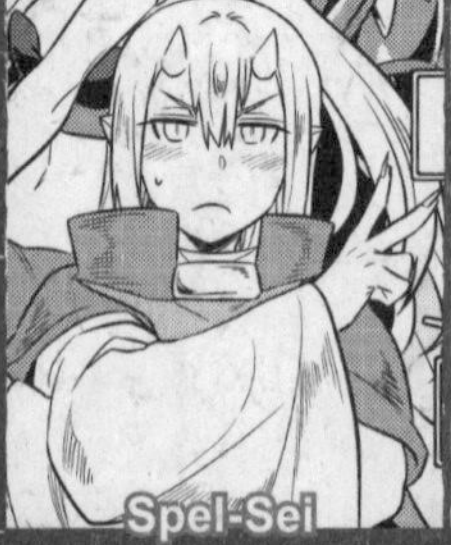
Spel-Sei

This unflappable half spell lord is older than Ogre-Rou, and is Blod-Sato's best friend. Although she's physically unremarkable, she can cast powerful magic spells.

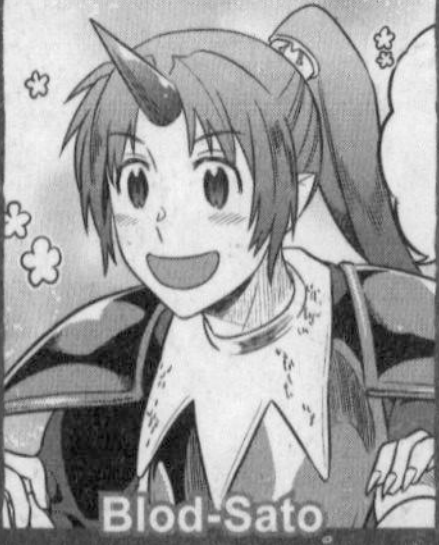
Blod-Sato

This half blood lord was Ogre-Rou's senior during his goblin days. She possesses prowess in melee combat, and can turn her own blood into weapons.

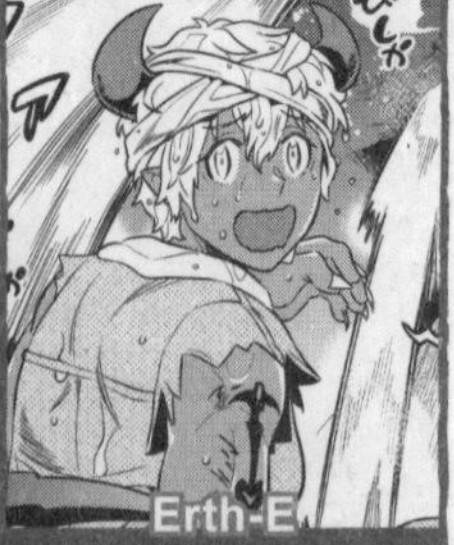
Erth-E

A half earth lord with an affinity for the earth element. While leading the elemental stone mining group, she discovers something amazing!

CHAPTER 29

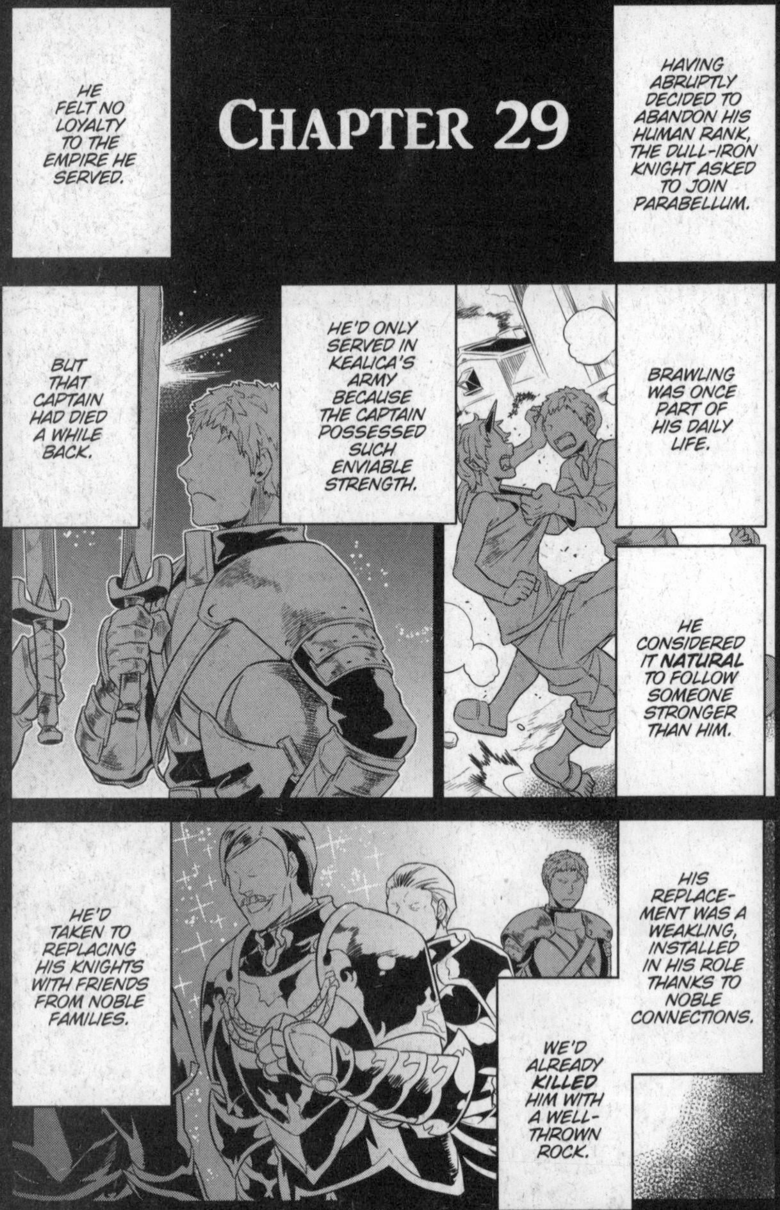
HAVING ABRUPTLY DECIDED TO ABANDON HIS HUMAN RANK, THE DULL-IRON KNIGHT ASKED TO JOIN PARABELLUM.
HE FELT NO LOYALTY TO THE EMPIRE HE SERVED.
BRAWLING WAS ONCE PART OF HIS DAILY LIFE.
HE CONSIDERED IT **NATURAL** TO FOLLOW SOMEONE STRONGER THAN HIM.
HE'D ONLY SERVED IN KEALICA'S ARMY BECAUSE THE CAPTAIN POSSESSED SUCH ENVIABLE STRENGTH.
BUT THAT CAPTAIN HAD DIED A WHILE BACK.
HIS REPLACEMENT WAS A WEAKLING, INSTALLED IN HIS ROLE THANKS TO NOBLE CONNECTIONS.
WE'D ALREADY **KILLED** HIM WITH A WELL-THROWN ROCK.
HE'D TAKEN TO REPLACING HIS KNIGHTS WITH FRIENDS FROM NOBLE FAMILIES.

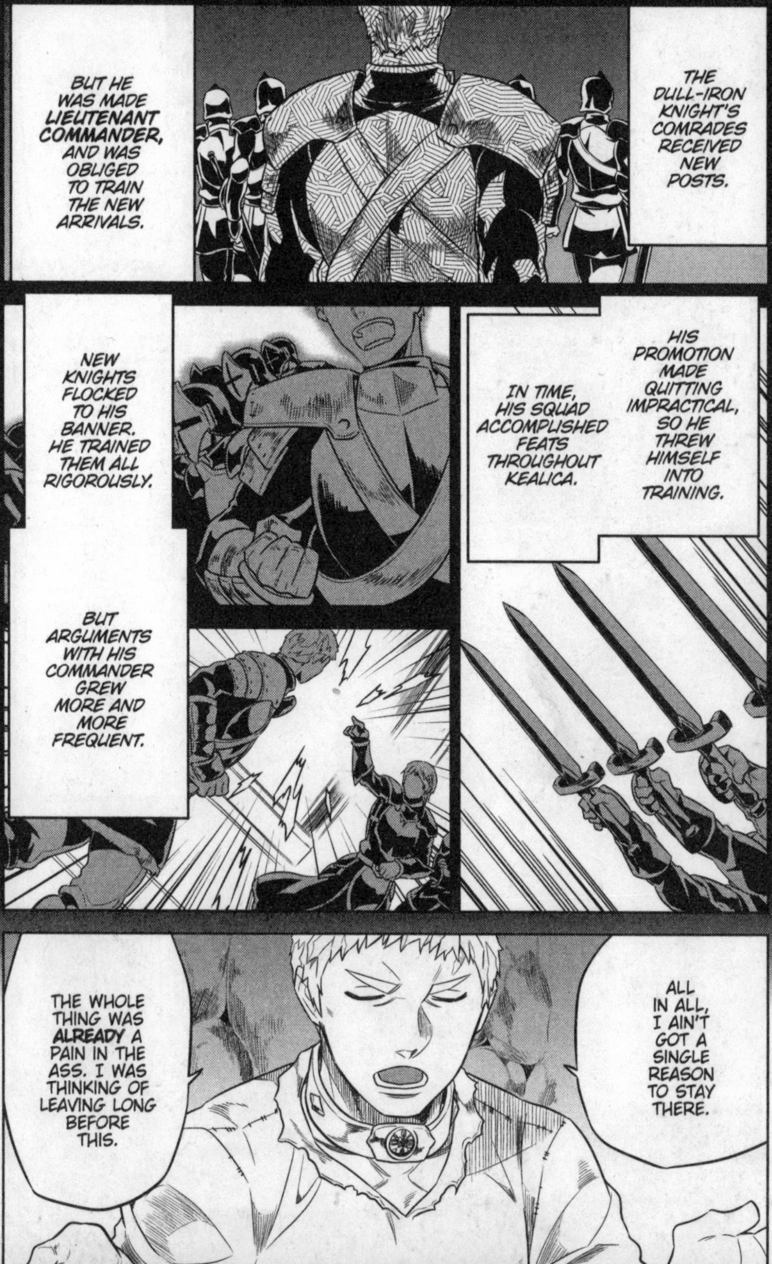
THE DULL-IRON KNIGHT'S COMRADES RECEIVED NEW POSTS.
BUT HE WAS MADE LIEUTENANT COMMANDER, AND WAS OBLIGED TO TRAIN THE NEW ARRIVALS.
HIS PROMOTION MADE QUITTING IMPRACTICAL, SO HE THREW HIMSELF INTO TRAINING.
IN TIME, HIS SQUAD ACCOMPLISHED FEATS THROUGHOUT KEALICA.
NEW KNIGHTS FLOCKED TO HIS BANNER. HE TRAINED THEM ALL RIGOROUSLY.
BUT ARGUMENTS WITH HIS COMMANDER GREW MORE AND MORE FREQUENT.
ALL IN ALL, I AIN'T GOT A SINGLE REASON TO STAY THERE.
THE WHOLE THING WAS ALREADY A PAIN IN THE ASS. I WAS THINKING OF LEAVING LONG BEFORE THIS.

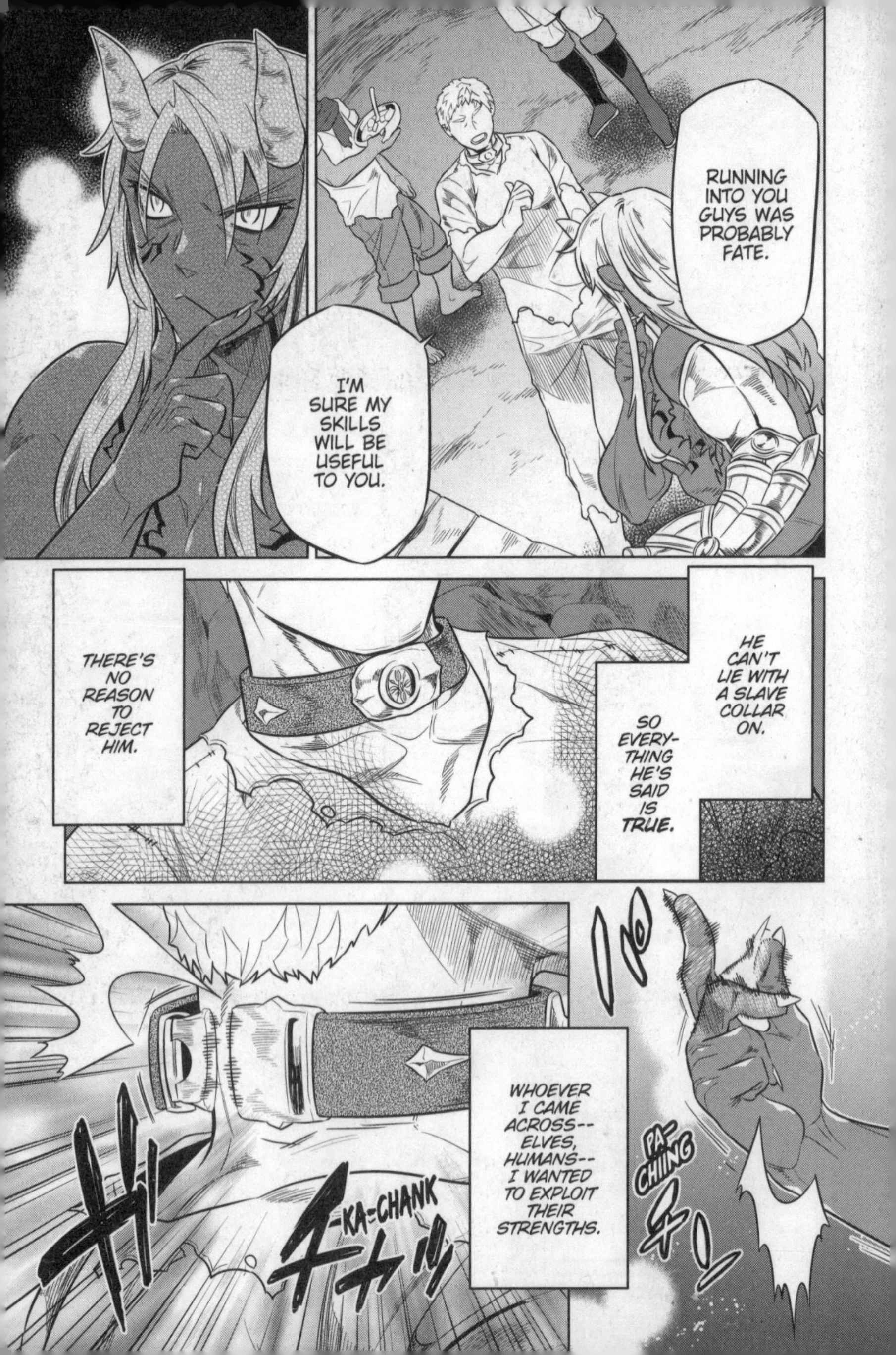
RUNNING INTO YOU GUYS WAS PROBABLY FATE.
I'M SURE MY SKILLS WILL BE USEFUL TO YOU.
HE CAN'T LIE WITH A SLAVE COLLAR ON.
SO EVERY-THING HE'S SAID IS TRUE.
THERE'S NO REASON TO REJECT HIM.
PA-CHIING
WHOEVER I CAME ACROSS-- ELVES, HUMANS-- I WANTED TO EXPLOIT THEIR STRENGTHS.
KA-CHANK

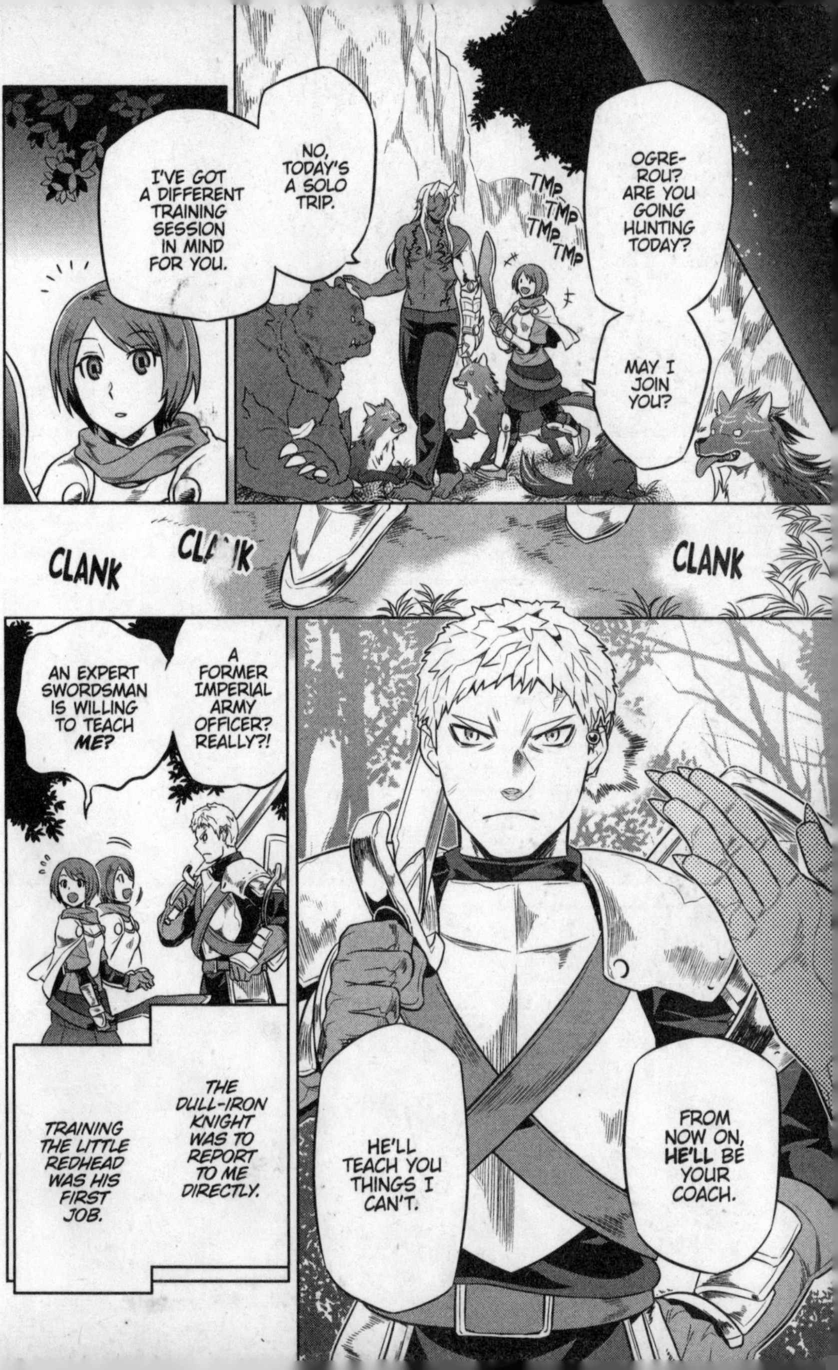
OGRE-ROU? ARE YOU GOING HUNTING TODAY?
MAY I JOIN YOU?
TMP TMP TMP TMP
NO, TODAY'S A SOLO TRIP.
I'VE GOT A DIFFERENT TRAINING SESSION IN MIND FOR YOU.
CLANK
CLANK
FROM NOW ON, HE'LL BE YOUR COACH.
HE'LL TEACH YOU THINGS I CAN'T.
A FORMER IMPERIAL ARMY OFFICER? REALLY?!
AN EXPERT SWORDSMAN IS WILLING TO TEACH *ME*?
THE DULL-IRON KNIGHT WAS TO REPORT TO ME DIRECTLY.
TRAINING THE LITTLE REDHEAD WAS HIS FIRST JOB.

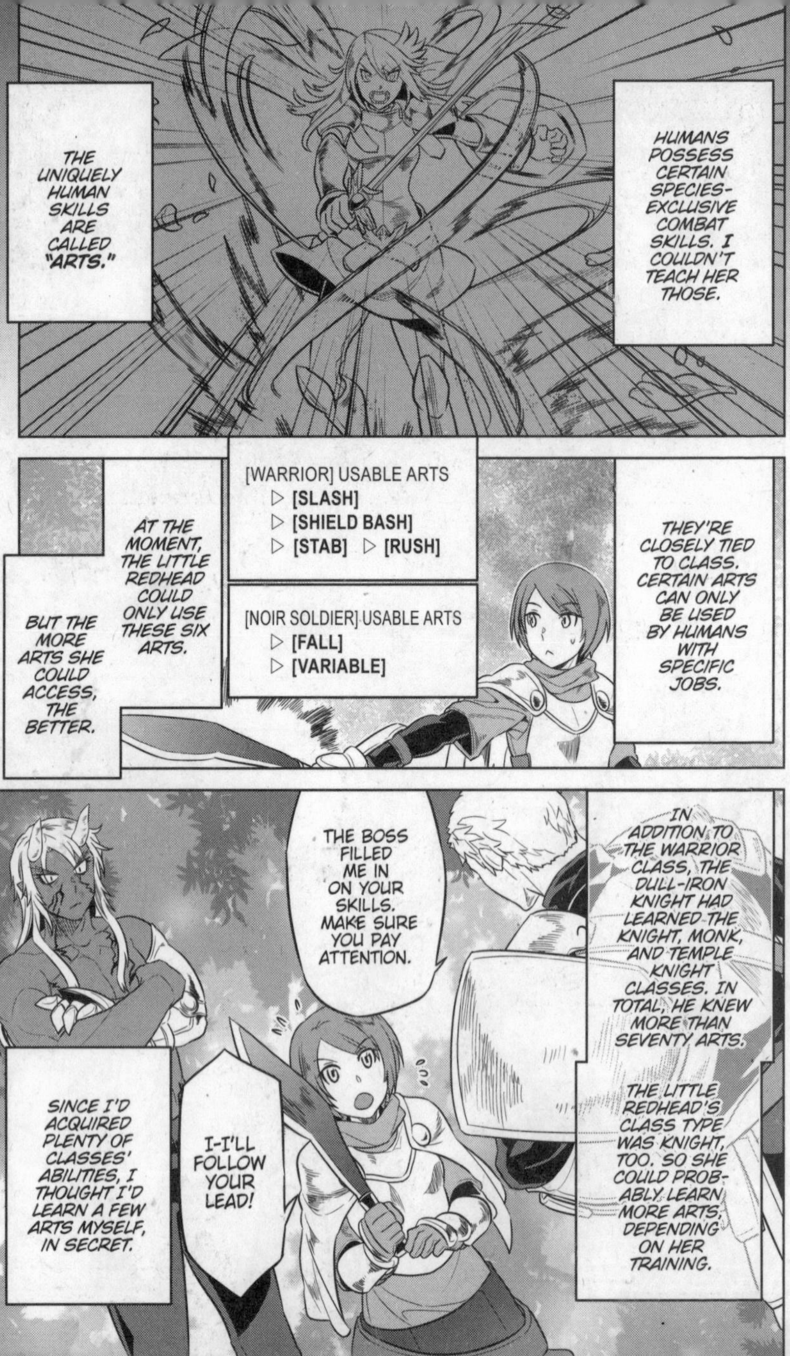
HUMANS POSSESS CERTAIN SPECIES-EXCLUSIVE COMBAT SKILLS. I COULDN'T TEACH HER THOSE.
THE UNIQUELY HUMAN SKILLS ARE CALLED "ARTS."
THEY'RE CLOSELY TIED TO CLASS. CERTAIN ARTS CAN ONLY BE USED BY HUMANS WITH SPECIFIC JOBS.
[WARRIOR] USABLE ARTS
▷ [SLASH]
▷ [SHIELD BASH]
▷ [STAB] ▷ [RUSH]
[NOIR SOLDIER] USABLE ARTS
▷ [FALL]
▷ [VARIABLE]
AT THE MOMENT, THE LITTLE REDHEAD COULD ONLY USE THESE SIX ARTS.
BUT THE MORE ARTS SHE COULD ACCESS, THE BETTER.
IN ADDITION TO THE WARRIOR CLASS, THE DULL-IRON KNIGHT HAD LEARNED THE KNIGHT, MONK, AND TEMPLE KNIGHT CLASSES. IN TOTAL, HE KNEW MORE THAN SEVENTY ARTS.
THE BOSS FILLED ME IN ON YOUR SKILLS. MAKE SURE YOU PAY ATTENTION.
THE LITTLE REDHEAD'S CLASS TYPE WAS KNIGHT, TOO. SO SHE COULD PROBABLY LEARN MORE ARTS, DEPENDING ON HER TRAINING.
I-I'LL FOLLOW YOUR LEAD!
SINCE I'D ACQUIRED PLENTY OF CLASSES' ABILITIES, I THOUGHT I'D LEARN A FEW ARTS MYSELF, IN SECRET.

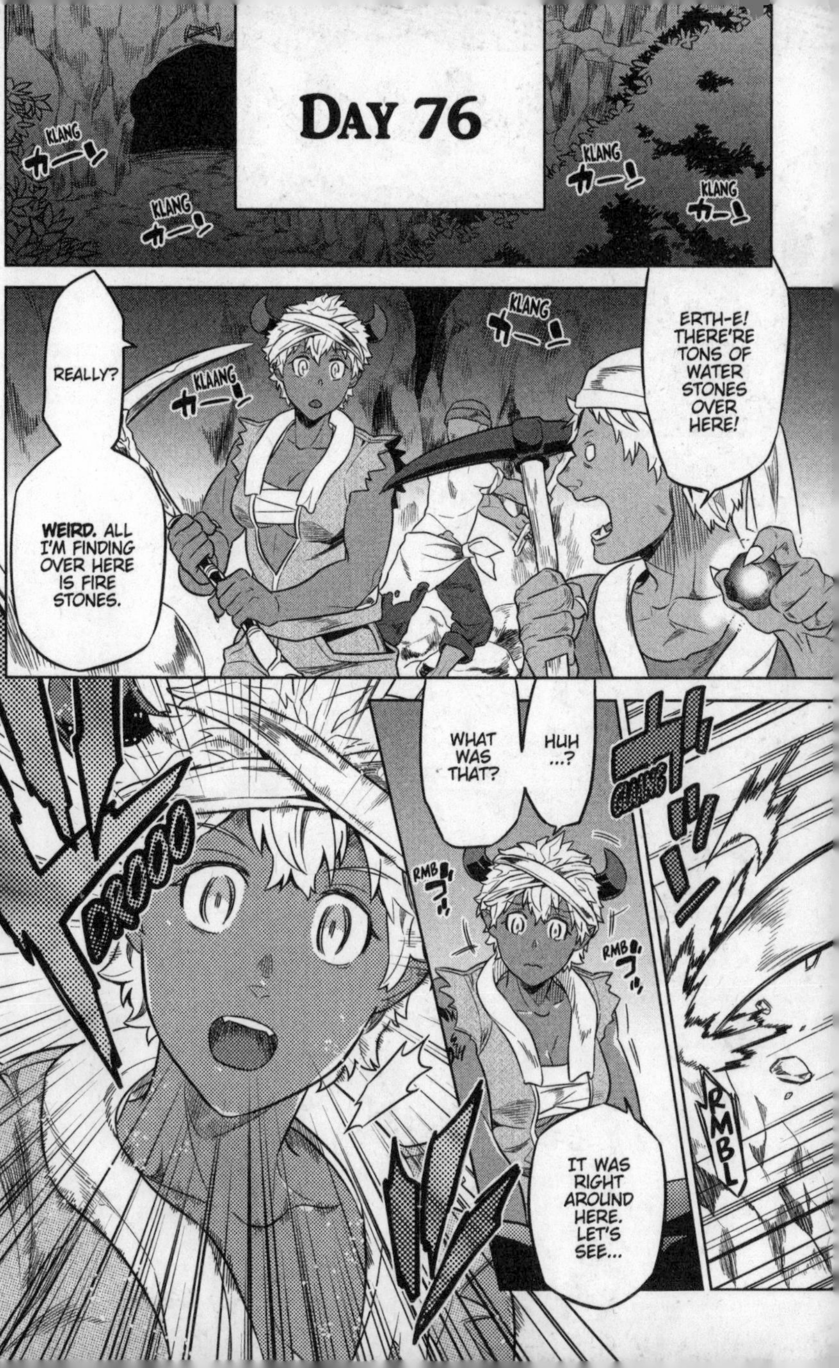
DAY 76
KLANG
KLANG
KLANG
KLANG
ERTH-E! THERE'RE TONS OF WATER STONES OVER HERE!
KLANG
KLAANG
REALLY?
WEIRD. ALL I'M FINDING OVER HERE IS FIRE STONES.
HUH ...?
WHAT WAS THAT?
RMB
RMB
RMBL
IT WAS RIGHT AROUND HERE. LET'S SEE...

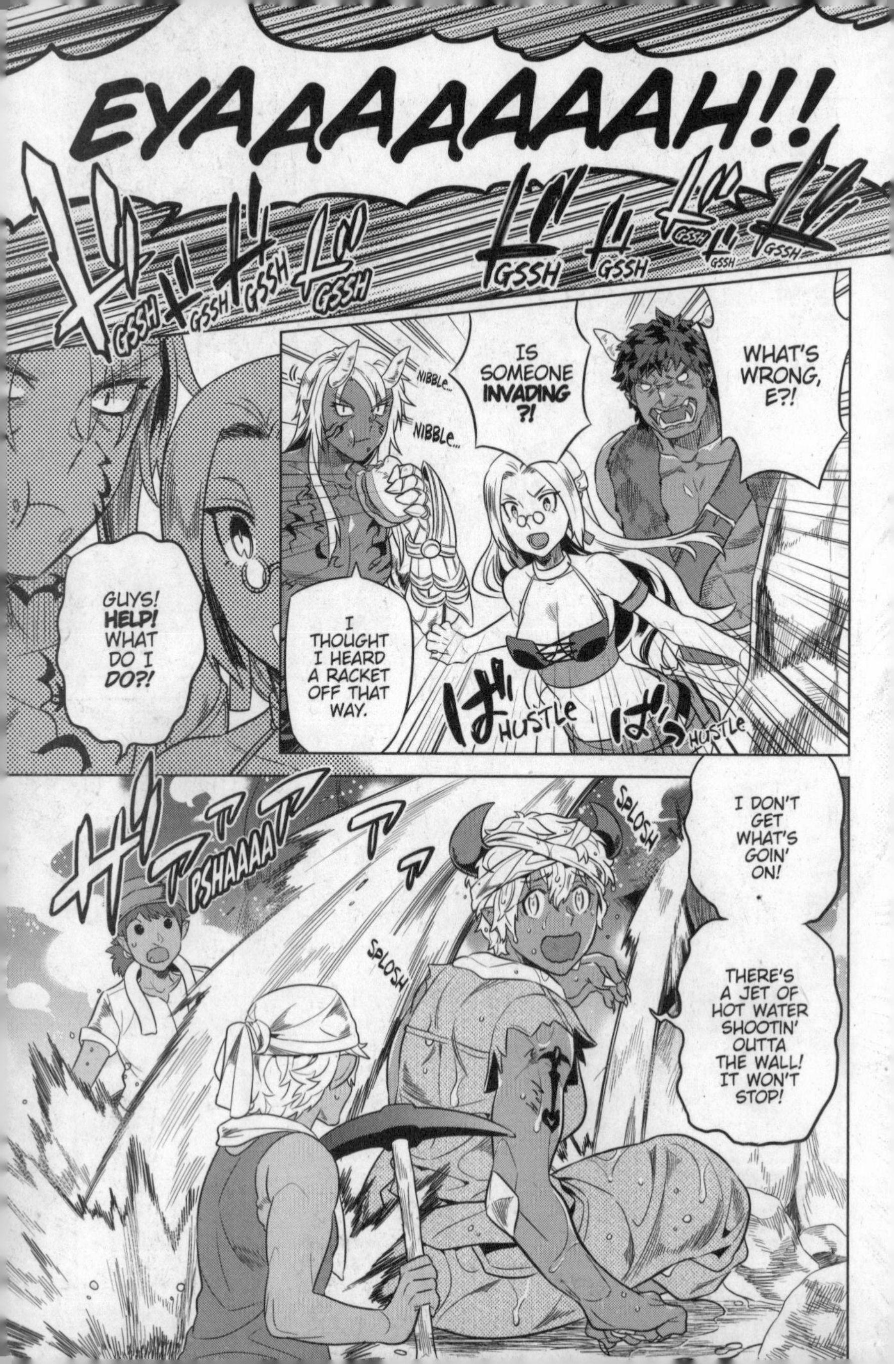
EYAAAAAAAH!!
GSSH GSSH GSSH GSSH GSSH GSSH GSSH GSSH GSSH
WHAT'S WRONG, E?!
IS SOMEONE INVADING?!
NIBBLE... NIBBLE...
I THOUGHT I HEARD A RACKET OFF THAT WAY.
HUSTLE HUSTLE
GUYS! HELP! WHAT DO I DO?!
I DON'T GET WHAT'S GOIN' ON!
SPLOSH
THERE'S A JET OF HOT WATER SHOOTIN' OUTTA THE WALL! IT WON'T STOP!
PSHAAAA
SPLOSH

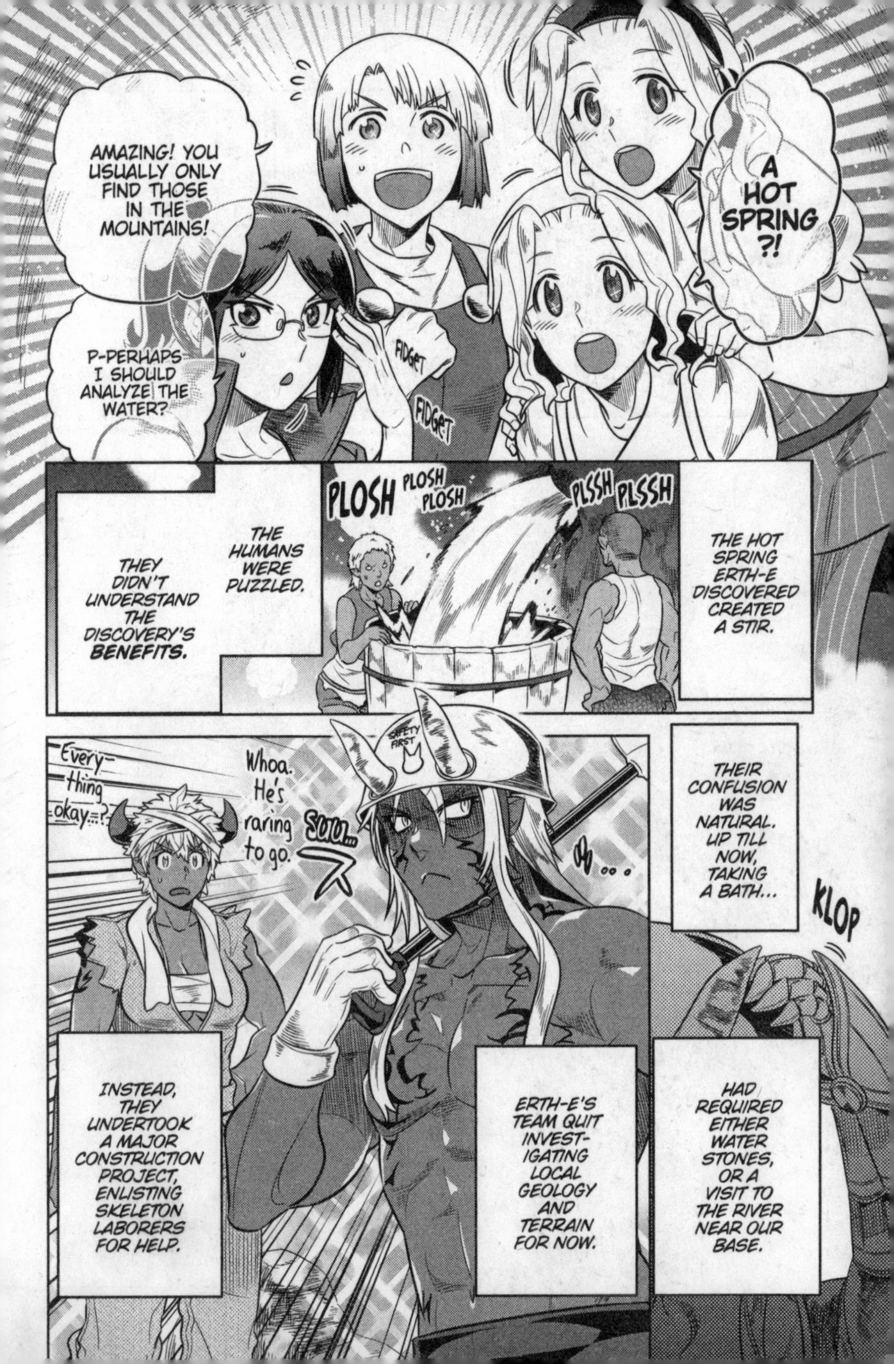

A HOT SPRING ?!
AMAZING! YOU USUALLY ONLY FIND THOSE IN THE MOUNTAINS!
FIDGET
FIDGET
P-PERHAPS I SHOULD ANALYZE THE WATER?
THE HOT SPRING ERTH-E DISCOVERED CREATED A STIR.
PLSSH PLSSH
PLOSH PLOSH
PLOSH
THE HUMANS WERE PUZZLED.
THEY DIDN'T UNDERSTAND THE DISCOVERY'S BENEFITS.
THEIR CONFUSION WAS NATURAL. UP TILL NOW, TAKING A BATH...
KLOP
HAD REQUIRED EITHER WATER STONES, OR A VISIT TO THE RIVER NEAR OUR BASE.
SAFETY FIRST
SOO...
Whoa. He's raring to go.
Every-thing okay...?
ERTH-E'S TEAM QUIT INVEST-IGATING LOCAL GEOLOGY AND TERRAIN FOR NOW.
INSTEAD, THEY UNDERTOOK A MAJOR CONSTRUCTION PROJECT, ENLISTING SKELETON LABORERS FOR HELP.

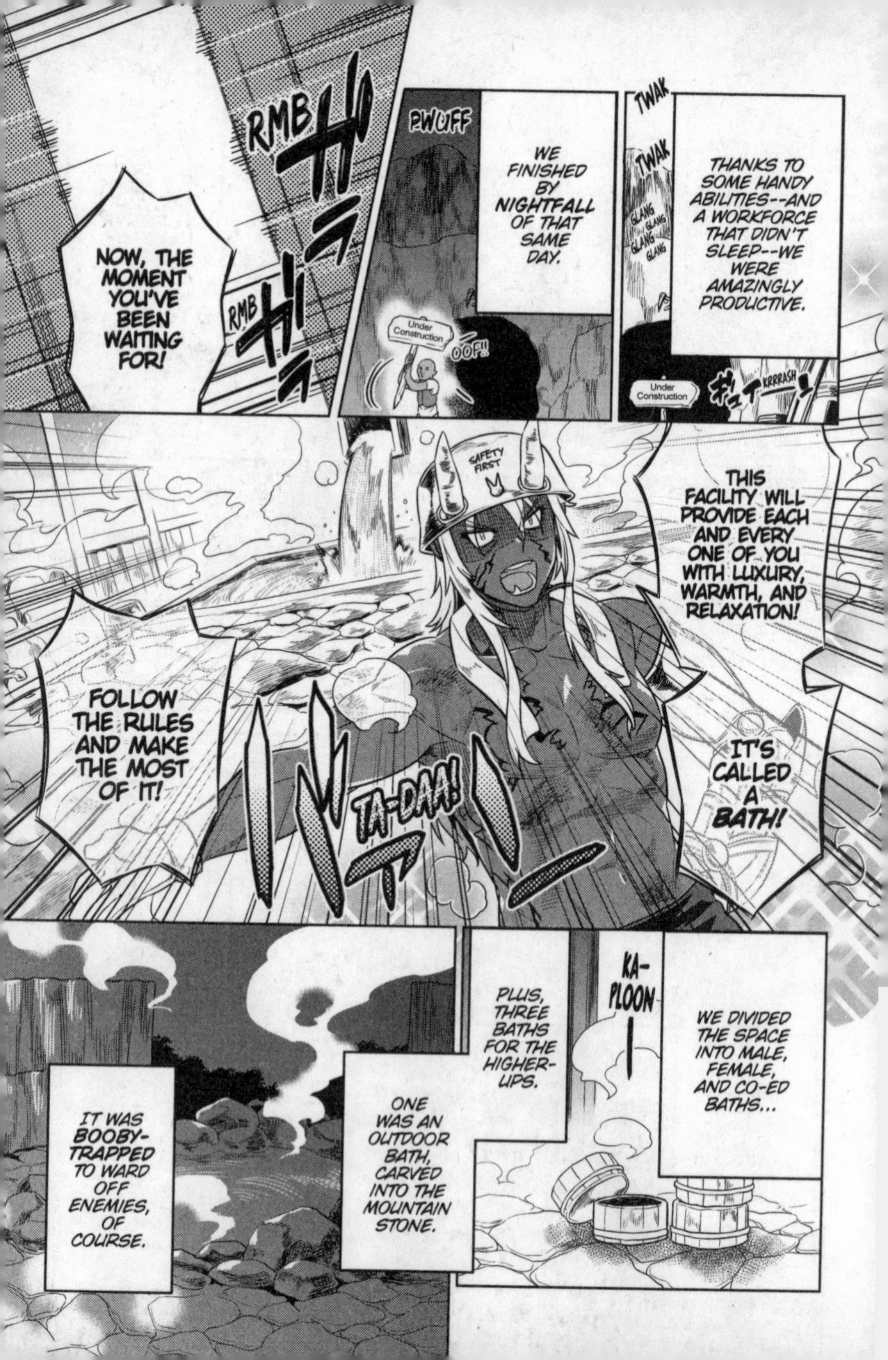
TWAK
TWAK
THANKS TO SOME HANDY ABILITIES--AND A WORKFORCE THAT DIDN'T SLEEP--WE WERE AMAZINGLY PRODUCTIVE.
GLANG GLANG GLANG GLANG
Under Construction
KRRRASH
P-WUFF
WE FINISHED BY NIGHTFALL OF THAT SAME DAY.
Under Construction
OOF!!
RMB
RMB
NOW, THE MOMENT YOU'VE BEEN WAITING FOR!
THIS FACILITY WILL PROVIDE EACH AND EVERY ONE OF YOU WITH LUXURY, WARMTH, AND RELAXATION!
SAFETY FIRST
IT'S CALLED A BATH!
FOLLOW THE RULES AND MAKE THE MOST OF IT!
TA-DAA!
WE DIVIDED THE SPACE INTO MALE, FEMALE, AND CO-ED BATHS...
KA-PLOON
PLUS, THREE BATHS FOR THE HIGHER-UPS.
ONE WAS AN OUTDOOR BATH, CARVED INTO THE MOUNTAIN STONE.
IT WAS BOOBY-TRAPPED TO WARD OFF ENEMIES, OF COURSE.

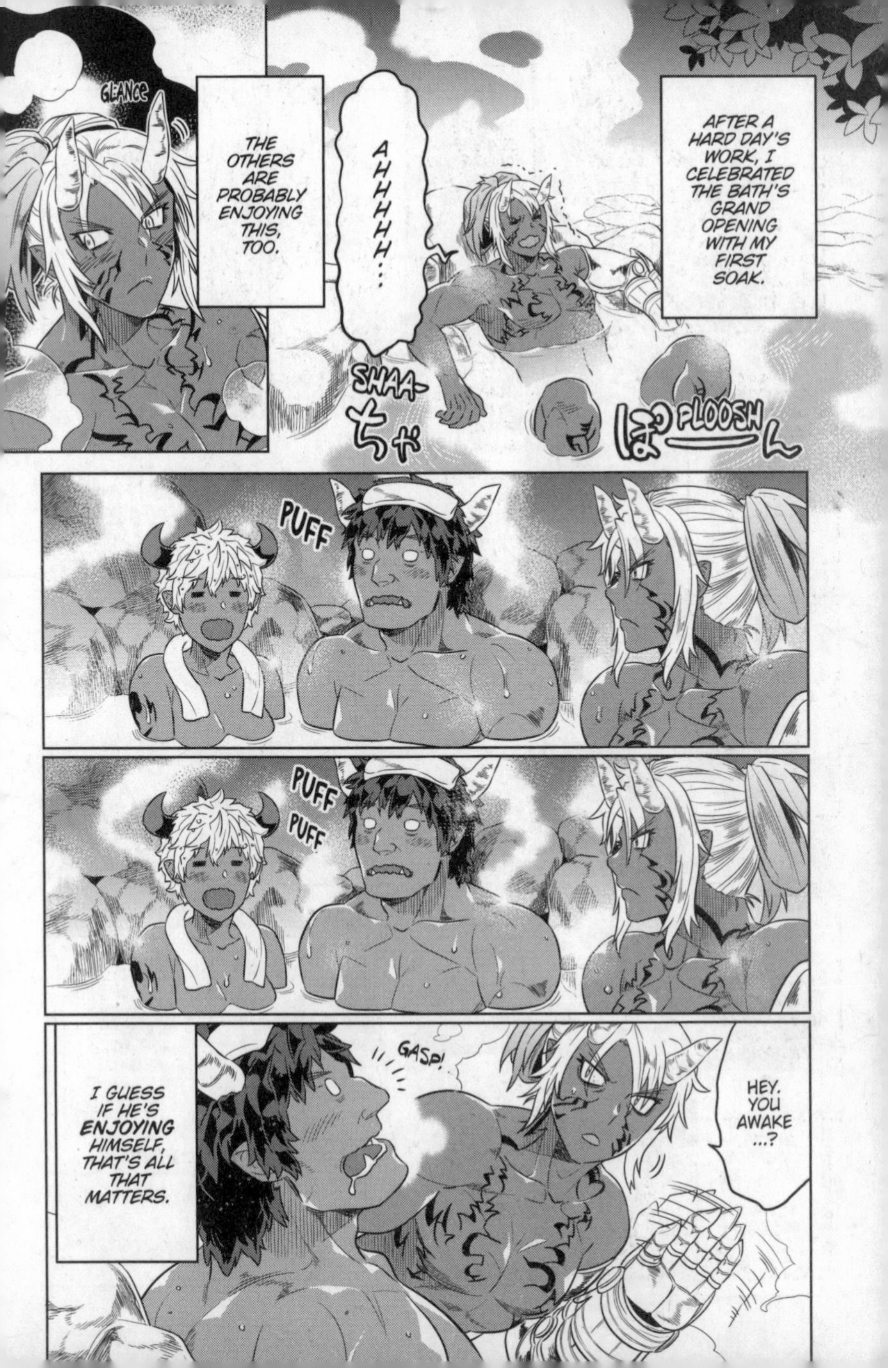
AFTER A HARD DAY'S WORK, I CELEBRATED THE BATH'S GRAND OPENING WITH MY FIRST SOAK.
AHHHHH...
SHAA- ちゃ
ぽ PLOOSH ん
THE OTHERS ARE PROBABLY ENJOYING THIS, TOO.
GLANCE
PUFF
PUFF
PUFF
HEY. YOU AWAKE ...?
GASP!
I GUESS IF HE'S ENJOYING HIMSELF, THAT'S ALL THAT MATTERS.

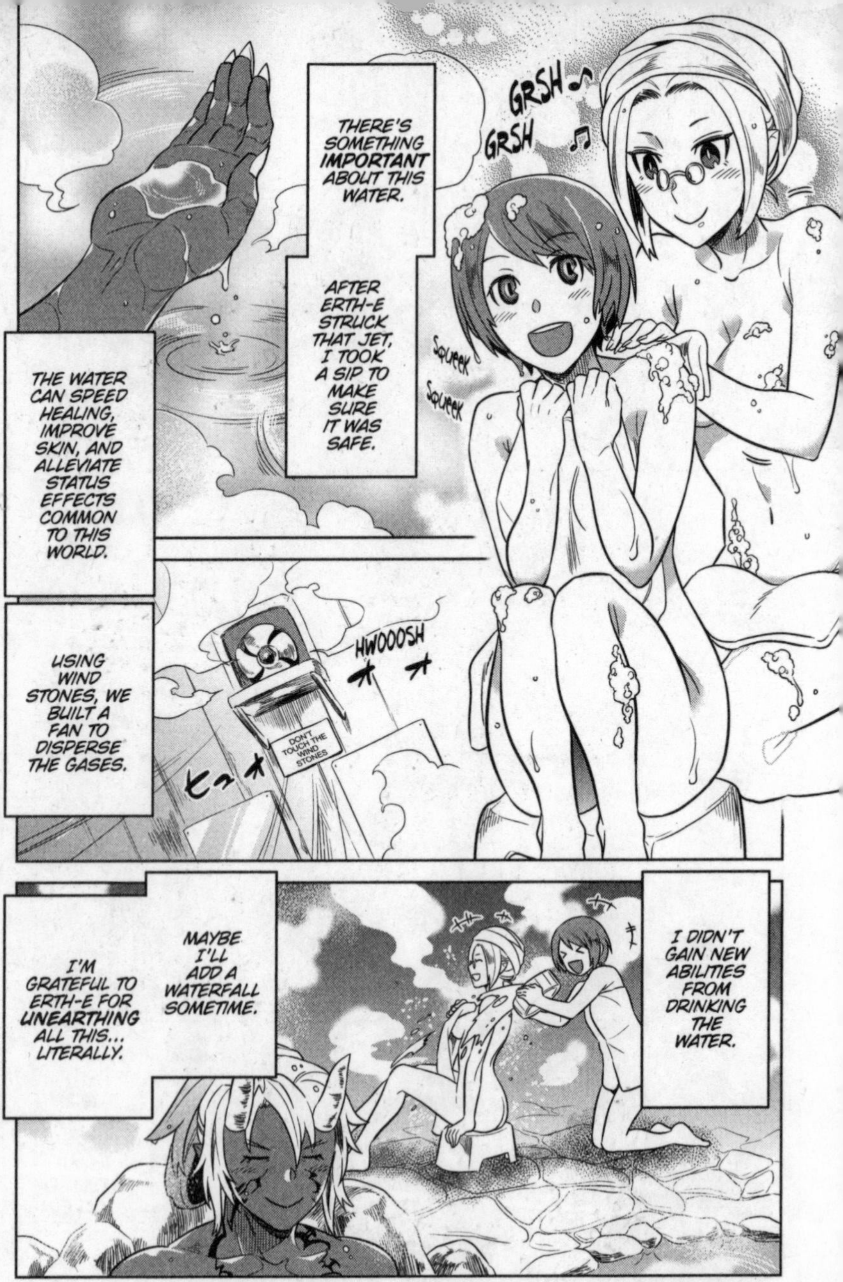
GRSH ♪
GRSH ♪
Squeek
Squeek
THERE'S SOMETHING IMPORTANT ABOUT THIS WATER.
AFTER ERTH-E STRUCK THAT JET, I TOOK A SIP TO MAKE SURE IT WAS SAFE.
THE WATER CAN SPEED HEALING, IMPROVE SKIN, AND ALLEVIATE STATUS EFFECTS COMMON TO THIS WORLD.
USING WIND STONES, WE BUILT A FAN TO DISPERSE THE GASES.
HWOOOSH
DON'T TOUCH THE WIND STONES
I DIDN'T GAIN NEW ABILITIES FROM DRINKING THE WATER.
MAYBE I'LL ADD A WATERFALL SOMETIME.
I'M GRATEFUL TO ERTH-E FOR UNEARTHING ALL THIS... LITERALLY.

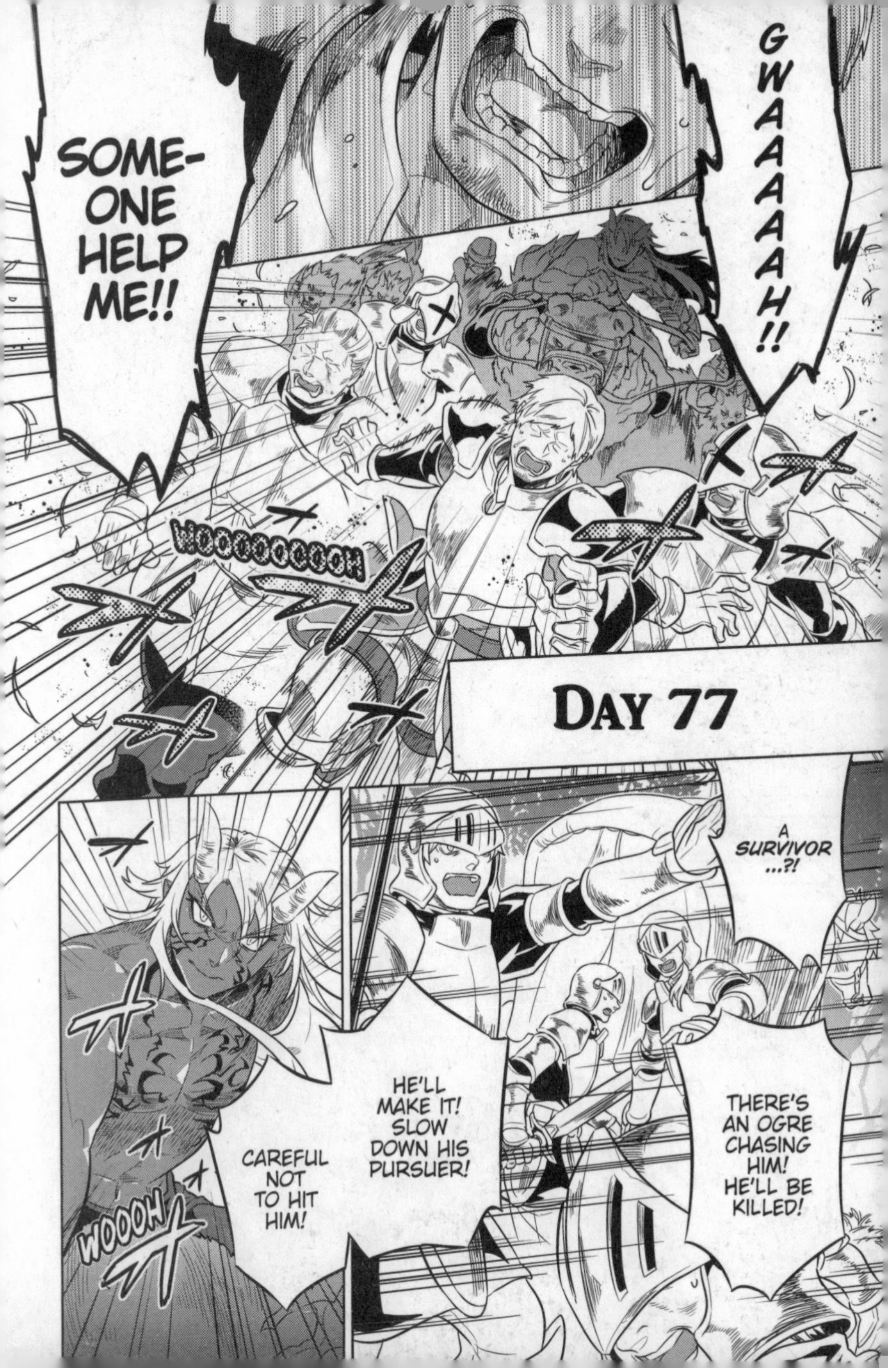
GWAAAAAAH!!
SOME-ONE HELP ME!!
WOOOOOOOOH
DAY 77
A SURVIVOR ...?!
THERE'S AN OGRE CHASING HIM! HE'LL BE KILLED!
HE'LL MAKE IT! SLOW DOWN HIS PURSUER!
CAREFUL NOT TO HIT HIM!
WOOOH

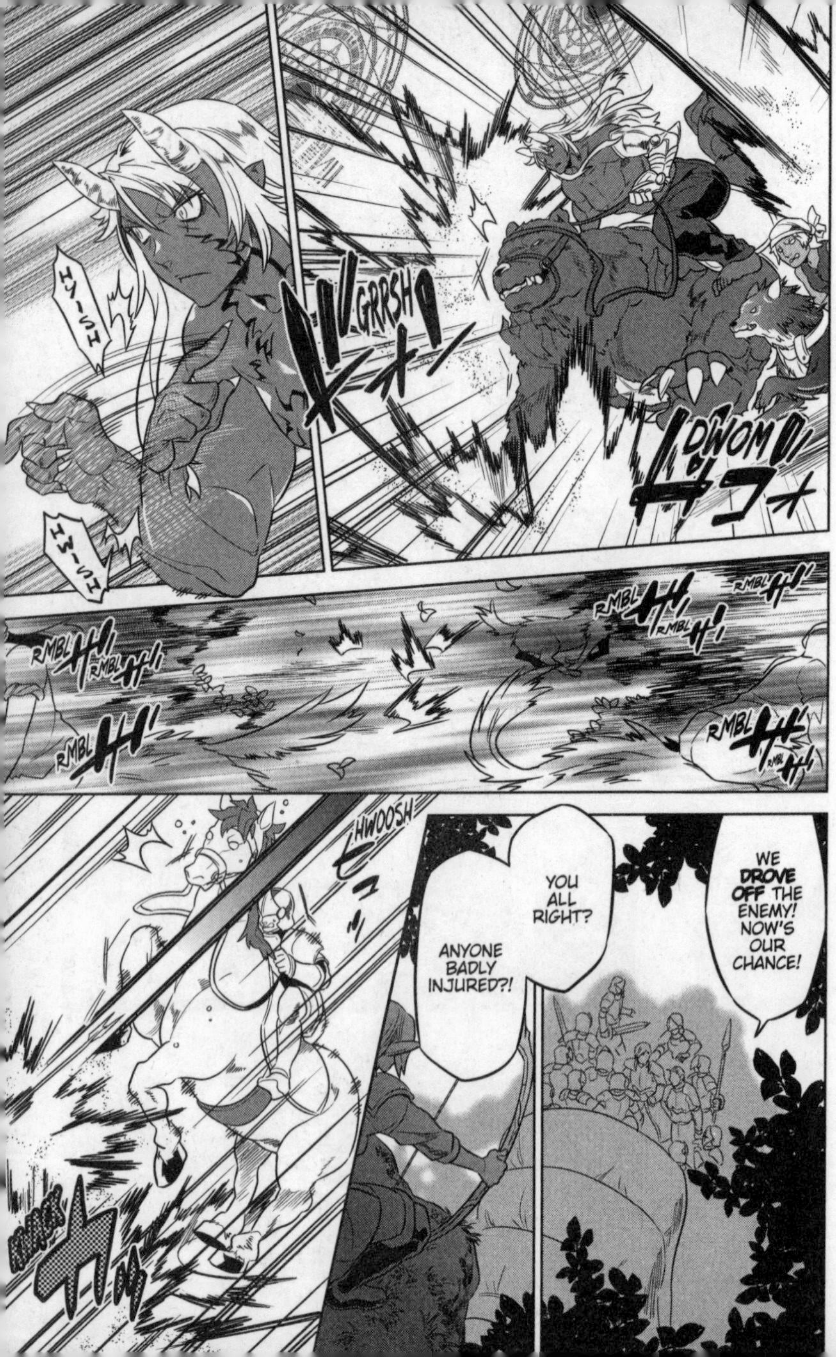
GRRSH
DWOM
HYISH
HWISH
RMBL RMBL
RMBL RMBL
RMBL RMBL
RMBL
RMBL RMBL
WE DROVE OFF THE ENEMY! NOW'S OUR CHANCE!
YOU ALL RIGHT?
ANYONE BADLY INJURED?!
HWOOSH

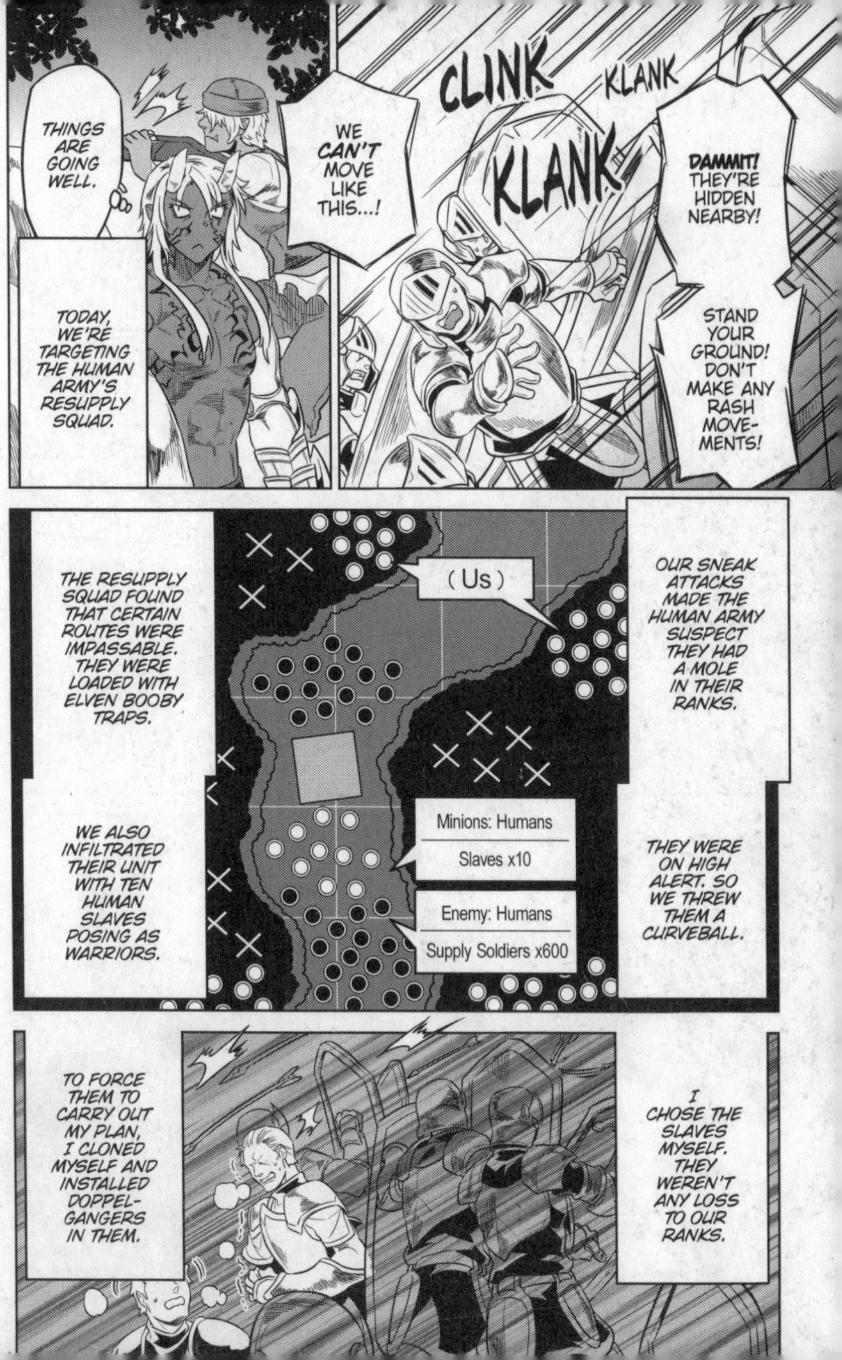
DAMMIT! THEY'RE HIDDEN NEARBY!
STAND YOUR GROUND! DON'T MAKE ANY RASH MOVE-MENTS!
CLINK
KLANK
KLANK
WE CAN'T MOVE LIKE THIS...!
THINGS ARE GOING WELL.
TODAY, WE'RE TARGETING THE HUMAN ARMY'S RESUPPLY SQUAD.
OUR SNEAK ATTACKS MADE THE HUMAN ARMY SUSPECT THEY HAD A MOLE IN THEIR RANKS.
THEY WERE ON HIGH ALERT. SO WE THREW THEM A CURVEBALL.
(Us)
Minions: Humans
Slaves x10
Enemy: Humans
Supply Soldiers x600
THE RESUPPLY SQUAD FOUND THAT CERTAIN ROUTES WERE IMPASSABLE. THEY WERE LOADED WITH ELVEN BOOBY TRAPS.
WE ALSO INFILTRATED THEIR UNIT WITH TEN HUMAN SLAVES POSING AS WARRIORS.
I CHOSE THE SLAVES MYSELF. THEY WEREN'T ANY LOSS TO OUR RANKS.
TO FORCE THEM TO CARRY OUT MY PLAN, I CLONED MYSELF AND INSTALLED DOPPEL-GANGERS IN THEM.

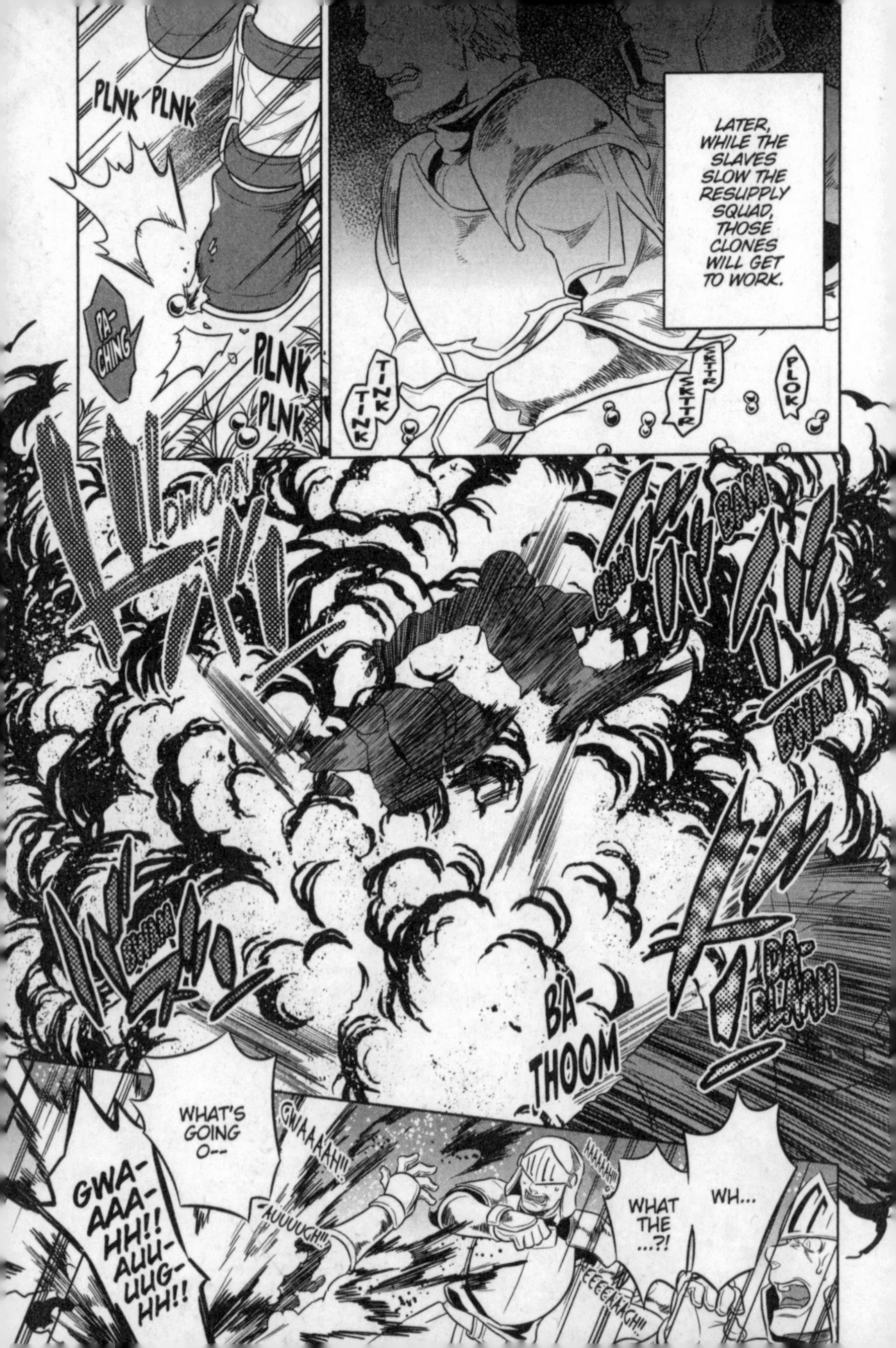
LATER, WHILE THE SLAVES SLOW THE RESUPPLY SQUAD, THOSE CLONES WILL GET TO WORK.
PLOK
SKTTR SKTTR
TINK TINK TINK
PLNK PLNK
PA-CHING
PLNK PLNK
BA-THOOM
WH...
WHAT THE ...?!
WHAT'S GOING O--
GWAA-AAA-HH!! AUU-UUG-HH!!

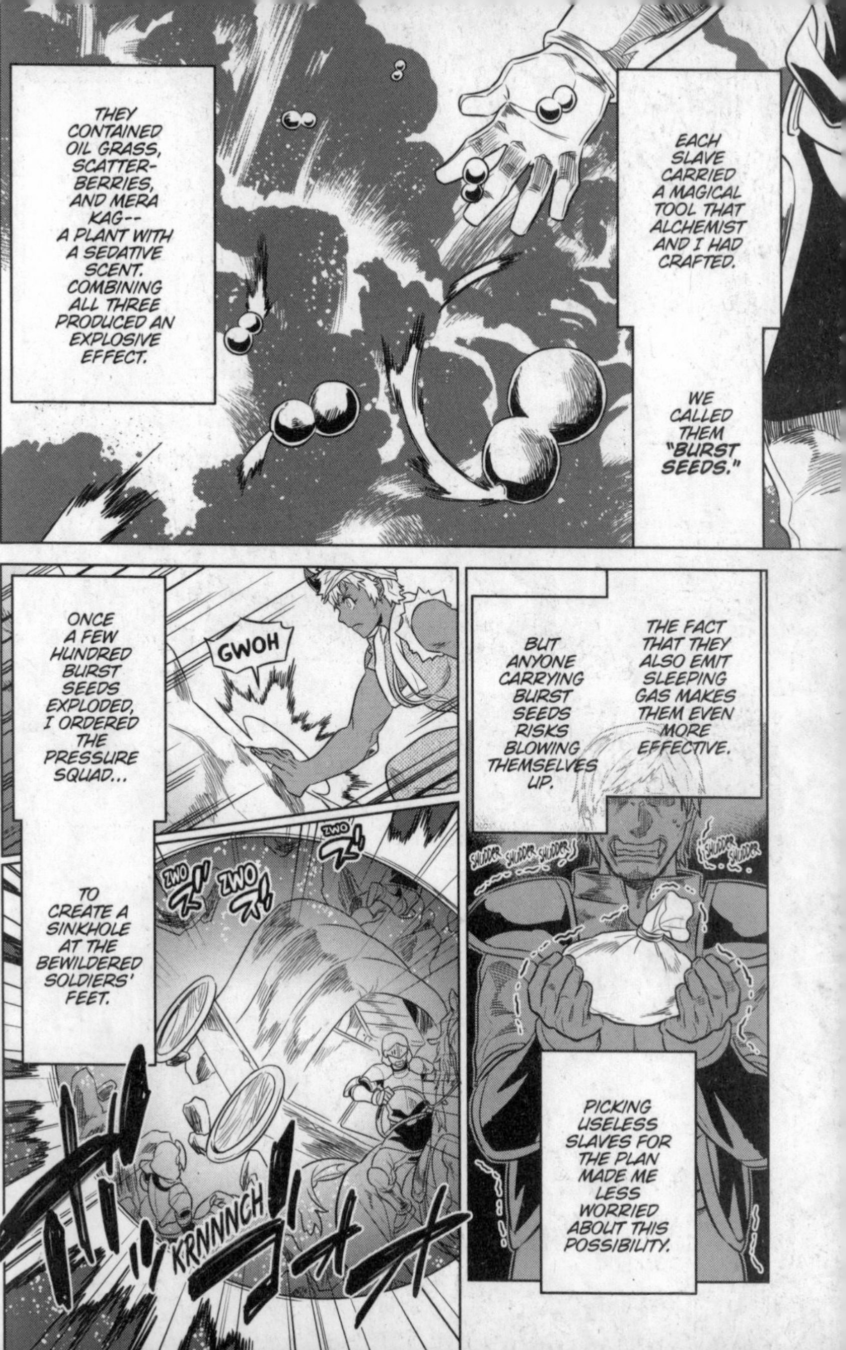
EACH SLAVE CARRIED A MAGICAL TOOL THAT ALCHEMIST AND I HAD CRAFTED.
WE CALLED THEM "BURST SEEDS."
THEY CONTAINED OIL GRASS, SCATTER-BERRIES, AND MERA KAG-- A PLANT WITH A SEDATIVE SCENT. COMBINING ALL THREE PRODUCED AN EXPLOSIVE EFFECT.
THE FACT THAT THEY ALSO EMIT SLEEPING GAS MAKES THEM EVEN MORE EFFECTIVE.
BUT ANYONE CARRYING BURST SEEDS RISKS BLOWING THEMSELVES UP.
SHUDDER SHUDDER SHUDDER
SHUDDER SHUDDER
PICKING USELESS SLAVES FOR THE PLAN MADE ME LESS WORRIED ABOUT THIS POSSIBILITY.
ONCE A FEW HUNDRED BURST SEEDS EXPLODED, I ORDERED THE PRESSURE SQUAD...
GWOH
TO CREATE A SINKHOLE AT THE BEWILDERED SOLDIERS' FEET.
ZWO
ZWO
ZWO
KRNNNCH

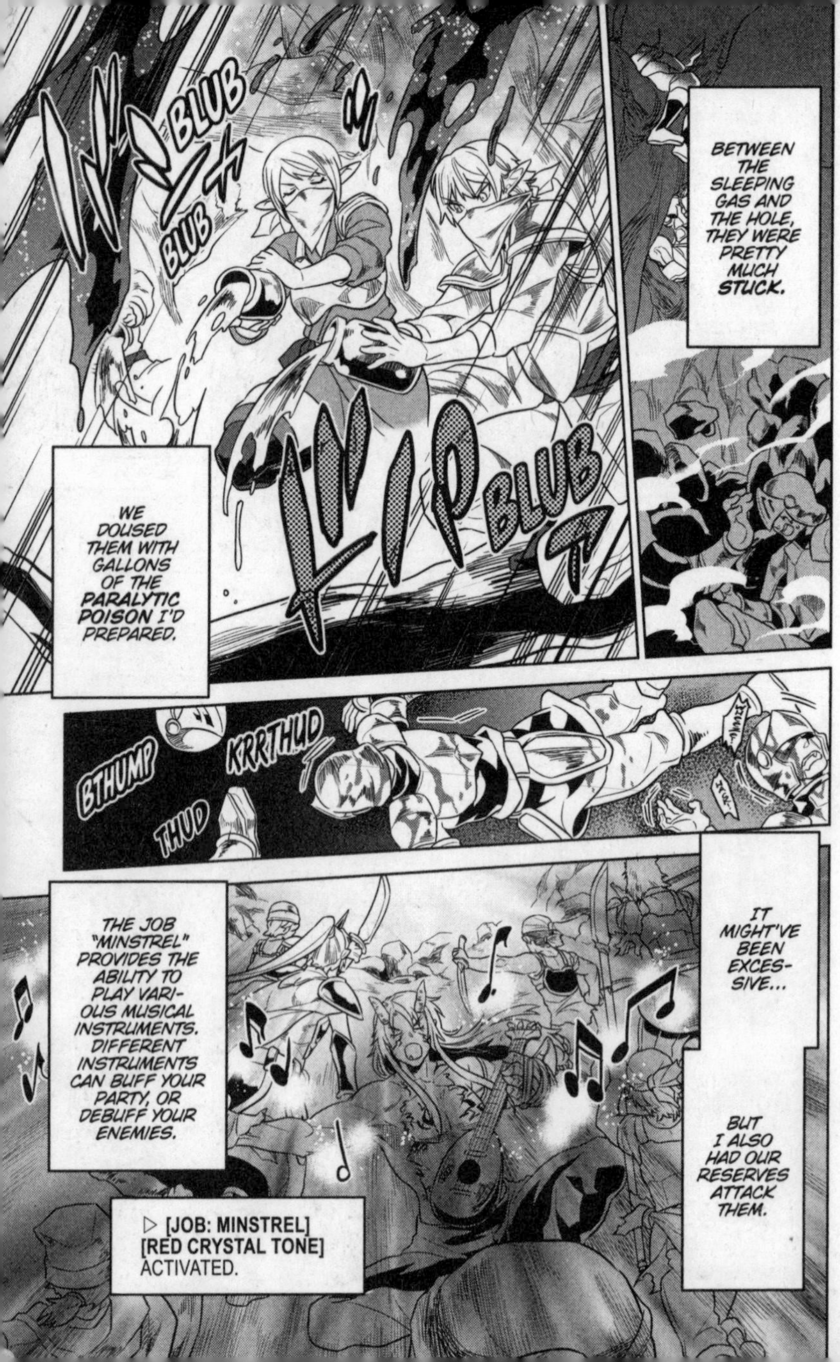
BETWEEN THE SLEEPING GAS AND THE HOLE, THEY WERE PRETTY MUCH STUCK.
BLUB
BLUB
WE DOUSED THEM WITH GALLONS OF THE PARALYTIC POISON I'D PREPARED.
BLUB
KRRTHUD
BTHUMP
THUD
IT MIGHT'VE BEEN EXCES-SIVE...
BUT I ALSO HAD OUR RESERVES ATTACK THEM.
THE JOB "MINSTREL" PROVIDES THE ABILITY TO PLAY VARI-OUS MUSICAL INSTRUMENTS. DIFFERENT INSTRUMENTS CAN BUFF YOUR PARTY, OR DEBUFF YOUR ENEMIES.
▷ [JOB: MINSTREL] [RED CRYSTAL TONE] ACTIVATED.

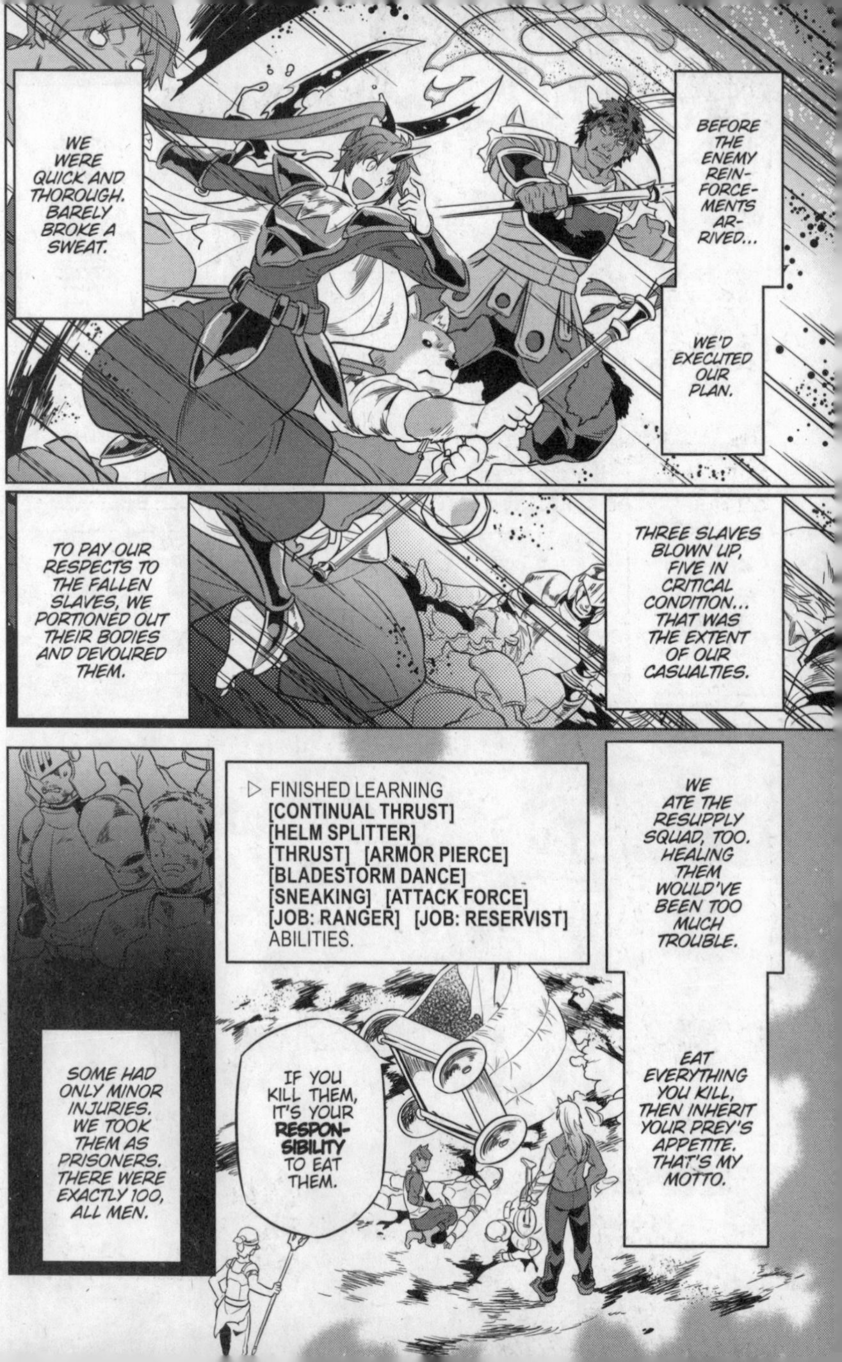
BEFORE THE ENEMY REIN-FORCE-MENTS AR-RIVED...
WE'D EXECUTED OUR PLAN.
WE WERE QUICK AND THOROUGH. BARELY BROKE A SWEAT.
THREE SLAVES BLOWN UP, FIVE IN CRITICAL CONDITION... THAT WAS THE EXTENT OF OUR CASUALTIES.
TO PAY OUR RESPECTS TO THE FALLEN SLAVES, WE PORTIONED OUT THEIR BODIES AND DEVOURED THEM.
WE ATE THE RESUPPLY SQUAD, TOO. HEALING THEM WOULD'VE BEEN TOO MUCH TROUBLE.
EAT EVERYTHING YOU KILL, THEN INHERIT YOUR PREY'S APPETITE. THAT'S MY MOTTO.
▷ FINISHED LEARNING [CONTINUAL THRUST] [HELM SPLITTER] [THRUST] [ARMOR PIERCE] [BLADESTORM DANCE] [SNEAKING] [ATTACK FORCE] [JOB: RANGER] [JOB: RESERVIST] ABILITIES.
IF YOU KILL THEM, IT'S YOUR RESPON-SIBILITY TO EAT THEM.
SOME HAD ONLY MINOR INJURIES. WE TOOK THEM AS PRISONERS. THERE WERE EXACTLY 100, ALL MEN.

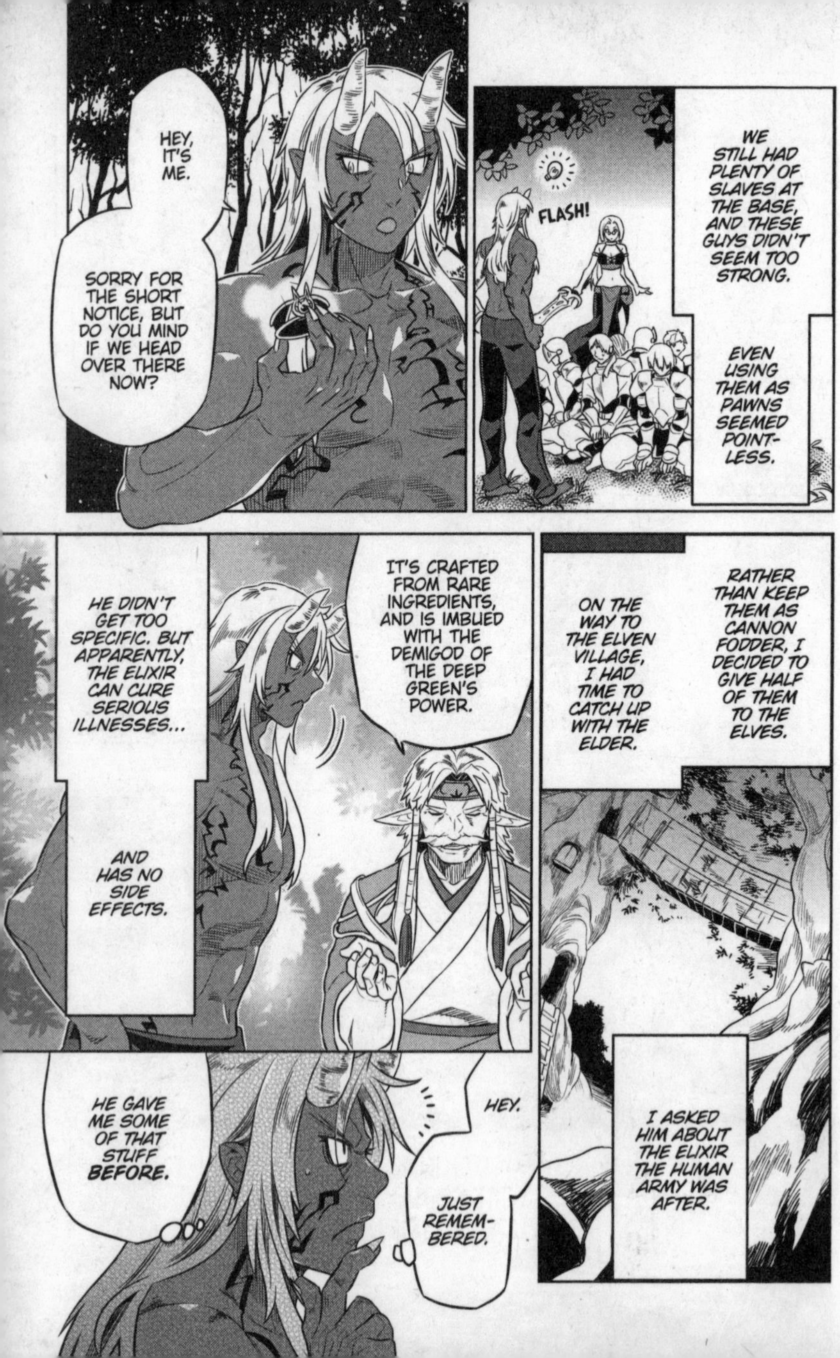
WE STILL HAD PLENTY OF SLAVES AT THE BASE, AND THESE GUYS DIDN'T SEEM TOO STRONG.
FLASH!
EVEN USING THEM AS PAWNS SEEMED POINT-LESS.
HEY, IT'S ME.
SORRY FOR THE SHORT NOTICE, BUT DO YOU MIND IF WE HEAD OVER THERE NOW?
RATHER THAN KEEP THEM AS CANNON FODDER, I DECIDED TO GIVE HALF OF THEM TO THE ELVES.
ON THE WAY TO THE ELVEN VILLAGE, I HAD TIME TO CATCH UP WITH THE ELDER.
I ASKED HIM ABOUT THE ELIXIR THE HUMAN ARMY WAS AFTER.
IT'S CRAFTED FROM RARE INGREDIENTS, AND IS IMBUED WITH THE DEMIGOD OF THE DEEP GREEN'S POWER.
HE DIDN'T GET TOO SPECIFIC. BUT APPARENTLY, THE ELIXIR CAN CURE SERIOUS ILLNESSES...
AND HAS NO SIDE EFFECTS.
HEY.
JUST REMEM-BERED.
HE GAVE ME SOME OF THAT STUFF BEFORE.

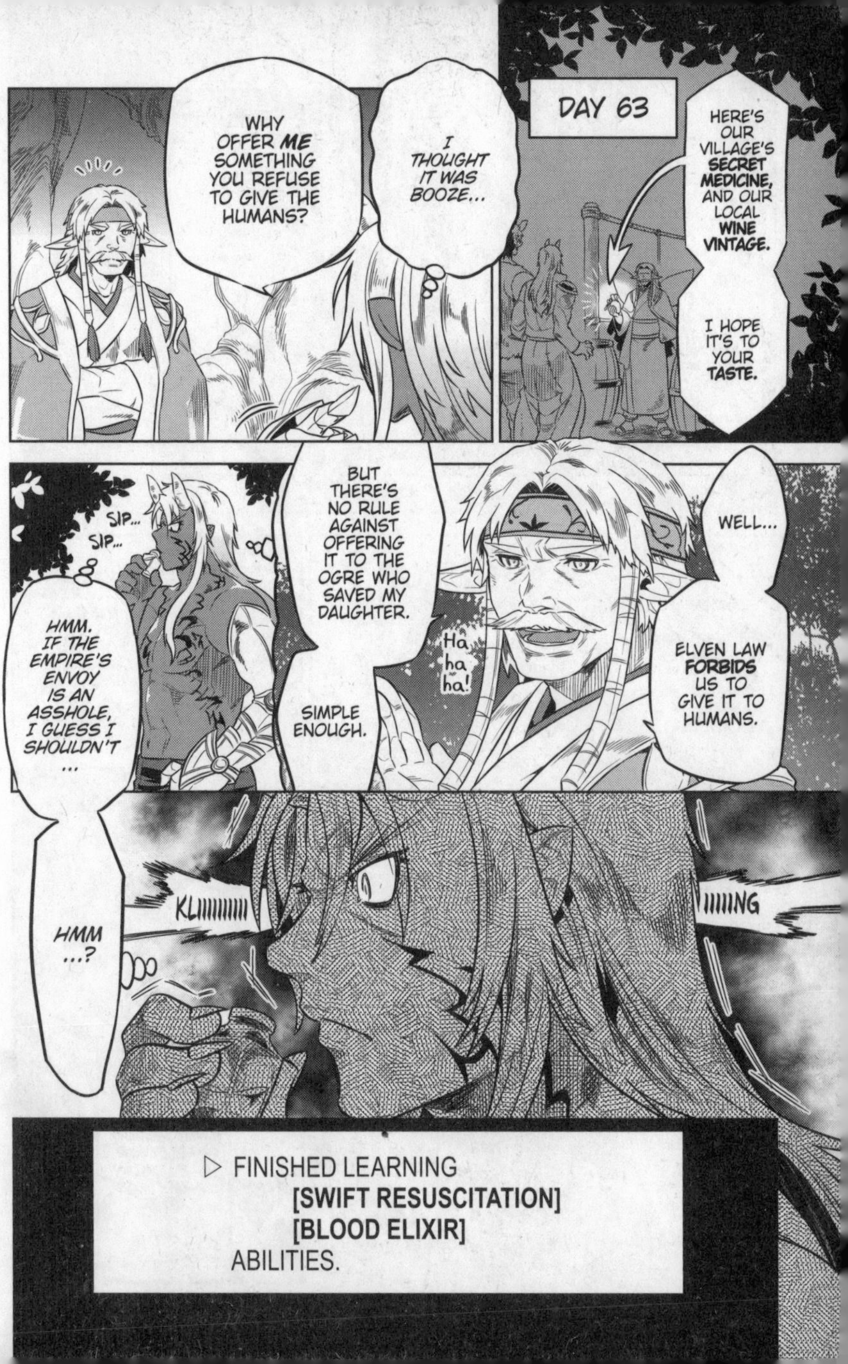
DAY 63
HERE'S OUR VILLAGE'S **SECRET MEDICINE,** AND OUR LOCAL **WINE VINTAGE.**
I HOPE IT'S TO YOUR **TASTE.**
I THOUGHT IT WAS BOOZE...
WHY OFFER **ME** SOMETHING YOU REFUSE TO GIVE THE HUMANS?
WELL...
ELVEN LAW **FORBIDS** US TO GIVE IT TO HUMANS.
BUT THERE'S NO RULE AGAINST OFFERING IT TO THE OGRE WHO SAVED MY DAUGHTER.
Ha ha ha!
SIMPLE ENOUGH.
SIP... SIP...
HMM. IF THE EMPIRE'S ENVOY IS AN ASSHOLE, I GUESS I SHOULDN'T ...
KLIIIIIIIIII IIIIING
HMM ...?
▷ FINISHED LEARNING
[SWIFT RESUSCITATION]
[BLOOD ELIXIR]
ABILITIES.

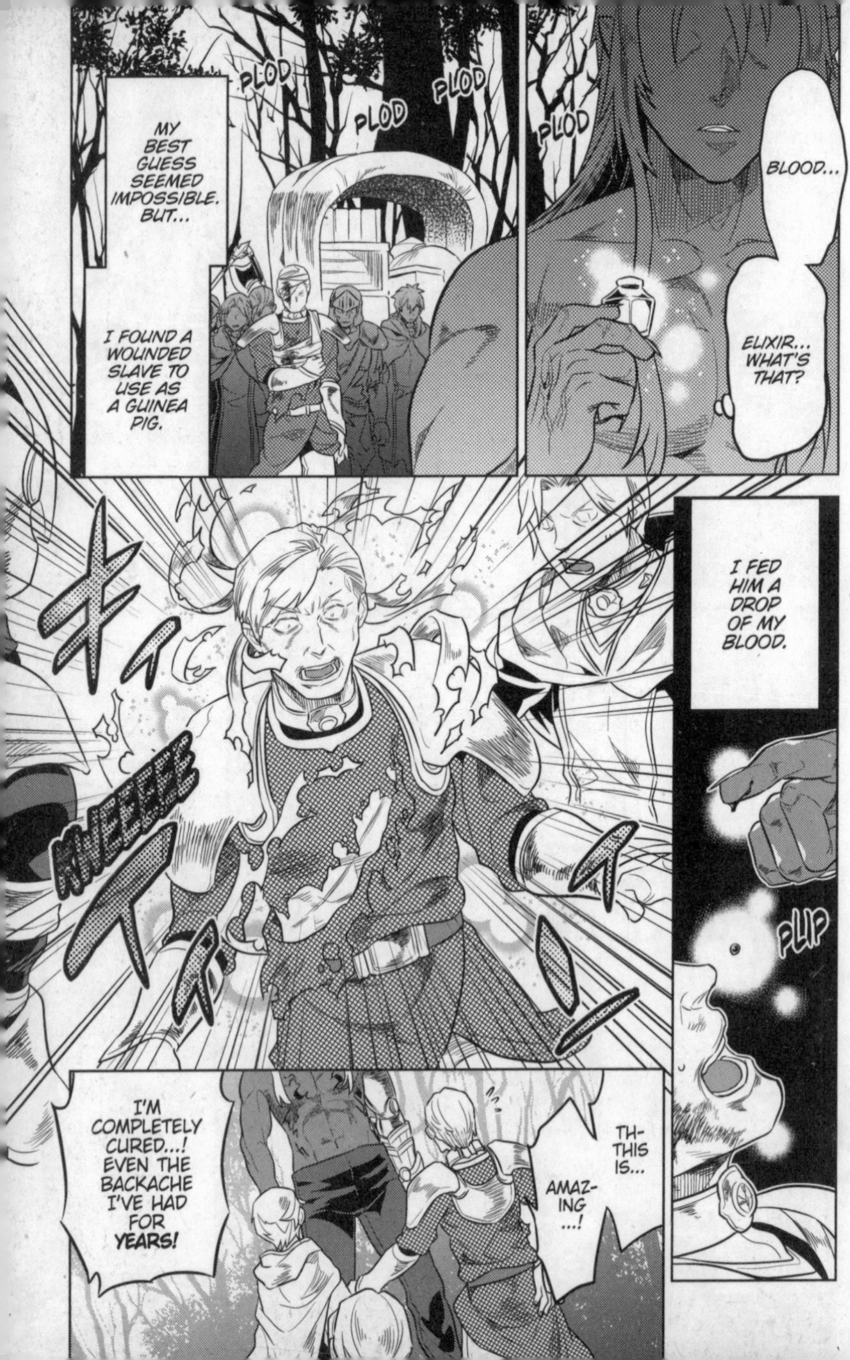
BLOOD...
ELIXIR... WHAT'S THAT?
PLOD
PLOD
PLOD
PLOD
MY BEST GUESS SEEMED IMPOSSIBLE. BUT...
I FOUND A WOUNDED SLAVE TO USE AS A GUINEA PIG.
I FED HIM A DROP OF MY BLOOD.
PLIP
KWEEEE
TH-THIS IS...
AMAZ-ING...!
I'M COMPLETELY CURED...! EVEN THE BACKACHE I'VE HAD FOR **YEARS!**

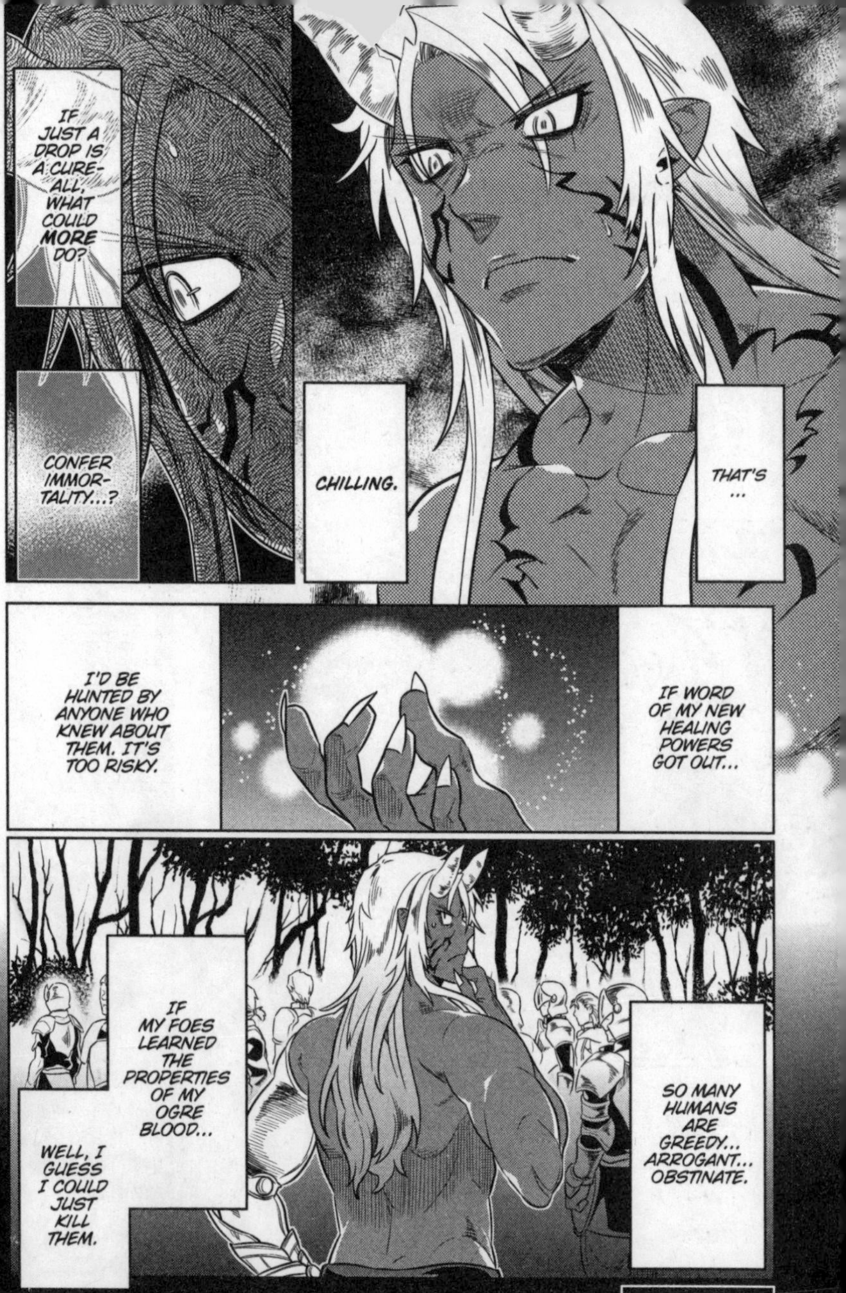
THAT'S ...
CHILLING.
IF JUST A DROP IS A CURE-ALL, WHAT COULD MORE DO?
CONFER IMMORTALITY...?
IF WORD OF MY NEW HEALING POWERS GOT OUT...
I'D BE HUNTED BY ANYONE WHO KNEW ABOUT THEM. IT'S TOO RISKY.
SO MANY HUMANS ARE GREEDY... ARROGANT... OBSTINATE.
IF MY FOES LEARNED THE PROPERTIES OF MY OGRE BLOOD...
WELL, I GUESS I COULD JUST KILL THEM.

▶ CONTINUE

Day 78

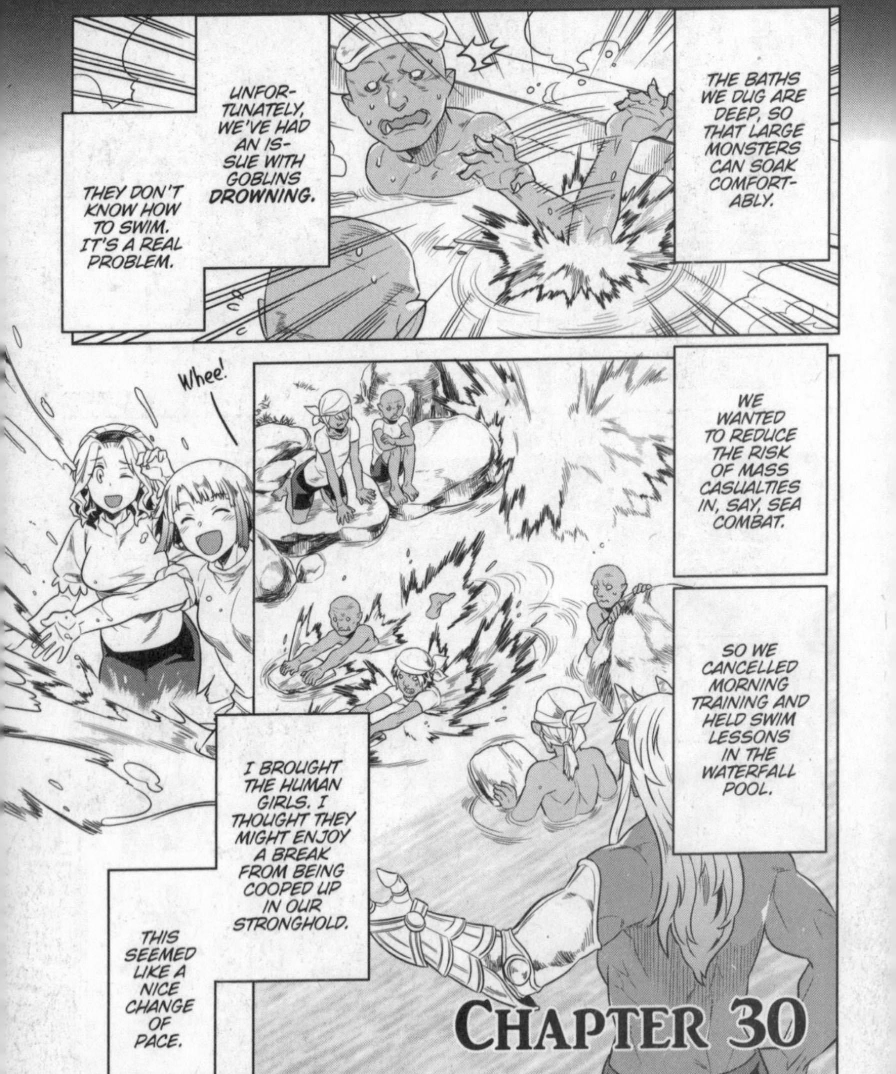
THE BATHS WE DUG ARE DEEP, SO THAT LARGE MONSTERS CAN SOAK COMFORTABLY.
UNFORTUNATELY, WE'VE HAD AN ISSUE WITH GOBLINS **DROWNING**.
THEY DON'T KNOW HOW TO SWIM. IT'S A REAL PROBLEM.
WE WANTED TO REDUCE THE RISK OF MASS CASUALTIES IN, SAY, SEA COMBAT.
SO WE CANCELLED MORNING TRAINING AND HELD SWIM LESSONS IN THE WATERFALL POOL.
Whee!
I BROUGHT THE HUMAN GIRLS. I THOUGHT THEY MIGHT ENJOY A BREAK FROM BEING COOPED UP IN OUR STRONGHOLD.
THIS SEEMED LIKE A NICE CHANGE OF PACE.
CHAPTER 30

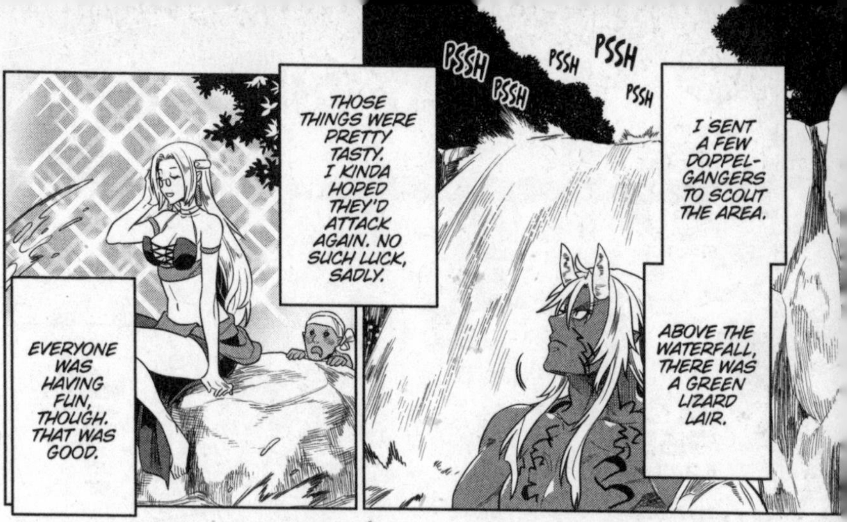
PSSH
PSSH
PSSH
PSSH
PSSH
I SENT A FEW DOPPEL-GANGERS TO SCOUT THE AREA.
ABOVE THE WATERFALL, THERE WAS A GREEN LIZARD LAIR.
THOSE THINGS WERE PRETTY TASTY. I KINDA HOPED THEY'D ATTACK AGAIN. NO SUCH LUCK, SADLY.
EVERYONE WAS HAVING FUN, THOUGH. THAT WAS GOOD.

DAY 79

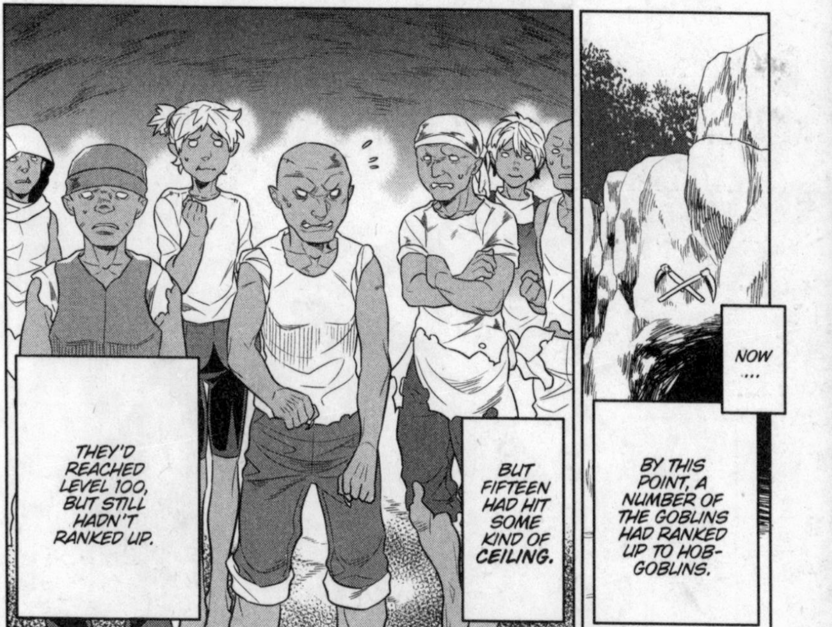
NOW ...
BY THIS POINT, A NUMBER OF THE GOBLINS HAD RANKED UP TO HOB-GOBLINS.
BUT FIFTEEN HAD HIT SOME KIND OF CEILING.
THEY'D REACHED LEVEL 100, BUT STILL HADN'T RANKED UP.

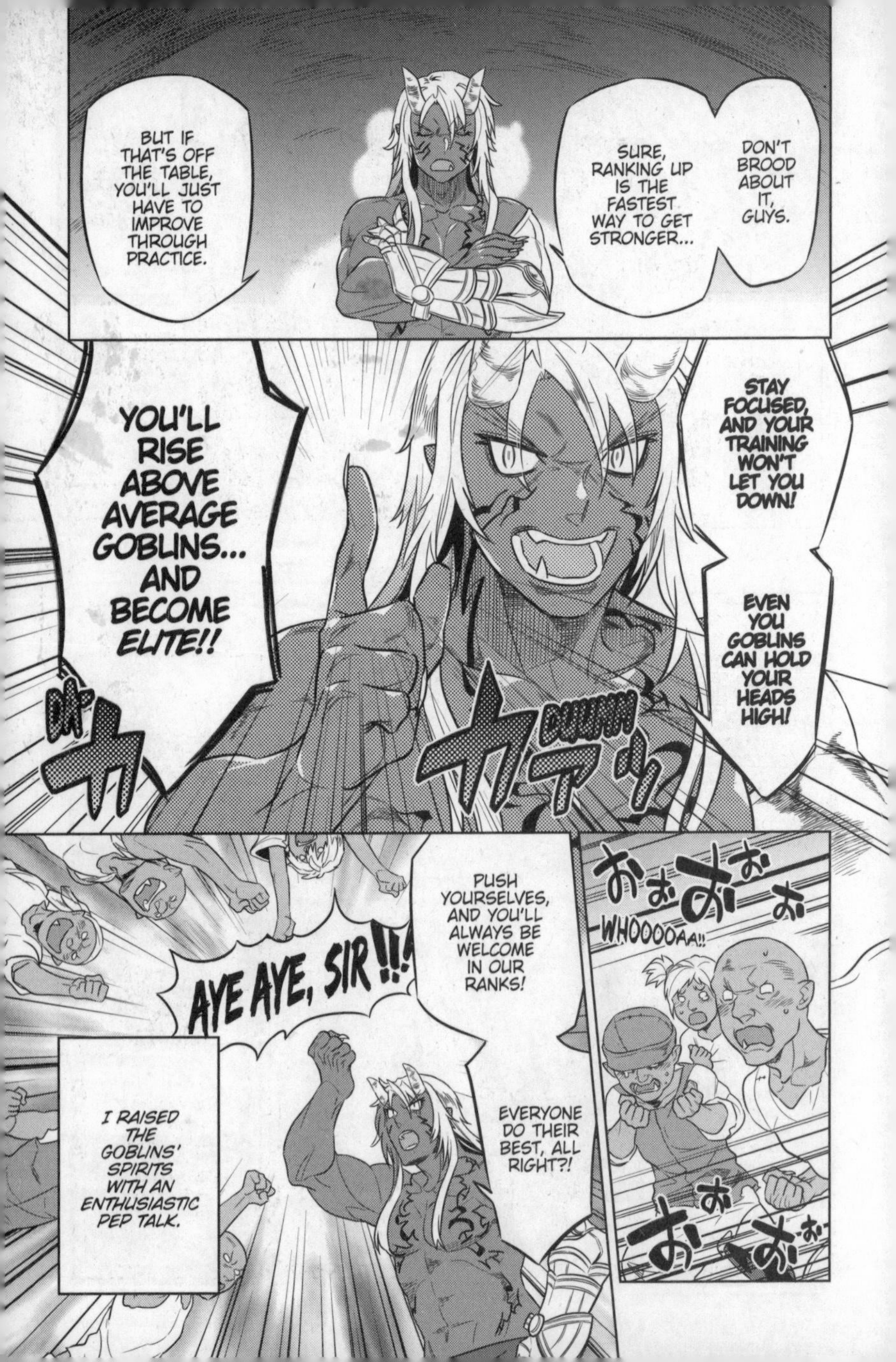
DON'T BROOD ABOUT IT, GUYS.
SURE, RANKING UP IS THE FASTEST WAY TO GET STRONGER...
BUT IF THAT'S OFF THE TABLE, YOU'LL JUST HAVE TO IMPROVE THROUGH PRACTICE.
STAY FOCUSED, AND YOUR TRAINING WON'T LET YOU DOWN!
EVEN YOU GOBLINS CAN HOLD YOUR HEADS HIGH!
カァッ
YOU'LL RISE ABOVE AVERAGE GOBLINS... AND BECOME ELITE!!
カッ
おぉおぉぉ
WHOOOOAA!!
PUSH YOURSELVES, AND YOU'LL ALWAYS BE WELCOME IN OUR RANKS!
EVERYONE DO THEIR BEST, ALL RIGHT?!
AYE AYE, SIR!!
I RAISED THE GOBLINS' SPIRITS WITH AN ENTHUSIASTIC PEP TALK.

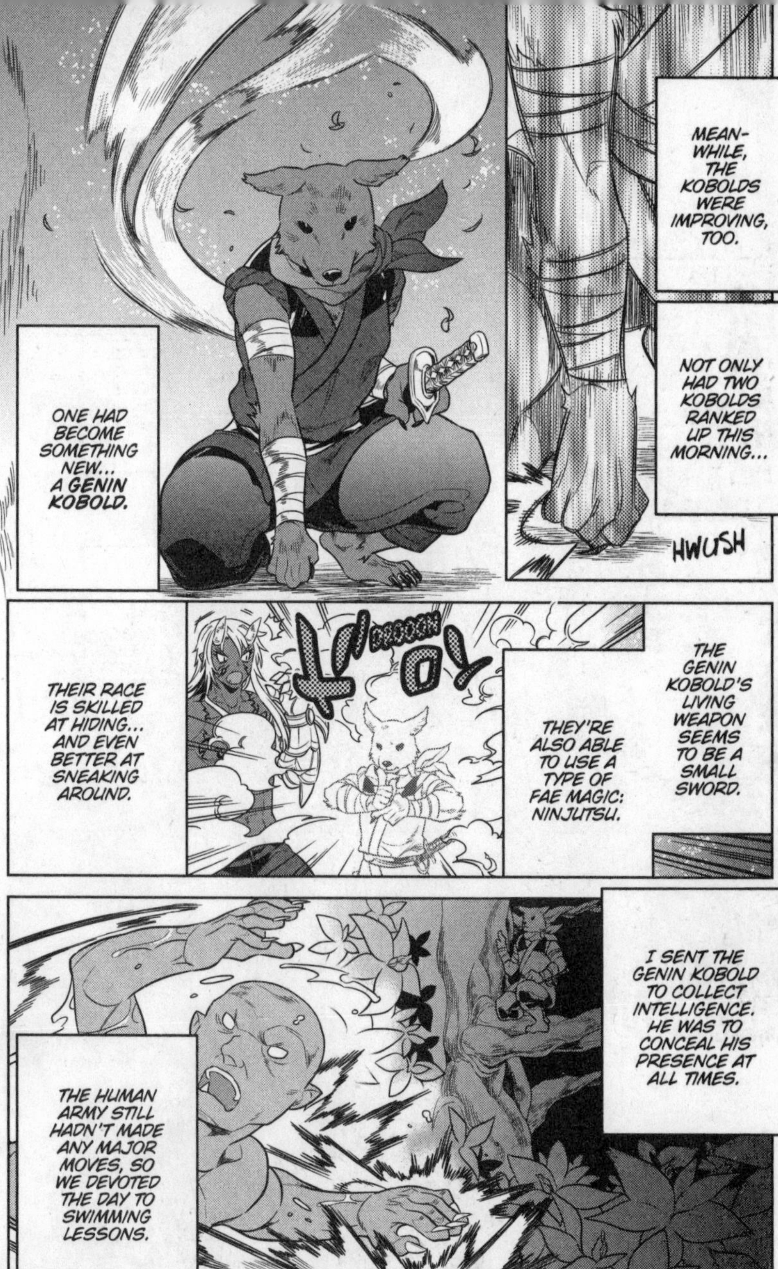
MEAN-WHILE, THE KOBOLDS WERE IMPROVING, TOO.
NOT ONLY HAD TWO KOBOLDS RANKED UP THIS MORNING...
HWUSH
ONE HAD BECOME SOMETHING NEW... A GENIN KOBOLD.
THE GENIN KOBOLD'S LIVING WEAPON SEEMS TO BE A SMALL SWORD.
THEY'RE ALSO ABLE TO USE A TYPE OF FAE MAGIC: NINJUTSU.
DROOOM
THEIR RACE IS SKILLED AT HIDING... AND EVEN BETTER AT SNEAKING AROUND.
I SENT THE GENIN KOBOLD TO COLLECT INTELLIGENCE. HE WAS TO CONCEAL HIS PRESENCE AT ALL TIMES.
THE HUMAN ARMY STILL HADN'T MADE ANY MAJOR MOVES, SO WE DEVOTED THE DAY TO SWIMMING LESSONS.

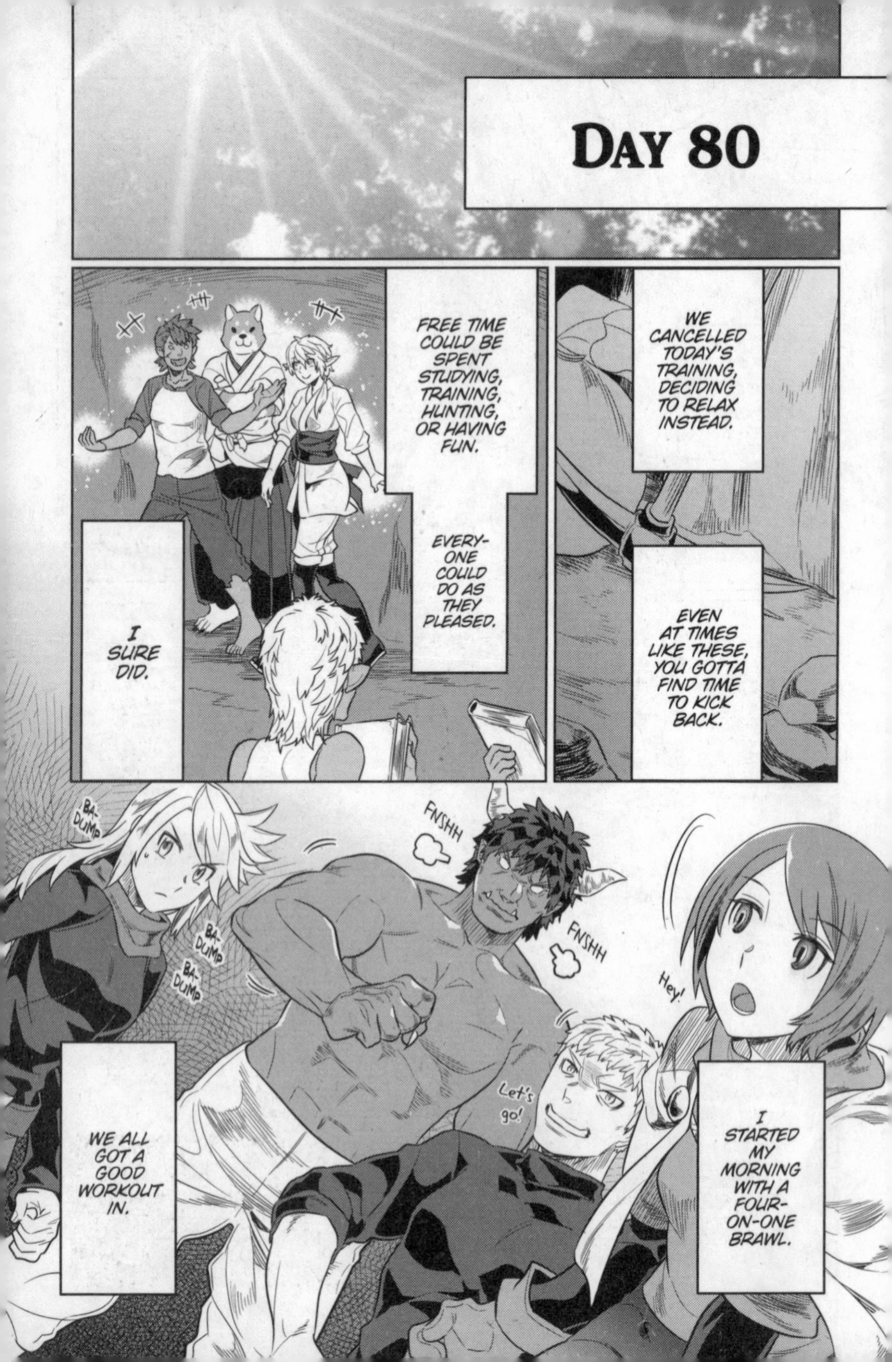
DAY 80
WE CANCELLED TODAY'S TRAINING, DECIDING TO RELAX INSTEAD.
EVEN AT TIMES LIKE THESE, YOU GOTTA FIND TIME TO KICK BACK.
FREE TIME COULD BE SPENT STUDYING, TRAINING, HUNTING, OR HAVING FUN.
EVERY-ONE COULD DO AS THEY PLEASED.
I SURE DID.
Hey!
I STARTED MY MORNING WITH A FOUR-ON-ONE BRAWL.
FNSHH
FNSHH
Let's go!
BA-DUMP
BA-DUMP
BA-DUMP
WE ALL GOT A GOOD WORKOUT IN.

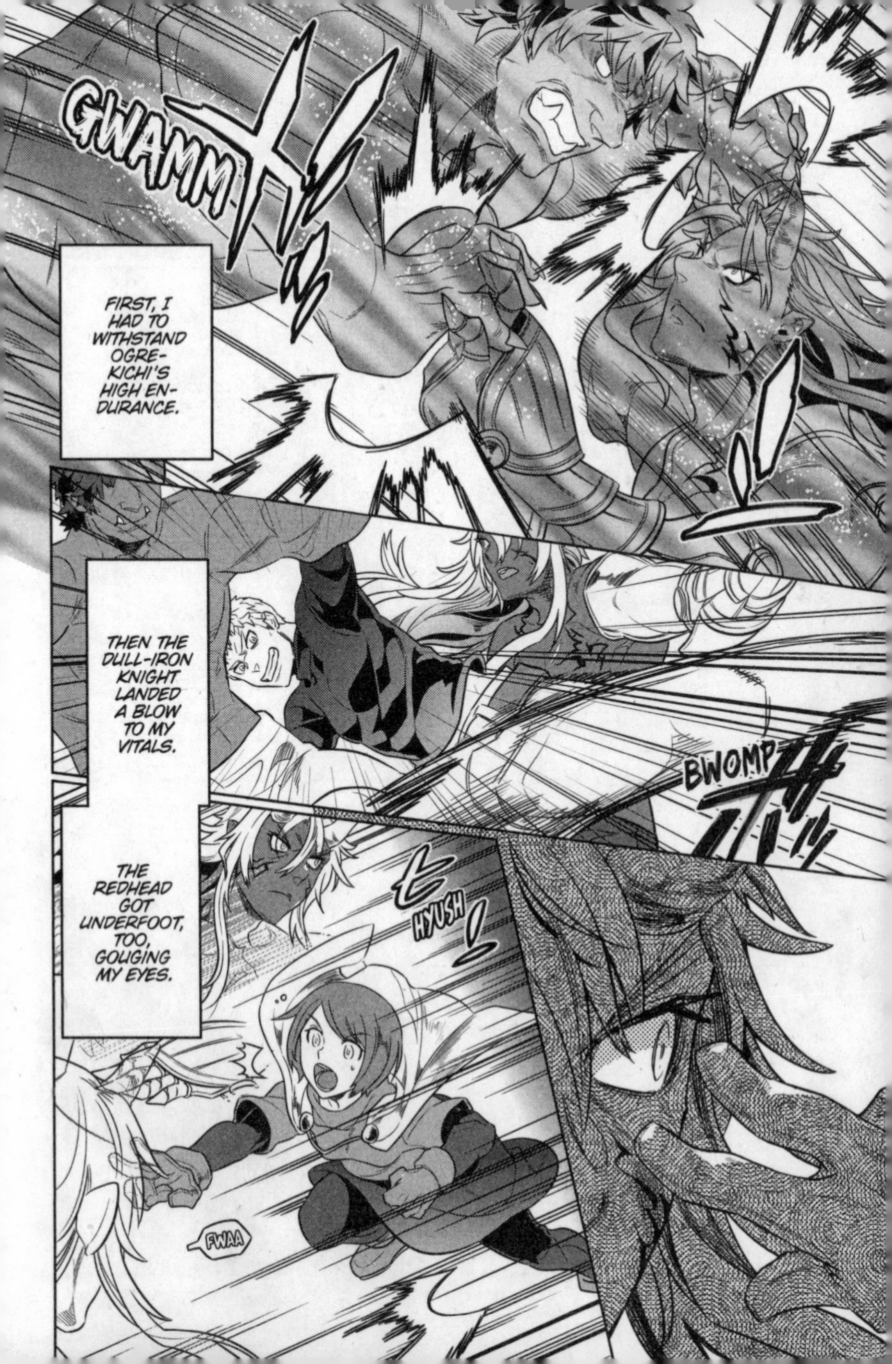
GWAMM
FIRST, I HAD TO WITHSTAND OGRE-KICHI'S HIGH EN-DURANCE.
BWOMP
THEN THE DULL-IRON KNIGHT LANDED A BLOW TO MY VITALS.
HYUSH
THE REDHEAD GOT UNDERFOOT, TOO, GOUGING MY EYES.
FWAA

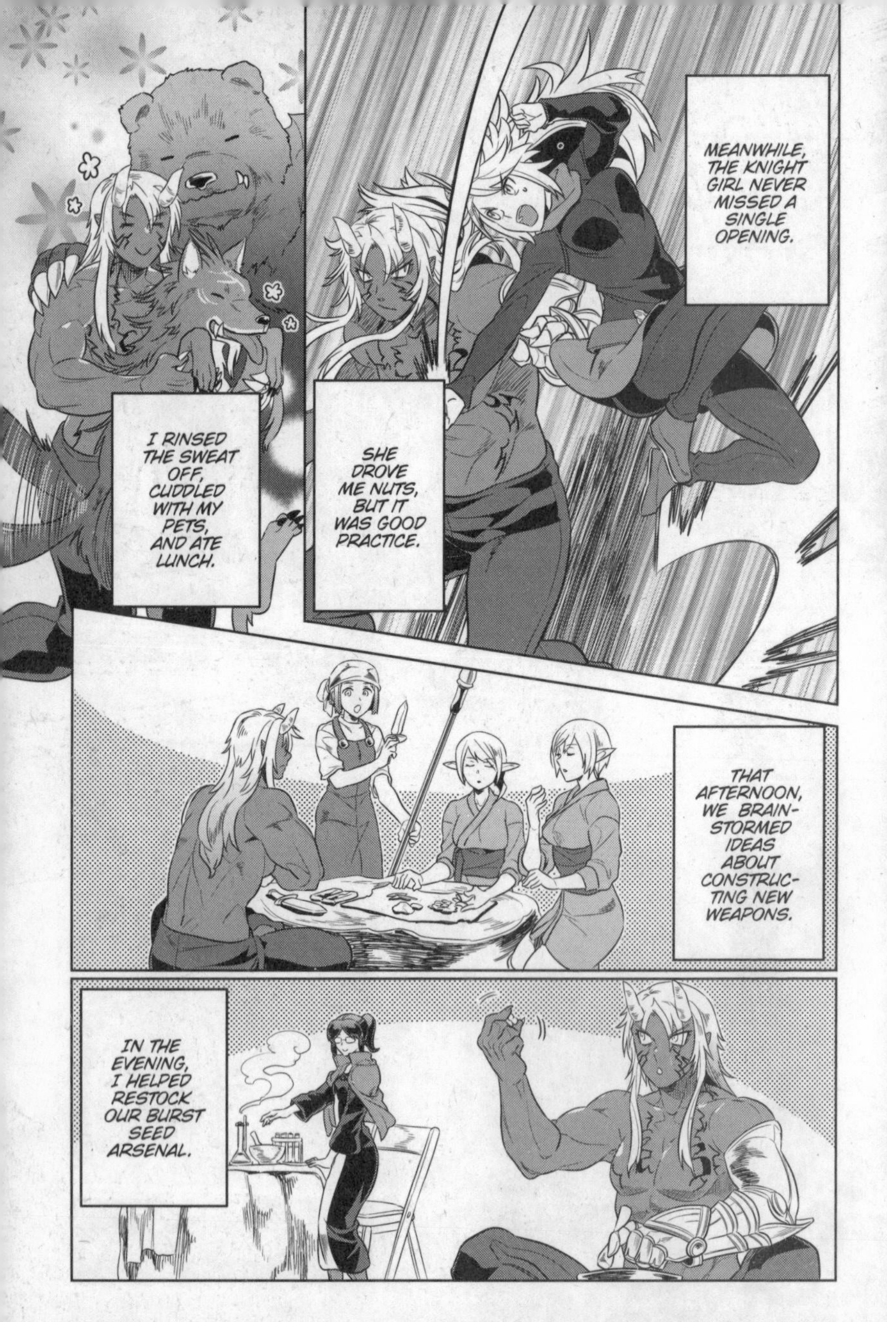
MEANWHILE, THE KNIGHT GIRL NEVER MISSED A SINGLE OPENING.
SHE DROVE ME NUTS, BUT IT WAS GOOD PRACTICE.
I RINSED THE SWEAT OFF, CUDDLED WITH MY PETS, AND ATE LUNCH.
THAT AFTERNOON, WE BRAIN-STORMED IDEAS ABOUT CONSTRUC-TING NEW WEAPONS.
IN THE EVENING, I HELPED RESTOCK OUR BURST SEED ARSENAL.

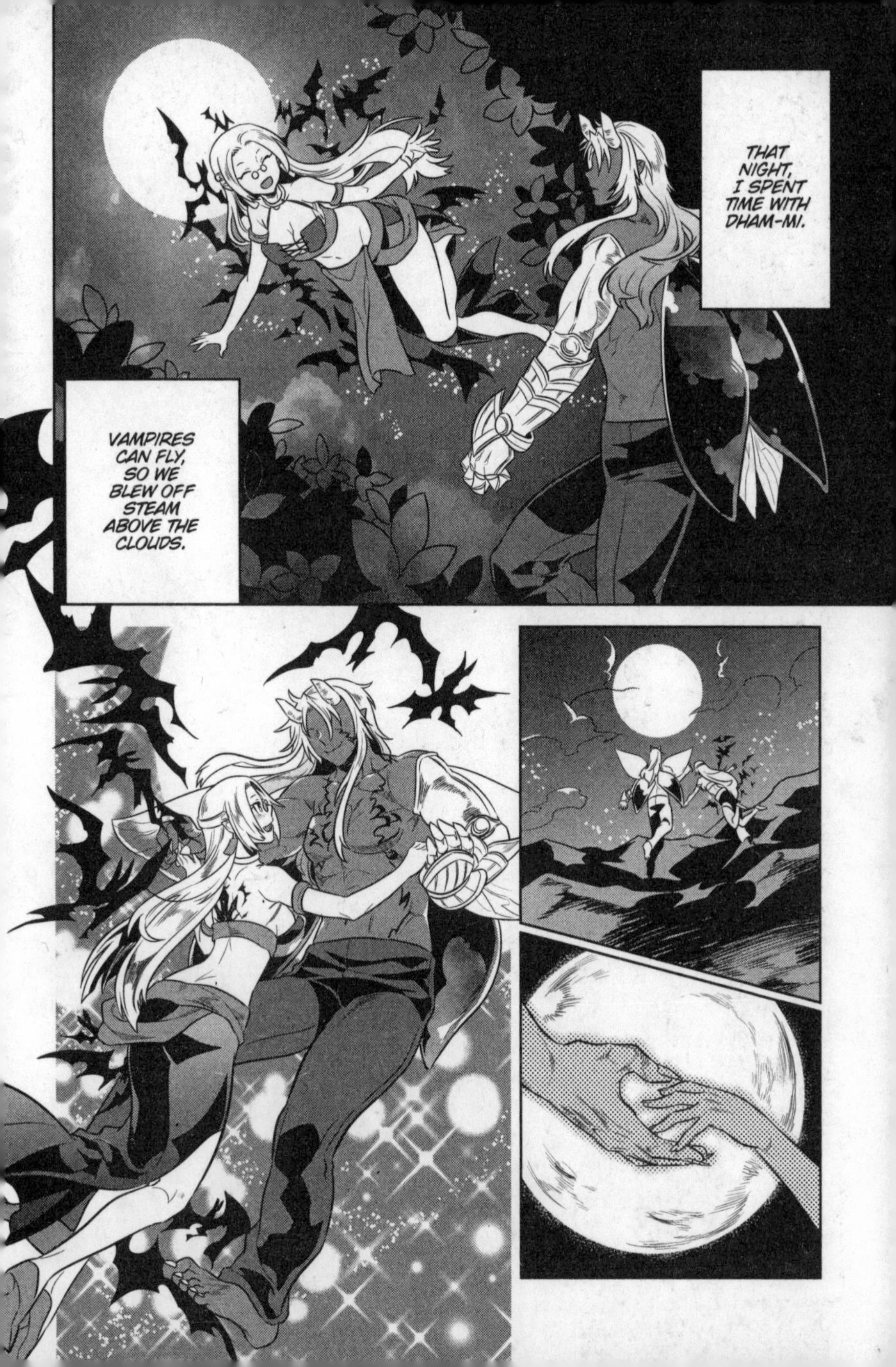
THAT NIGHT, I SPENT TIME WITH DHAM-MI.
VAMPIRES CAN FLY, SO WE BLEW OFF STEAM ABOVE THE CLOUDS.

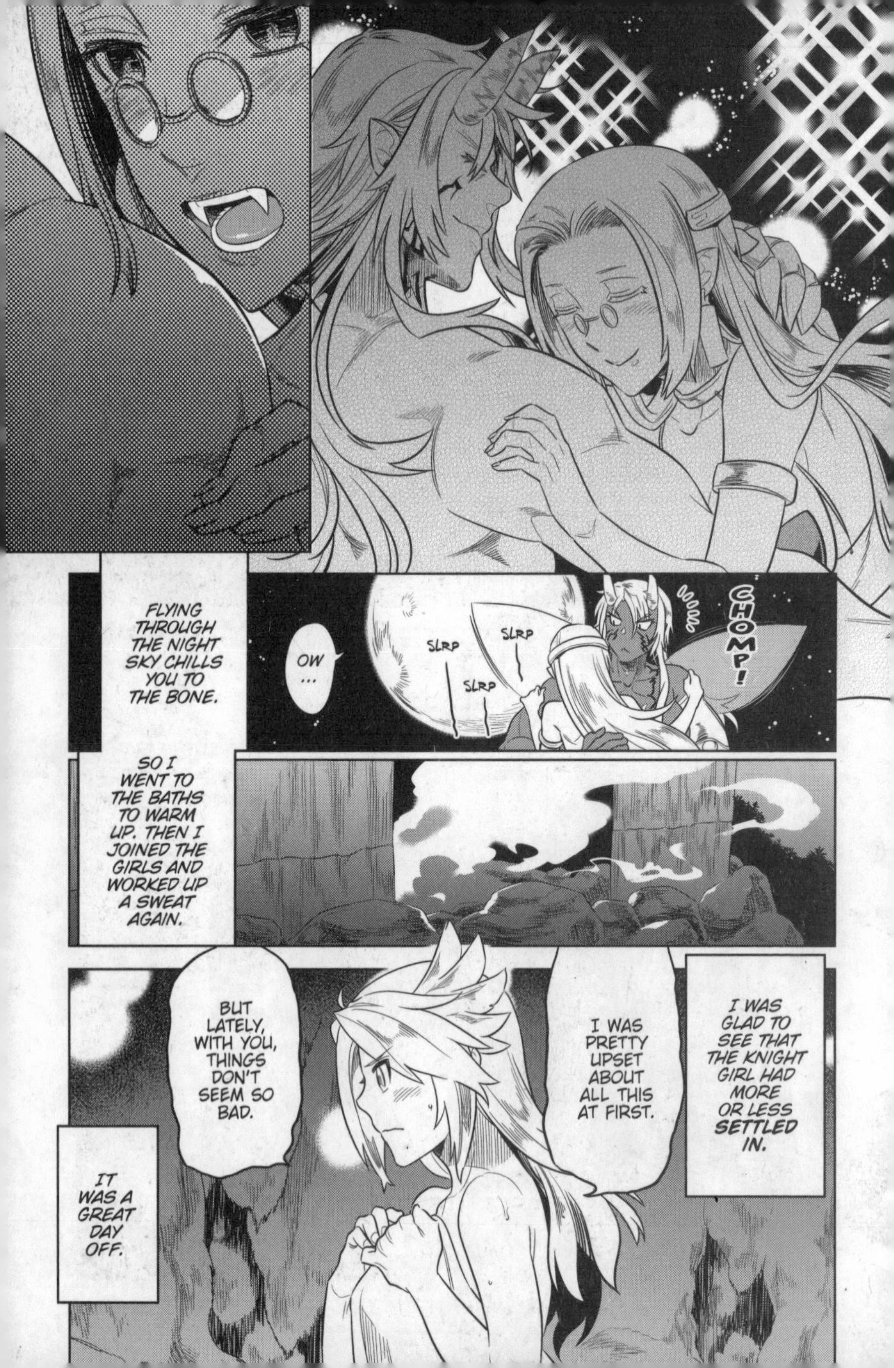
CHOMP!
SLRP
SLRP
SLRP
OW ...
FLYING THROUGH THE NIGHT SKY CHILLS YOU TO THE BONE.
SO I WENT TO THE BATHS TO WARM UP. THEN I JOINED THE GIRLS AND WORKED UP A SWEAT AGAIN.
I WAS GLAD TO SEE THAT THE KNIGHT GIRL HAD MORE OR LESS **SETTLED IN.**
I WAS PRETTY UPSET ABOUT ALL THIS AT FIRST.
BUT LATELY, WITH YOU, THINGS DON'T SEEM SO BAD.
IT WAS A GREAT DAY OFF.

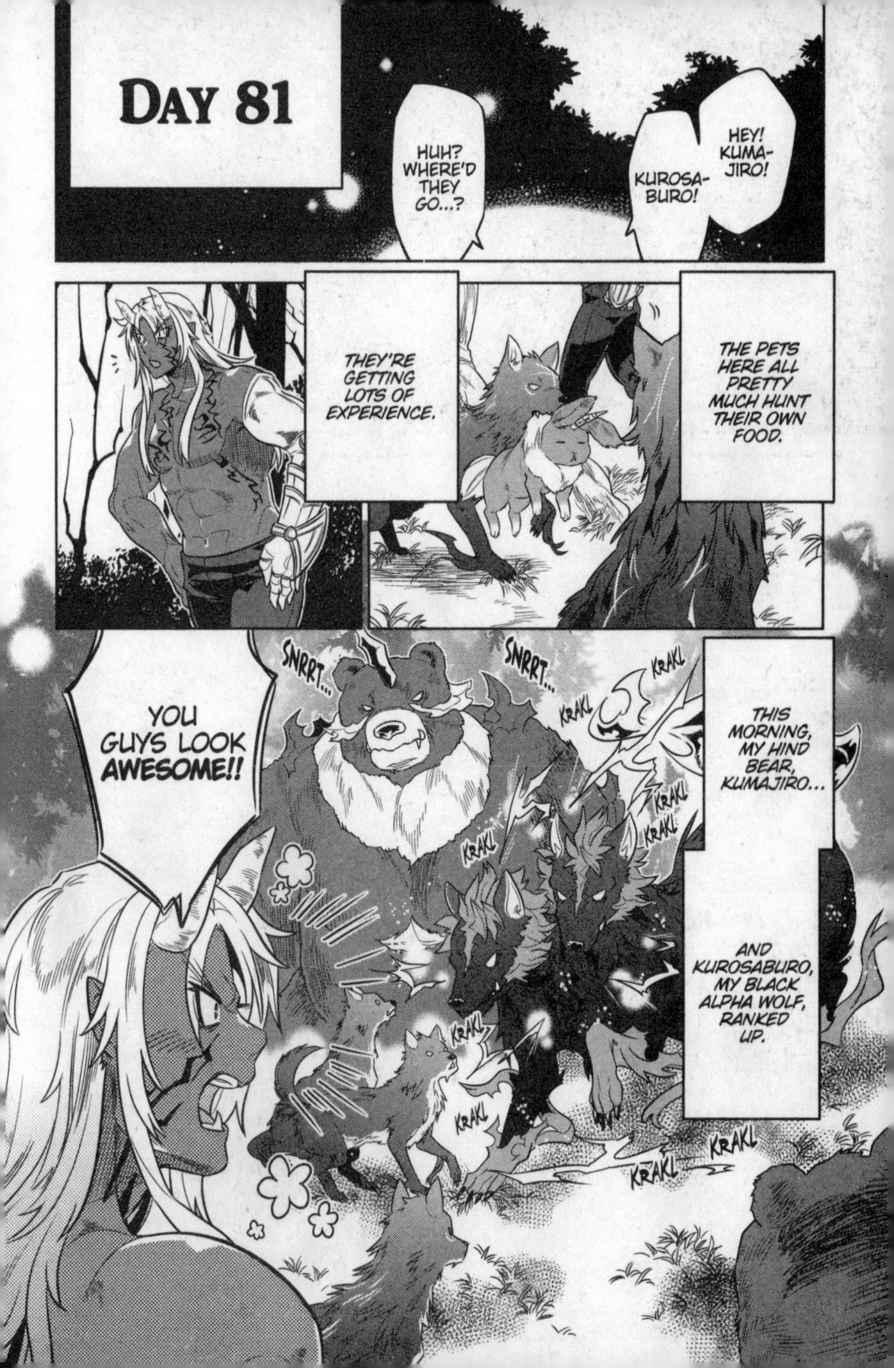
HEY! KUMA-JIRO!
KUROSA-BURO!
HUH? WHERE'D THEY GO...?
DAY 81
THE PETS HERE ALL PRETTY MUCH HUNT THEIR OWN FOOD.
THEY'RE GETTING LOTS OF EXPERIENCE.
THIS MORNING, MY HIND BEAR, KUMAJIRO...
AND KUROSABURO, MY BLACK ALPHA WOLF, RANKED UP.
KRAKL
KRAKL
KRAKL
KRAKL
SNRRT...
KRAKL
SNRRT...
KRAKL
KRAKL
KRAKL
KRAKL
KRAKL
YOU GUYS LOOK **AWESOME!!**

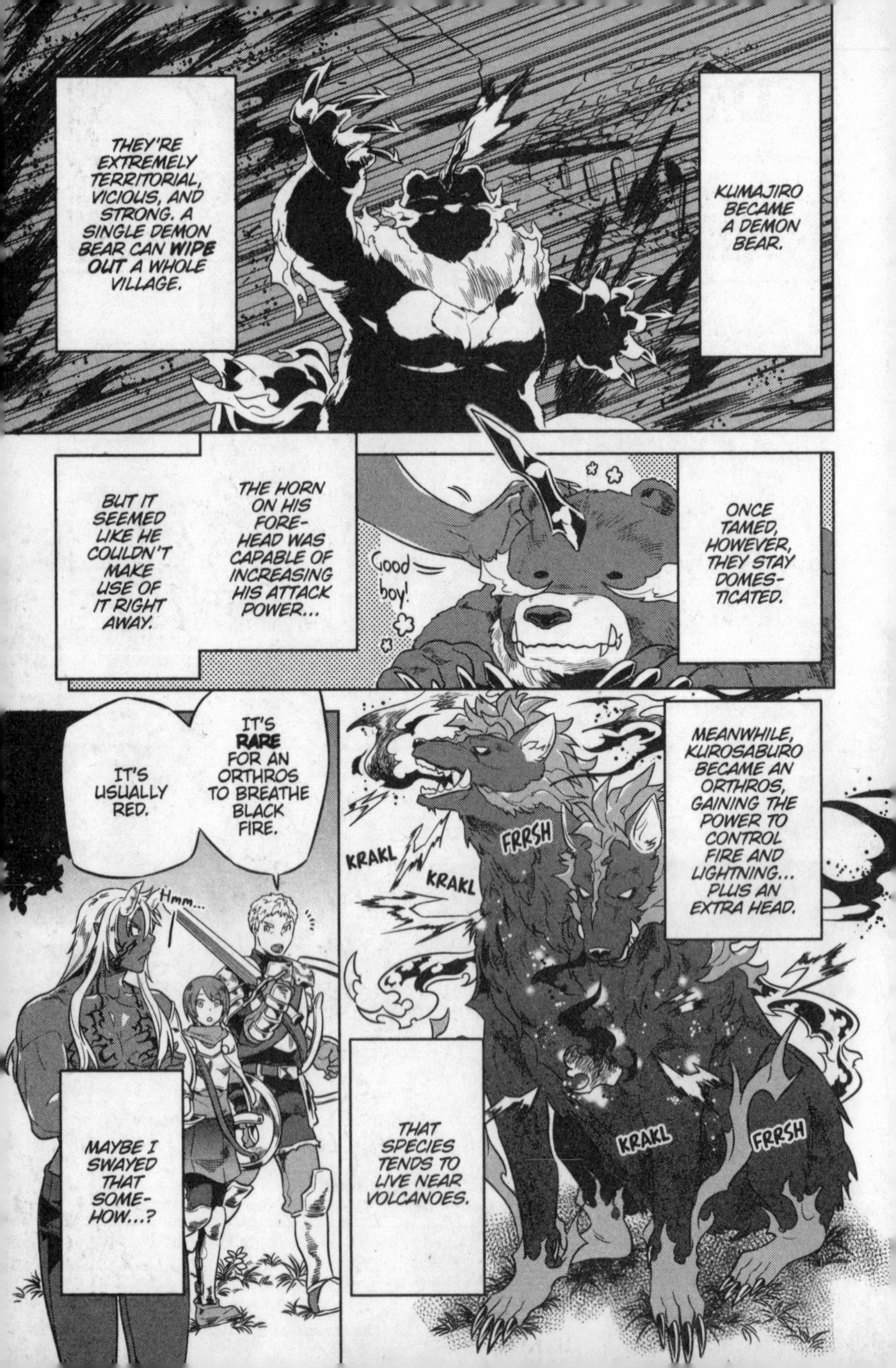
KUMAJIRO BECAME A DEMON BEAR.
THEY'RE EXTREMELY TERRITORIAL, VICIOUS, AND STRONG. A SINGLE DEMON BEAR CAN WIPE OUT A WHOLE VILLAGE.
ONCE TAMED, HOWEVER, THEY STAY DOMESTICATED.
Good boy!
THE HORN ON HIS FOREHEAD WAS CAPABLE OF INCREASING HIS ATTACK POWER...
BUT IT SEEMED LIKE HE COULDN'T MAKE USE OF IT RIGHT AWAY.
MEANWHILE, KUROSABURO BECAME AN ORTHROS, GAINING THE POWER TO CONTROL FIRE AND LIGHTNING... PLUS AN EXTRA HEAD.
FRRSH
KRAKL
KRAKL
KRAKL
FRRSH
THAT SPECIES TENDS TO LIVE NEAR VOLCANOES.
IT'S RARE FOR AN ORTHROS TO BREATHE BLACK FIRE.
IT'S USUALLY RED.
Hmm...
MAYBE I SWAYED THAT SOMEHOW...?

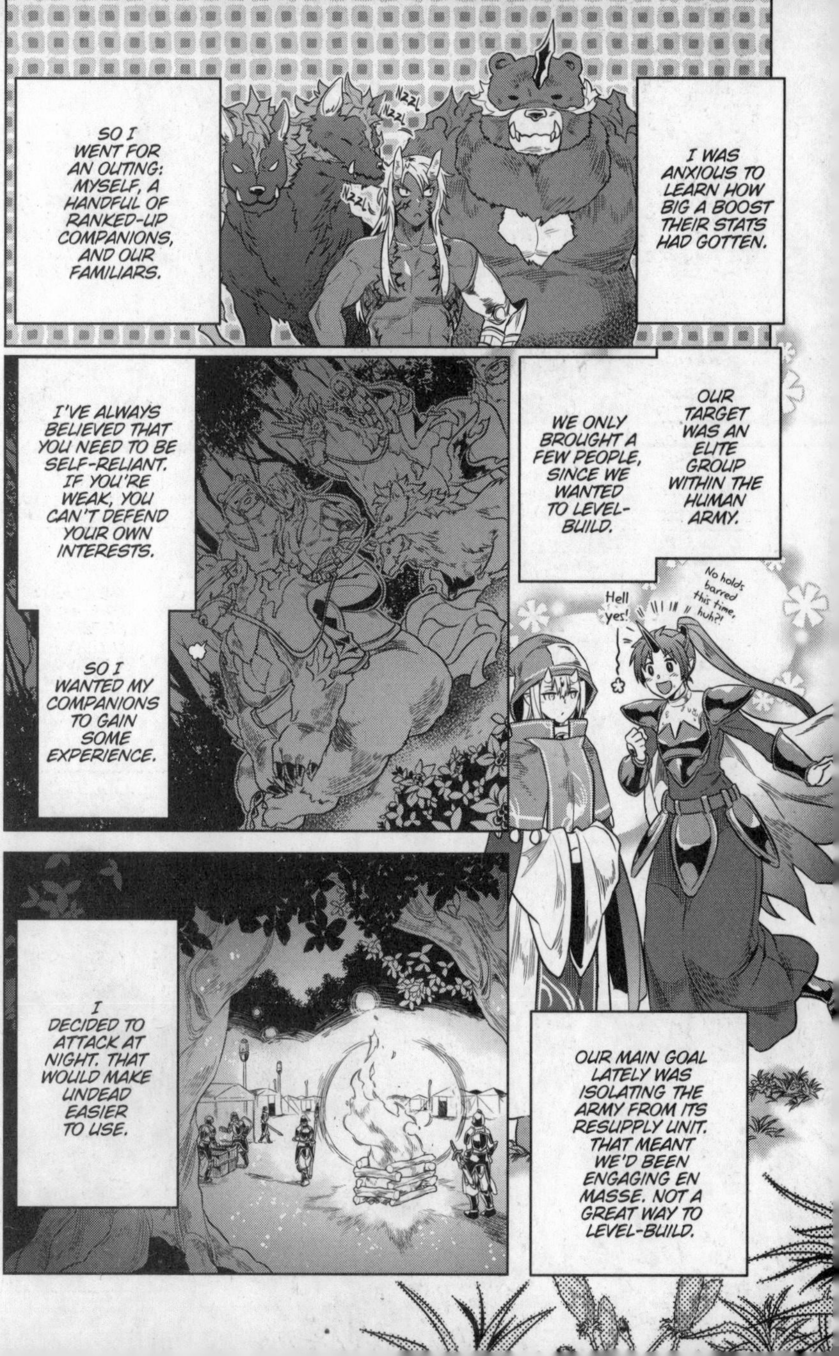
I WAS ANXIOUS TO LEARN HOW BIG A BOOST THEIR STATS HAD GOTTEN.
NZZL
NZZL
SO I WENT FOR AN OUTING: MYSELF, A HANDFUL OF RANKED-UP COMPANIONS, AND OUR FAMILIARS.
NZZL
OUR TARGET WAS AN ELITE GROUP WITHIN THE HUMAN ARMY.
WE ONLY BROUGHT A FEW PEOPLE, SINCE WE WANTED TO LEVEL-BUILD.
No holds barred this time, huh?!
Hell yes!
OUR MAIN GOAL LATELY WAS ISOLATING THE ARMY FROM ITS RESUPPLY UNIT. THAT MEANT WE'D BEEN ENGAGING EN MASSE. NOT A GREAT WAY TO LEVEL-BUILD.
I'VE ALWAYS BELIEVED THAT YOU NEED TO BE SELF-RELIANT. IF YOU'RE WEAK, YOU CAN'T DEFEND YOUR OWN INTERESTS.
SO I WANTED MY COMPANIONS TO GAIN SOME EXPERIENCE.
I DECIDED TO ATTACK AT NIGHT. THAT WOULD MAKE UNDEAD EASIER TO USE.

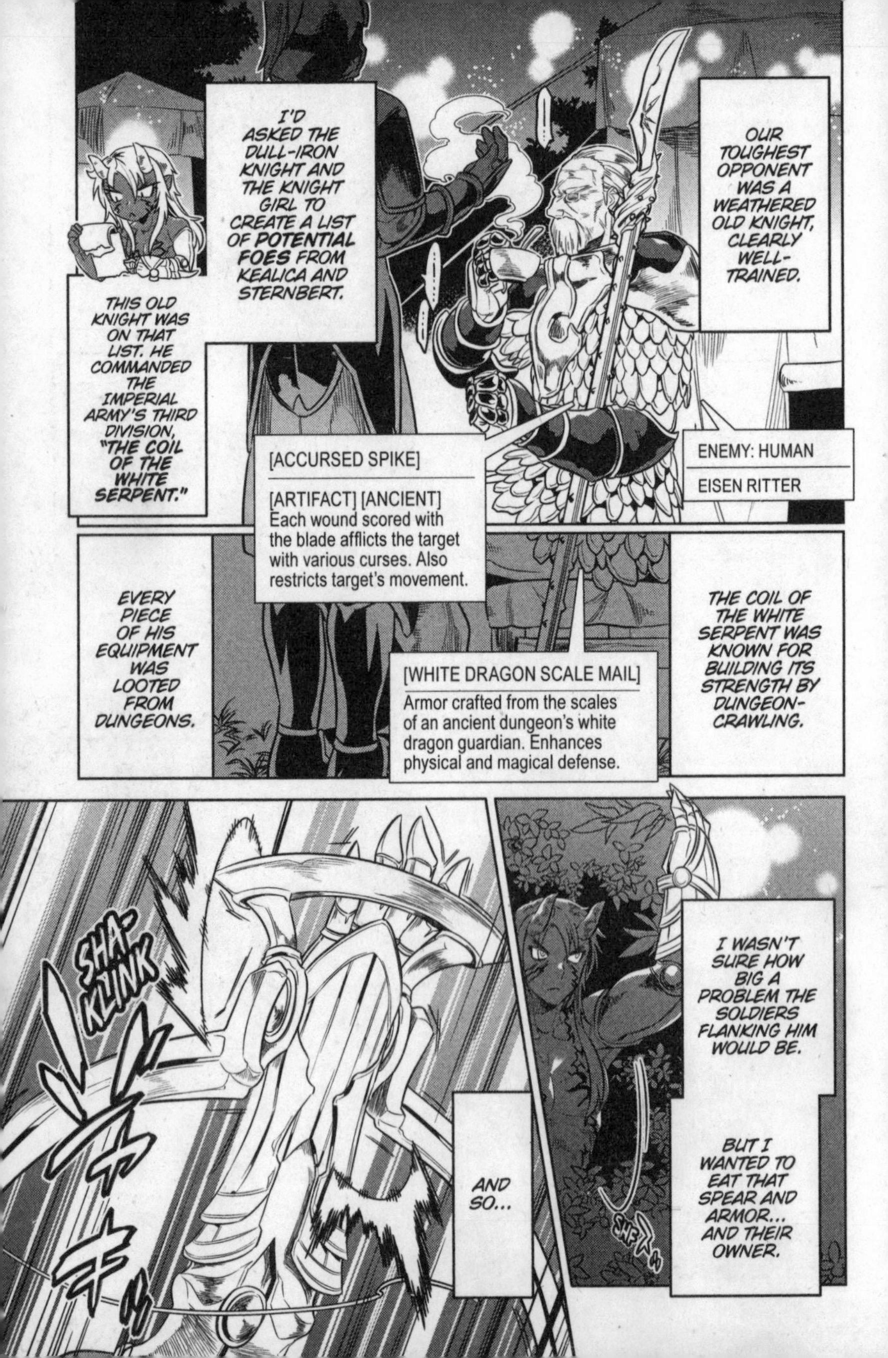

OUR TOUGHEST OPPONENT WAS A WEATHERED OLD KNIGHT, CLEARLY WELL-TRAINED.
I'D ASKED THE DULL-IRON KNIGHT AND THE KNIGHT GIRL TO CREATE A LIST OF **POTENTIAL FOES** FROM KEALICA AND STERNBERT.
THIS OLD KNIGHT WAS ON THAT LIST. HE COMMANDED THE IMPERIAL ARMY'S THIRD DIVISION, **"THE COIL OF THE WHITE SERPENT."**
ENEMY: HUMAN
EISEN RITTER
[ACCURSED SPIKE]
[ARTIFACT] [ANCIENT]
Each wound scored with the blade afflicts the target with various curses. Also restricts target's movement.
THE COIL OF THE WHITE SERPENT WAS KNOWN FOR BUILDING ITS STRENGTH BY DUNGEON-CRAWLING.
[WHITE DRAGON SCALE MAIL]
Armor crafted from the scales of an ancient dungeon's white dragon guardian. Enhances physical and magical defense.
EVERY PIECE OF HIS EQUIPMENT WAS LOOTED FROM DUNGEONS.
I WASN'T SURE HOW BIG A PROBLEM THE SOLDIERS FLANKING HIM WOULD BE.
BUT I WANTED TO EAT THAT SPEAR AND ARMOR... AND THEIR OWNER.
AND SO...
SHA-KLINK

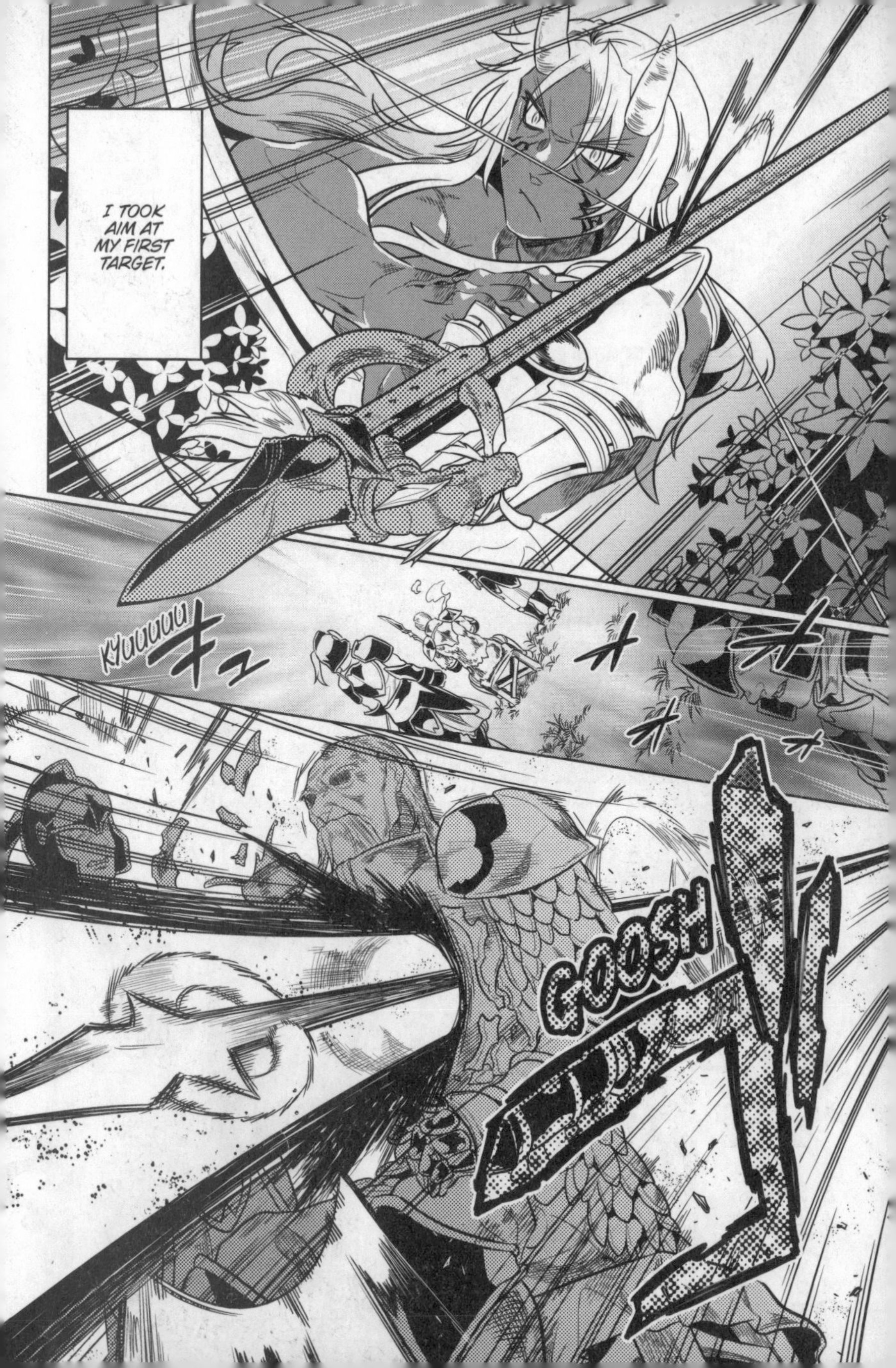
I TOOK AIM AT MY FIRST TARGET.
KYUUUUU
キュ
GOOSH

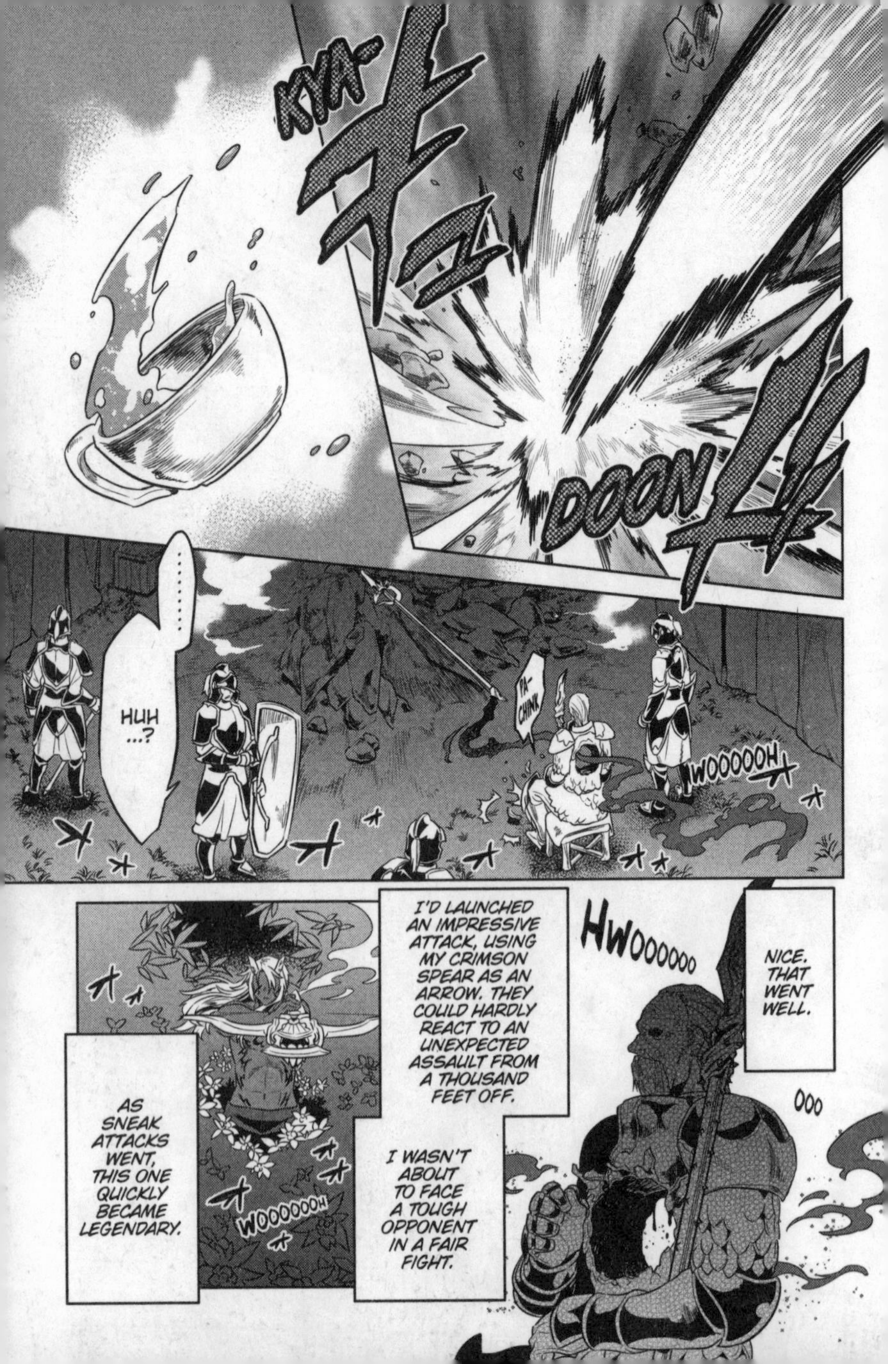
KYA-
DOOON!!
PA-CHINK
WOOOOOH
......
HUH ...?
NICE. THAT WENT WELL.
HWOOOOOO
OOO
I'D LAUNCHED AN IMPRESSIVE ATTACK, USING MY CRIMSON SPEAR AS AN ARROW. THEY COULD HARDLY REACT TO AN UNEXPECTED ASSAULT FROM A THOUSAND FEET OFF.
I WASN'T ABOUT TO FACE A TOUGH OPPONENT IN A FAIR FIGHT.
AS SNEAK ATTACKS WENT, THIS ONE QUICKLY BECAME LEGENDARY.
WOOOOOOH

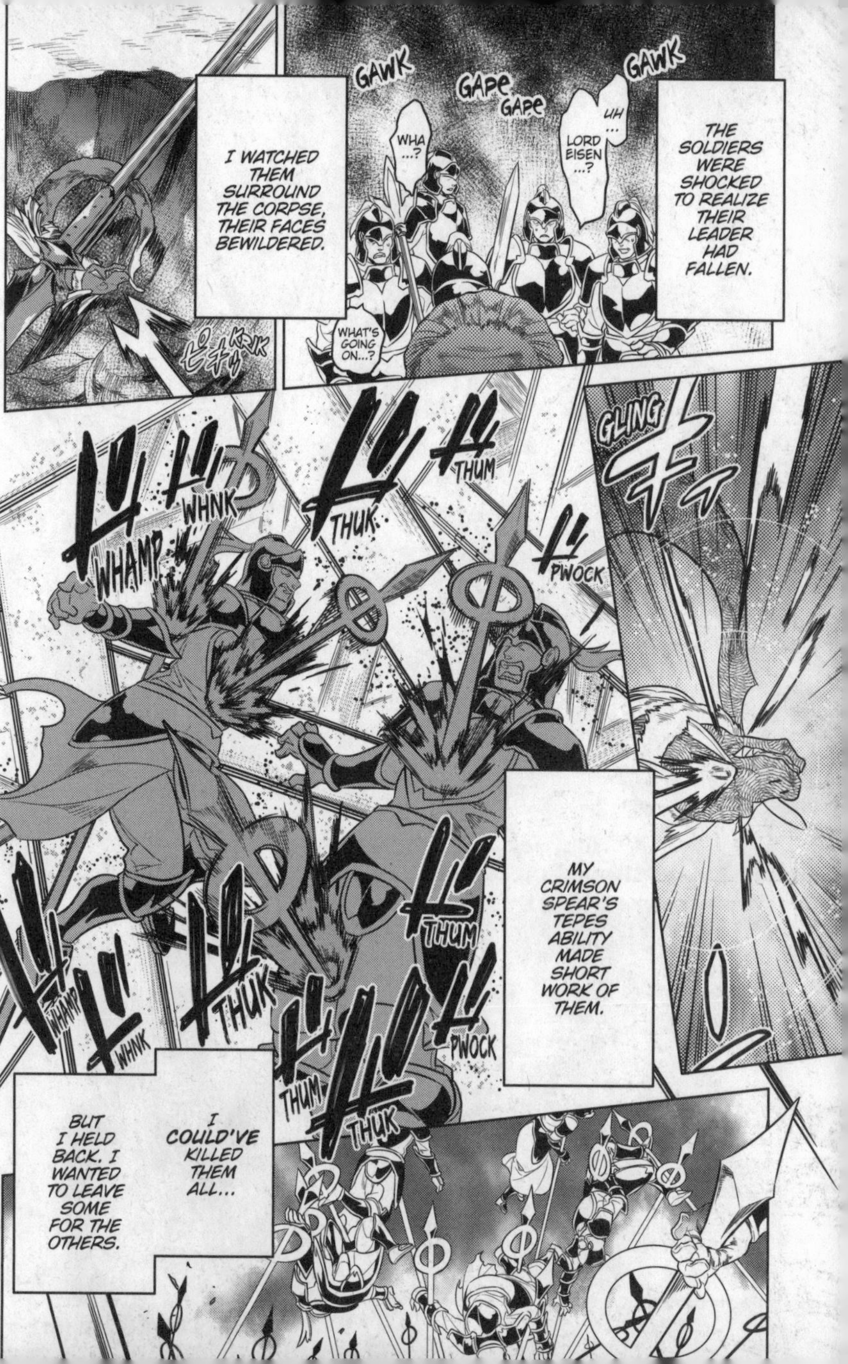
THE SOLDIERS WERE SHOCKED TO REALIZE THEIR LEADER HAD FALLEN.
GAWK
GAPE GAPE
GAWK
UH...
LORD EISEN...?
WHA...?
WHAT'S GOING ON...?
I WATCHED THEM SURROUND THE CORPSE, THEIR FACES BEWILDERED.
KRIK
GLING
THUM
THUK
WHNK
WHAMP
PWOCK
MY CRIMSON SPEAR'S TEPES ABILITY MADE SHORT WORK OF THEM.
THUM
PWOCK
THUK
WHAMP
WHNK
THUM
THUK
I COULD'VE KILLED THEM ALL...
BUT I HELD BACK. I WANTED TO LEAVE SOME FOR THE OTHERS.

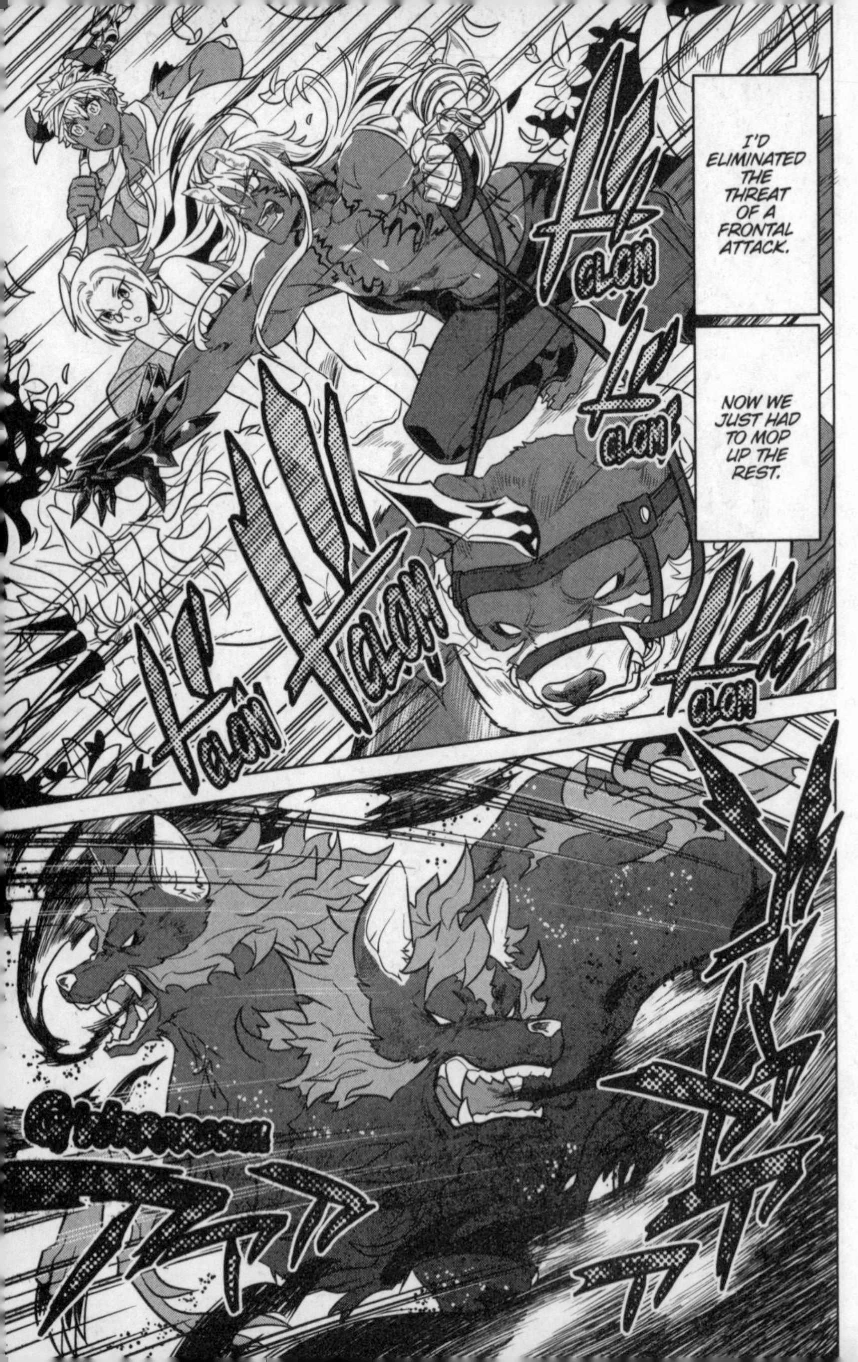
I'D ELIMINATED THE THREAT OF A FRONTAL ATTACK.
CLOP
CLOP
NOW WE JUST HAD TO MOP UP THE REST.
CLOP
CLOP
CLOP

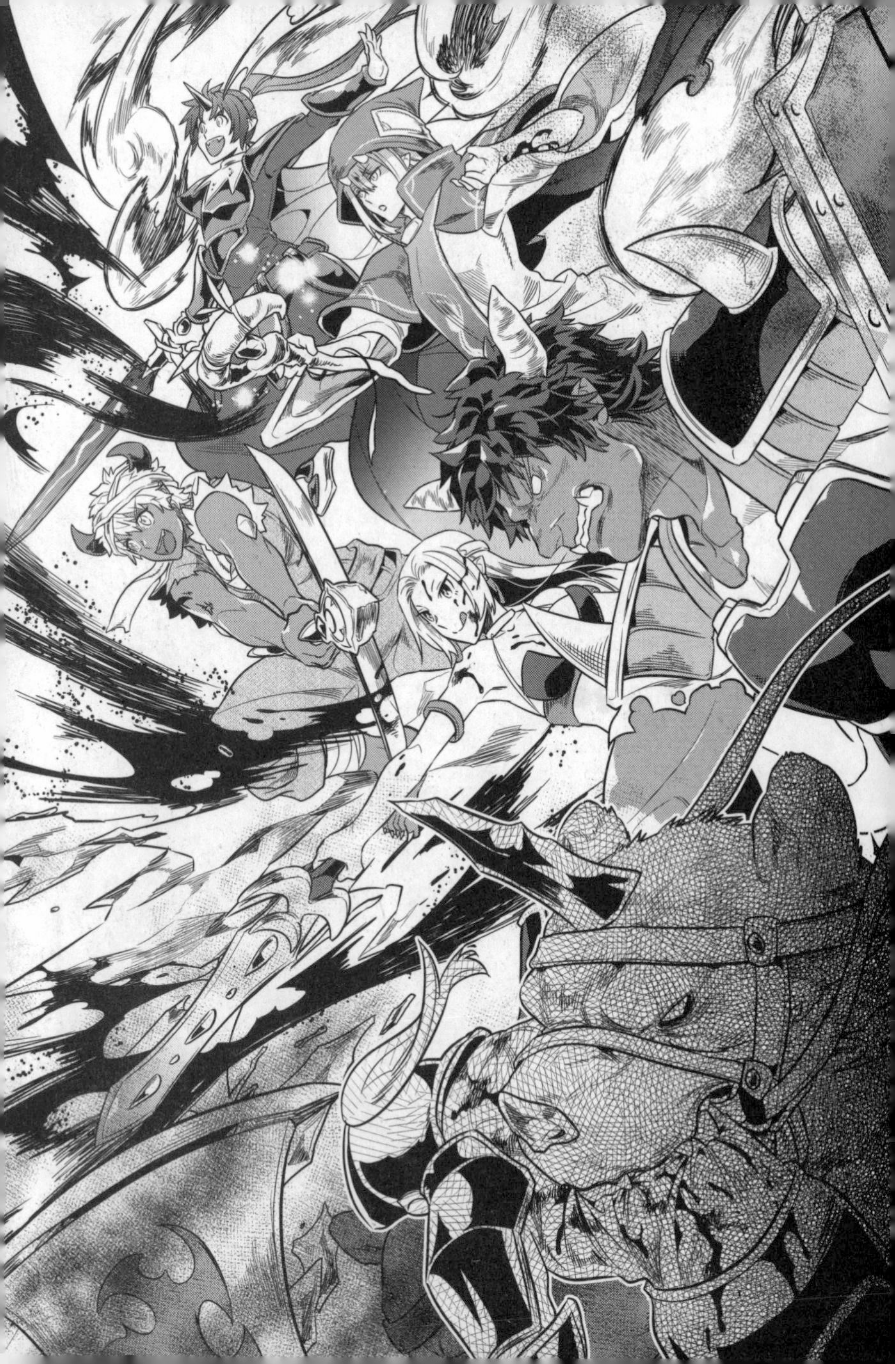

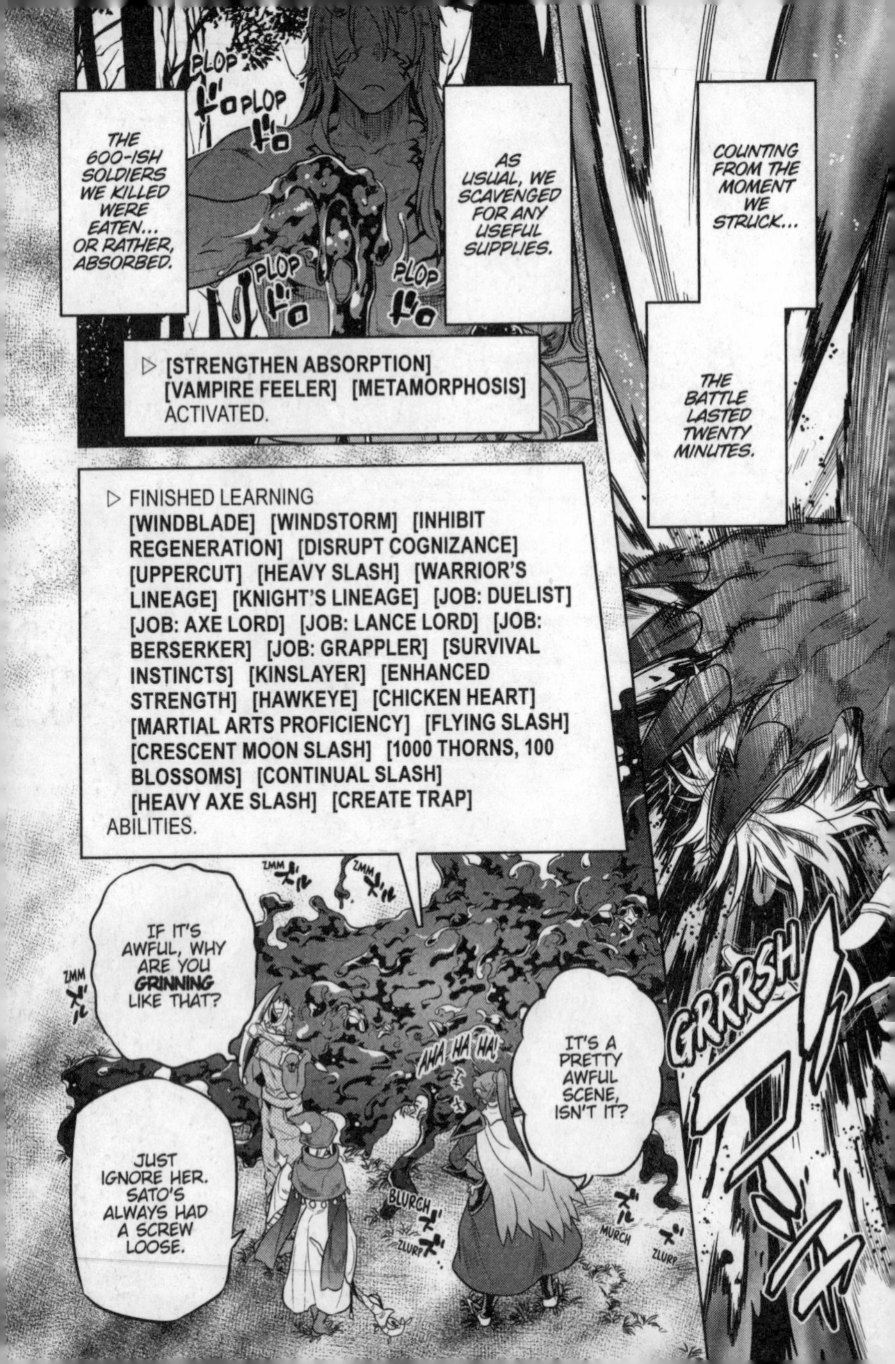
COUNTING FROM THE MOMENT WE STRUCK...
THE BATTLE LASTED TWENTY MINUTES.
AS USUAL, WE SCAVENGED FOR ANY USEFUL SUPPLIES.
PLOP
PLOP
THE 600-ISH SOLDIERS WE KILLED WERE EATEN... OR RATHER, ABSORBED.
PLOP
PLOP
▷ [STRENGTHEN ABSORPTION] [VAMPIRE FEELER] [METAMORPHOSIS] ACTIVATED.
GRRRSH
▷ FINISHED LEARNING [WINDBLADE] [WINDSTORM] [INHIBIT REGENERATION] [DISRUPT COGNIZANCE] [UPPERCUT] [HEAVY SLASH] [WARRIOR'S LINEAGE] [KNIGHT'S LINEAGE] [JOB: DUELIST] [JOB: AXE LORD] [JOB: LANCE LORD] [JOB: BERSERKER] [JOB: GRAPPLER] [SURVIVAL INSTINCTS] [KINSLAYER] [ENHANCED STRENGTH] [HAWKEYE] [CHICKEN HEART] [MARTIAL ARTS PROFICIENCY] [FLYING SLASH] [CRESCENT MOON SLASH] [1000 THORNS, 100 BLOSSOMS] [CONTINUAL SLASH] [HEAVY AXE SLASH] [CREATE TRAP] ABILITIES.
ZMM
ZMM
IT'S A PRETTY AWFUL SCENE, ISN'T IT?
AHA HA HA!
IF IT'S AWFUL, WHY ARE YOU GRINNING LIKE THAT?
ZMM
JUST IGNORE HER. SATO'S ALWAYS HAD A SCREW LOOSE.
ZLURP
MURCH
BLURCH
ZLURP

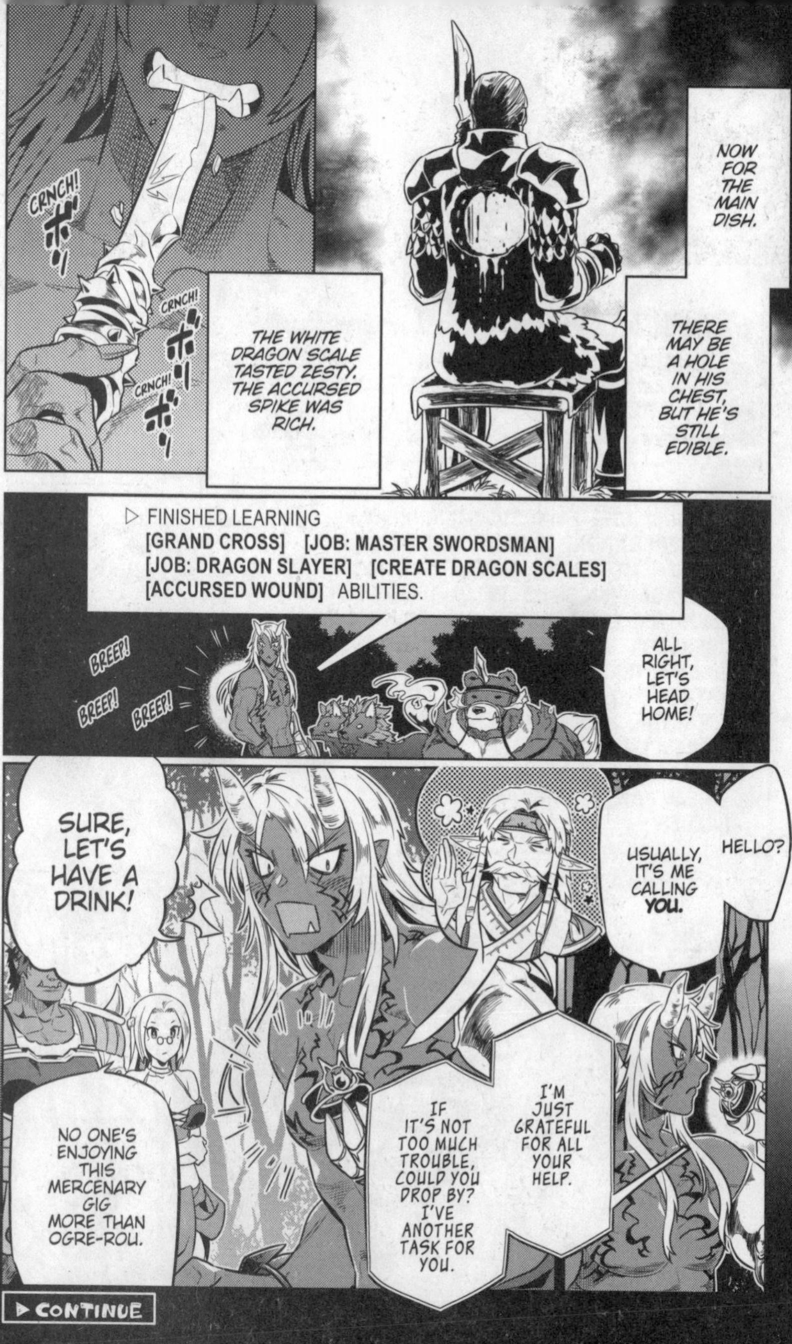
NOW FOR THE MAIN DISH.
THERE MAY BE A HOLE IN HIS CHEST, BUT HE'S STILL EDIBLE.
THE WHITE DRAGON SCALE TASTED ZESTY. THE ACCURSED SPIKE WAS RICH.
CRNCH!
CRNCH!
CRNCH!
▷ FINISHED LEARNING [GRAND CROSS] [JOB: MASTER SWORDSMAN] [JOB: DRAGON SLAYER] [CREATE DRAGON SCALES] [ACCURSED WOUND] ABILITIES.
ALL RIGHT, LET'S HEAD HOME!
BREEP!
BREEP!
BREEP!
HELLO?
USUALLY, IT'S ME CALLING **YOU.**
SURE, LET'S HAVE A DRINK!
I'M JUST GRATEFUL FOR ALL YOUR HELP.
IF IT'S NOT TOO MUCH TROUBLE, COULD YOU DROP BY? I'VE ANOTHER TASK FOR YOU.
NO ONE'S ENJOYING THIS MERCENARY GIG MORE THAN OGRE-ROU.
▶ CONTINUE

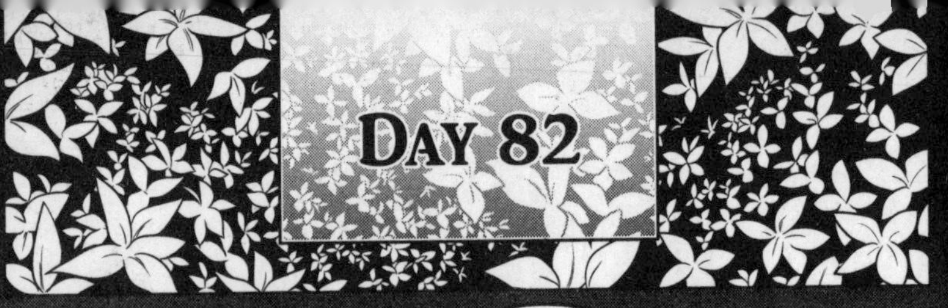
DAY 82

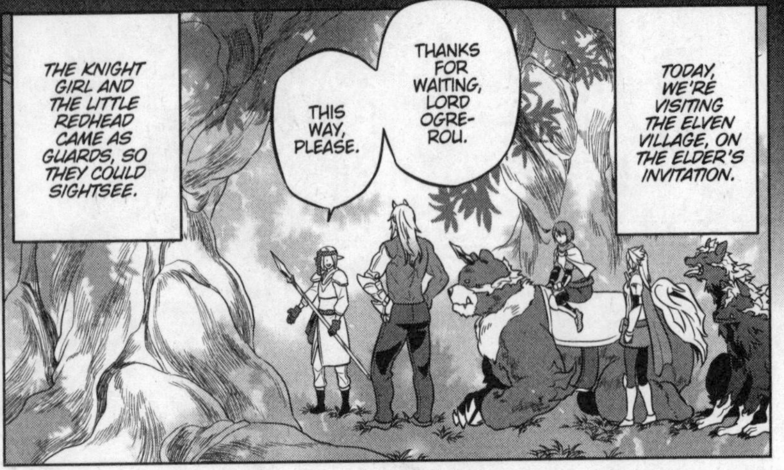
TODAY, WE'RE VISITING THE ELVEN VILLAGE, ON THE ELDER'S INVITATION.
THANKS FOR WAITING, LORD OGRE-ROU.
THIS WAY, PLEASE.
THE KNIGHT GIRL AND THE LITTLE REDHEAD CAME AS GUARDS, SO THEY COULD SIGHTSEE.

CHAPTER 31

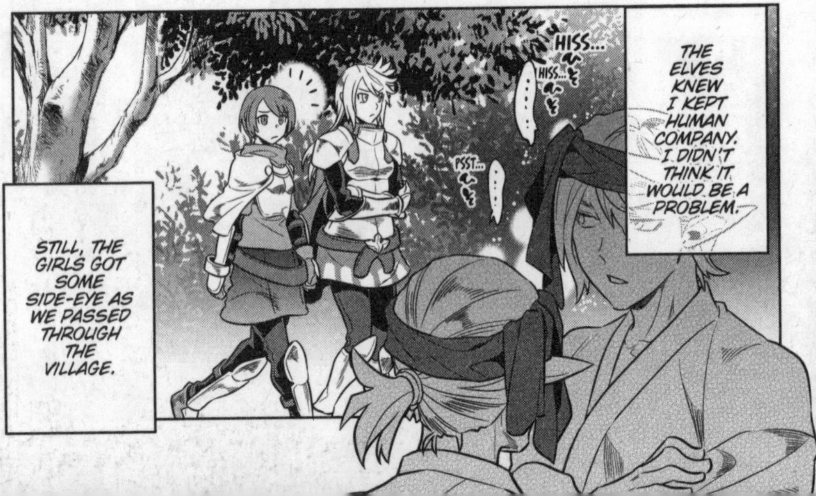
THE ELVES KNEW I KEPT HUMAN COMPANY. I DIDN'T THINK IT WOULD BE A PROBLEM.
HISS...
HISS...
...
PSST...
...
STILL, THE GIRLS GOT SOME SIDE-EYE AS WE PASSED THROUGH THE VILLAGE.

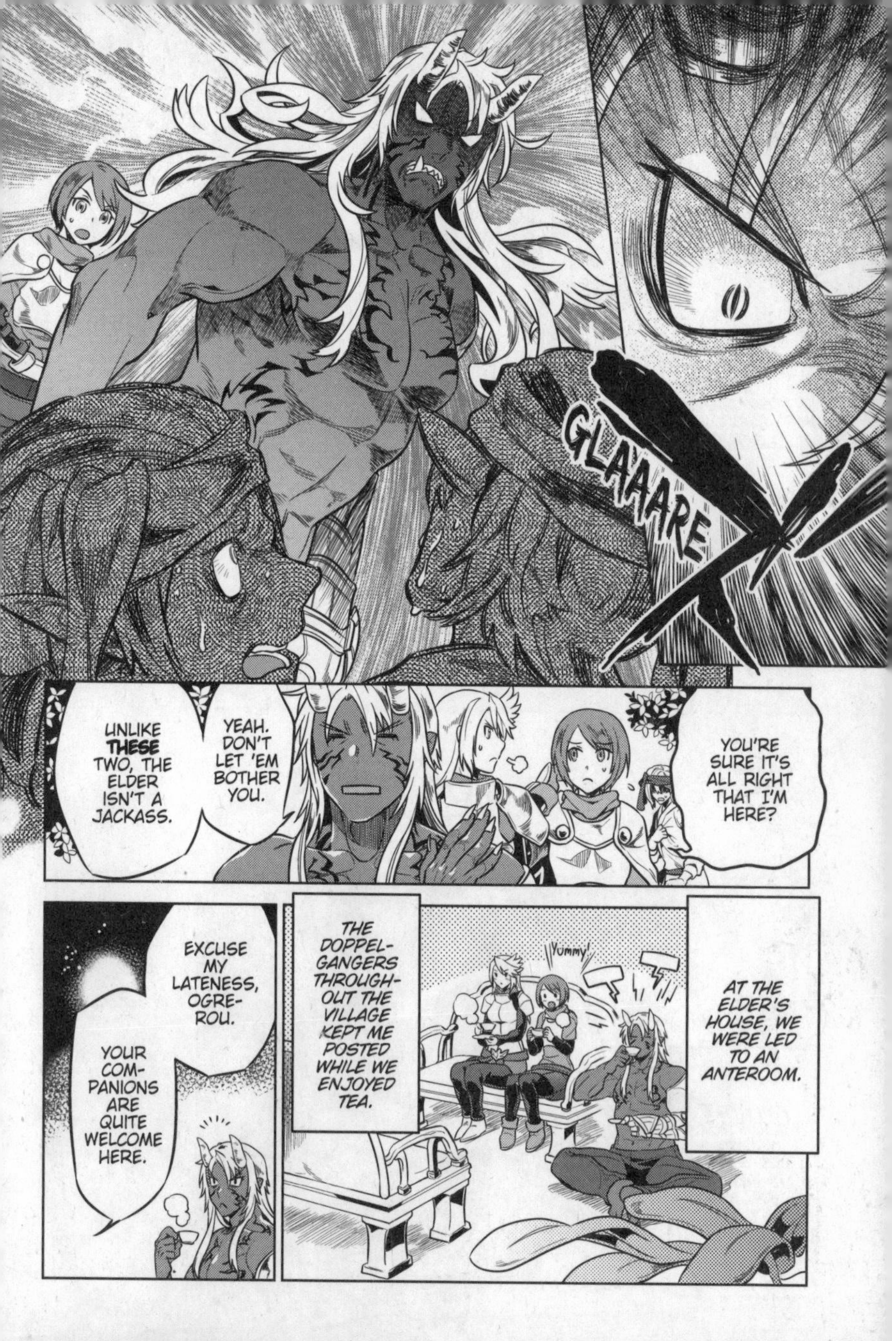

GLAAARE
YOU'RE SURE IT'S ALL RIGHT THAT I'M HERE?
YEAH. DON'T LET 'EM BOTHER YOU.
UNLIKE **THESE** TWO, THE ELDER ISN'T A JACKASS.
AT THE ELDER'S HOUSE, WE WERE LED TO AN ANTEROOM.
Yummy!
THE DOPPEL-GANGERS THROUGH-OUT THE VILLAGE KEPT ME POSTED WHILE WE ENJOYED TEA.
EXCUSE MY LATENESS, OGRE-ROU.
YOUR COM-PANIONS ARE QUITE WELCOME HERE.

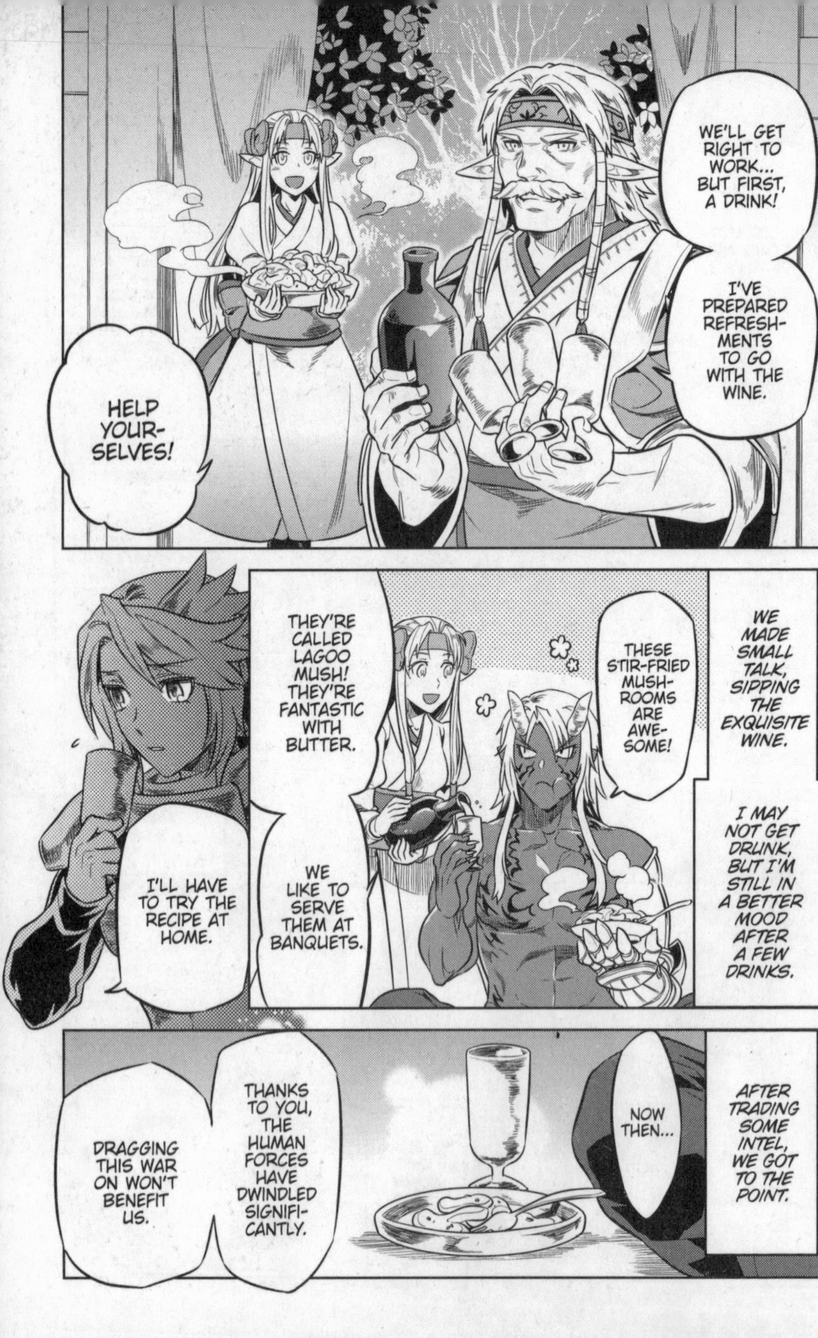

WE'LL GET RIGHT TO WORK... BUT FIRST, A DRINK!
I'VE PREPARED REFRESHMENTS TO GO WITH THE WINE.
HELP YOURSELVES!
WE MADE SMALL TALK, SIPPING THE EXQUISITE WINE.
I MAY NOT GET DRUNK, BUT I'M STILL IN A BETTER MOOD AFTER A FEW DRINKS.
THESE STIR-FRIED MUSHROOMS ARE AWESOME!
THEY'RE CALLED LAGOO MUSH! THEY'RE FANTASTIC WITH BUTTER.
WE LIKE TO SERVE THEM AT BANQUETS.
I'LL HAVE TO TRY THE RECIPE AT HOME.
AFTER TRADING SOME INTEL, WE GOT TO THE POINT.
NOW THEN...
THANKS TO YOU, THE HUMAN FORCES HAVE DWINDLED SIGNIFICANTLY.
DRAGGING THIS WAR ON WON'T BENEFIT US.

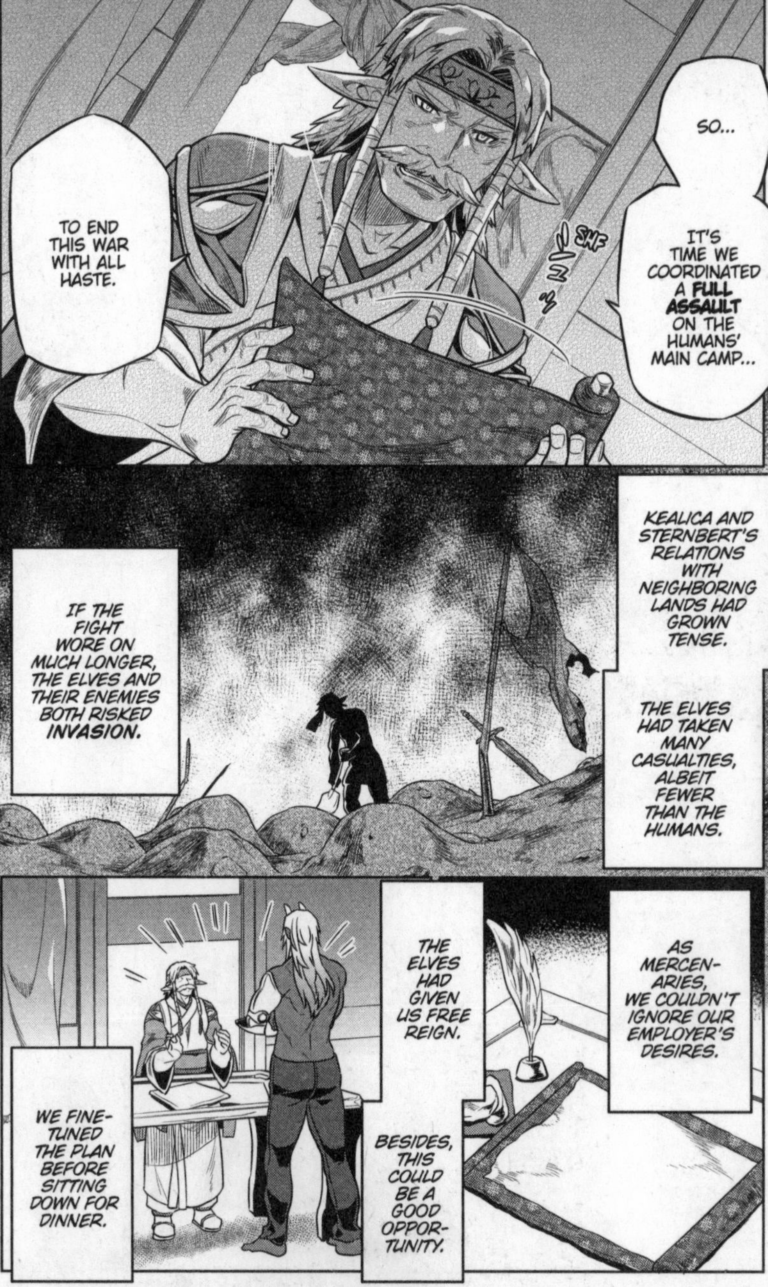
SO...
IT'S TIME WE COORDINATED A **FULL ASSAULT** ON THE HUMANS' MAIN CAMP...
SHF
TO END THIS WAR WITH ALL HASTE.
KEALICA AND STERNBERT'S RELATIONS WITH NEIGHBORING LANDS HAD GROWN TENSE.
THE ELVES HAD TAKEN MANY CASUALTIES, ALBEIT FEWER THAN THE HUMANS.
IF THE FIGHT WORE ON MUCH LONGER, THE ELVES AND THEIR ENEMIES BOTH RISKED **INVASION.**
AS MERCEN-ARIES, WE COULDN'T IGNORE OUR EMPLOYER'S DESIRES.
THE ELVES HAD GIVEN US FREE REIGN.
BESIDES, THIS COULD BE A GOOD OPPOR-TUNITY.
WE FINE-TUNED THE PLAN BEFORE SITTING DOWN FOR DINNER.

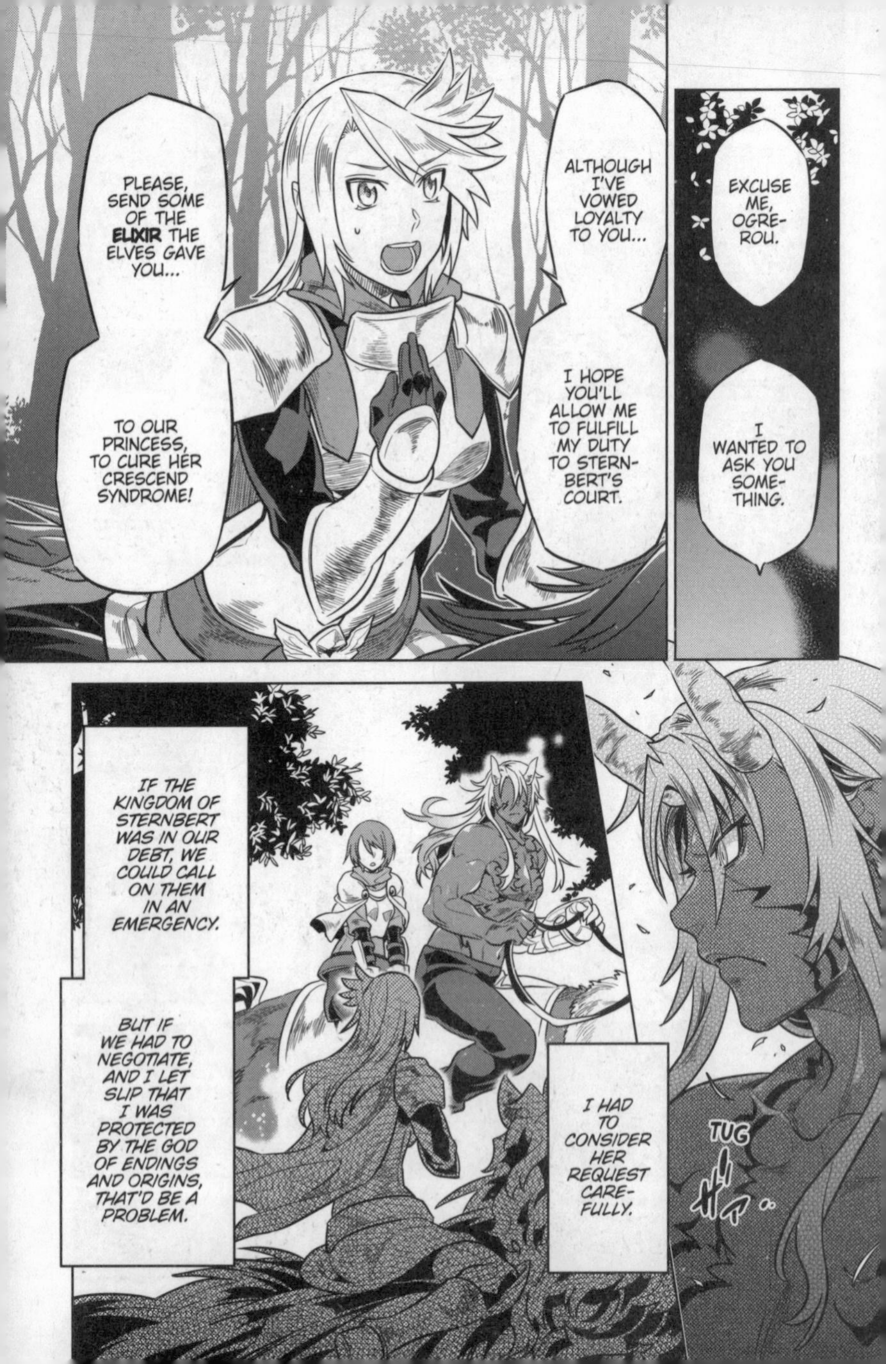
EXCUSE ME, OGRE-ROU.
I WANTED TO ASK YOU SOME-THING.
ALTHOUGH I'VE VOWED LOYALTY TO YOU...
I HOPE YOU'LL ALLOW ME TO FULFILL MY DUTY TO STERN-BERT'S COURT.
PLEASE, SEND SOME OF THE ELIXIR THE ELVES GAVE YOU...
TO OUR PRINCESS, TO CURE HER CRESCEND SYNDROME!
TUG
I HAD TO CONSIDER HER REQUEST CARE-FULLY.
IF THE KINGDOM OF STERNBERT WAS IN OUR DEBT, WE COULD CALL ON THEM IN AN EMERGENCY.
BUT IF WE HAD TO NEGOTIATE, AND I LET SLIP THAT I WAS PROTECTED BY THE GOD OF ENDINGS AND ORIGINS, THAT'D BE A PROBLEM.

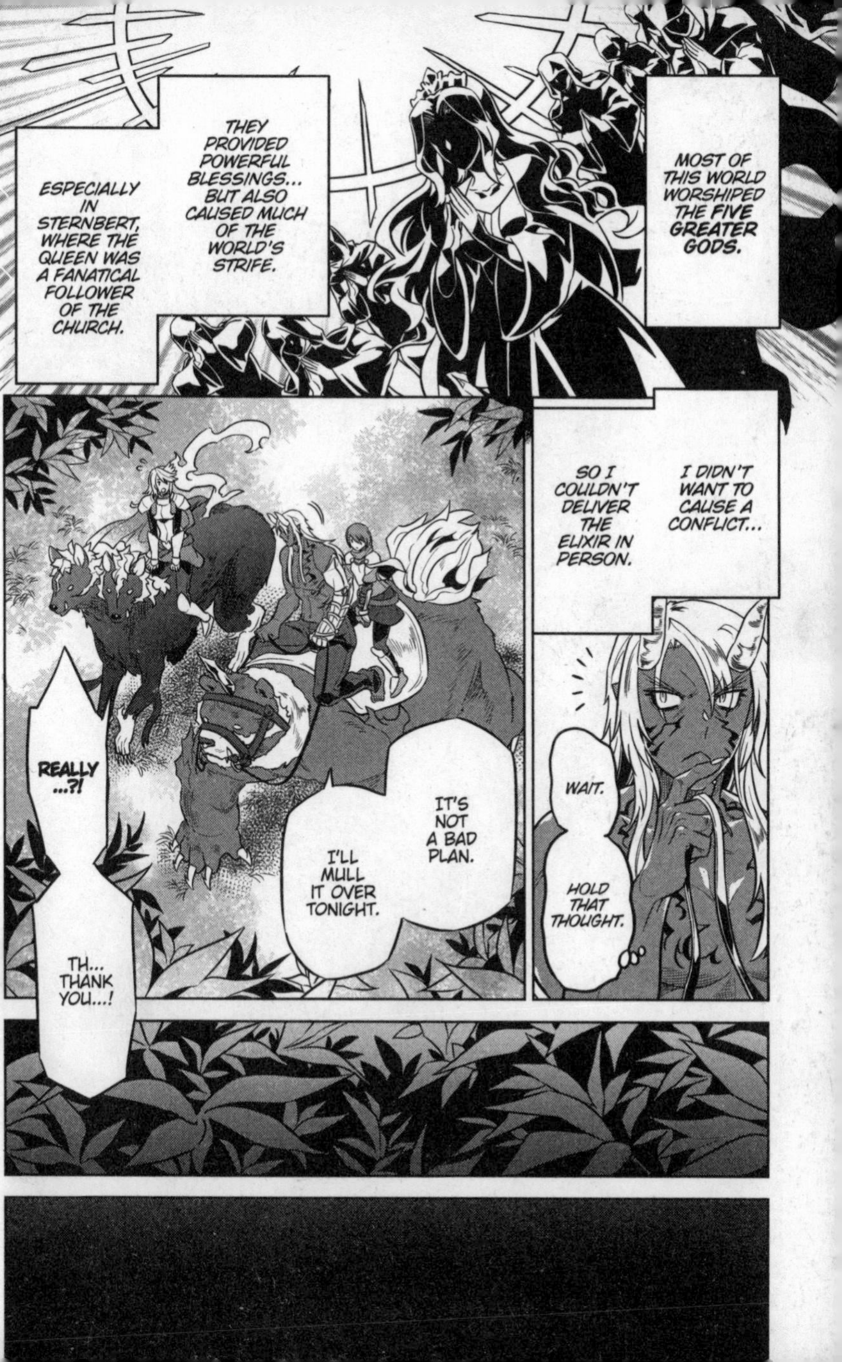
MOST OF THIS WORLD WORSHIPED THE **FIVE GREATER GODS.**
THEY PROVIDED POWERFUL BLESSINGS... BUT ALSO CAUSED MUCH OF THE WORLD'S STRIFE.
ESPECIALLY IN STERNBERT, WHERE THE QUEEN WAS A FANATICAL FOLLOWER OF THE CHURCH.
I DIDN'T WANT TO CAUSE A CONFLICT...
SO I COULDN'T DELIVER THE ELIXIR IN PERSON.
WAIT.
HOLD THAT THOUGHT.
IT'S NOT A BAD PLAN.
I'LL MULL IT OVER TONIGHT.
REALLY ...?!
TH... THANK YOU...!

Day 83

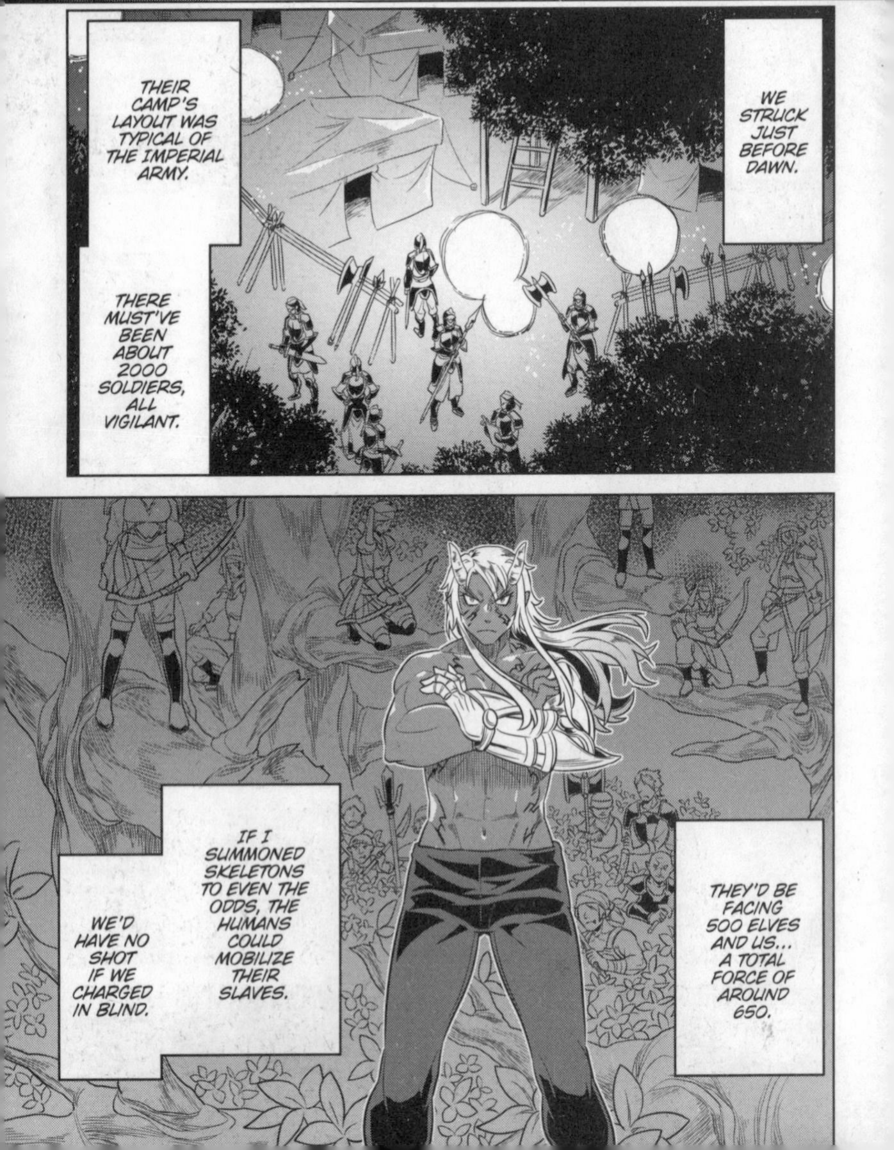
WE STRUCK JUST BEFORE DAWN.
THEIR CAMP'S LAYOUT WAS TYPICAL OF THE IMPERIAL ARMY.
THERE MUST'VE BEEN ABOUT 2000 SOLDIERS, ALL VIGILANT.
THEY'D BE FACING 500 ELVES AND US... A TOTAL FORCE OF AROUND 650.
IF I SUMMONED SKELETONS TO EVEN THE ODDS, THE HUMANS COULD MOBILIZE THEIR SLAVES.
WE'D HAVE NO SHOT IF WE CHARGED IN BLIND.

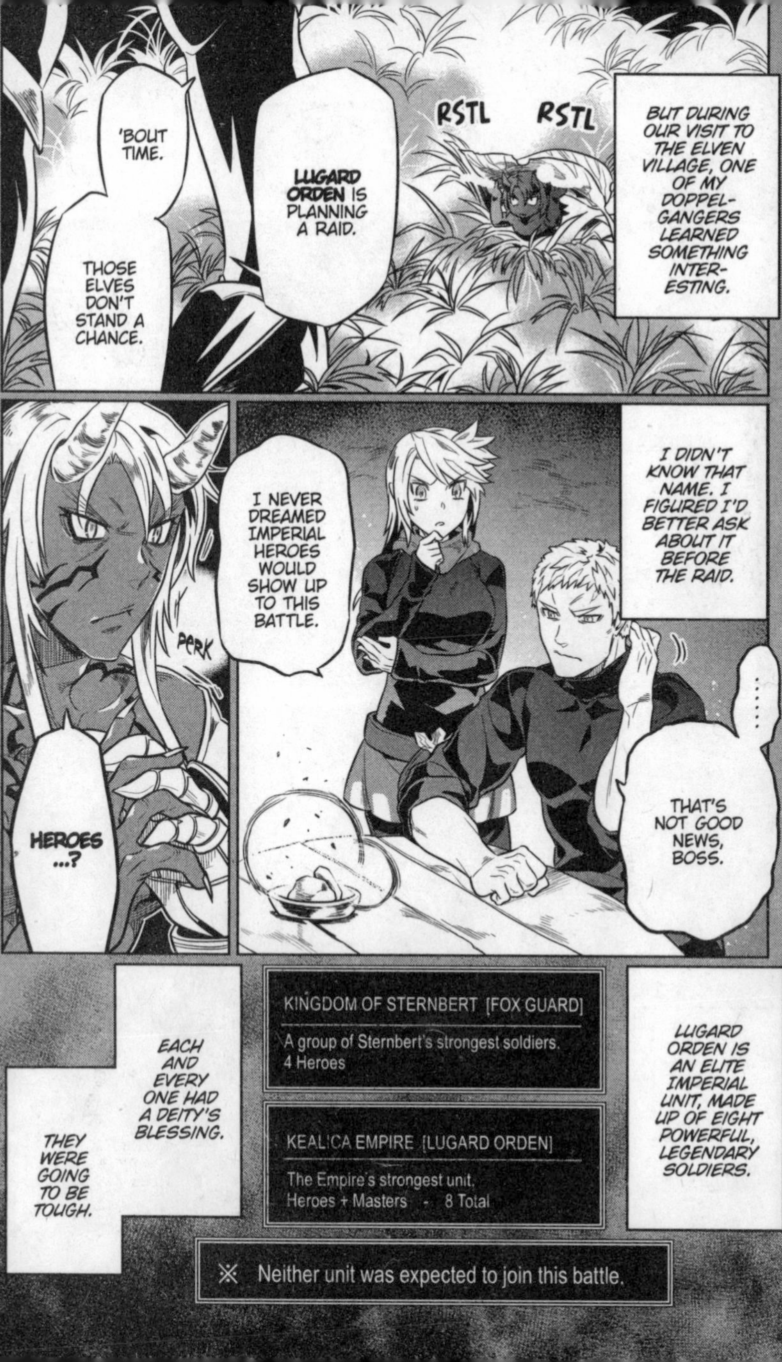
BUT DURING OUR VISIT TO THE ELVEN VILLAGE, ONE OF MY DOPPEL-GANGERS LEARNED SOMETHING INTER-ESTING.
RSTL RSTL
LUGARD ORDEN IS PLANNING A RAID.
'BOUT TIME.
THOSE ELVES DON'T STAND A CHANCE.
I DIDN'T KNOW THAT NAME. I FIGURED I'D BETTER ASK ABOUT IT BEFORE THE RAID.
......
THAT'S NOT GOOD NEWS, BOSS.
I NEVER DREAMED IMPERIAL HEROES WOULD SHOW UP TO THIS BATTLE.
PERK
HEROES ...?
LUGARD ORDEN IS AN ELITE IMPERIAL UNIT, MADE UP OF EIGHT POWERFUL, LEGENDARY SOLDIERS.
KINGDOM OF STERNBERT [FOX GUARD]
A group of Sternbert's strongest soldiers.
4 Heroes
KEALICA EMPIRE [LUGARD ORDEN]
The Empire's strongest unit.
Heroes + Masters - 8 Total
EACH AND EVERY ONE HAD A DEITY'S BLESSING.
THEY WERE GOING TO BE TOUGH.
※ Neither unit was expected to join this battle.

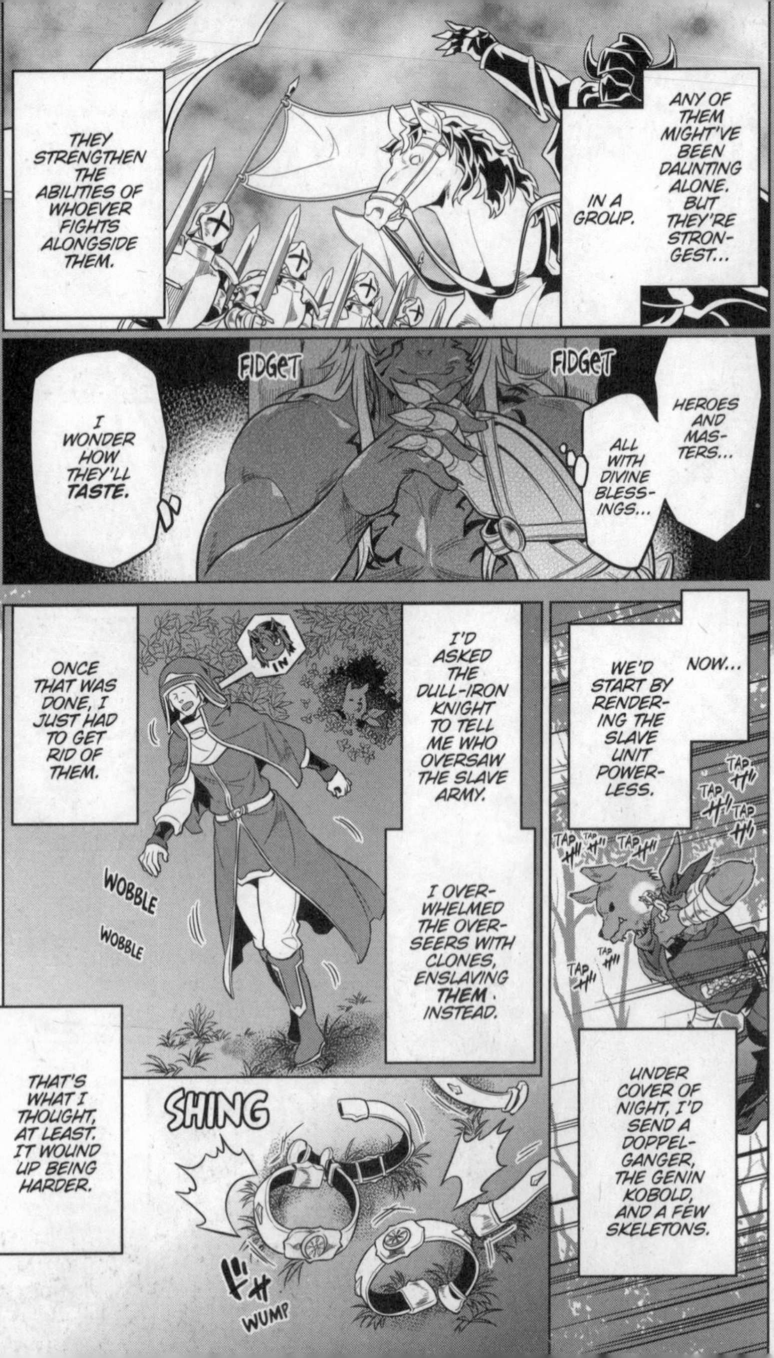
ANY OF THEM MIGHT'VE BEEN DAUNTING ALONE. BUT THEY'RE STRONGEST...
IN A GROUP.
THEY STRENGTHEN THE ABILITIES OF WHOEVER FIGHTS ALONGSIDE THEM.
HEROES AND MASTERS...
ALL WITH DIVINE BLESSINGS...
FIDGET
FIDGET
I WONDER HOW THEY'LL TASTE.
NOW...
WE'D START BY RENDERING THE SLAVE UNIT POWERLESS.
TAP TAP TAP TAP TAP TAP TAP TAP
UNDER COVER OF NIGHT, I'D SEND A DOPPELGANGER, THE GENIN KOBOLD, AND A FEW SKELETONS.
I'D ASKED THE DULL-IRON KNIGHT TO TELL ME WHO OVERSAW THE SLAVE ARMY.
I OVERWHELMED THE OVERSEERS WITH CLONES, ENSLAVING THEM INSTEAD.
IN
ONCE THAT WAS DONE, I JUST HAD TO GET RID OF THEM.
WOBBLE
WOBBLE
SHING
THAT'S WHAT I THOUGHT, AT LEAST. IT WOUND UP BEING HARDER.
WUMP

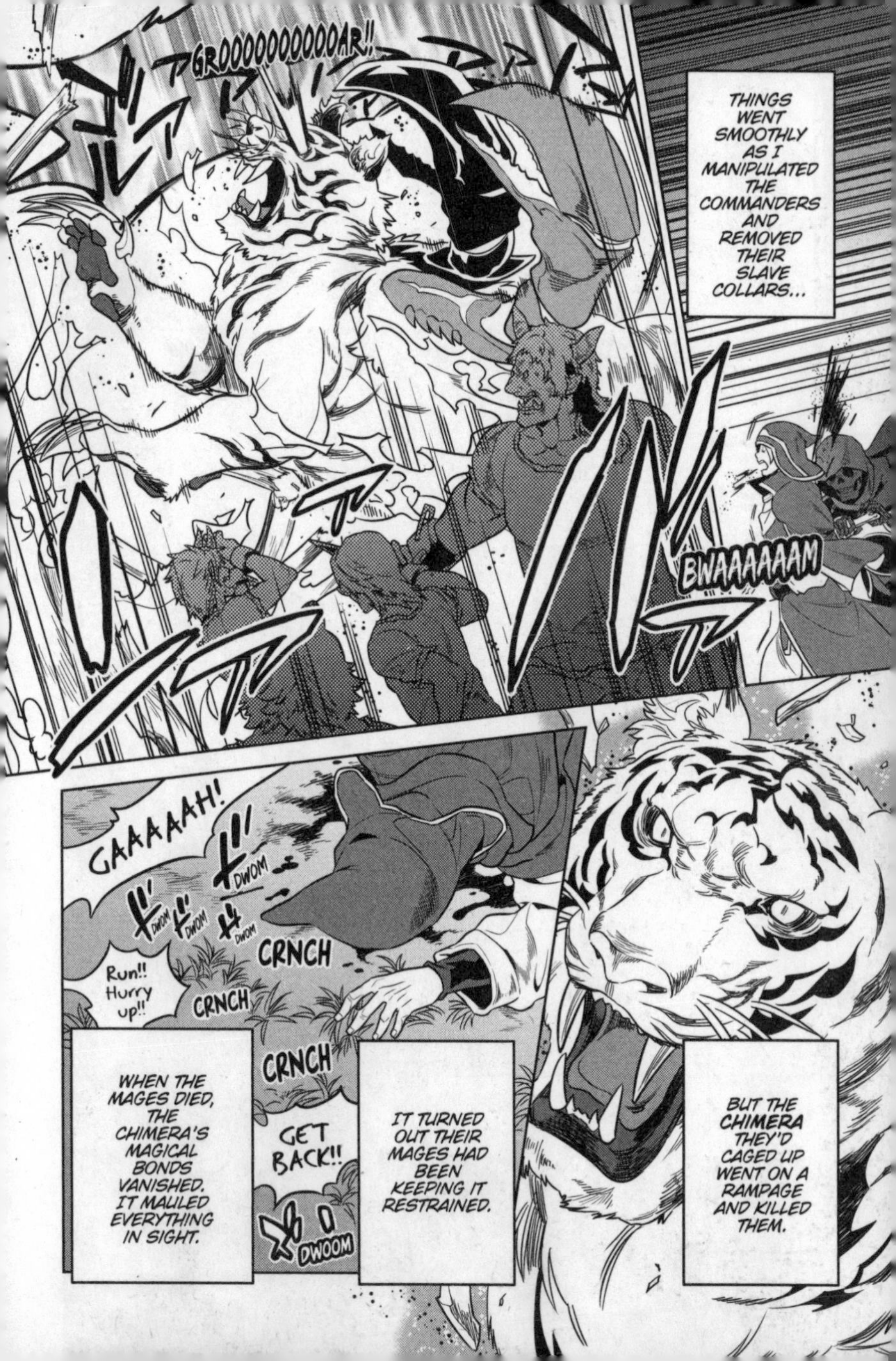
THINGS WENT SMOOTHLY AS I MANIPULATED THE COMMANDERS AND REMOVED THEIR SLAVE COLLARS...
GROOOOOOOOOOAR!!
BWAAAAAAM
BUT THE CHIMERA THEY'D CAGED UP WENT ON A RAMPAGE AND KILLED THEM.
GAAAAAH!
DWOM
DWOM
DWOM
DWOM
CRNCH
CRNCH
CRNCH
Run!! Hurry up!!
IT TURNED OUT THEIR MAGES HAD BEEN KEEPING IT RESTRAINED.
GET BACK!!
DWOOM
WHEN THE MAGES DIED, THE CHIMERA'S MAGICAL BONDS VANISHED. IT MAULED EVERYTHING IN SIGHT.

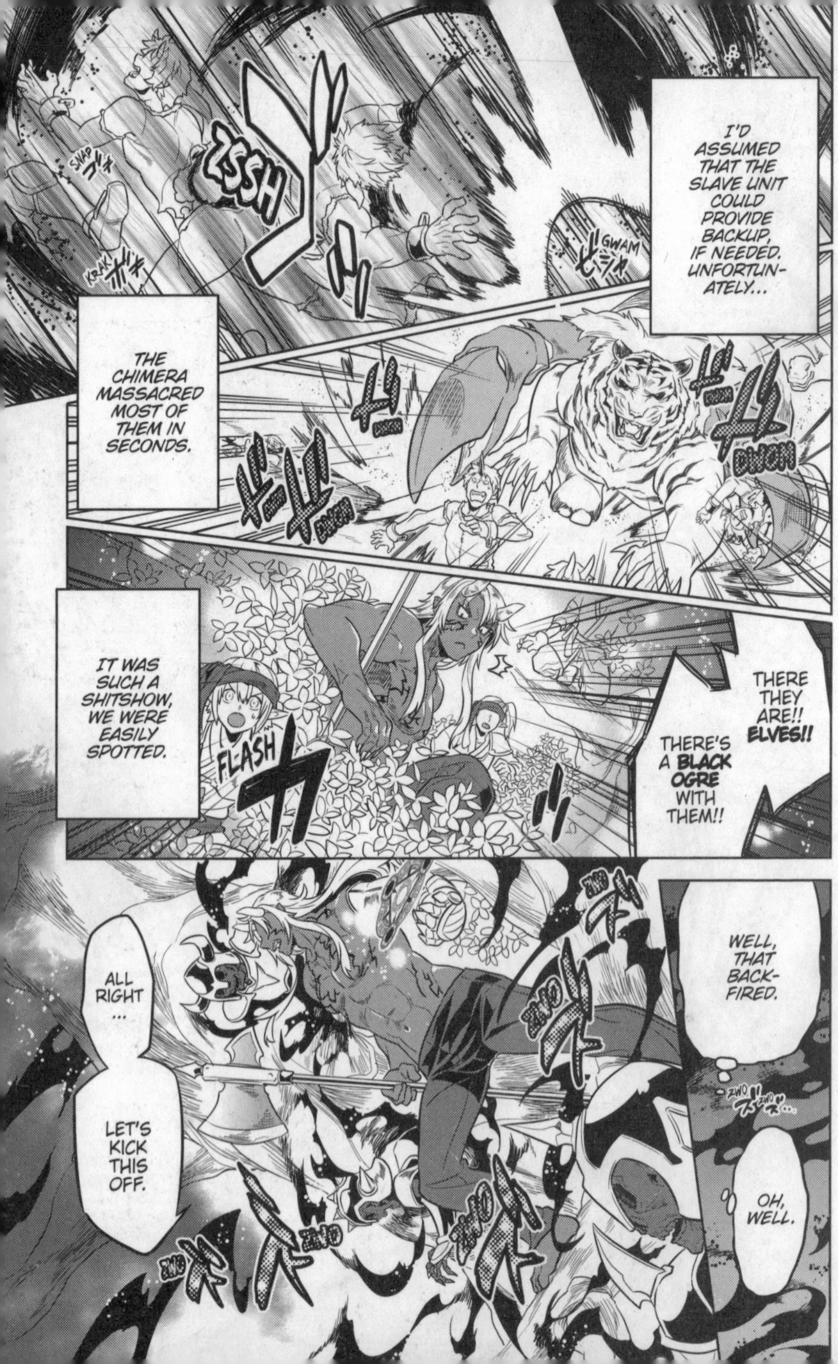
I'D ASSUMED THAT THE SLAVE UNIT COULD PROVIDE BACKUP, IF NEEDED. UNFORTUNATELY...
GWAM
ZASH
SNAP
KRAK
DWOM
THE CHIMERA MASSACRED MOST OF THEM IN SECONDS.
THERE THEY ARE!! ELVES!!
THERE'S A BLACK OGRE WITH THEM!!
FLASH
IT WAS SUCH A SHITSHOW, WE WERE EASILY SPOTTED.
WELL, THAT BACKFIRED.
ZWO
OH, WELL.
ALL RIGHT...
LET'S KICK THIS OFF.

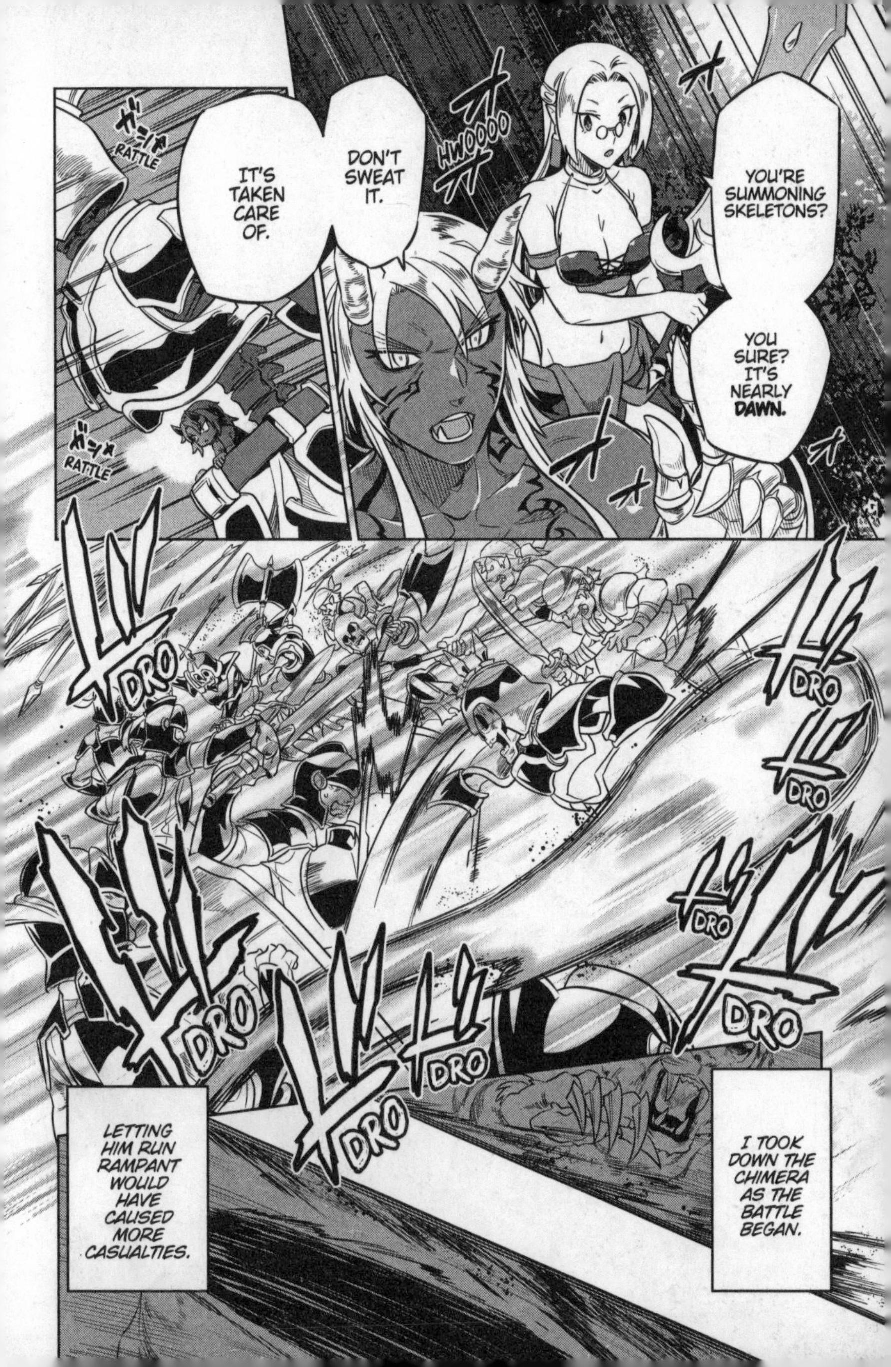

YOU'RE SUMMONING SKELETONS?
YOU SURE? IT'S NEARLY **DAWN.**
HWOOOO
DON'T SWEAT IT.
IT'S TAKEN CARE OF.
RATTLE
RATTLE
DRO
DRO
DRO
DRO
DRO
DRO
DRO
DRO
I TOOK DOWN THE CHIMERA AS THE BATTLE BEGAN.
LETTING HIM RUN RAMPANT WOULD HAVE CAUSED MORE CASUALTIES.

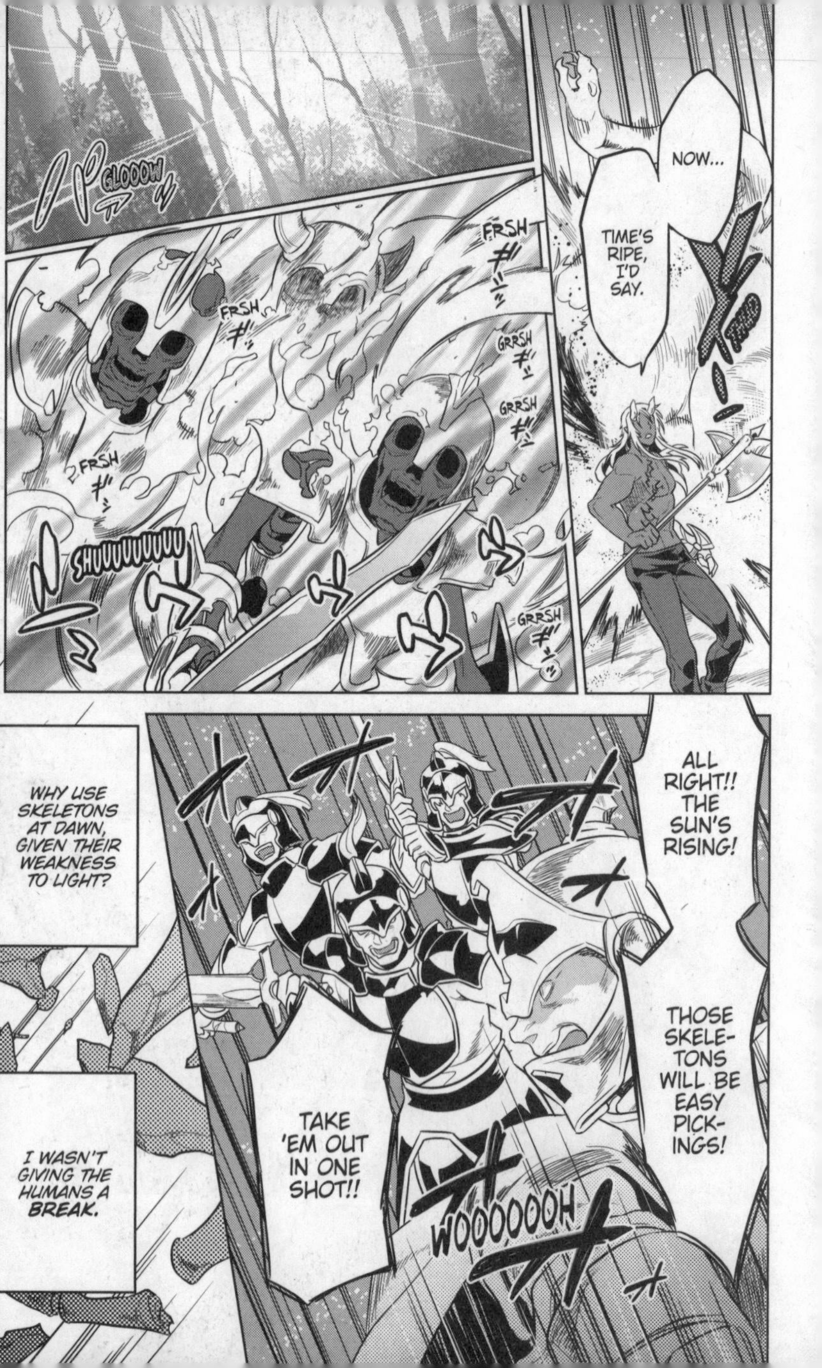
NOW...
TIME'S RIPE, I'D SAY.
THD
GLOOOW
FRSH
FRSH
GRRSH
GRRSH
GRRSH
FRSH
SHUUUUUUUUU
ALL RIGHT!! THE SUN'S RISING!
THOSE SKELETONS WILL BE EASY PICKINGS!
TAKE 'EM OUT IN ONE SHOT!!
WOOOOOOH
WHY USE SKELETONS AT DAWN, GIVEN THEIR WEAKNESS TO LIGHT?
I WASN'T GIVING THE HUMANS A BREAK.

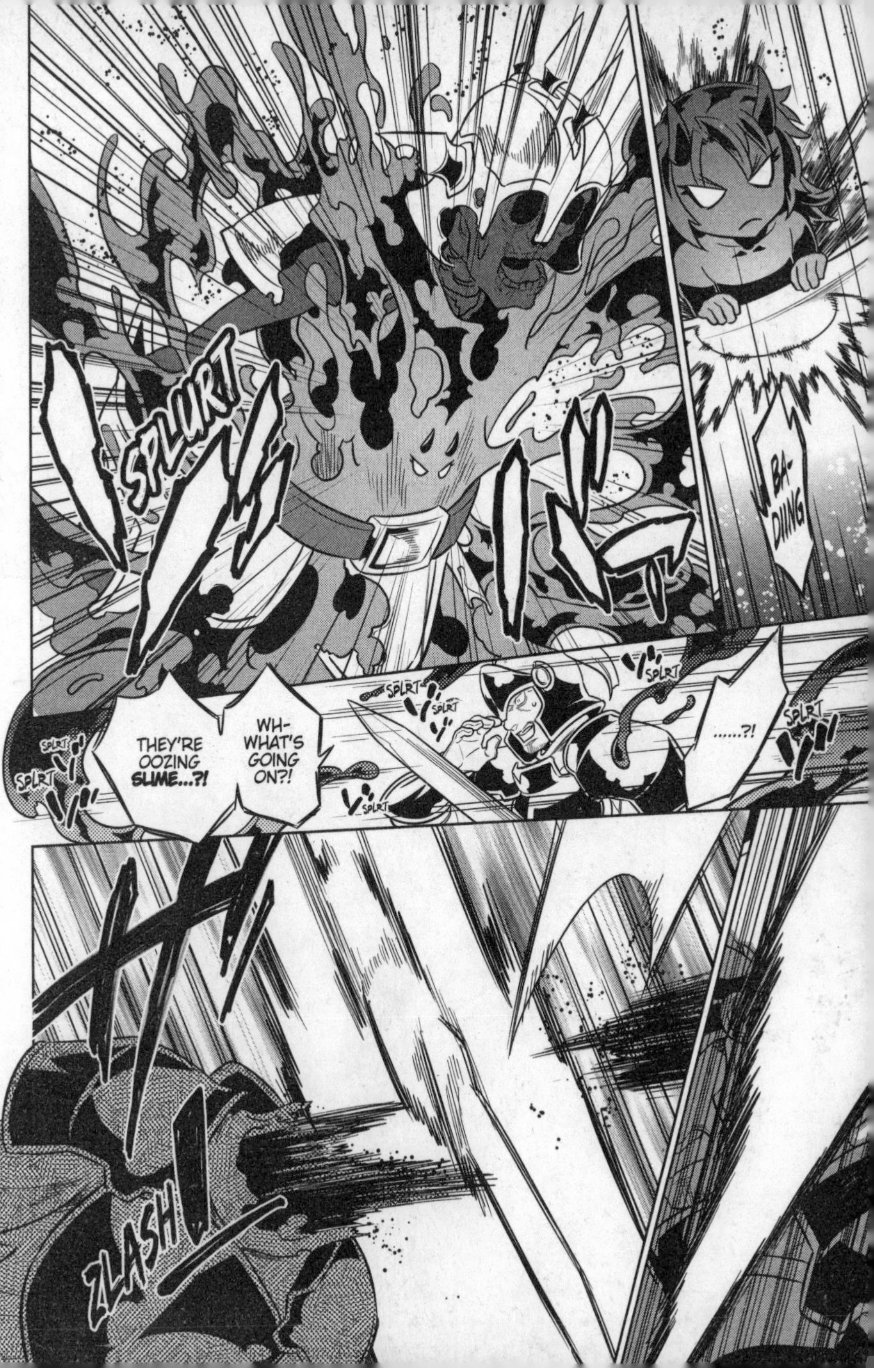
BA-DIING
SPLURT
SPLRT
......?!
SPLRT
SPLRT
SPLRT
SPLRT
WH-WHAT'S GOING ON?!
THEY'RE OOZING **SLIME**...?!
SPLRT
SPLRT
ZLASH

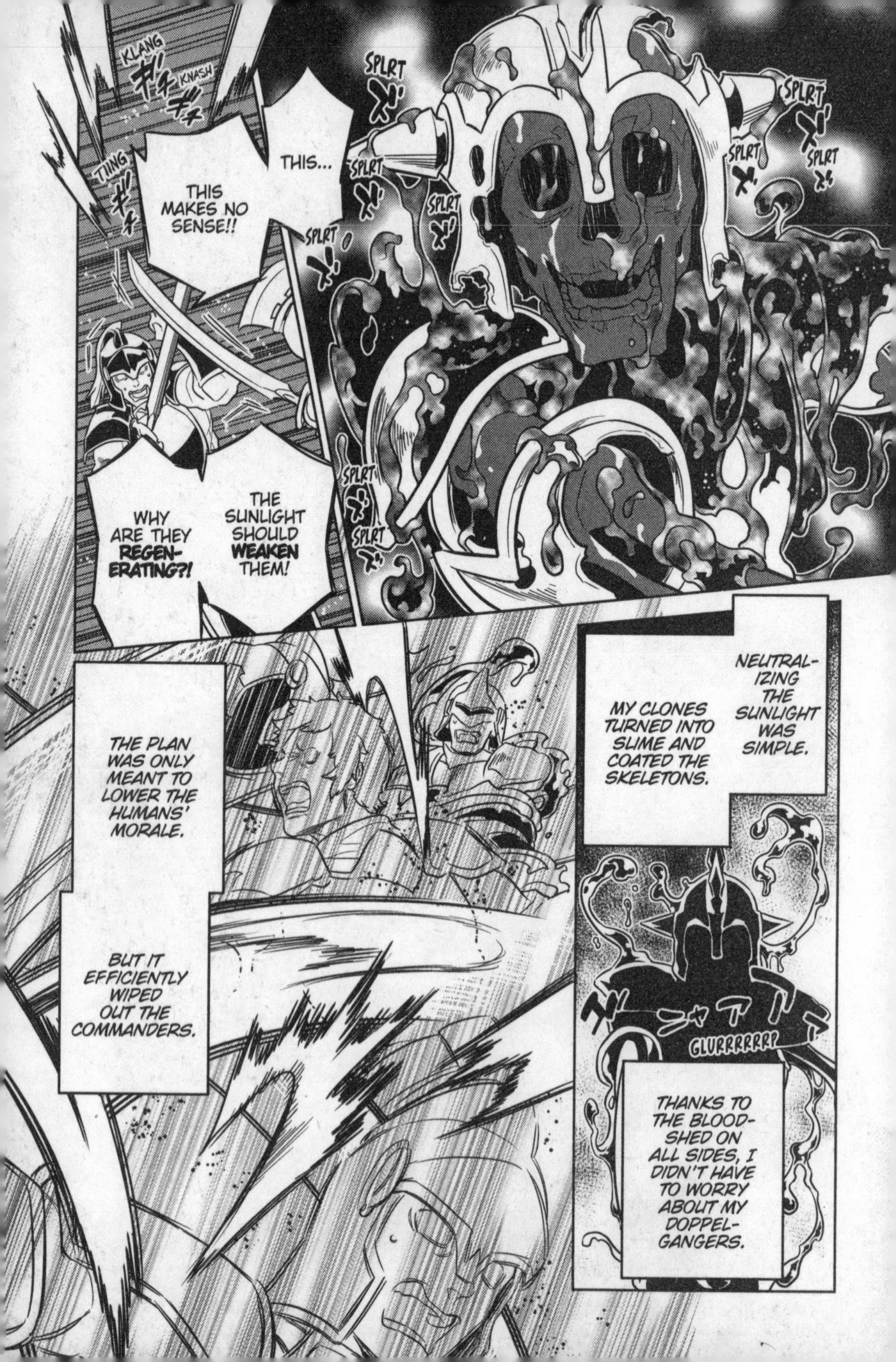
SPLRT
SPLRT
SPLRT
SPLRT
SPLRT
SPLRT
SPLRT
SPLRT
SPLRT
KLANG
KNASH
TIING
THIS...
THIS MAKES NO SENSE!!
THE SUNLIGHT SHOULD WEAKEN THEM!
WHY ARE THEY REGEN-ERATING?!
NEUTRAL-IZING THE SUNLIGHT WAS SIMPLE.
MY CLONES TURNED INTO SLIME AND COATED THE SKELETONS.
GLURRRRRRP
THANKS TO THE BLOOD-SHED ON ALL SIDES, I DIDN'T HAVE TO WORRY ABOUT MY DOPPEL-GANGERS.
THE PLAN WAS ONLY MEANT TO LOWER THE HUMANS' MORALE.
BUT IT EFFICIENTLY WIPED OUT THE COMMANDERS.

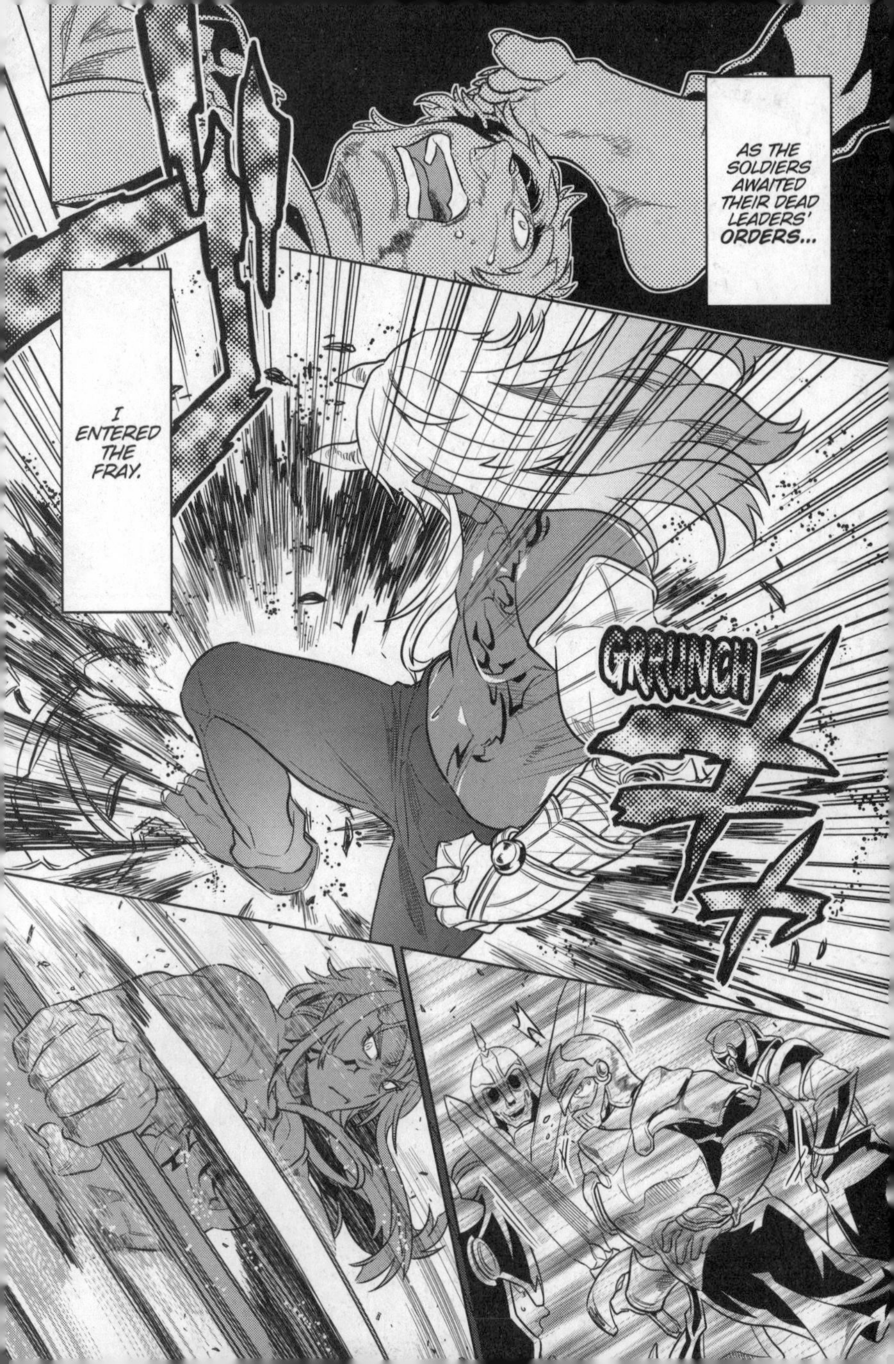
AS THE SOLDIERS AWAITED THEIR DEAD LEADERS' ORDERS...
I ENTERED THE FRAY.
GRRUNCH

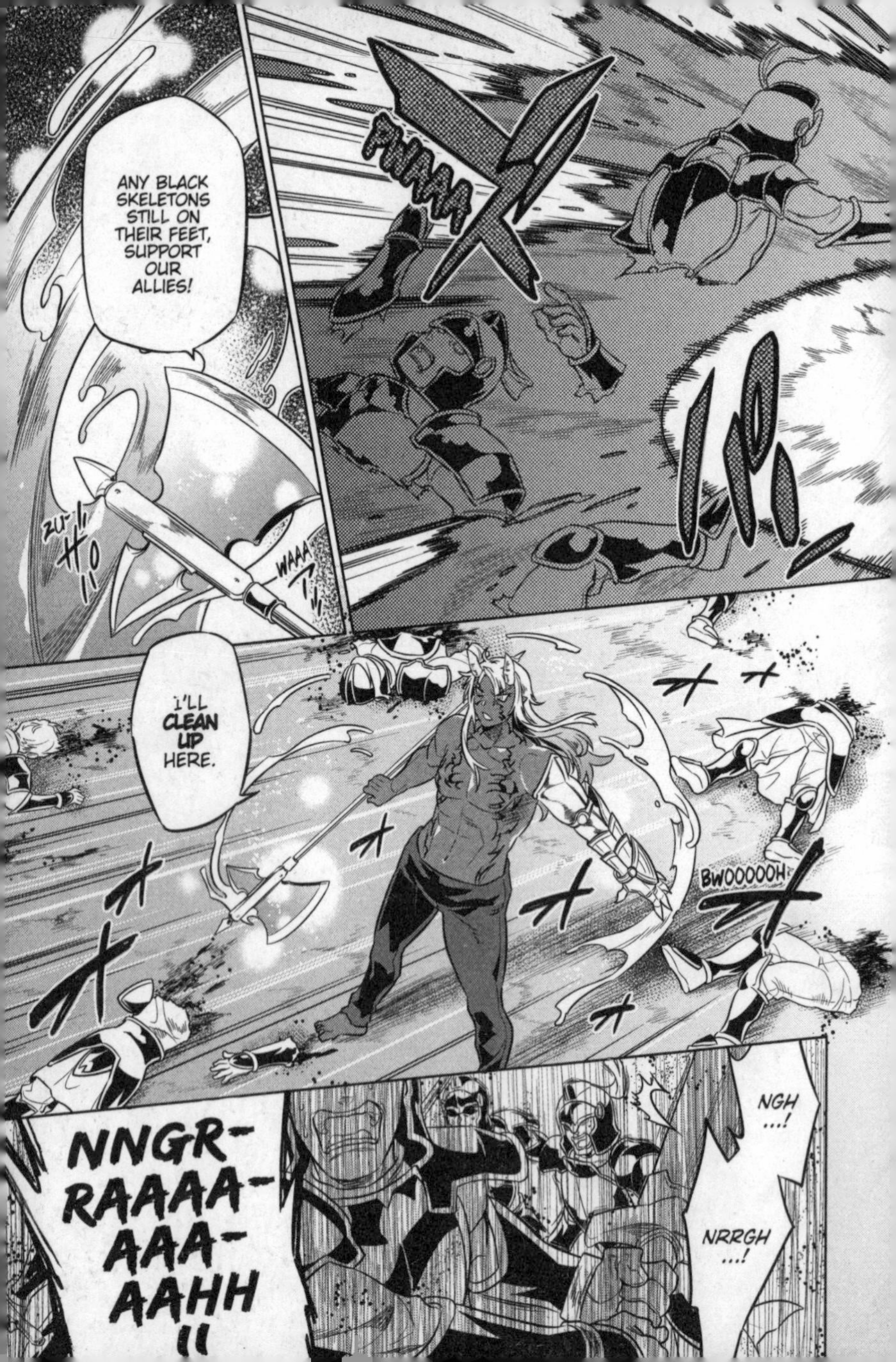
PWAAA
ANY BLACK SKELETONS STILL ON THEIR FEET, SUPPORT OUR ALLIES!
ZU-
WAAA
I'LL **CLEAN UP** HERE.
BWOOOOOH
NGH ...!
NRRGH ...!
NNGR-RAAAA-AAA-AAHH !!

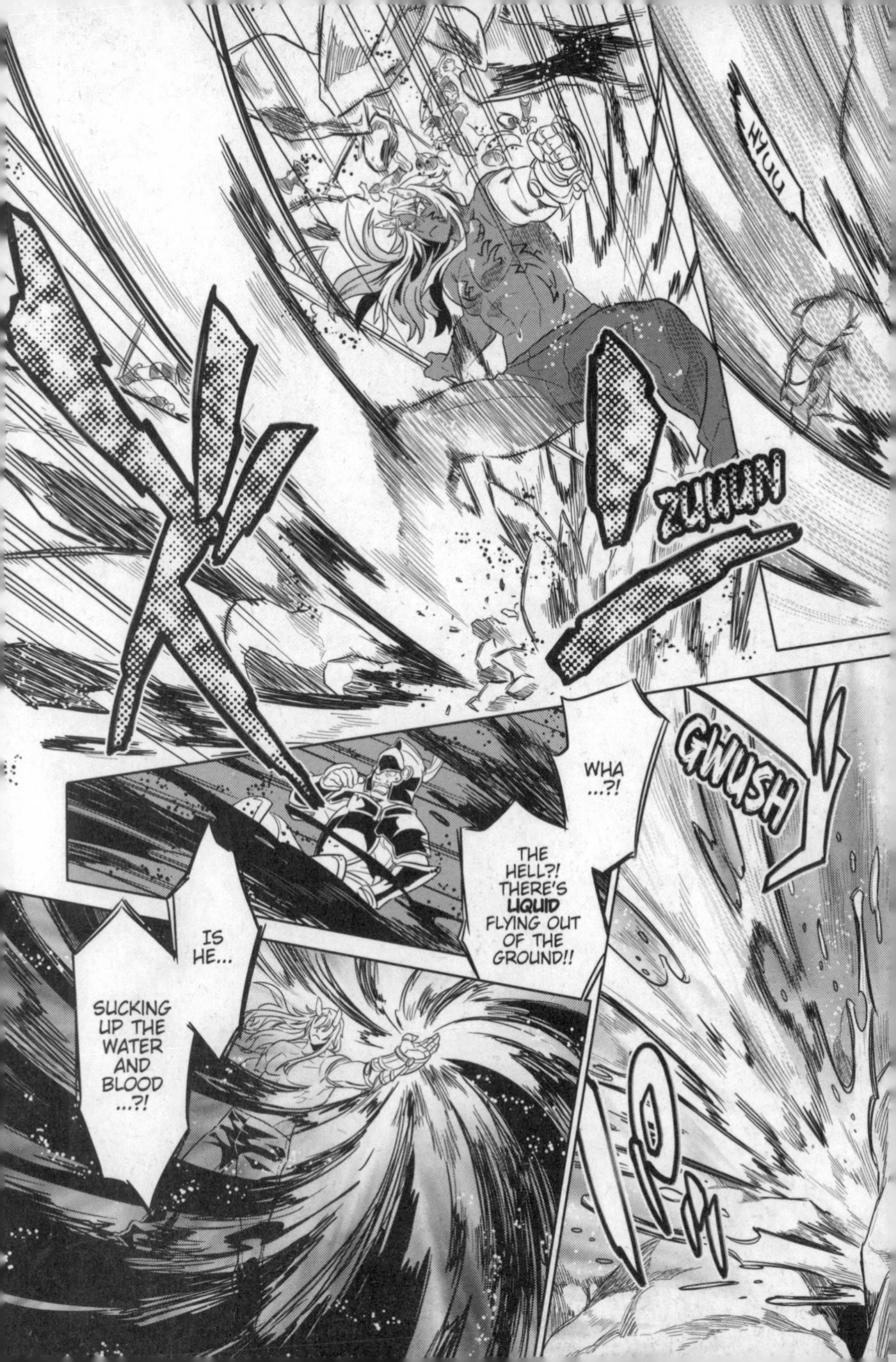
HYUU
ZUWUN
GWUSH
WHA ...?!
THE HELL?! THERE'S **LIQUID** FLYING OUT OF THE GROUND!!
IS HE...
SUCKING UP THE WATER AND BLOOD ...?!

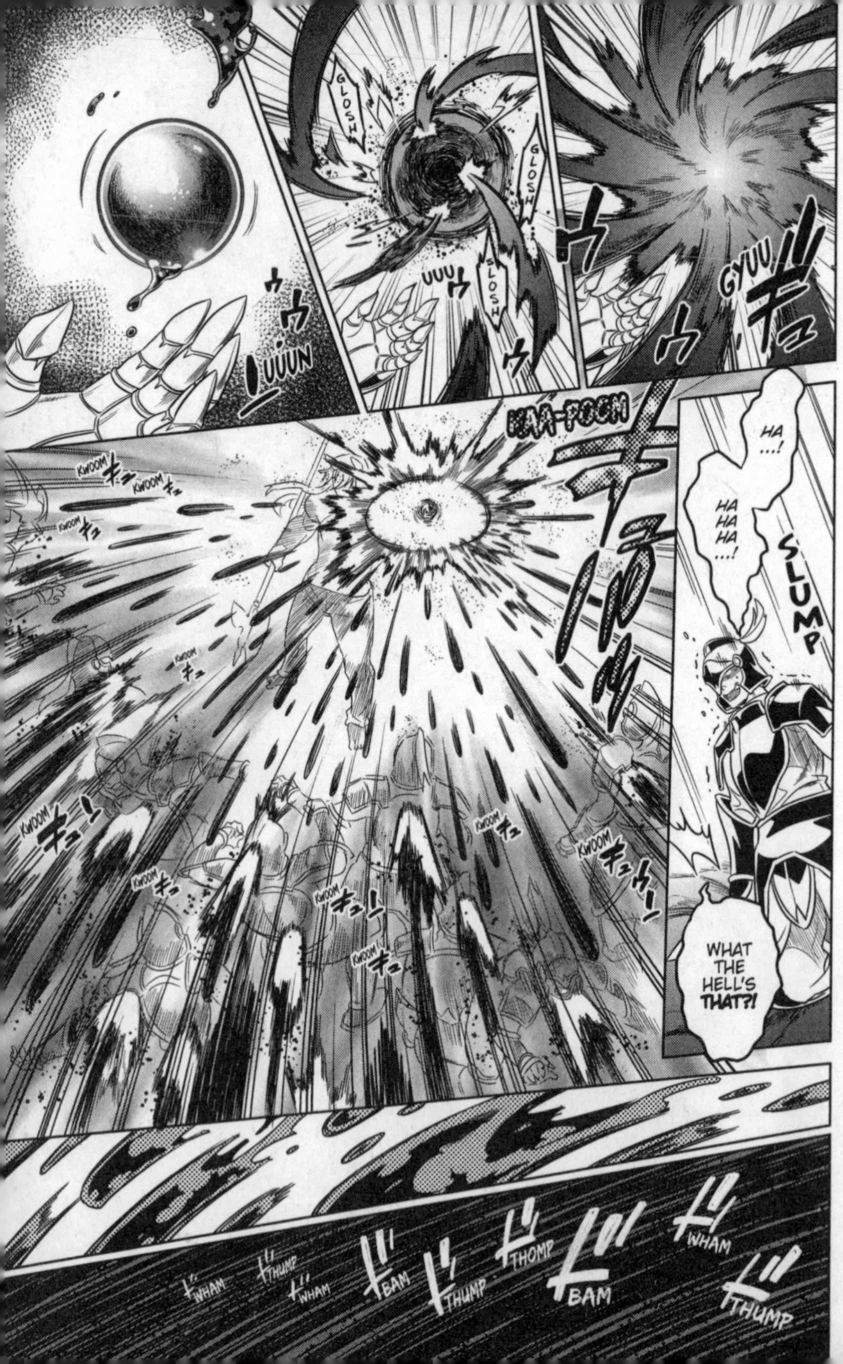
GYUU
GLOSH
GLOSH
UUUウ
SLOSH
ウ
ウウ
UUUN
HA...!
HA HA HA...!
SLUMP
WHAT THE HELL'S THAT?!
KAA-POOM
KWOOM
KWOOM
KWOOM
KWOOM
KWOOM
KWOOM
KWOOM
KWOOM
KWOOM
KWOOM
WHAM
THUMP
BAM
THOMP
THUMP
BAM
WHAM
THUMP
WHAM
WHAM

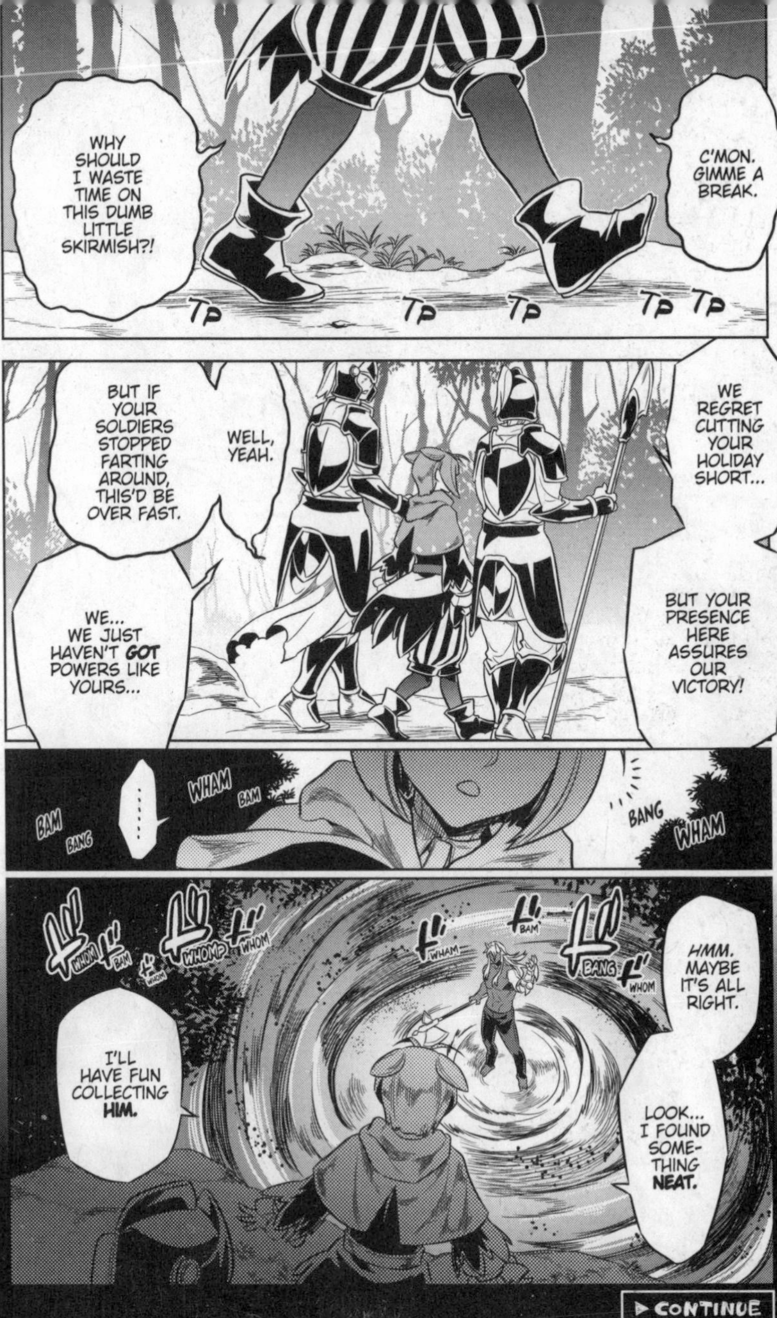
C'MON. GIMME A BREAK.
WHY SHOULD I WASTE TIME ON THIS DUMB LITTLE SKIRMISH?!
Tp Tp Tp Tp Tp
WE REGRET CUTTING YOUR HOLIDAY SHORT...
BUT YOUR PRESENCE HERE ASSURES OUR VICTORY!
WELL, YEAH.
BUT IF YOUR SOLDIERS STOPPED FARTING AROUND, THIS'D BE OVER FAST.
WE... WE JUST HAVEN'T **GOT** POWERS LIKE YOURS...
BANG WHAM
......
WHAM BAM
BAM BANG
BAM BANG WHOM
WHAM
WHOM WHOMP WHOM BAM WHOM
HMM. MAYBE IT'S ALL RIGHT.
LOOK... I FOUND SOME-THING **NEAT.**
I'LL HAVE FUN COLLECTING **HIM.**

▶ CONTINUE

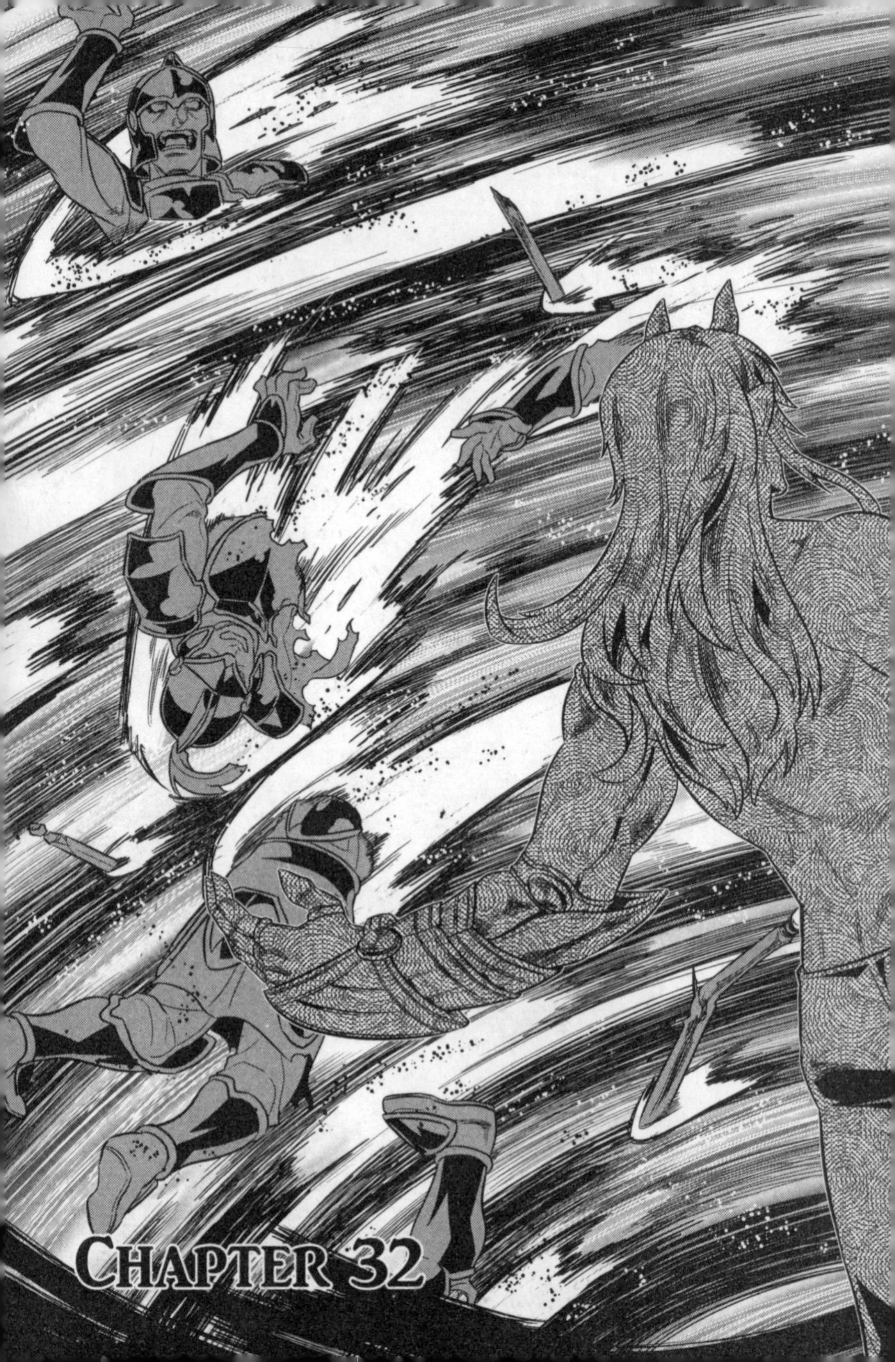
CHAPTER 32

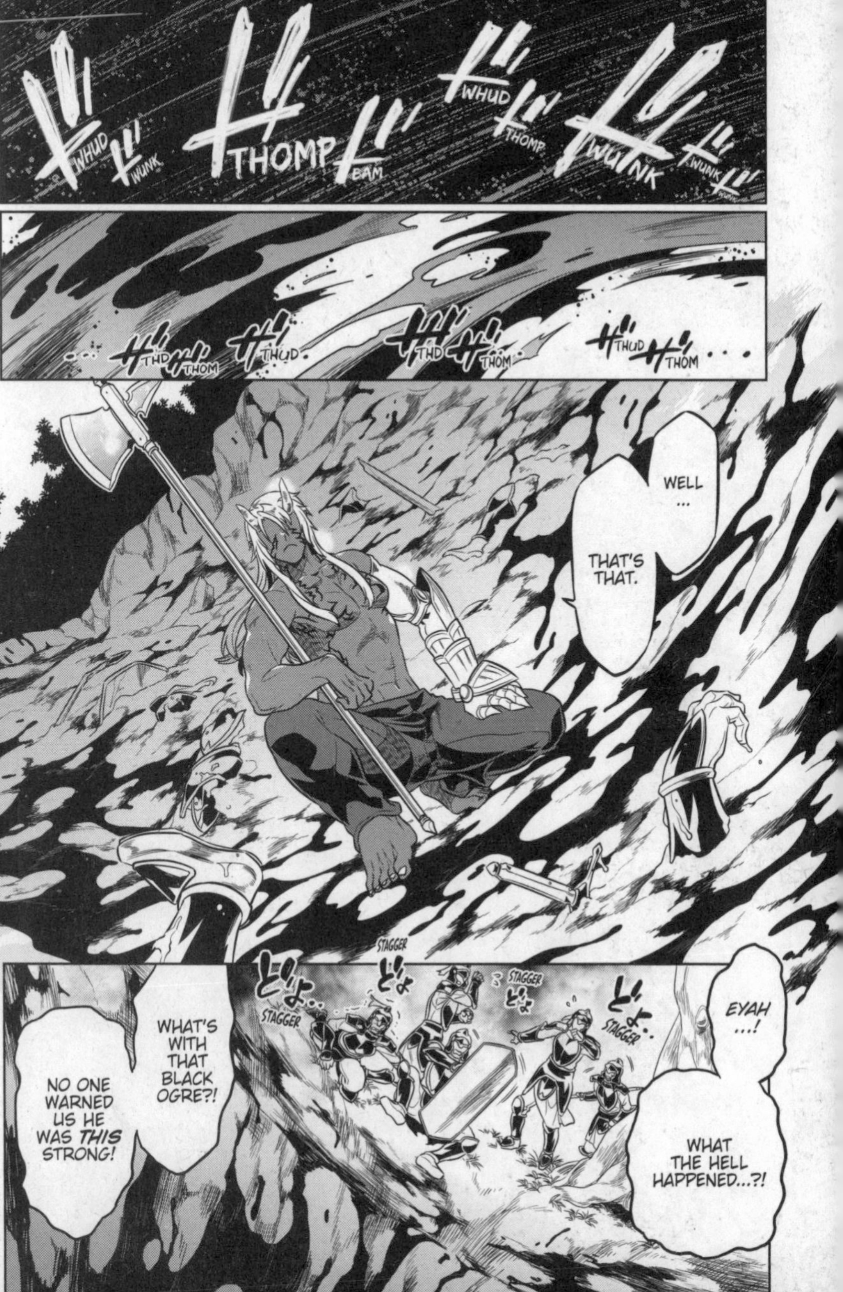
WUNK
WUNK
WUNK
THOMP
WHUD
BAM
THOMP
WUNK
WHUD
THOM
THUD
THOM
THD
THUD
THOM
THD
WELL ...
THAT'S THAT.
EYAH ...!
WHAT THE HELL HAPPENED...?!
STAGGER
STAGGER
STAGGER
STAGGER
WHAT'S WITH THAT BLACK OGRE?!
NO ONE WARNED US HE WAS *THIS* STRONG!

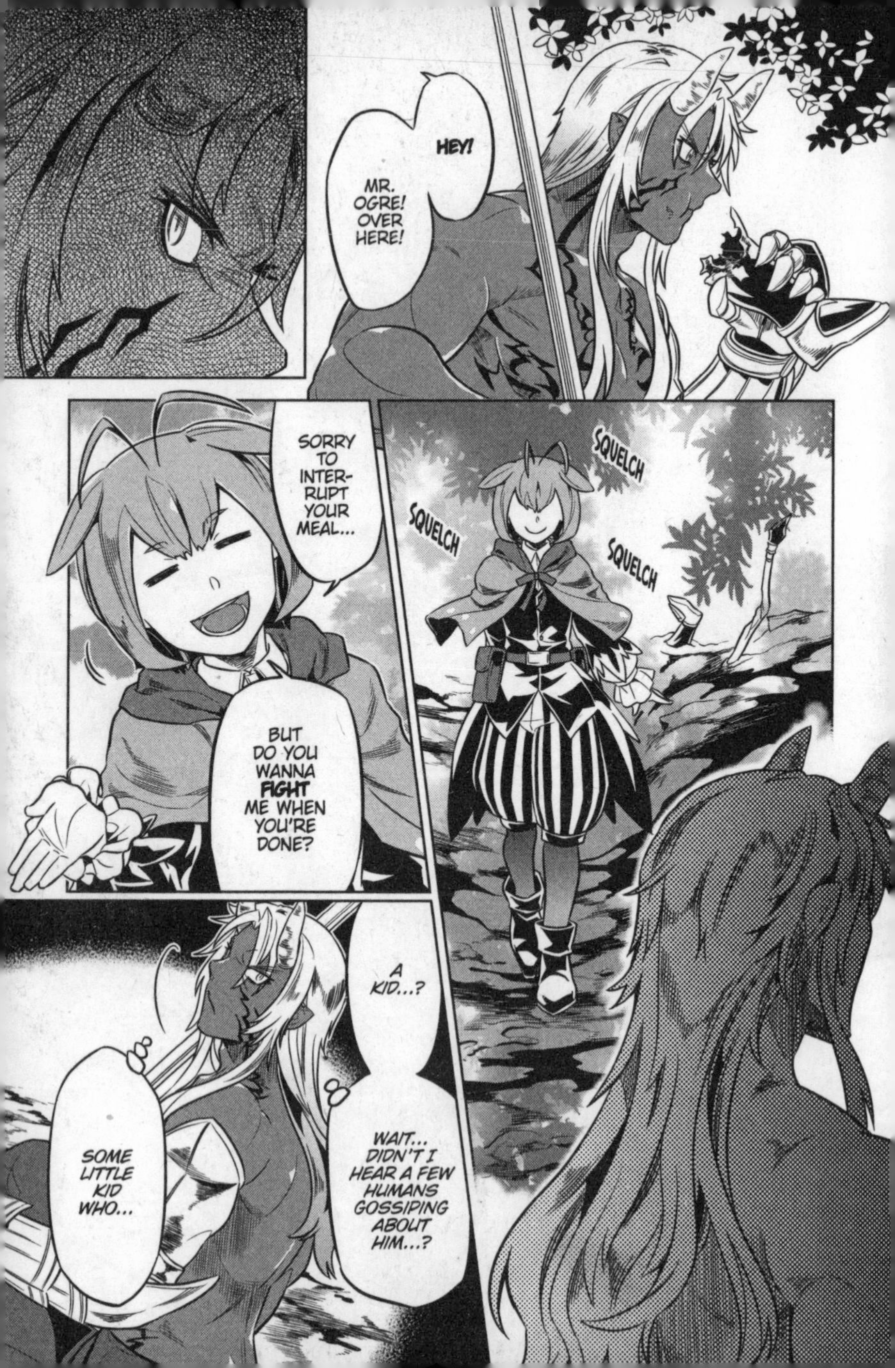
HEY!
MR. OGRE! OVER HERE!
SQUELCH
SQUELCH
SQUELCH
SORRY TO INTER-RUPT YOUR MEAL...
BUT DO YOU WANNA **FIGHT** ME WHEN YOU'RE DONE?
A KID...?
WAIT... DIDN'T I HEAR A FEW HUMANS GOSSIPING ABOUT HIM...?
SOME LITTLE KID WHO...

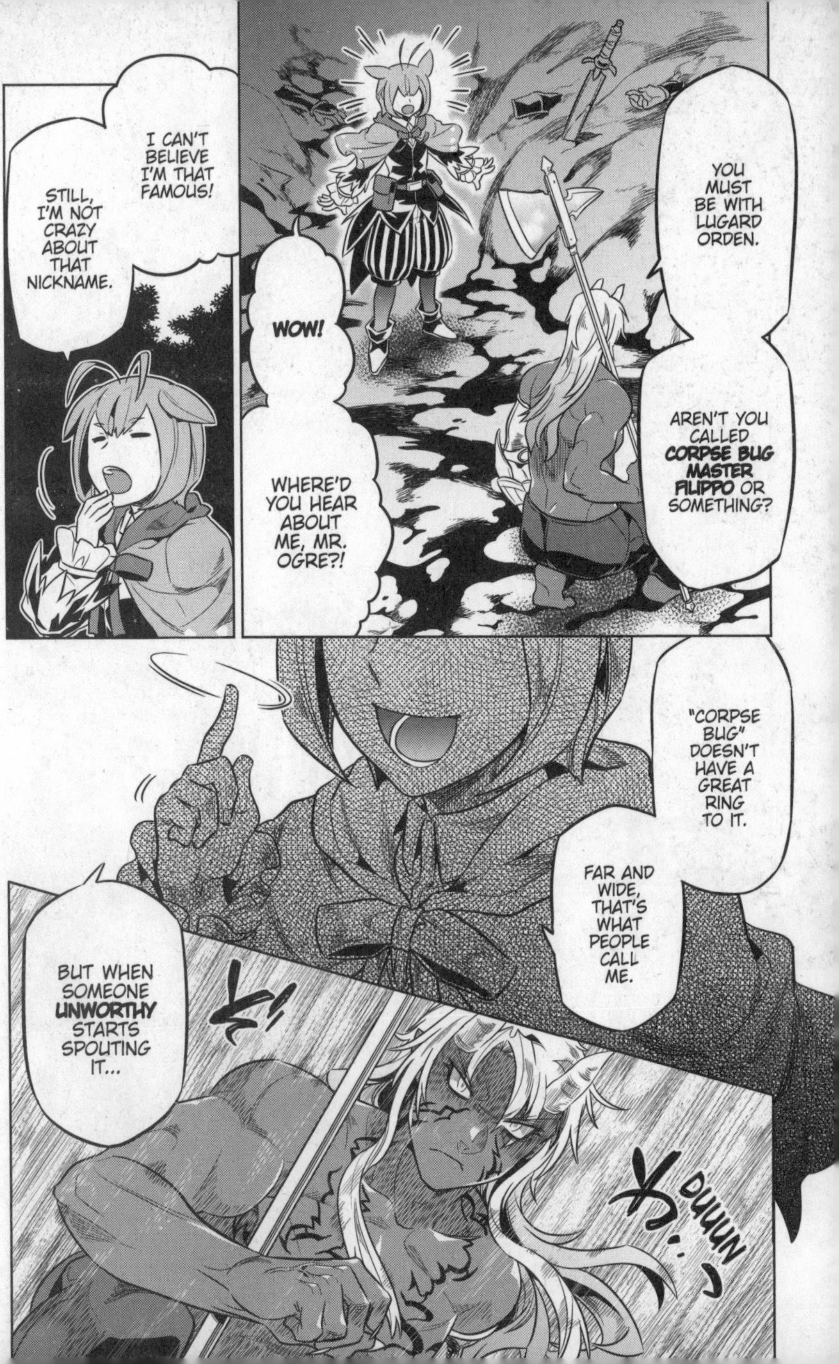

YOU MUST BE WITH LUGARD ORDEN.
AREN'T YOU CALLED **CORPSE BUG MASTER FILIPPO** OR SOMETHING?
WOW!
WHERE'D YOU HEAR ABOUT ME, MR. OGRE?!
I CAN'T BELIEVE I'M THAT FAMOUS!
STILL, I'M NOT CRAZY ABOUT THAT NICKNAME.
"CORPSE BUG" DOESN'T HAVE A GREAT RING TO IT.
FAR AND WIDE, THAT'S WHAT PEOPLE CALL ME.
BUT WHEN SOMEONE **UNWORTHY** STARTS SPOUTING IT...
DUUUN

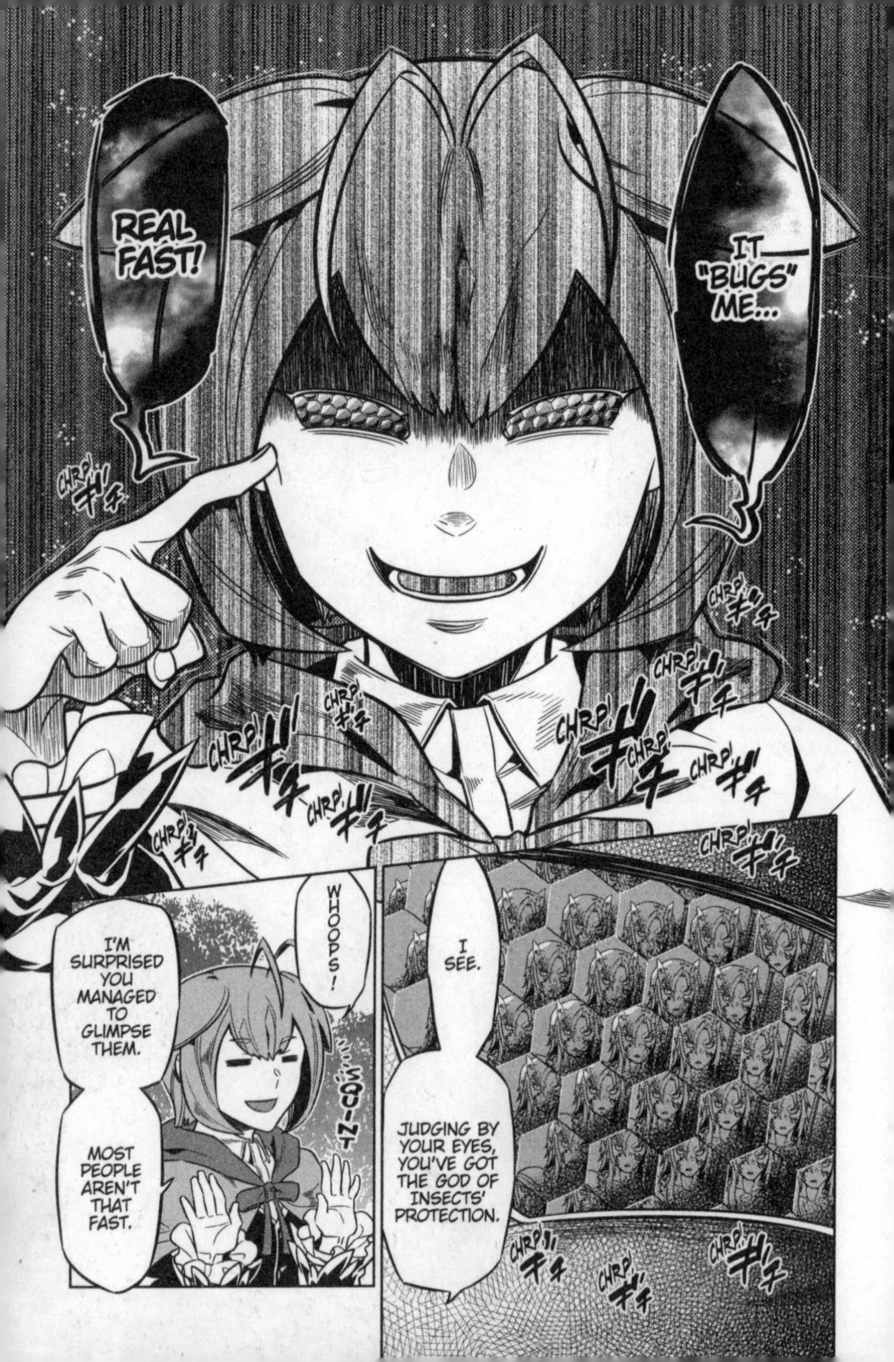
IT "BUGS" ME...
REAL FAST!
CHRP!
CHRP!
CHRP!
CHRP!
CHRP!
CHRP!
CHRP!
CHRP!
CHRP!
CHRP!
I SEE.
JUDGING BY YOUR EYES, YOU'VE GOT THE GOD OF INSECTS' PROTECTION.
CHRP!
CHRP!
CHRP!
WHOOPS!
I'M SURPRISED YOU MANAGED TO GLIMPSE THEM.
SQUINT
MOST PEOPLE AREN'T THAT FAST.

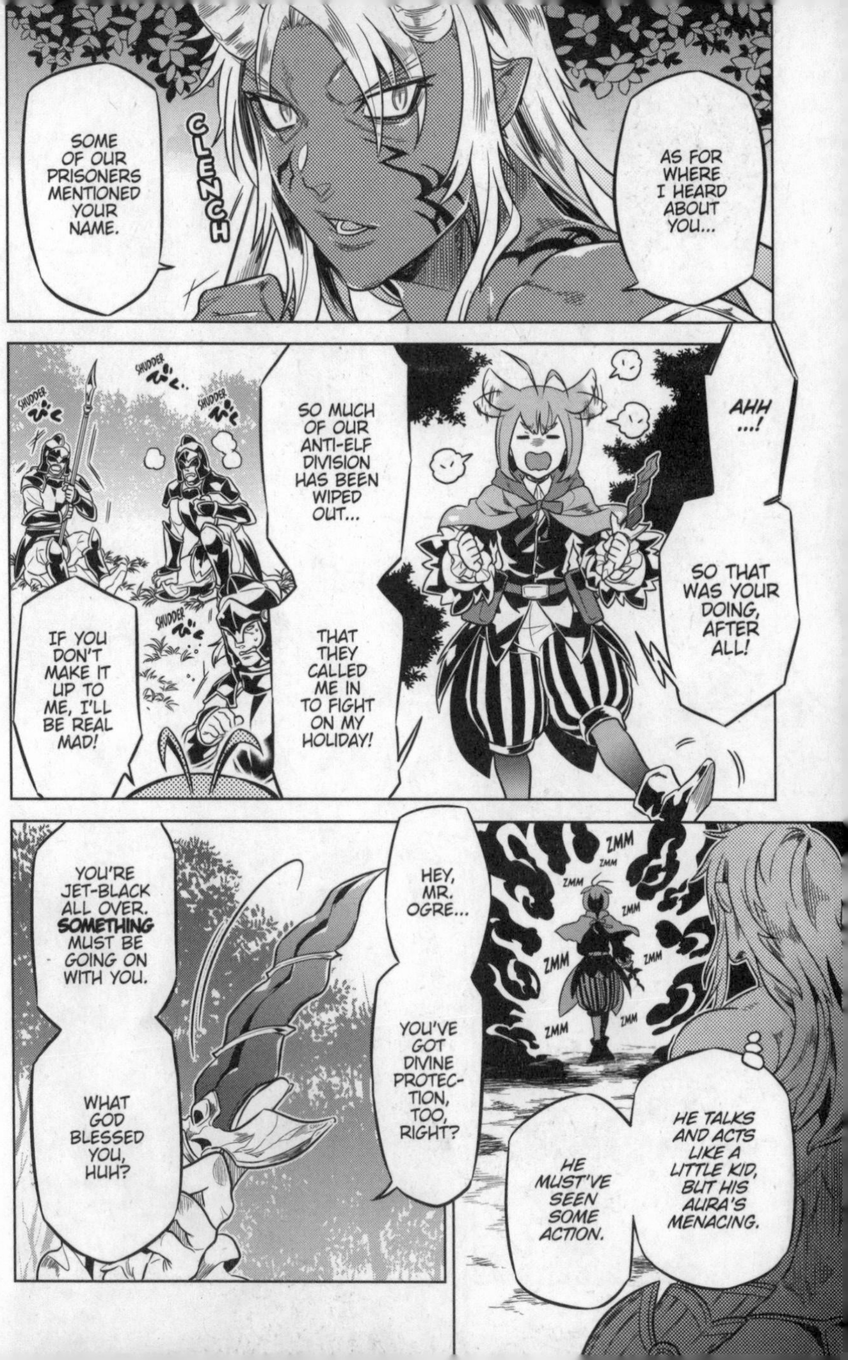

AS FOR WHERE I HEARD ABOUT YOU...
CLENCH
SOME OF OUR PRISONERS MENTIONED YOUR NAME.
AHH ...!
SO THAT WAS YOUR DOING, AFTER ALL!
SO MUCH OF OUR ANTI-ELF DIVISION HAS BEEN WIPED OUT...
THAT THEY CALLED ME IN TO FIGHT ON MY HOLIDAY!
IF YOU DON'T MAKE IT UP TO ME, I'LL BE REAL MAD!
SHUDDER
SHUDDER
SHUDDER
SHUDDER
ZMM
ZMM
ZMM
ZMM
ZMM
ZMM
ZMM
ZMM
HE TALKS AND ACTS LIKE A LITTLE KID, BUT HIS AURA'S MENACING.
HE MUST'VE SEEN SOME ACTION.
HEY, MR. OGRE...
YOU'VE GOT DIVINE PROTECTION, TOO, RIGHT?
YOU'RE JET-BLACK ALL OVER. SOMETHING MUST BE GOING ON WITH YOU.
WHAT GOD BLESSED YOU, HUH?

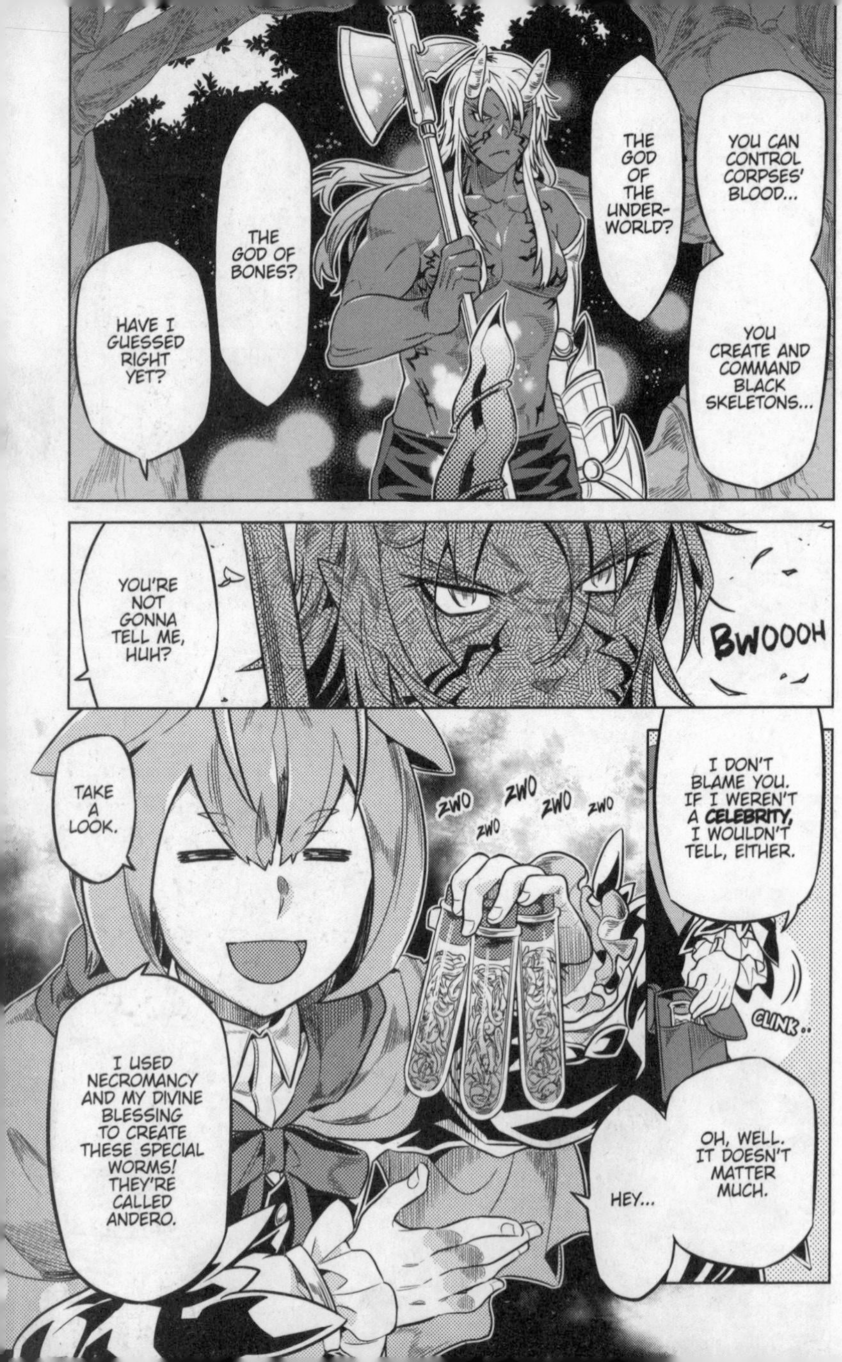
YOU CAN CONTROL CORPSES' BLOOD...
YOU CREATE AND COMMAND BLACK SKELETONS...
THE GOD OF THE UNDER-WORLD?
THE GOD OF BONES?
HAVE I GUESSED RIGHT YET?
BWOOOH
YOU'RE NOT GONNA TELL ME, HUH?
I DON'T BLAME YOU. IF I WEREN'T A **CELEBRITY,** I WOULDN'T TELL, EITHER.
ZWO ZWO ZWO ZWO ZWO
TAKE A LOOK.
CLINK..
OH, WELL. IT DOESN'T MATTER MUCH.
HEY...
I USED NECROMANCY AND MY DIVINE BLESSING TO CREATE THESE SPECIAL WORMS! THEY'RE CALLED ANDERO.

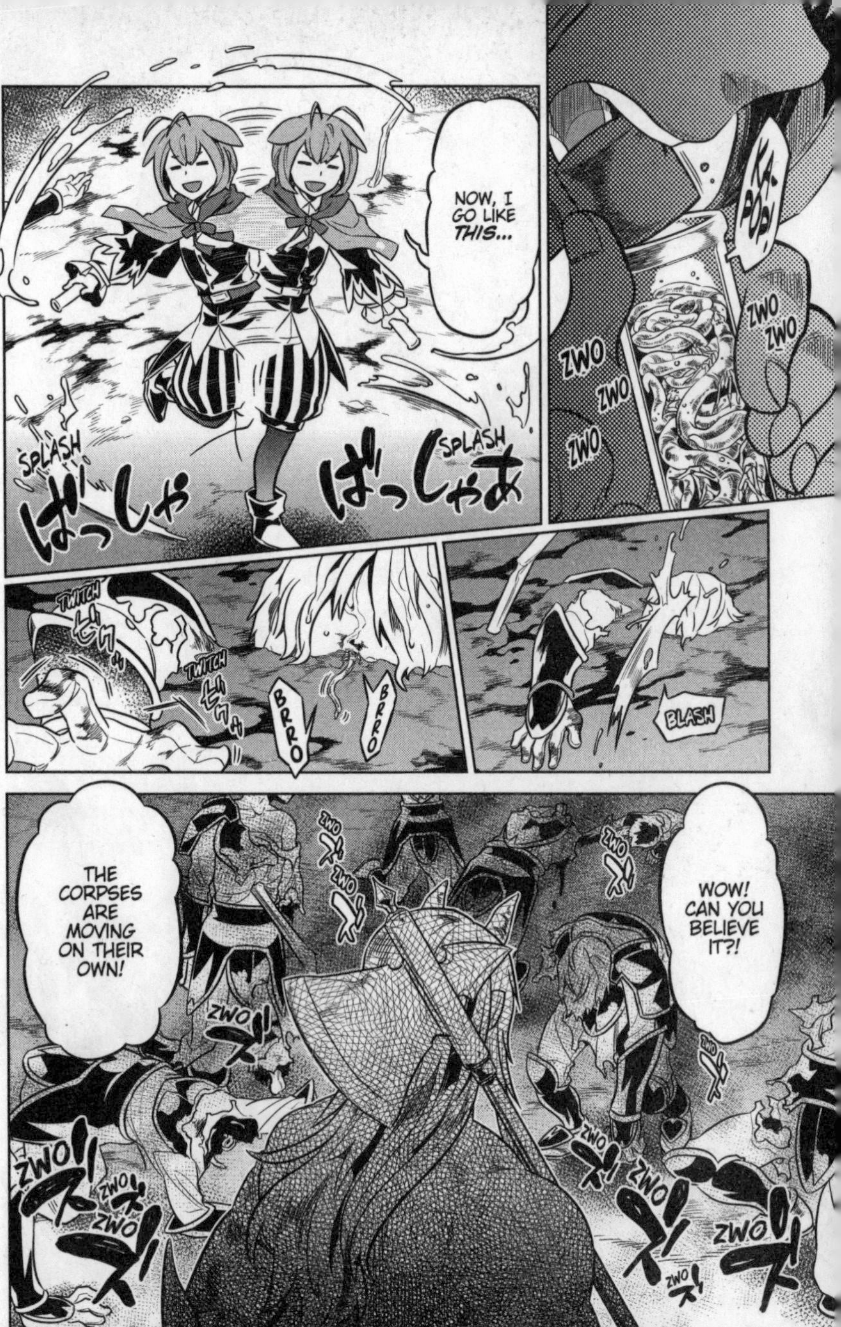

KA-POP!
ZWO ZWO
ZWO
ZWO
ZWO
NOW, I GO LIKE THIS...
SPLASH
ばっしゃあ
SPLASH
ばっしゃ
BLASH
BRRO
BRRO
TWITCH
TWITCH
WOW! CAN YOU BELIEVE IT?!
THE CORPSES ARE MOVING ON THEIR OWN!
ZWO
ZWO
ZWO
ZWO
ZWO
ZWO
ZWO
ZWO
ZWO
ZWO

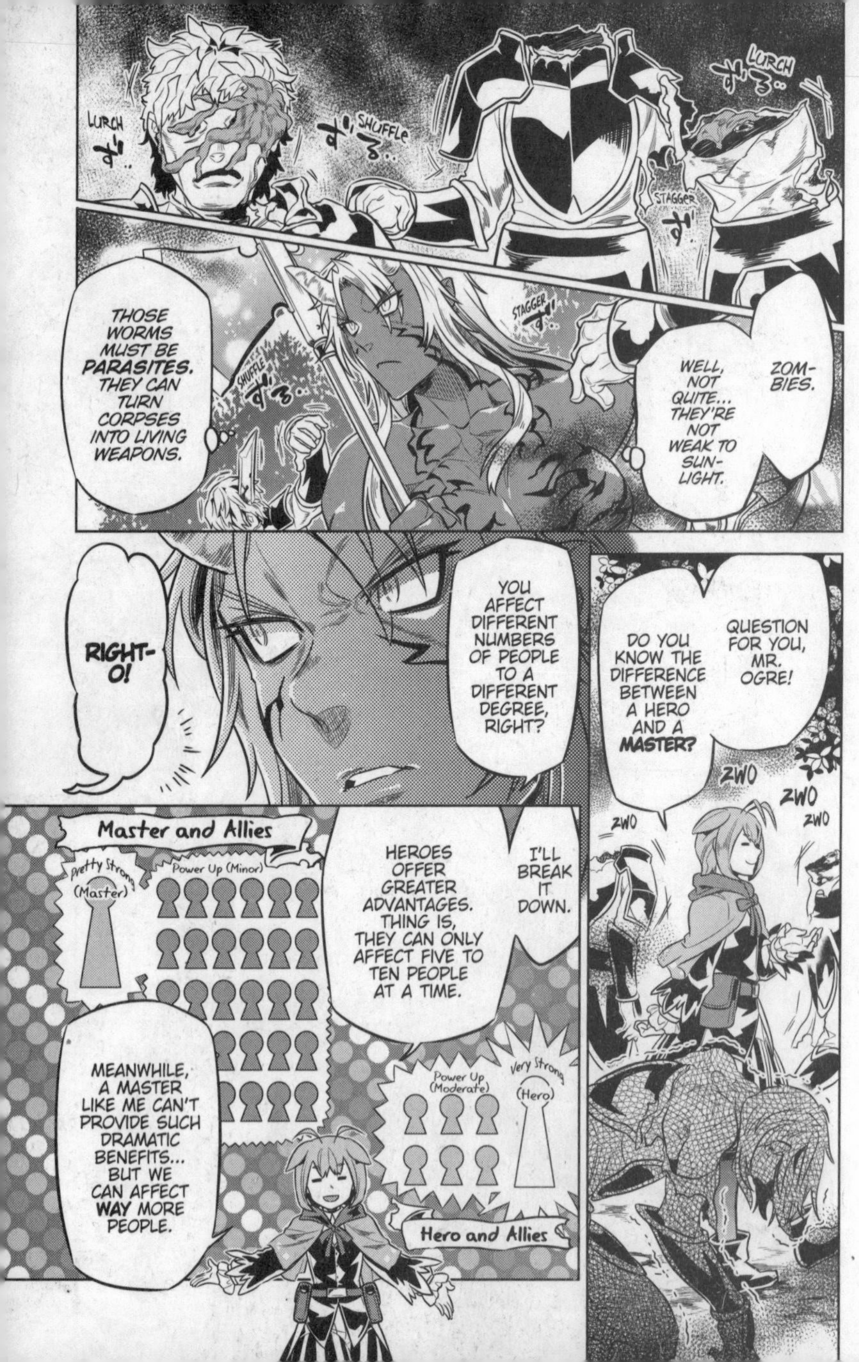
LURCH
STAGGER
SHUFFLE
LURCH
ZOMBIES.
WELL, NOT QUITE... THEY'RE NOT WEAK TO SUNLIGHT.
STAGGER
SHUFFLE
THOSE WORMS MUST BE **PARASITES.** THEY CAN TURN CORPSES INTO LIVING WEAPONS.
QUESTION FOR YOU, MR. OGRE!
DO YOU KNOW THE DIFFERENCE BETWEEN A HERO AND A **MASTER?**
ZWO
ZWO
ZWO
ZWO
YOU AFFECT DIFFERENT NUMBERS OF PEOPLE TO A DIFFERENT DEGREE, RIGHT?
RIGHT-O!
I'LL BREAK IT DOWN.
HEROES OFFER GREATER ADVANTAGES. THING IS, THEY CAN ONLY AFFECT FIVE TO TEN PEOPLE AT A TIME.
Master and Allies
Pretty Strong
(Master)
Power Up (Minor)
Power Up (Moderate)
Very Strong
(Hero)
Hero and Allies
MEANWHILE, A MASTER LIKE ME CAN'T PROVIDE SUCH DRAMATIC BENEFITS... BUT WE CAN AFFECT **WAY** MORE PEOPLE.

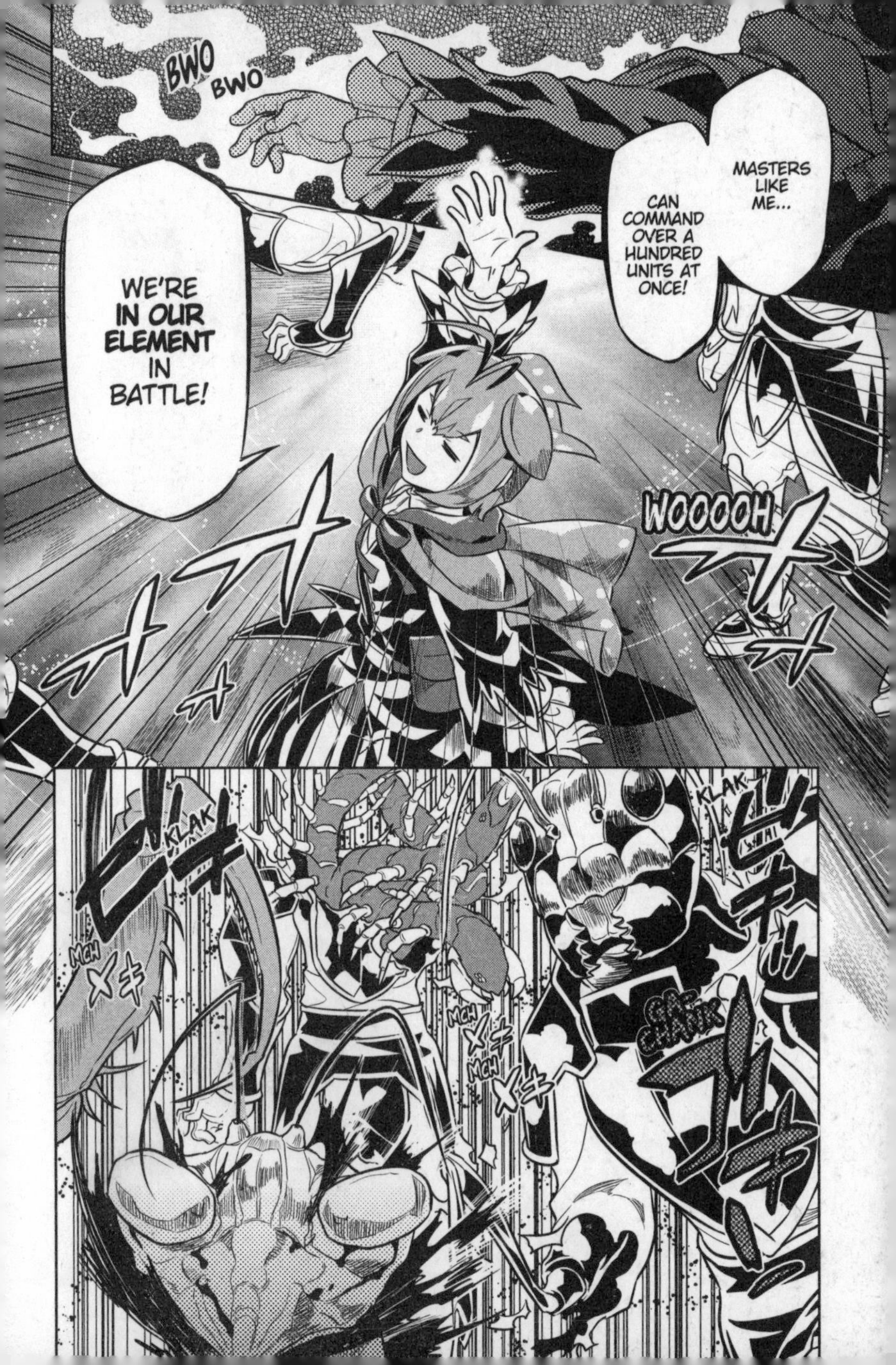

BWO BWO
MASTERS LIKE ME...
CAN COMMAND OVER A HUNDRED UNITS AT ONCE!
WE'RE IN OUR ELEMENT IN BATTLE!
WOOOOH
KLAK
KLAK
MCH
MCH
MCH

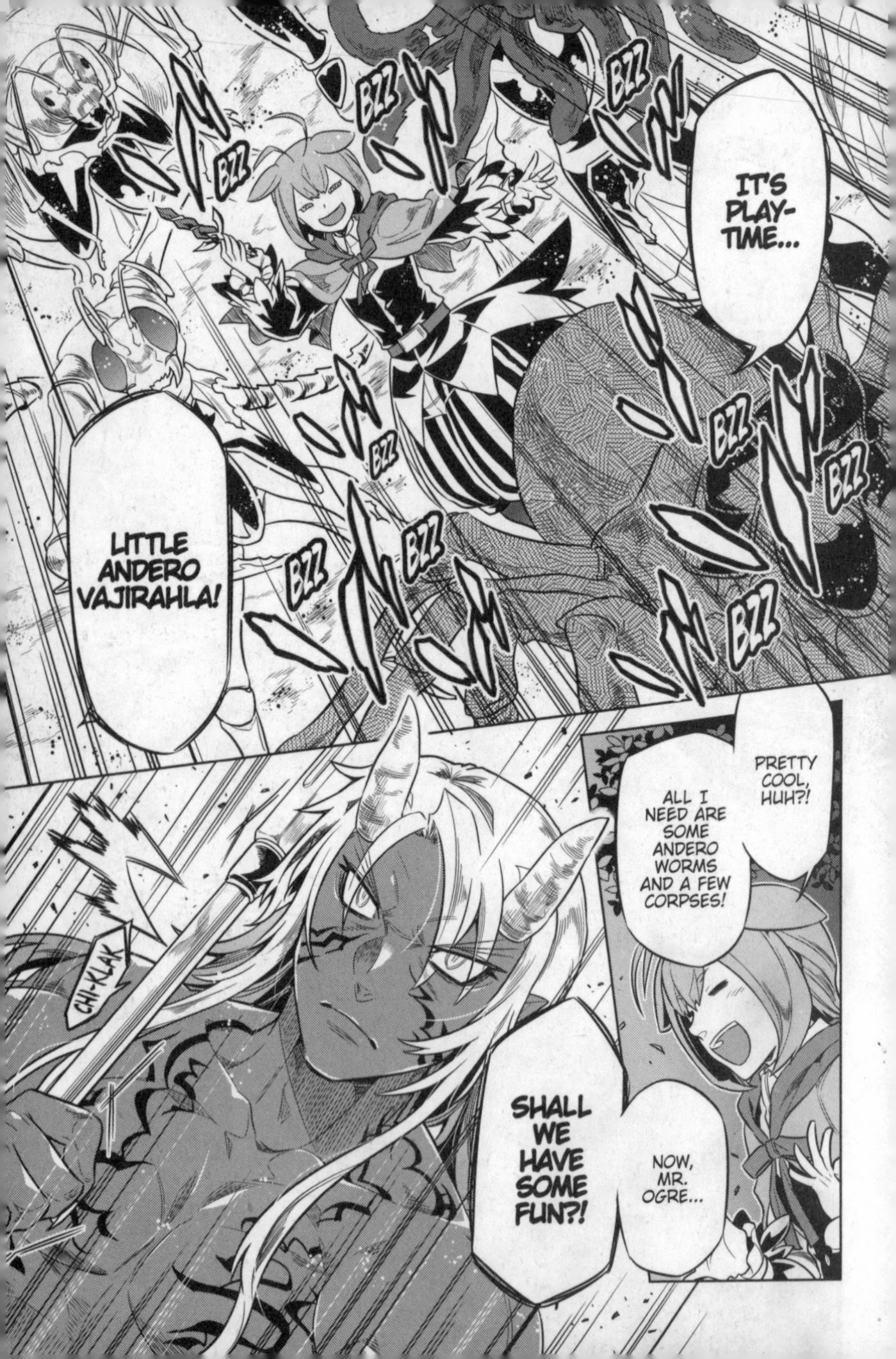

IT'S PLAY-TIME...
BZZ
BZZ
BZZ
BZZ
BZZ
BZZ
BZZ
BZZ
BZZ
LITTLE ANDERO VAJIRAHLA!
PRETTY COOL, HUH?!
ALL I NEED ARE SOME ANDERO WORMS AND A FEW CORPSES!
NOW, MR. OGRE...
SHALL WE HAVE SOME FUN?!
CHI-KLAK

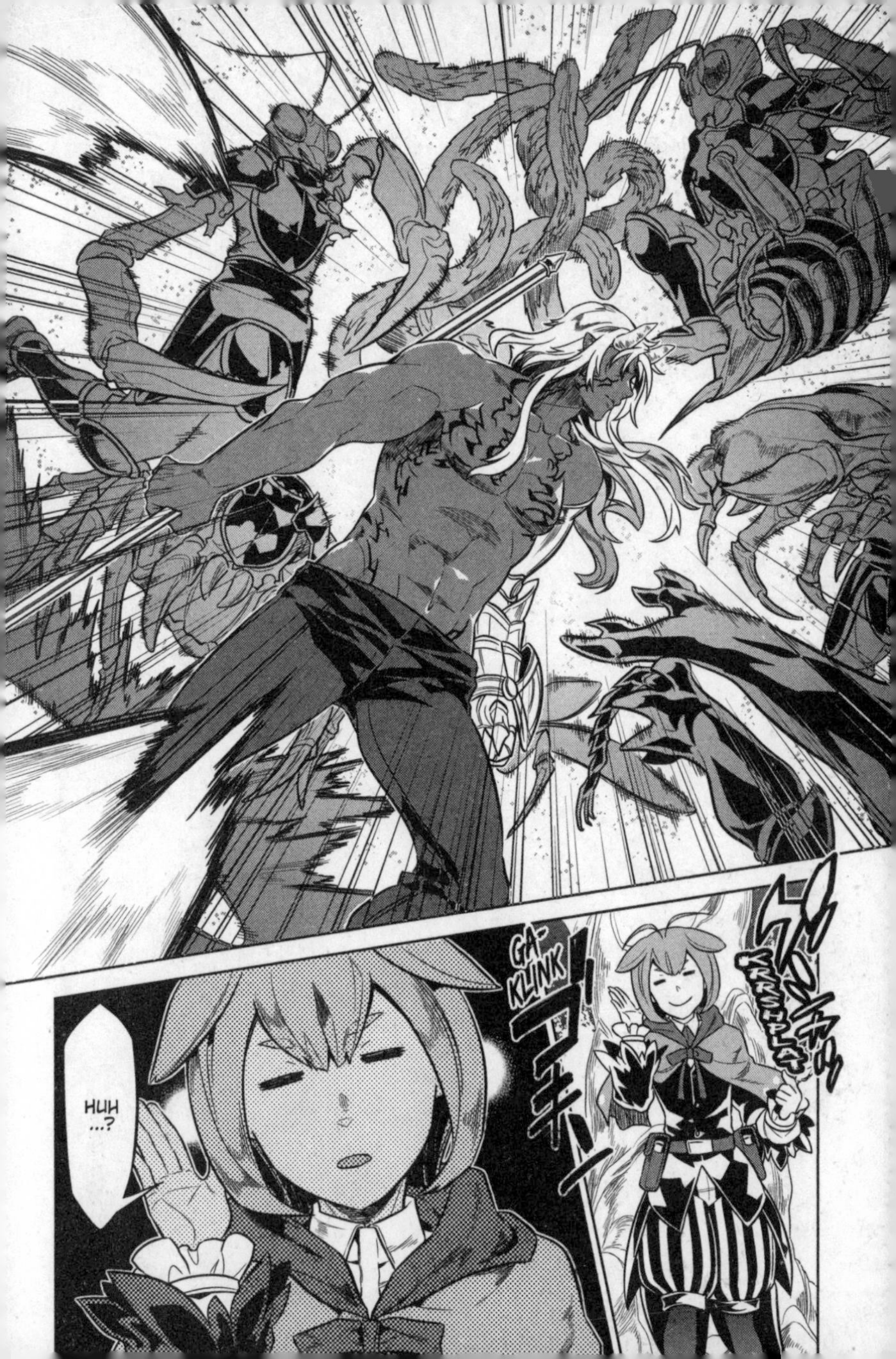
KRRSHPLAT
GA-KLINK
HUH ...?

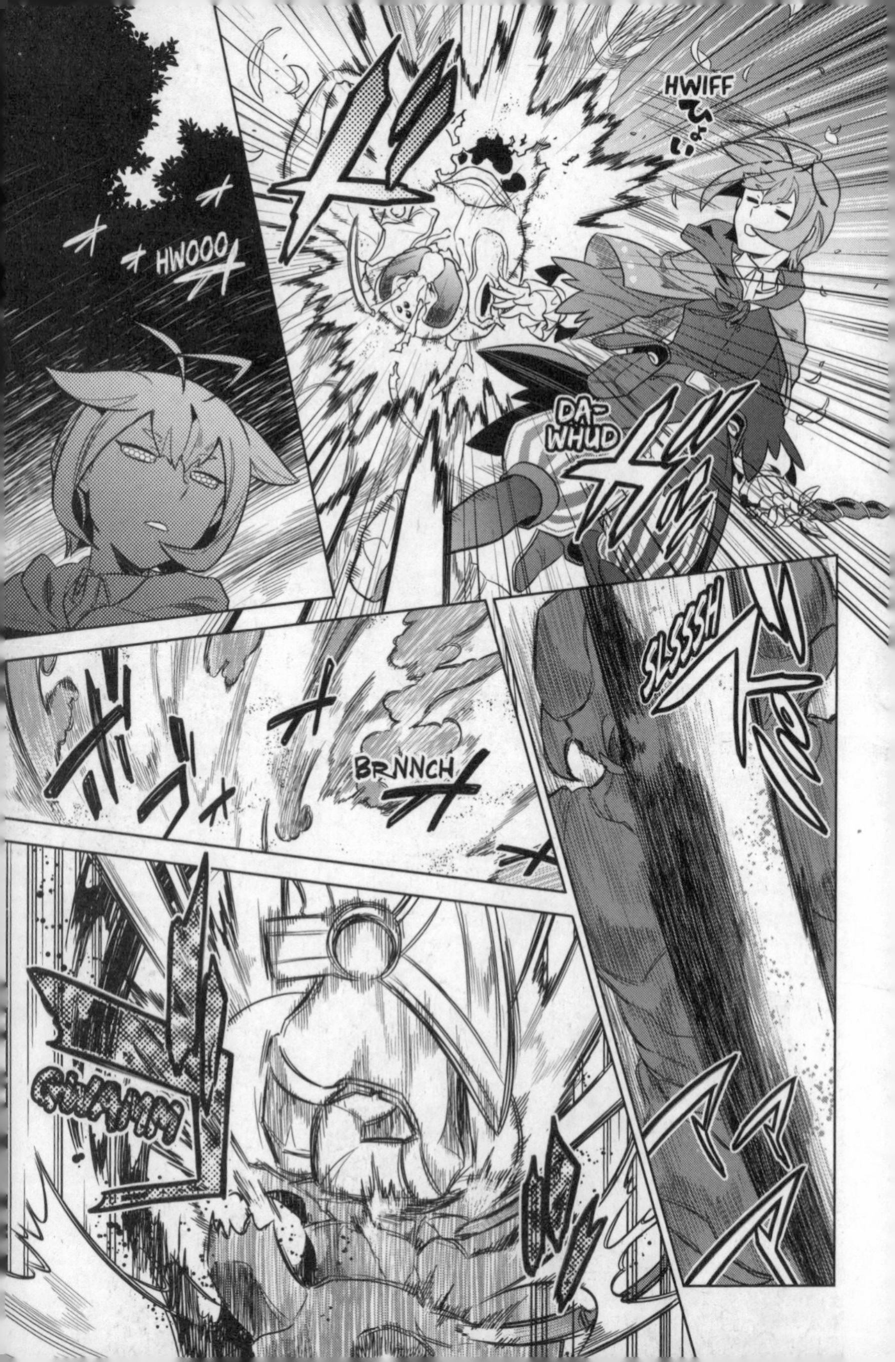
HWIFF
ひょい
DA-WHUD
HWOOO
SLSSSH
BRNNCH

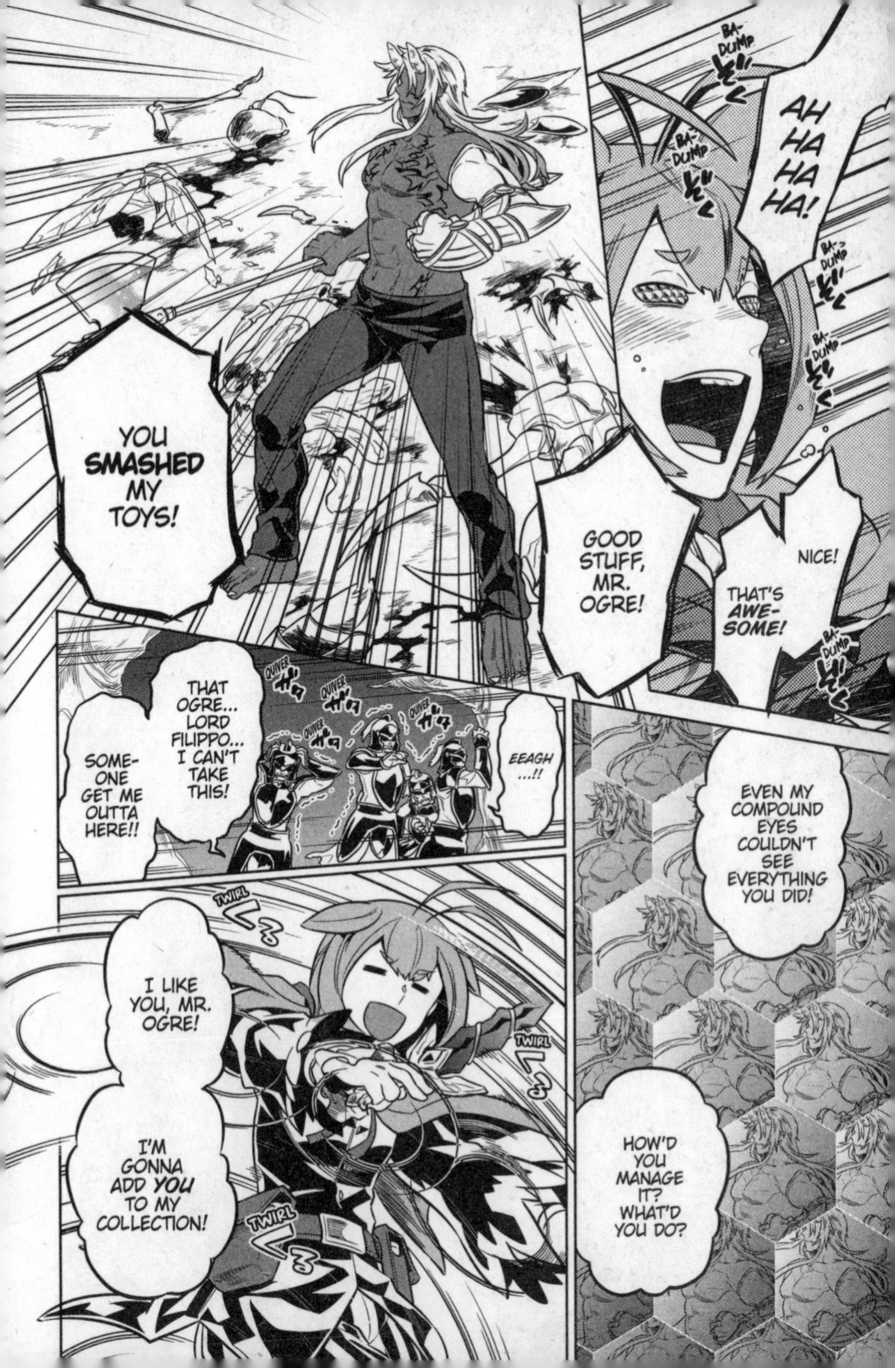
BA-DUMP
AH HA HA HA HA!
BA-DUMP
BA-DUMP
BA-DUMP
NICE!
THAT'S AWESOME!
GOOD STUFF, MR. OGRE!
BA-DUMP
YOU SMASHED MY TOYS!
EVEN MY COMPOUND EYES COULDN'T SEE EVERYTHING YOU DID!
HOW'D YOU MANAGE IT? WHAT'D YOU DO?
EEAGH ...!!
QUIVER
QUIVER
QUIVER
QUIVER
THAT OGRE... LORD FILIPPO... I CAN'T TAKE THIS!
SOME-ONE GET ME OUTTA HERE!!
TWIRL
I LIKE YOU, MR. OGRE!
TWIRL
I'M GONNA ADD YOU TO MY COLLECTION!
TWIRL

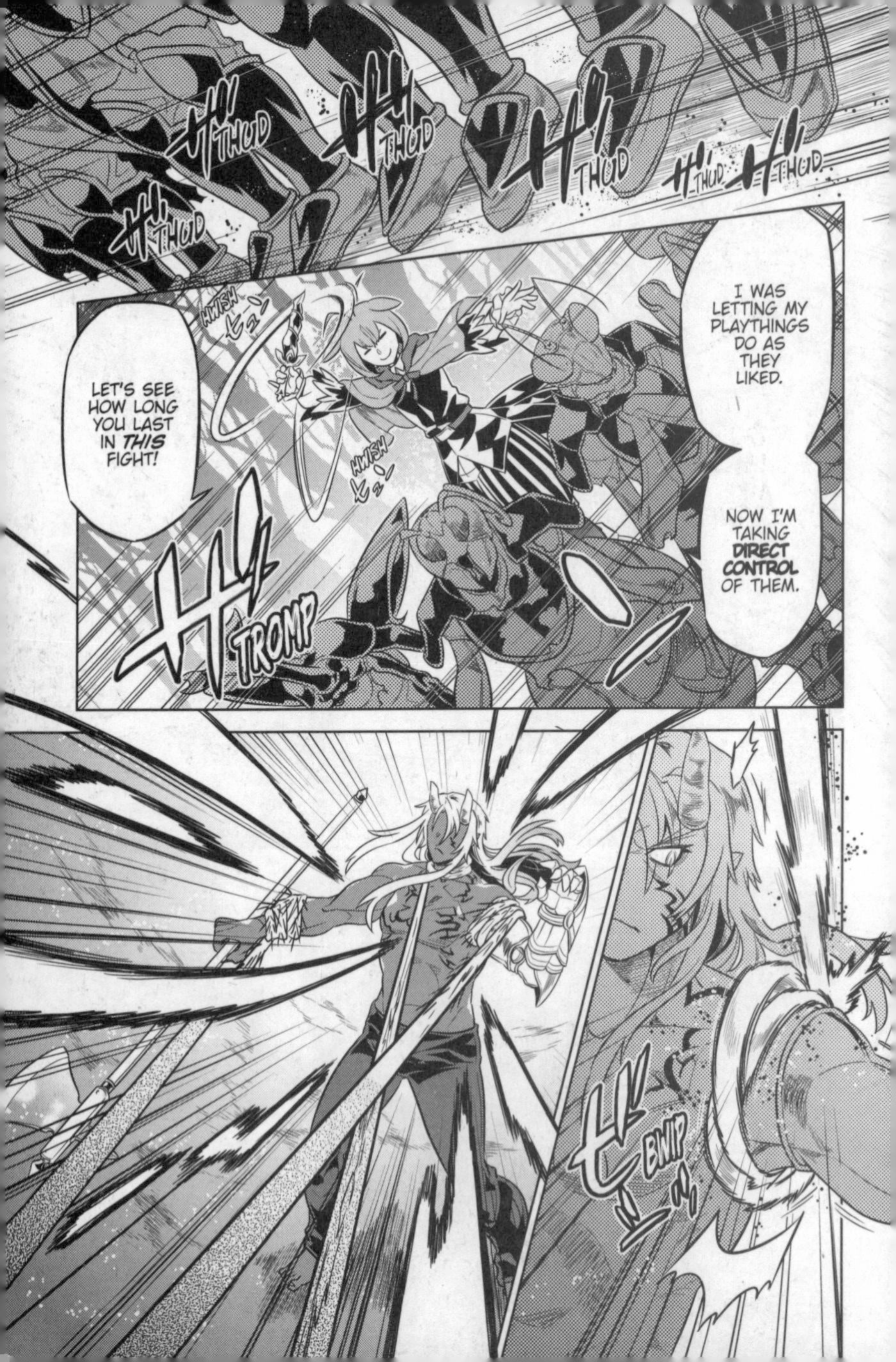
THUD
THUD
THUD
THUD
THUD
THUD
I WAS LETTING MY PLAYTHINGS DO AS THEY LIKED.
NOW I'M TAKING **DIRECT CONTROL** OF THEM.
HWISH
HWISH
LET'S SEE HOW LONG YOU LAST IN *THIS* FIGHT!
TROMP
BWIP

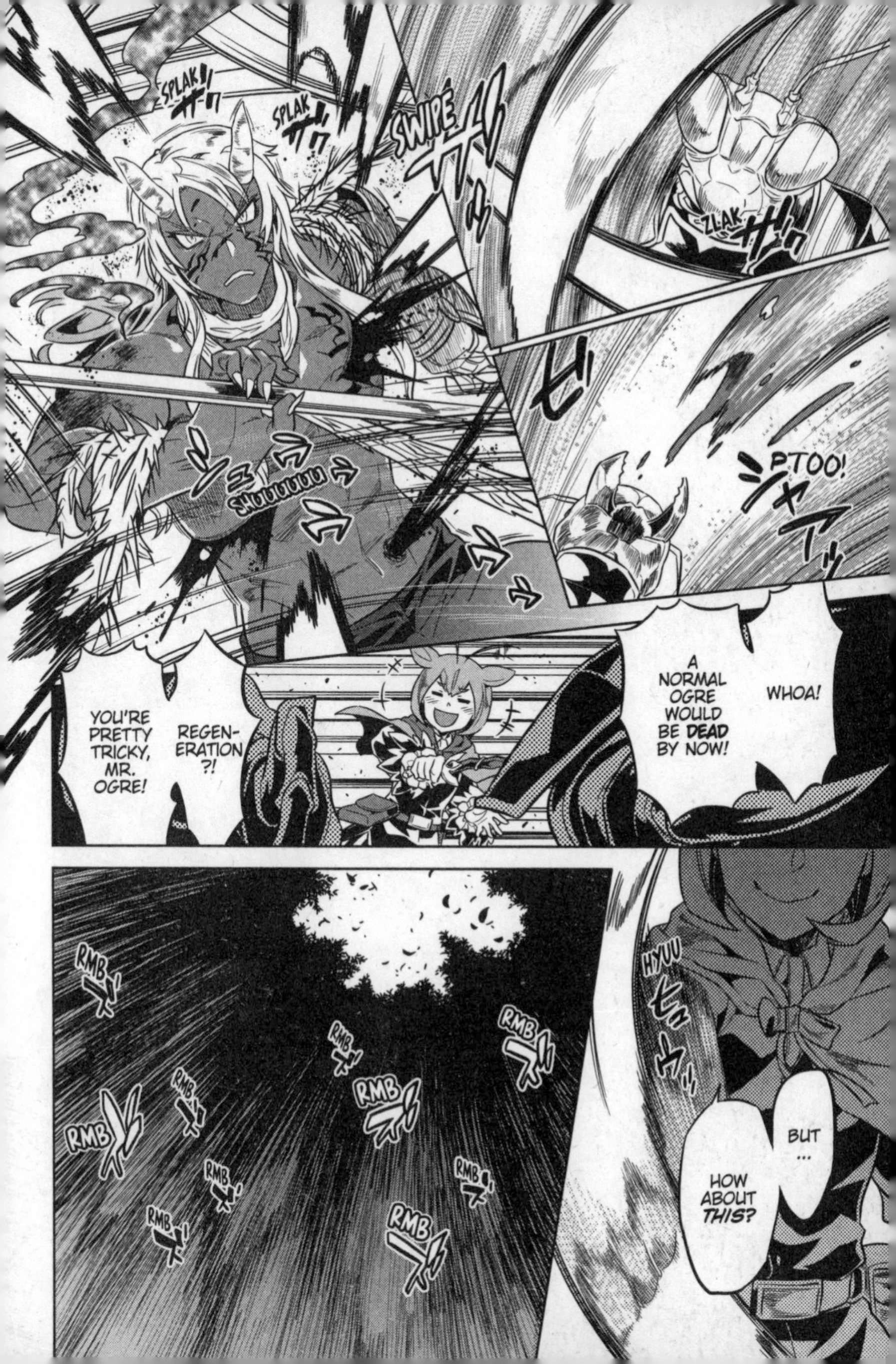

ZLAK
PTOO!
SWIPE
SPLAK
SPLAK
SHOOOOOOO
WHOA!
A NORMAL OGRE WOULD BE DEAD BY NOW!
REGEN-ERATION?!
YOU'RE PRETTY TRICKY, MR. OGRE!
HYUU
BUT...
HOW ABOUT THIS?
RMB
RMB
RMB
RMB
RMB
RMB
RMB
RMB
RMB
RMB

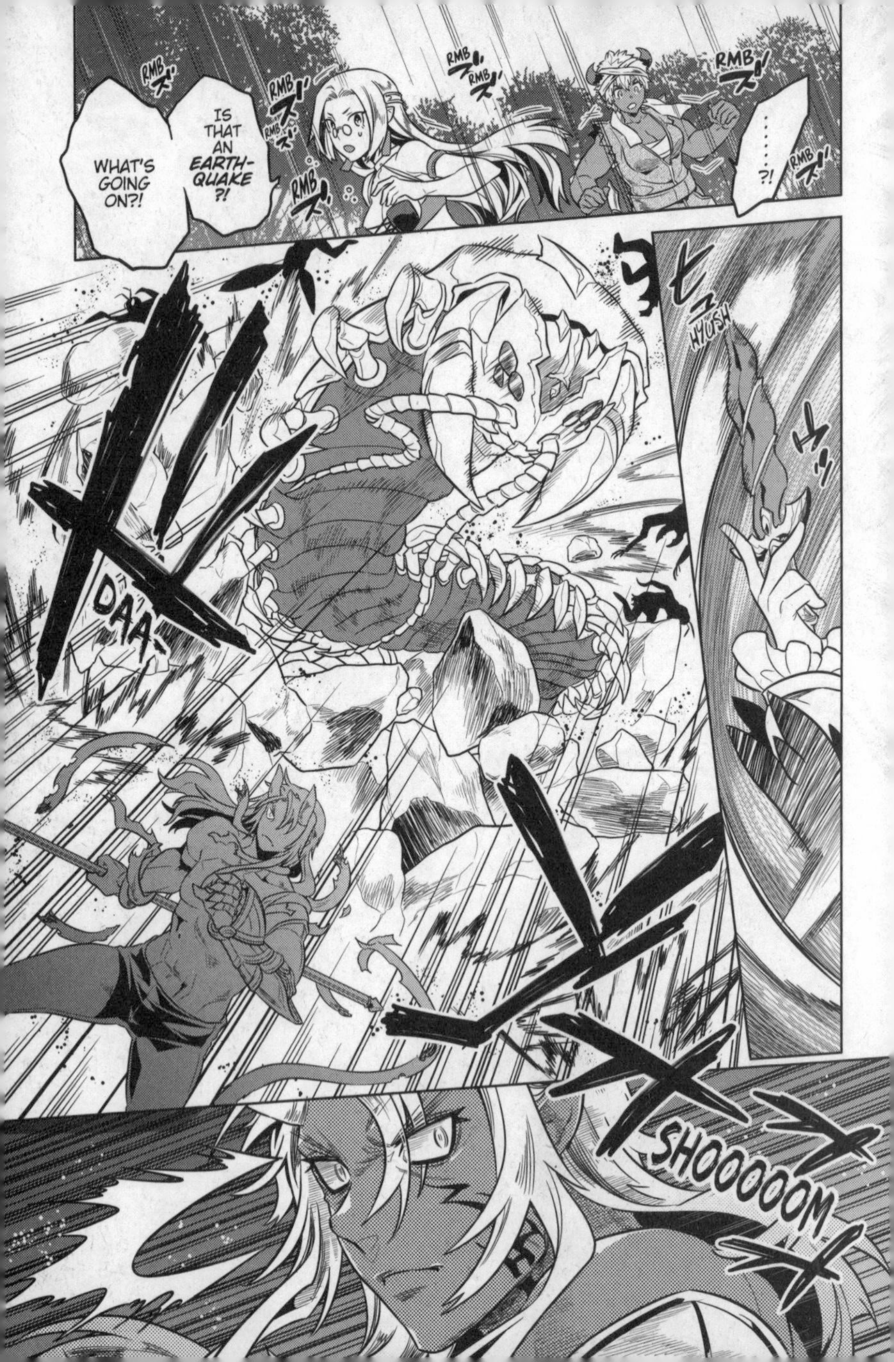
RMB
RMB
......?!
RMB
RMB
IS THAT AN EARTHQUAKE?!
RMB
RMB
RMB
WHAT'S GOING ON?!
RMB
HYUSH
DAA
SHOOOOOM

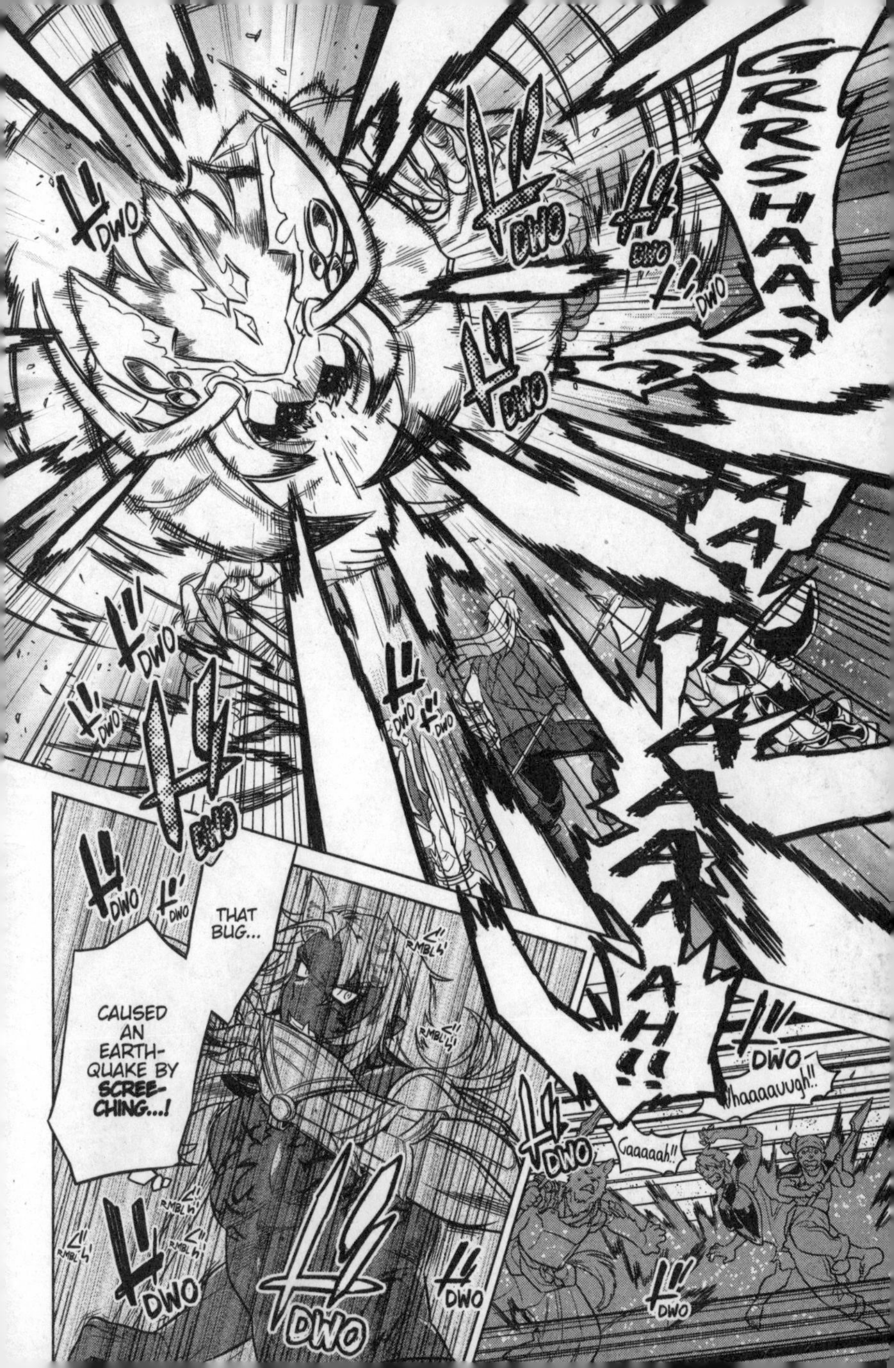

GRRSHAAAAAAAAAAAH!!
DWO
DWO
DWO
DWO
DWO
DWO
DWO
DWO
DWO
DWO
DWO
DWO
Whaaaauugh!!
Gaaaaah!!
DWO
DWO
DWO
THAT BUG...
CAUSED AN EARTHQUAKE BY SCREECHING...!
RMBL
RMBL
RMBL
RMBL
RMBL
DWO
DWO

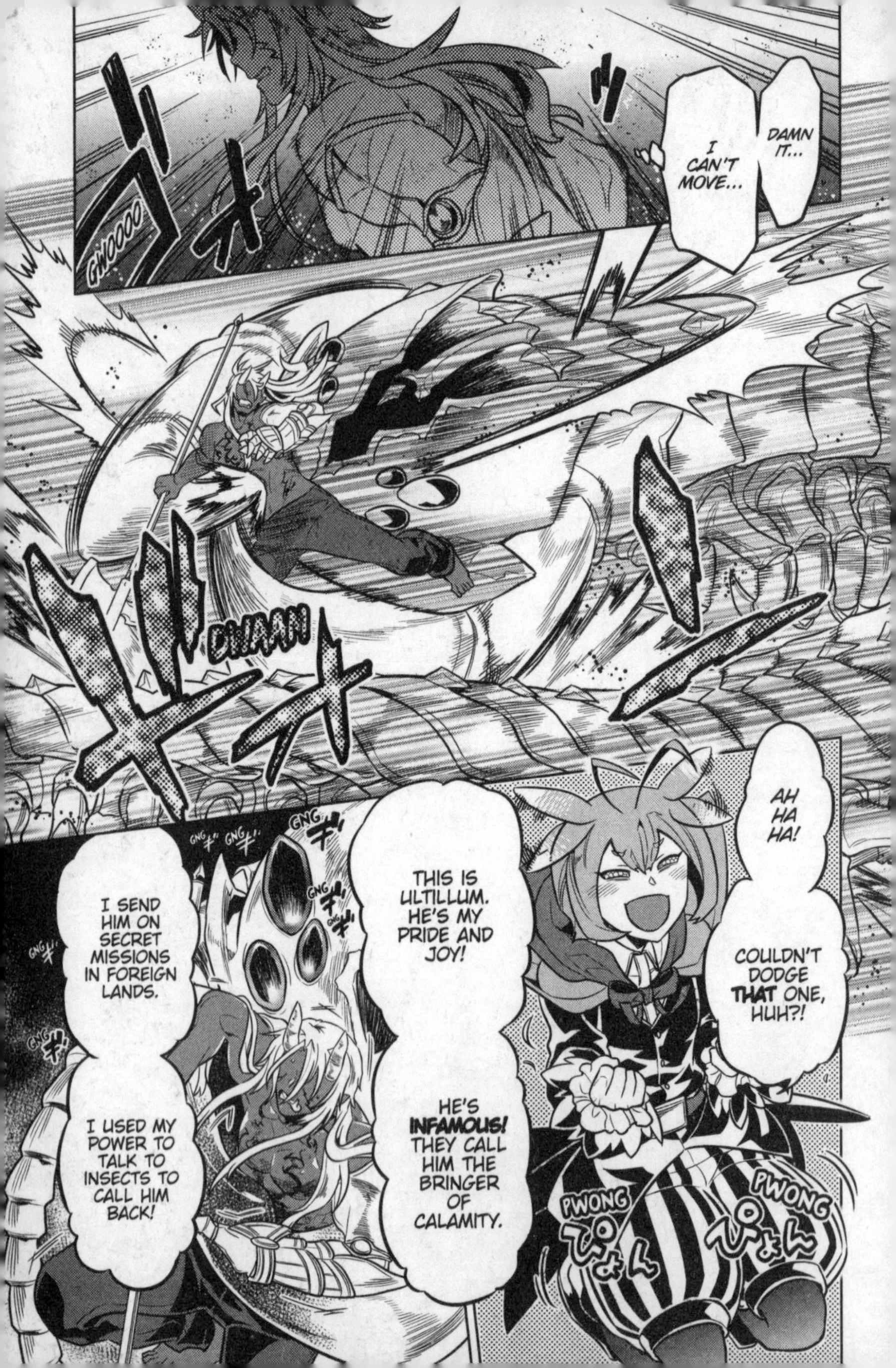
DAMN IT...
I CAN'T MOVE...
GWOOOO
DWAAN
AH HA HA!
COULDN'T DODGE **THAT** ONE, HUH?!
THIS IS ULTILLUM. HE'S MY PRIDE AND JOY!
HE'S **INFAMOUS!** THEY CALL HIM THE BRINGER OF CALAMITY.
PWONG ぴょん
PWONG ぴょん
GNG ギ
GNG ギ
GNG ギ
GNG ギ
GNG ギ
GNG ギ
I SEND HIM ON SECRET MISSIONS IN FOREIGN LANDS.
I USED MY POWER TO TALK TO INSECTS TO CALL HIM BACK!

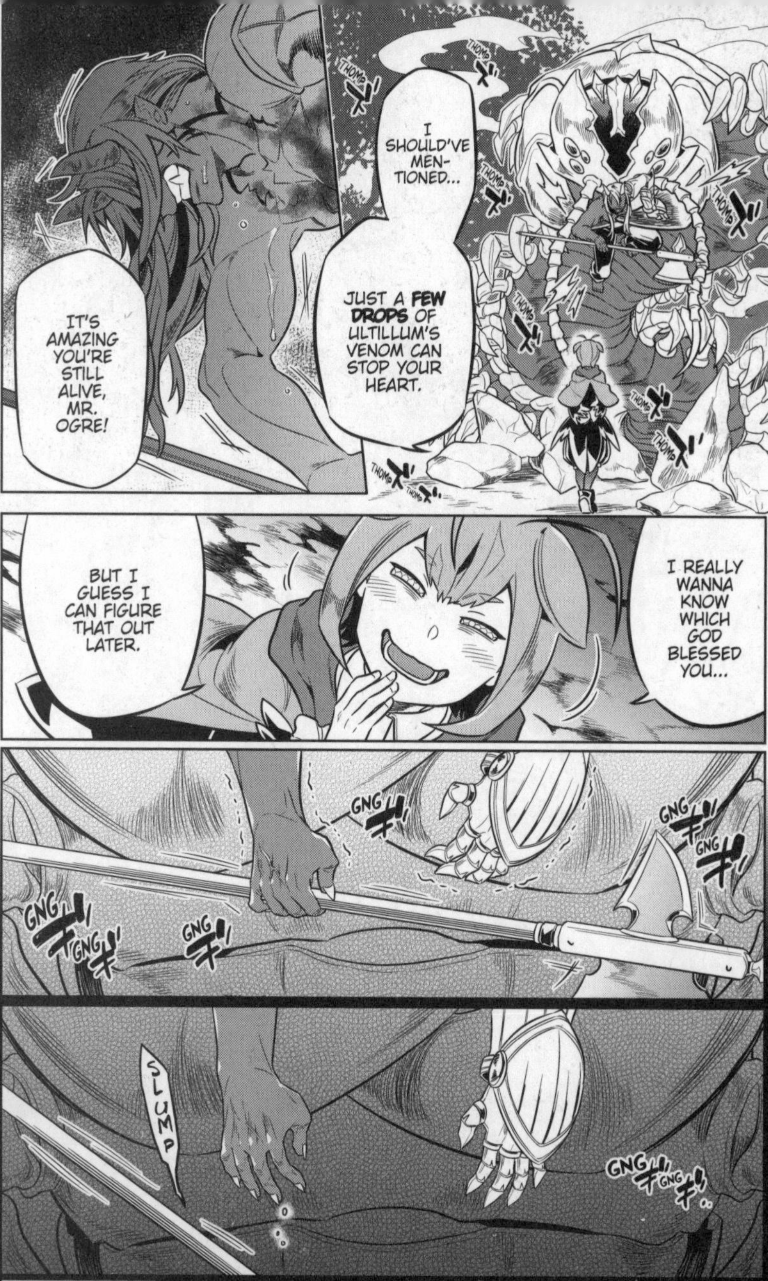
THOMP
THOMP
THOMP
THOMP
THOMP
THOMP
I SHOULD'VE MENTIONED...
JUST A **FEW DROPS** OF ULTILLUM'S VENOM CAN STOP YOUR HEART.
THOMP
THOMP
IT'S AMAZING YOU'RE STILL ALIVE, MR. OGRE!
I REALLY WANNA KNOW WHICH GOD BLESSED YOU...
BUT I GUESS I CAN FIGURE THAT OUT LATER.
GNG
GNG
GNG
GNG
GNG
GNG
GNG
GNG
SLUMP

▶ CONTINUE

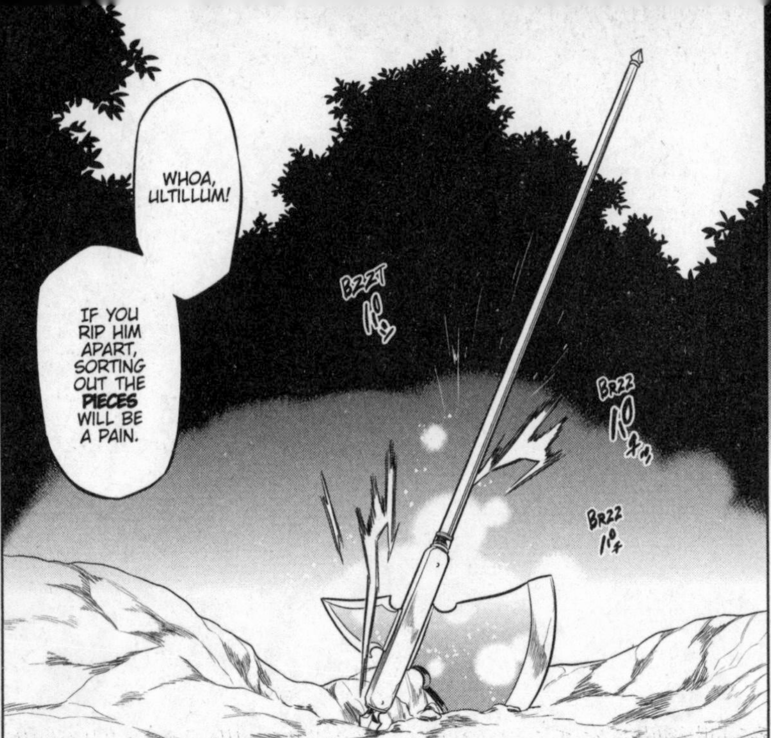
WHOA, ULTILLUM!
BZZT
IF YOU RIP HIM APART, SORTING OUT THE PIECES WILL BE A PAIN.
BRZZ
BRZZ

CHAPTER 33

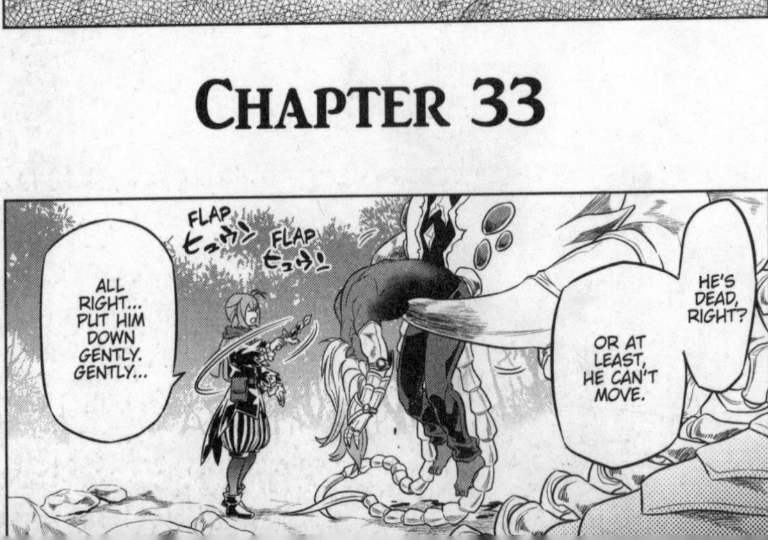
HE'S DEAD, RIGHT?
OR AT LEAST, HE CAN'T MOVE.
FLAP
FLAP
ALL RIGHT... PUT HIM DOWN GENTLY. GENTLY...

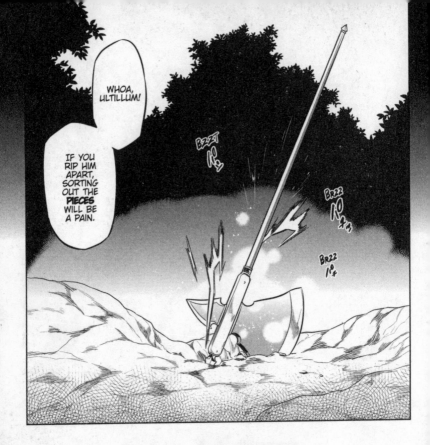

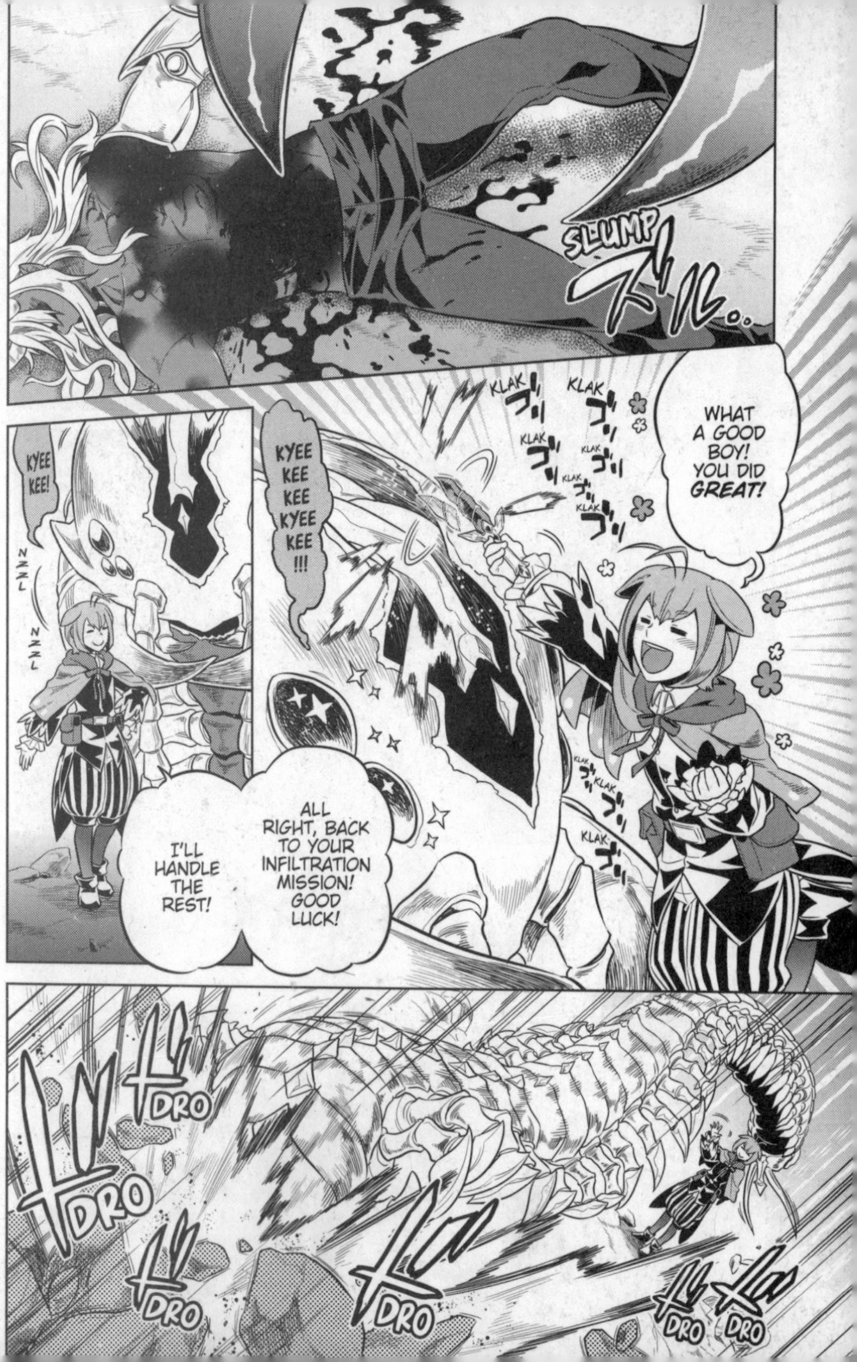
SLUMP
WHAT A GOOD BOY! YOU DID GREAT!
KLAK KLAK KLAK KLAK KLAK KLAK
KYEE KEE KEE KYEE KEE!!!
KLAK KLAK KLAK
ALL RIGHT, BACK TO YOUR INFILTRATION MISSION! GOOD LUCK!
KYEE KEE!
NZZL
NZZL
I'LL HANDLE THE REST!
DRO
DRO
DRO
DRO
DRO
DRO

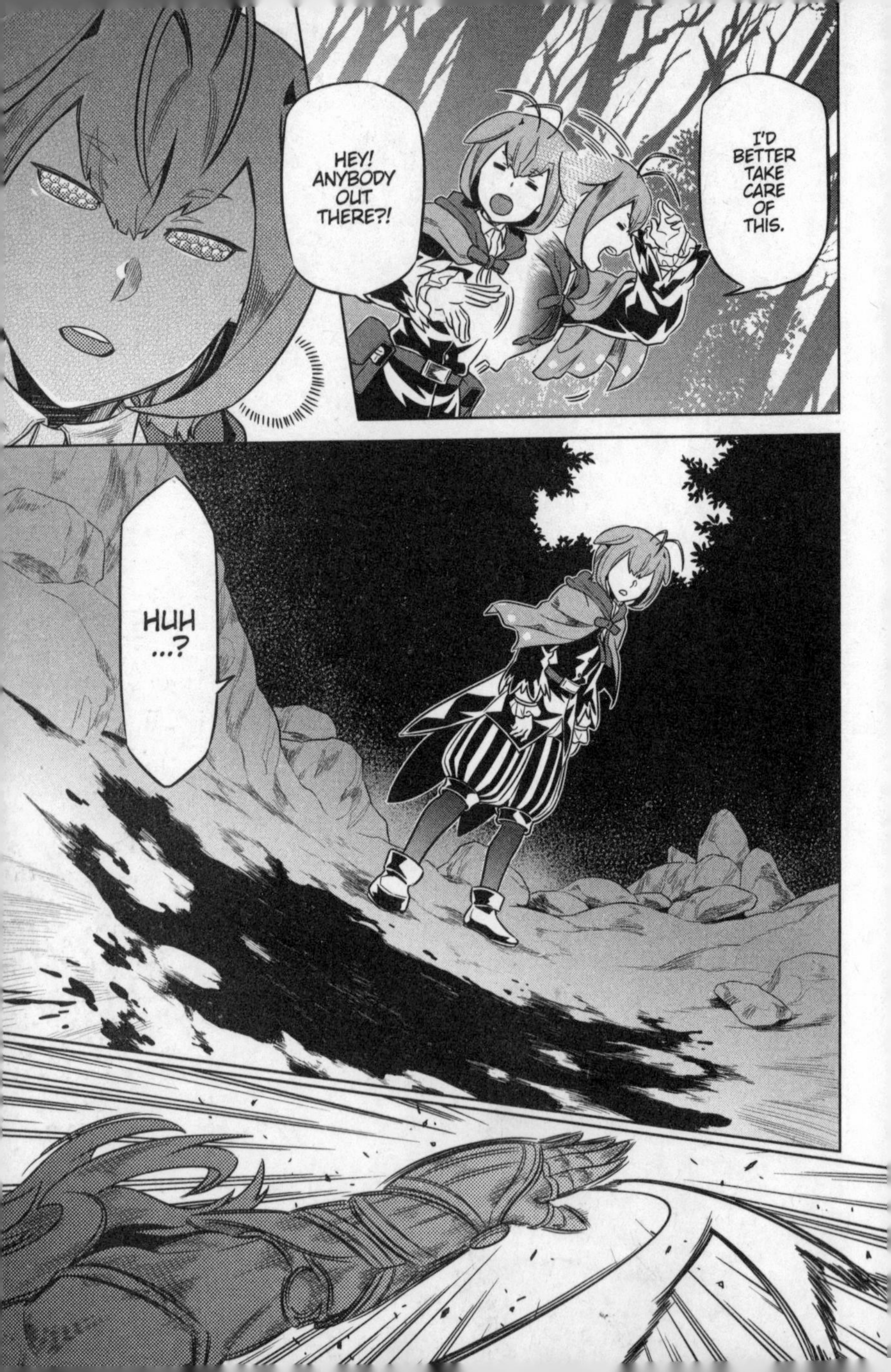
I'D BETTER TAKE CARE OF THIS.
HEY! ANYBODY OUT THERE?!
HUH ...?

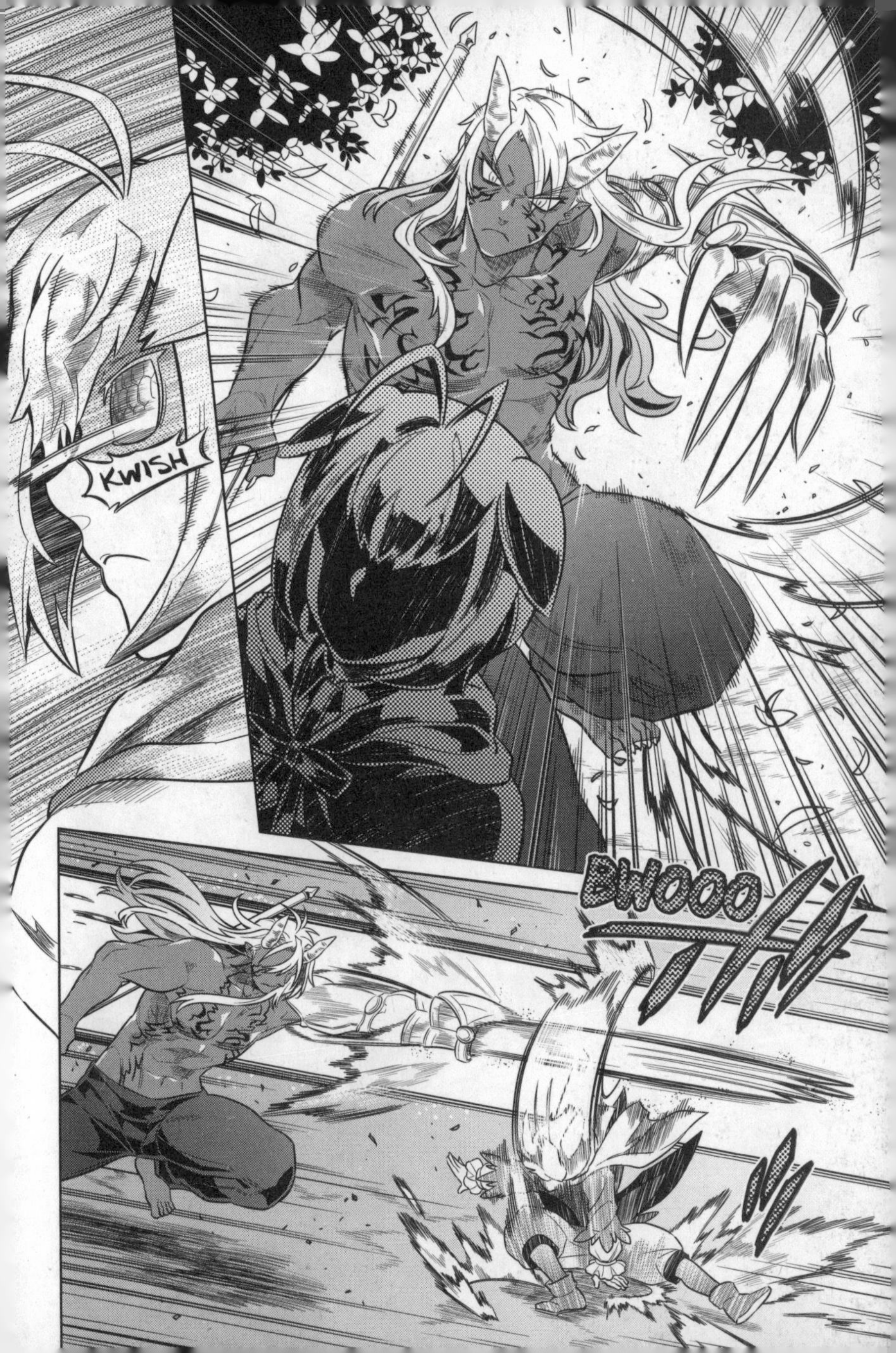
KWISH
BWOOO

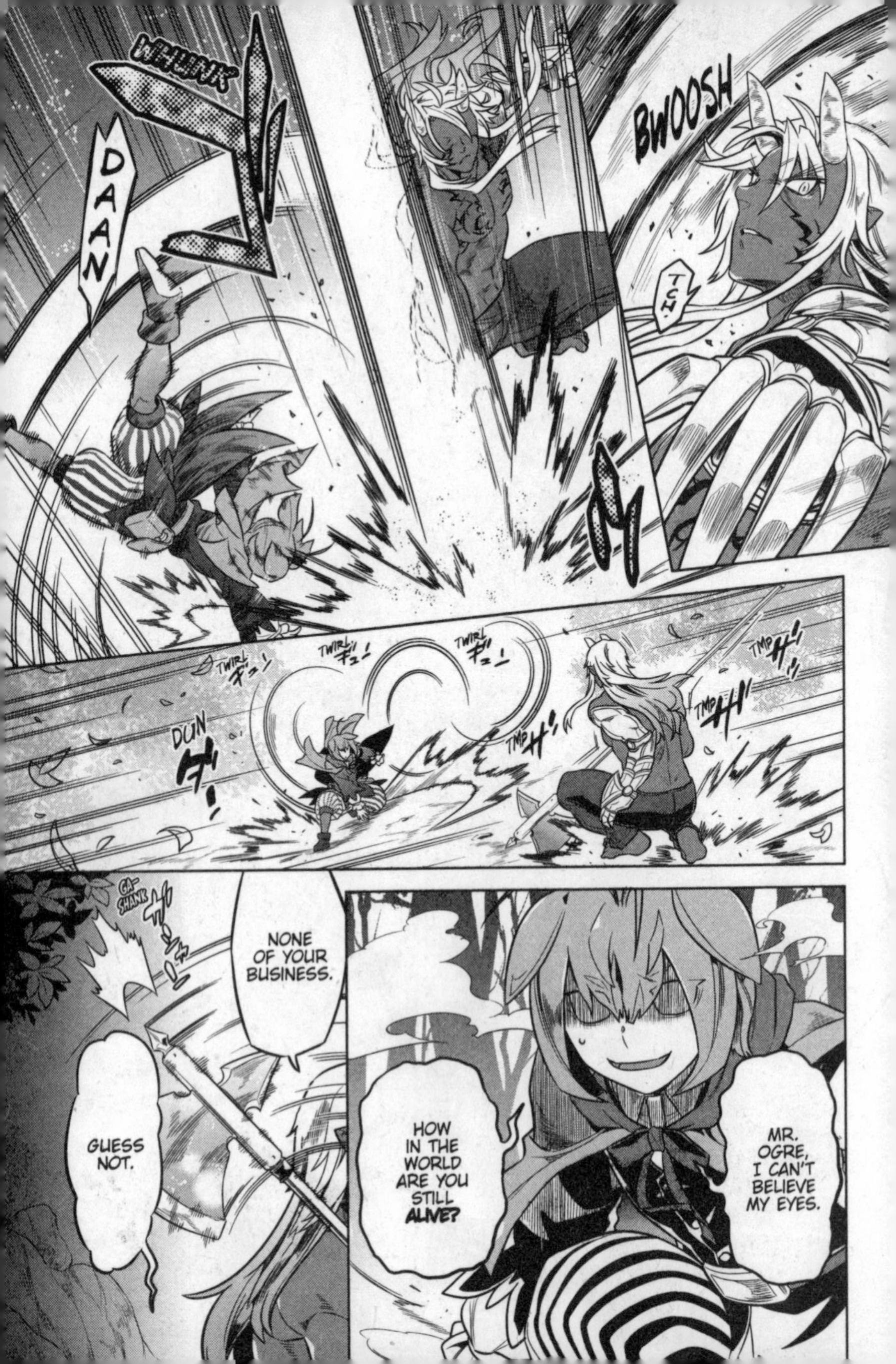
BWOOSH
TCH.
WHUNK
DAAN
TMP
TMP
TMP
TWIRL
TWIRL
TWIRL
DUN
MR. OGRE, I CAN'T BELIEVE MY EYES.
HOW IN THE WORLD ARE YOU STILL **ALIVE?**
NONE OF YOUR BUSINESS.
GA-SHANK
GUESS NOT.

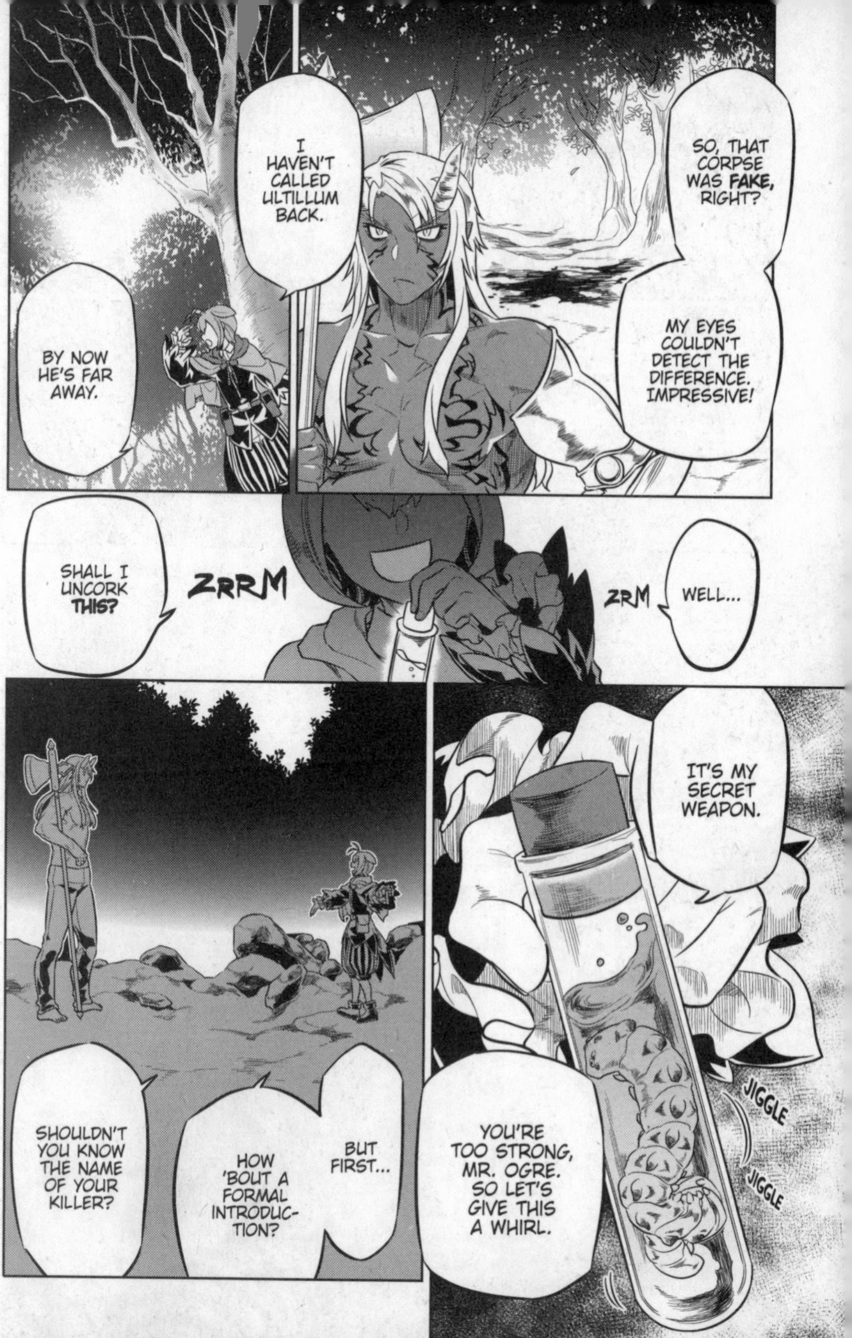
SO, THAT CORPSE WAS FAKE, RIGHT?
MY EYES COULDN'T DETECT THE DIFFERENCE. IMPRESSIVE!
I HAVEN'T CALLED ULTILLUM BACK.
BY NOW HE'S FAR AWAY.
WELL...
ZRM
ZRRM
SHALL I UNCORK THIS?
IT'S MY SECRET WEAPON.
YOU'RE TOO STRONG, MR. OGRE. SO LET'S GIVE THIS A WHIRL.
JIGGLE
JIGGLE
BUT FIRST...
HOW 'BOUT A FORMAL INTRODUCTION?
SHOULDN'T YOU KNOW THE NAME OF YOUR KILLER?

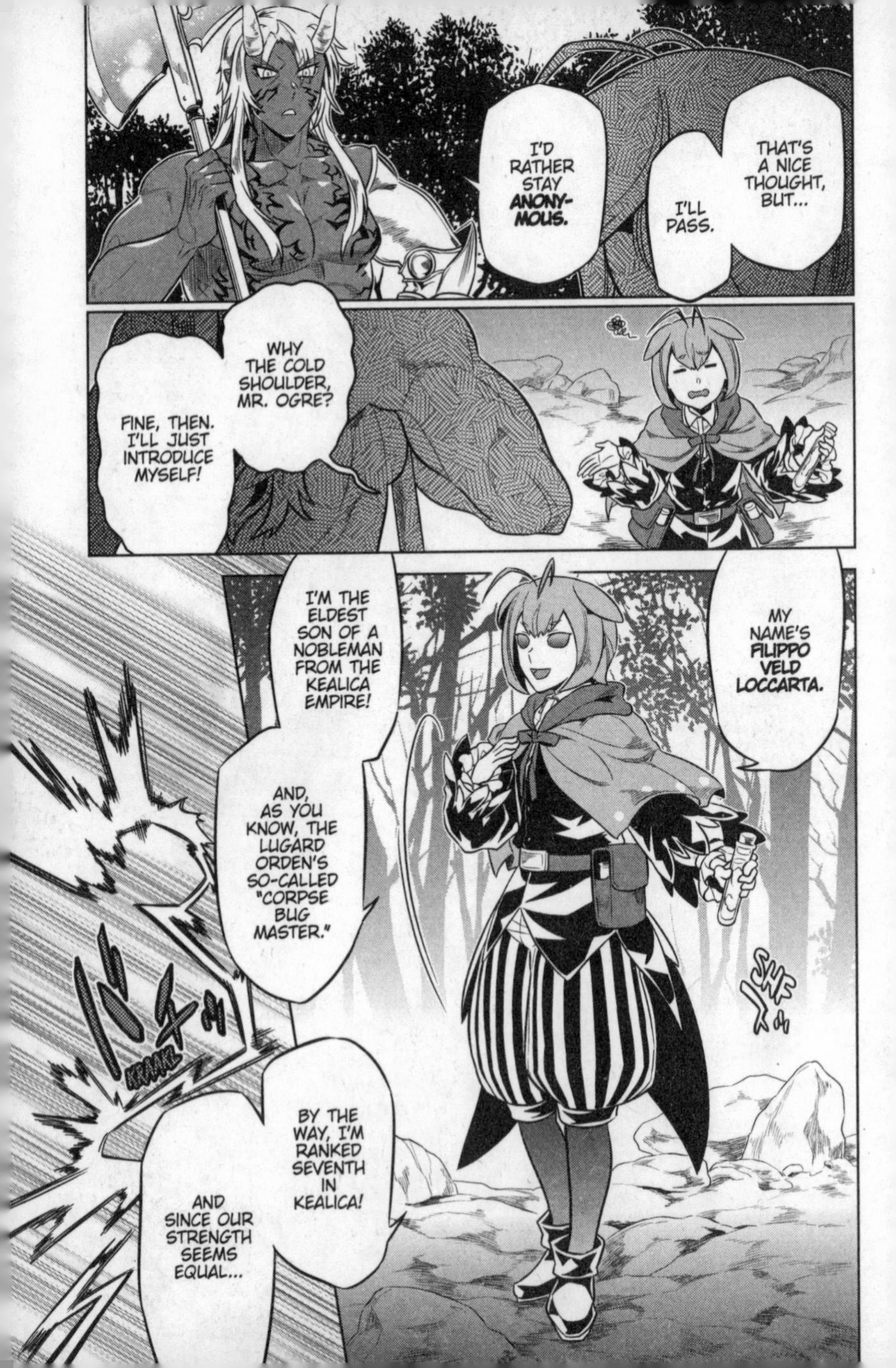
THAT'S A NICE THOUGHT, BUT...
I'LL PASS.
I'D RATHER STAY ANONYMOUS.
WHY THE COLD SHOULDER, MR. OGRE?
FINE, THEN. I'LL JUST INTRODUCE MYSELF!
MY NAME'S FILIPPO VELD LOCCARTA.
I'M THE ELDEST SON OF A NOBLEMAN FROM THE KEALICA EMPIRE!
AND, AS YOU KNOW, THE LUGARD ORDEN'S SO-CALLED "CORPSE BUG MASTER."
SHF
BY THE WAY, I'M RANKED SEVENTH IN KEALICA!
AND SINCE OUR STRENGTH SEEMS EQUAL...

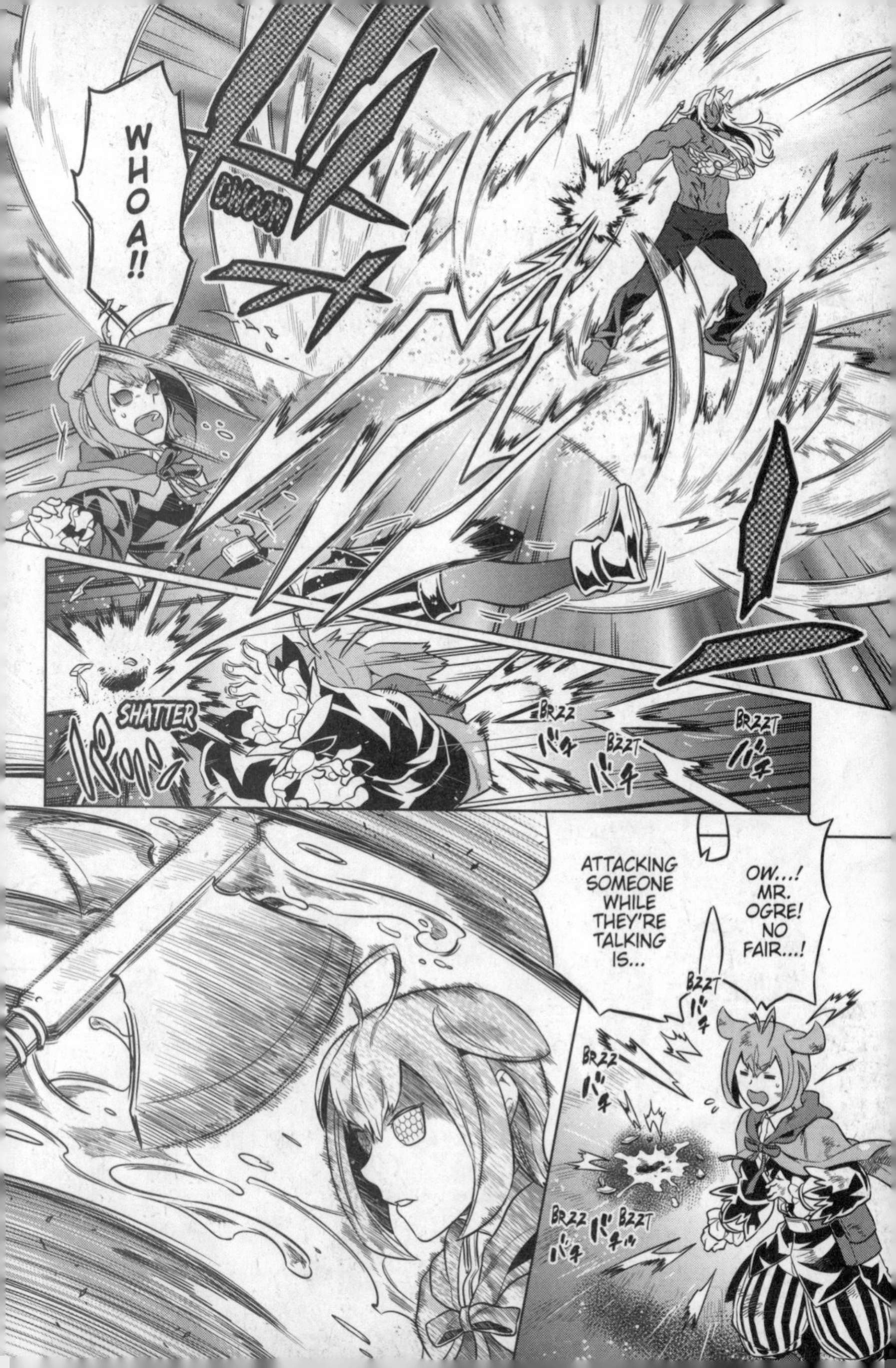
WHOA!!
SHATTER
BRZZ
バチ
BZZT
バチ
BRZZT
バチ
OW...! MR. OGRE! NO FAIR...!
ATTACKING SOMEONE WHILE THEY'RE TALKING IS...
BZZT
バチ
BRZZ
バチ
BRZZ
バチ
BZZT
バチッ

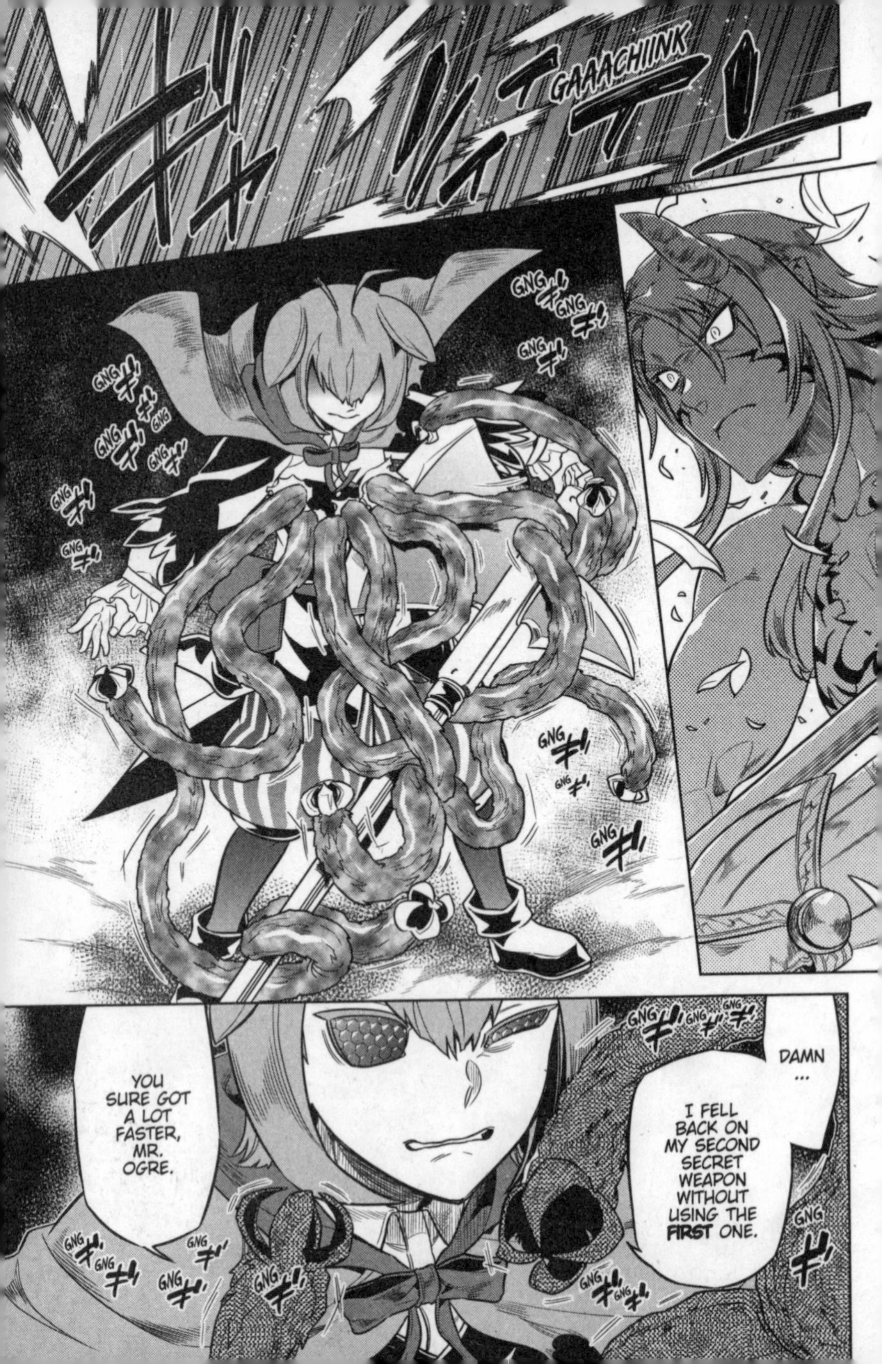
GAAACHIINK
GNG GNG
GNG
GNG GNG
GNG GNG
GNG
GNG
GNG
GNG
GNG
GNG
GNG GNG GNG
DAMN ...
I FELL BACK ON MY SECOND SECRET WEAPON WITHOUT USING THE **FIRST** ONE.
GNG
YOU SURE GOT A LOT FASTER, MR. OGRE.
GNG GNG
GNG GNG GNG
GNG

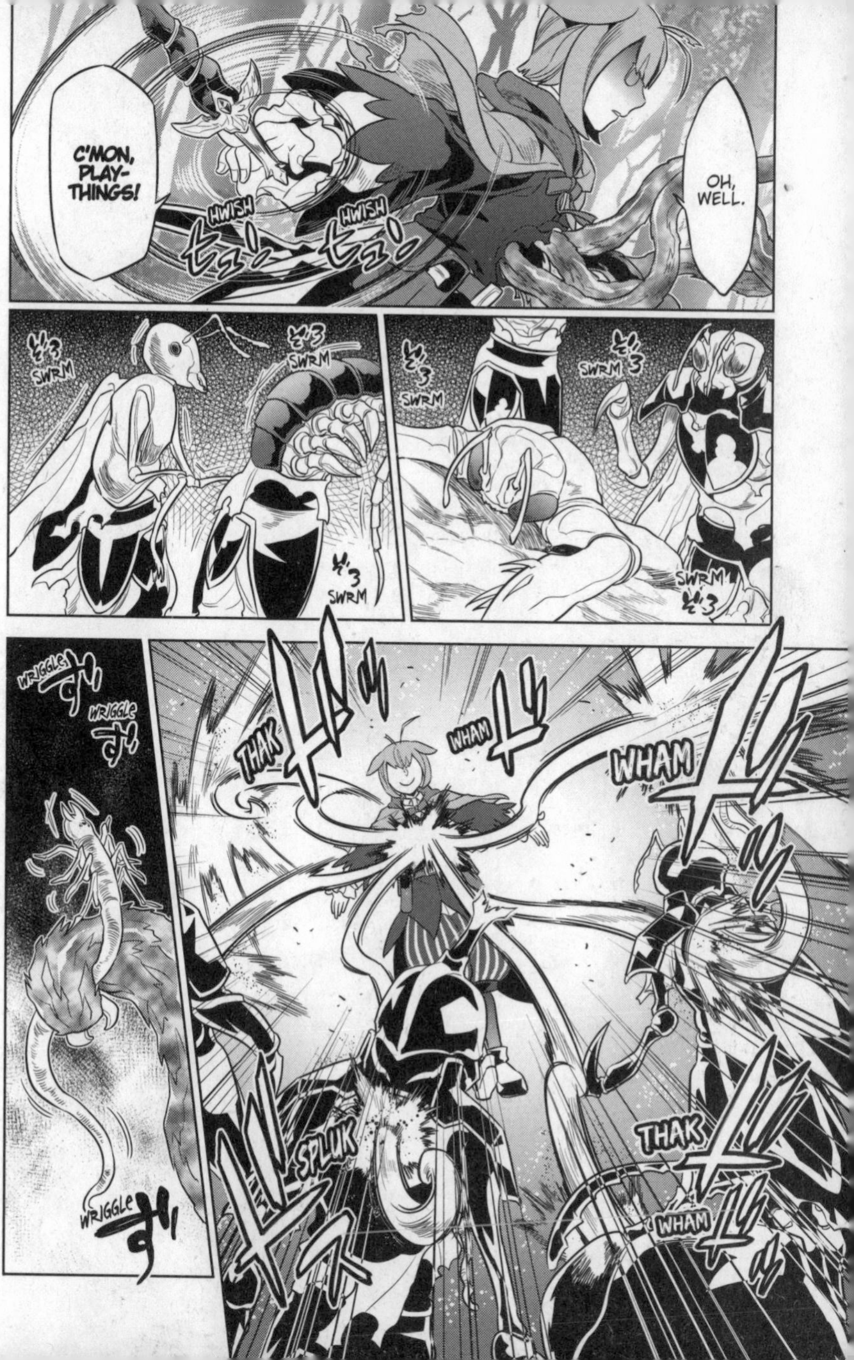
OH, WELL.
C'MON, PLAY-THINGS!
HWISH
HWISH
SWRM
SWRM
SWRM
SWRM
SWRM
WHAM
WHAM
THAK
THAK
WHAM
SPLUK
WRIGGLE
WRIGGLE
WRIGGLE

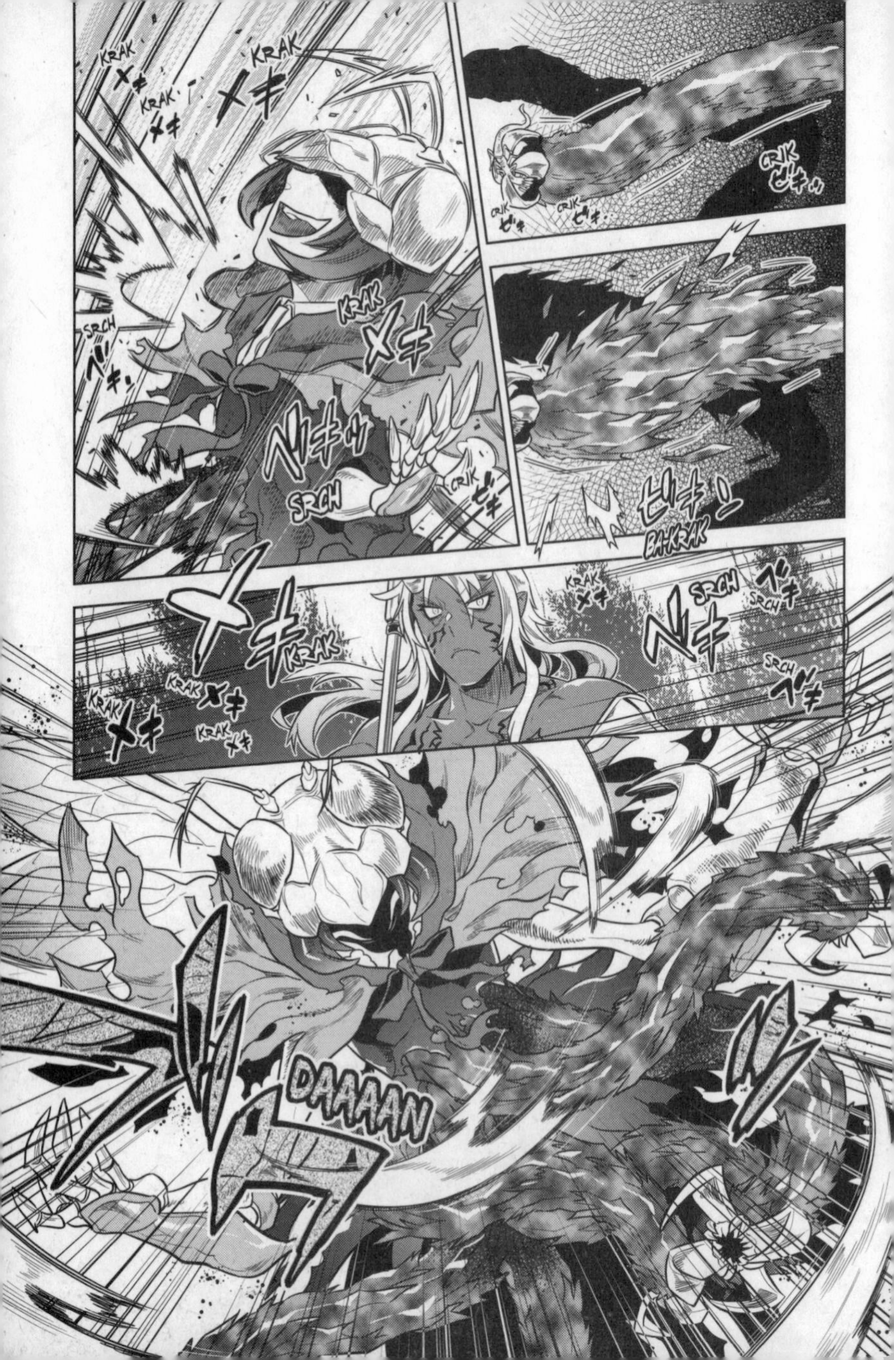
CRIK
CRIK
CRIK
BA-KRAK
KRAK
KRAK
KRAK
KRAK
SRCH
SRCH
CRIK
SRCH
SRCH
SRCH
KRAK
KRAK
KRAK
KRAK
KRAK
KRAK
DAAAAN

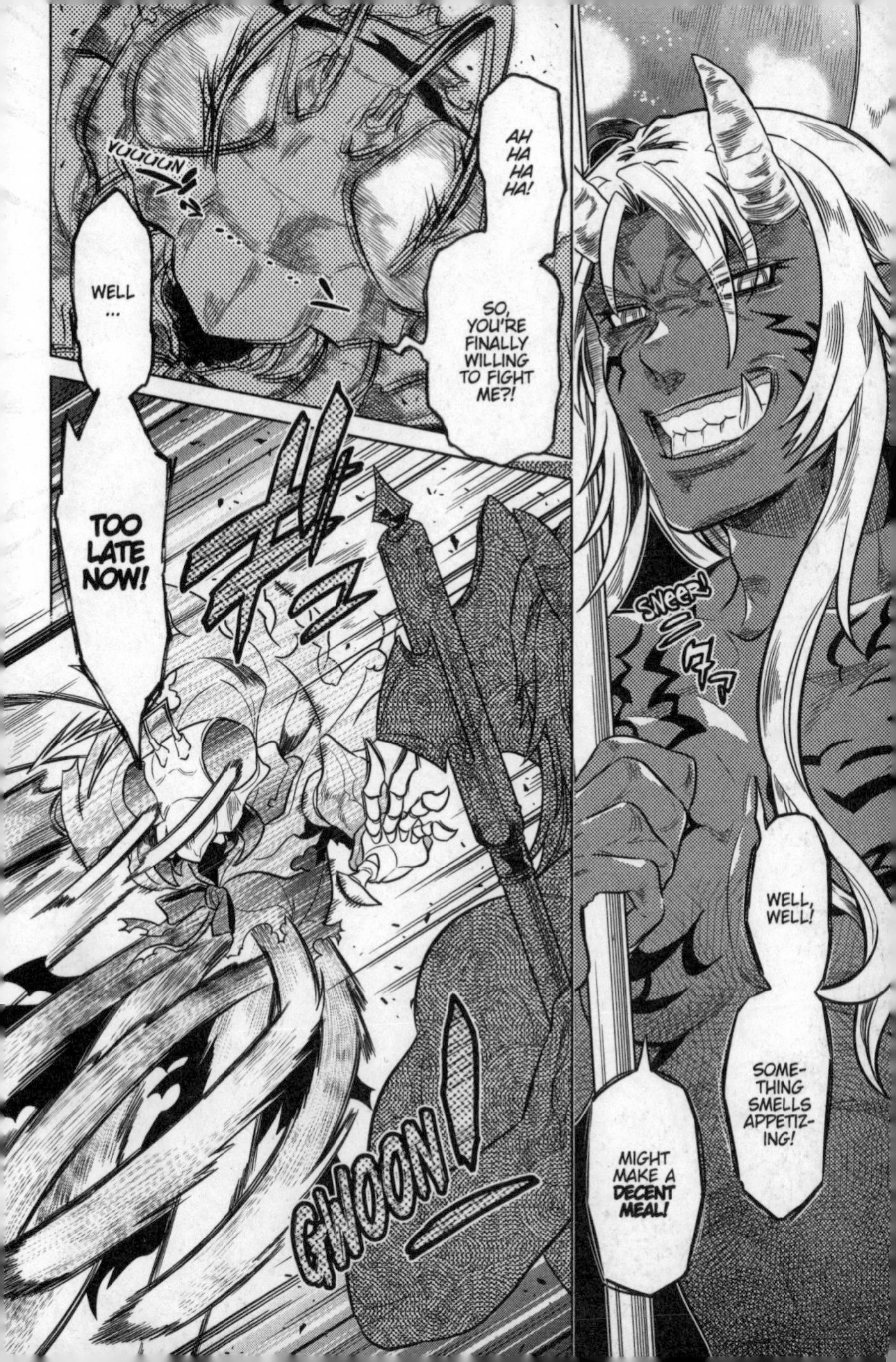
SNEER!
WELL, WELL!
SOME-THING SMELLS APPETIZ-ING!
MIGHT MAKE A DECENT MEAL!
AH HA HA HA!
SO, YOU'RE FINALLY WILLING TO FIGHT ME?!
VUUUUUN
WELL ...
TOO LATE NOW!
GWOON!

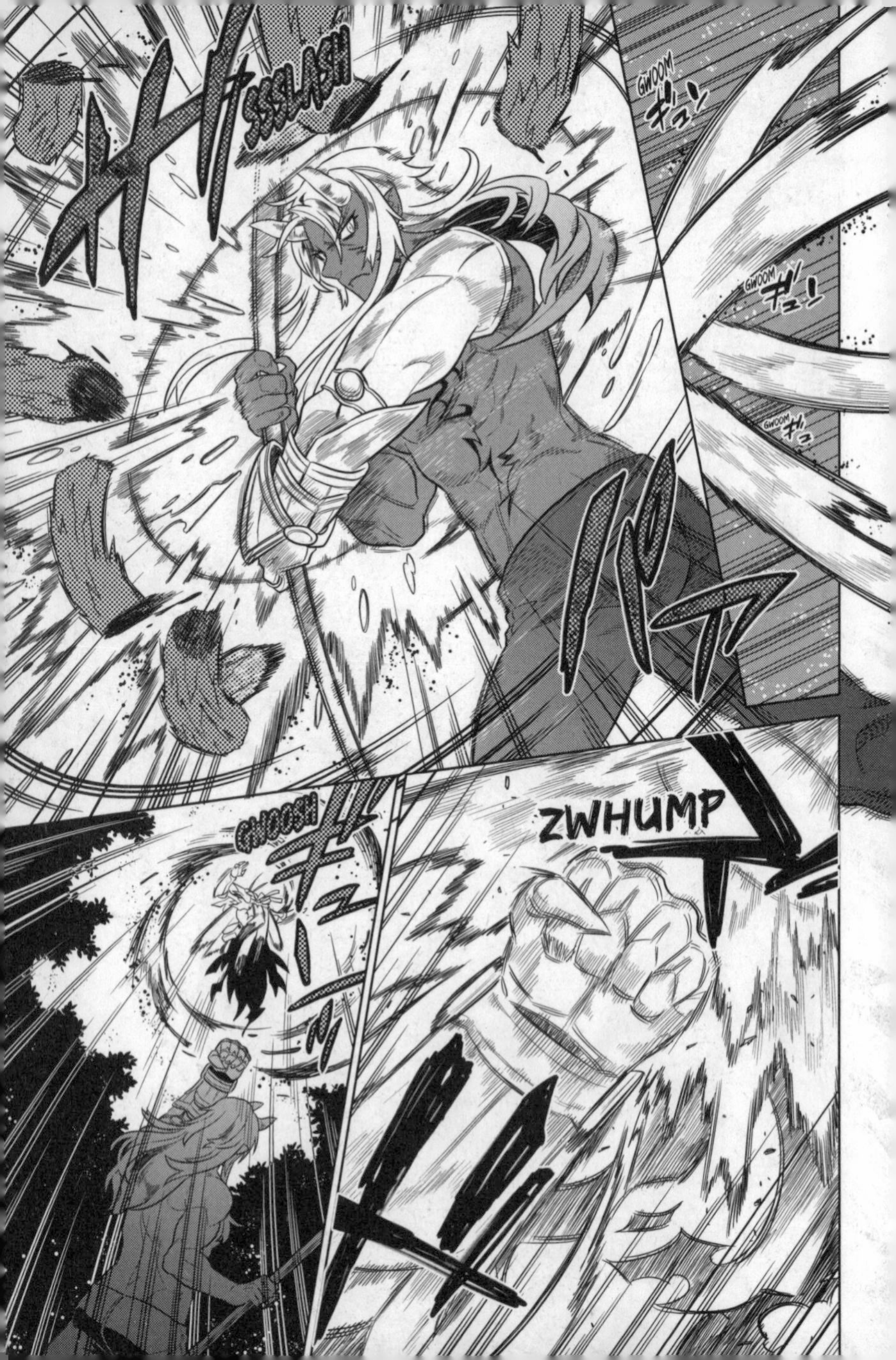
GWOOM
GWOOM
GWOOM
SSSLASH
ZWHUMP
GWOOSH

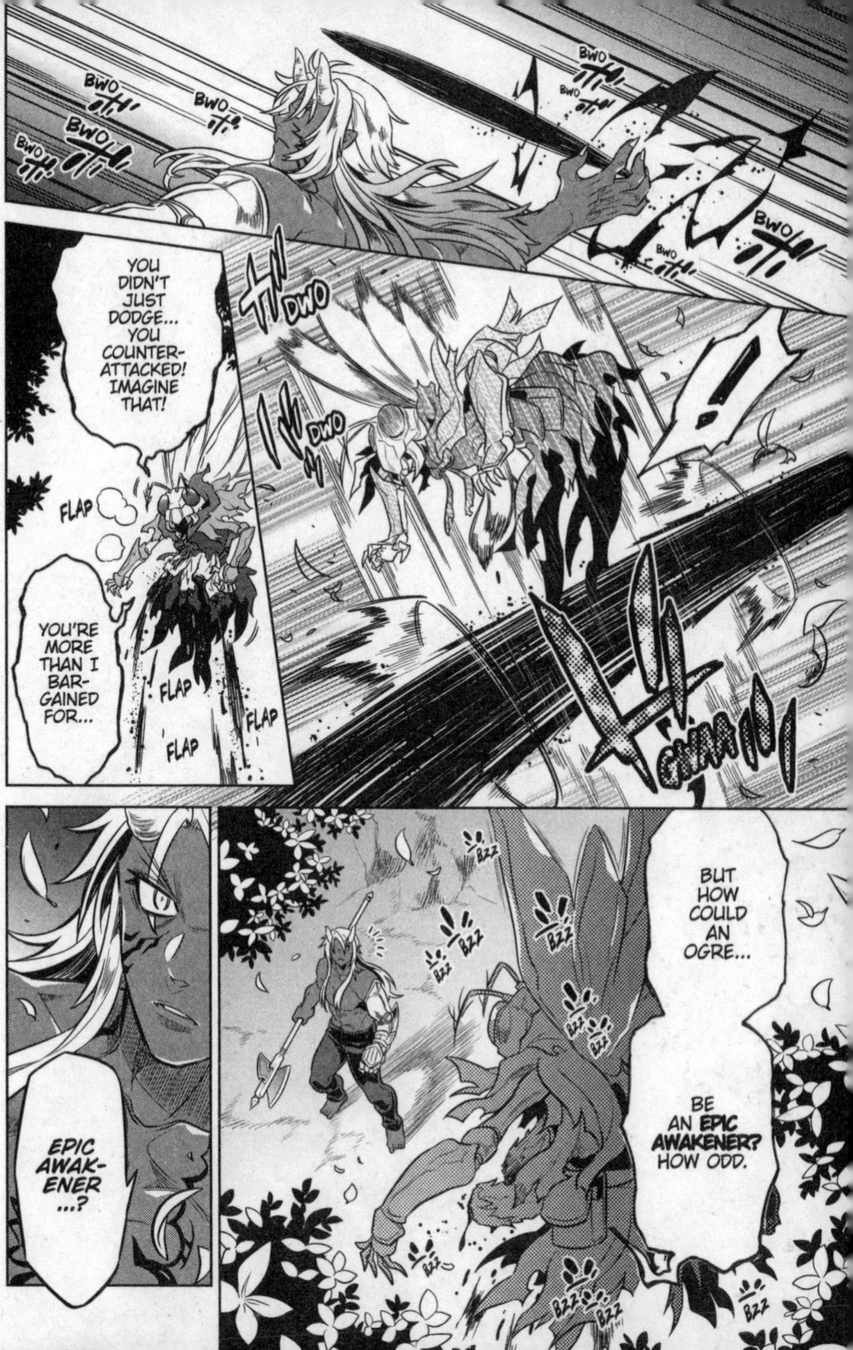
BWO
BWO
BWO
BWO
BWO
BWO
BWO
BWO
DWO
DWO
GWAA
YOU DIDN'T JUST DODGE... YOU COUNTER-ATTACKED! IMAGINE THAT!
FLAP
YOU'RE MORE THAN I BAR-GAINED FOR...
FLAP
FLAP
FLAP
BZZ
BZZ
BZZ
BUT HOW COULD AN OGRE...
BE AN **EPIC AWAKENER?** HOW ODD.
BZZ
BZZ
BZZ
BZZ
BZZ
BZZ
EPIC AWAK-ENER ...?

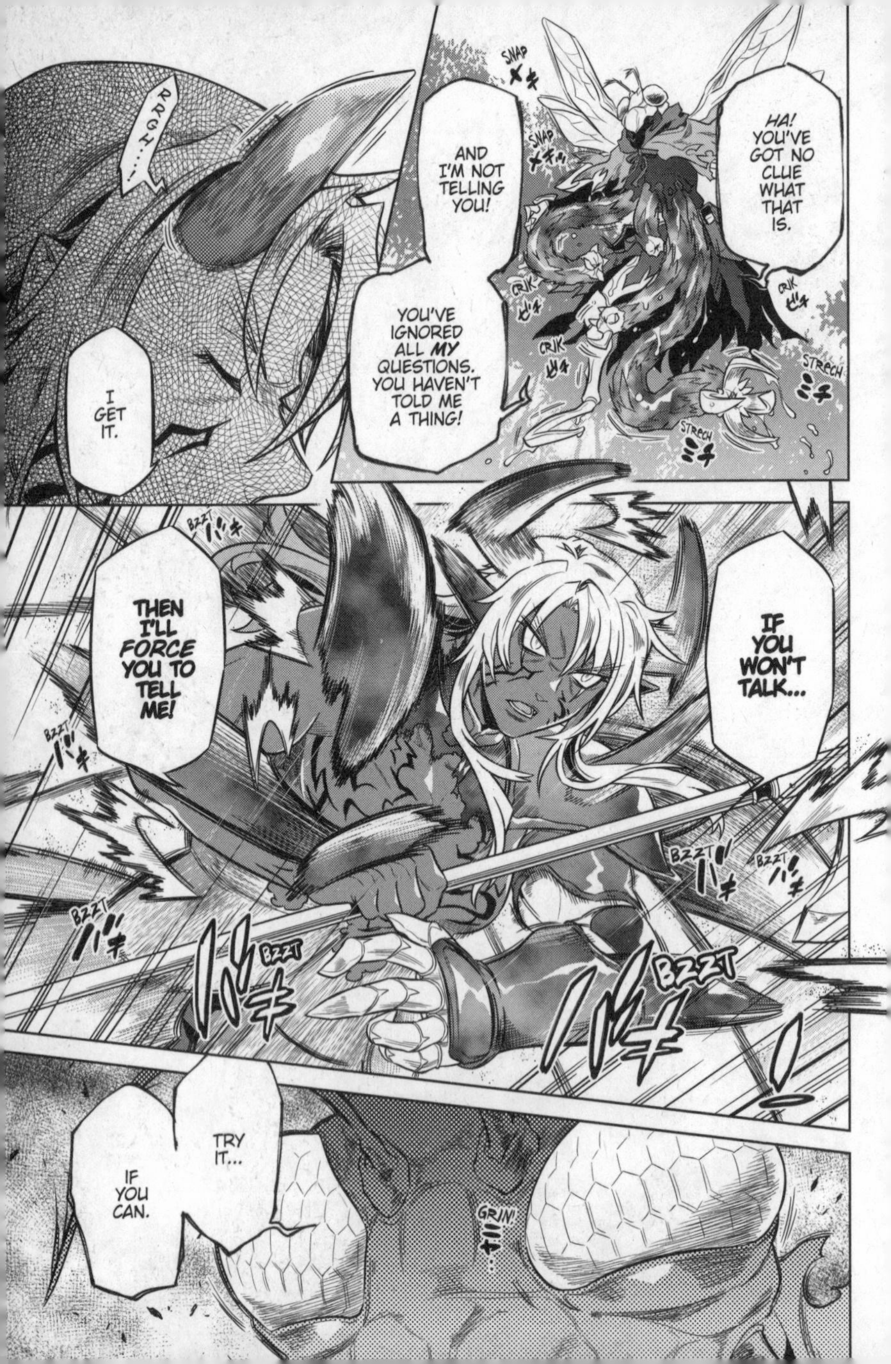
HA! YOU'VE GOT NO CLUE WHAT THAT IS.
SNAP
SNAP
AND I'M NOT TELLING YOU!
CRIK
CRIK
CRIK
STRECH
STRECH
YOU'VE IGNORED ALL *MY* QUESTIONS. YOU HAVEN'T TOLD ME A THING!
RRGH...!
I GET IT.
IF YOU WON'T TALK...
BZZT
BZZT
THEN I'LL *FORCE* YOU TO TELL ME!
BZZT
BZZT
BZZT
BZZT
BZZT
TRY IT...
IF YOU CAN.
GRIN!

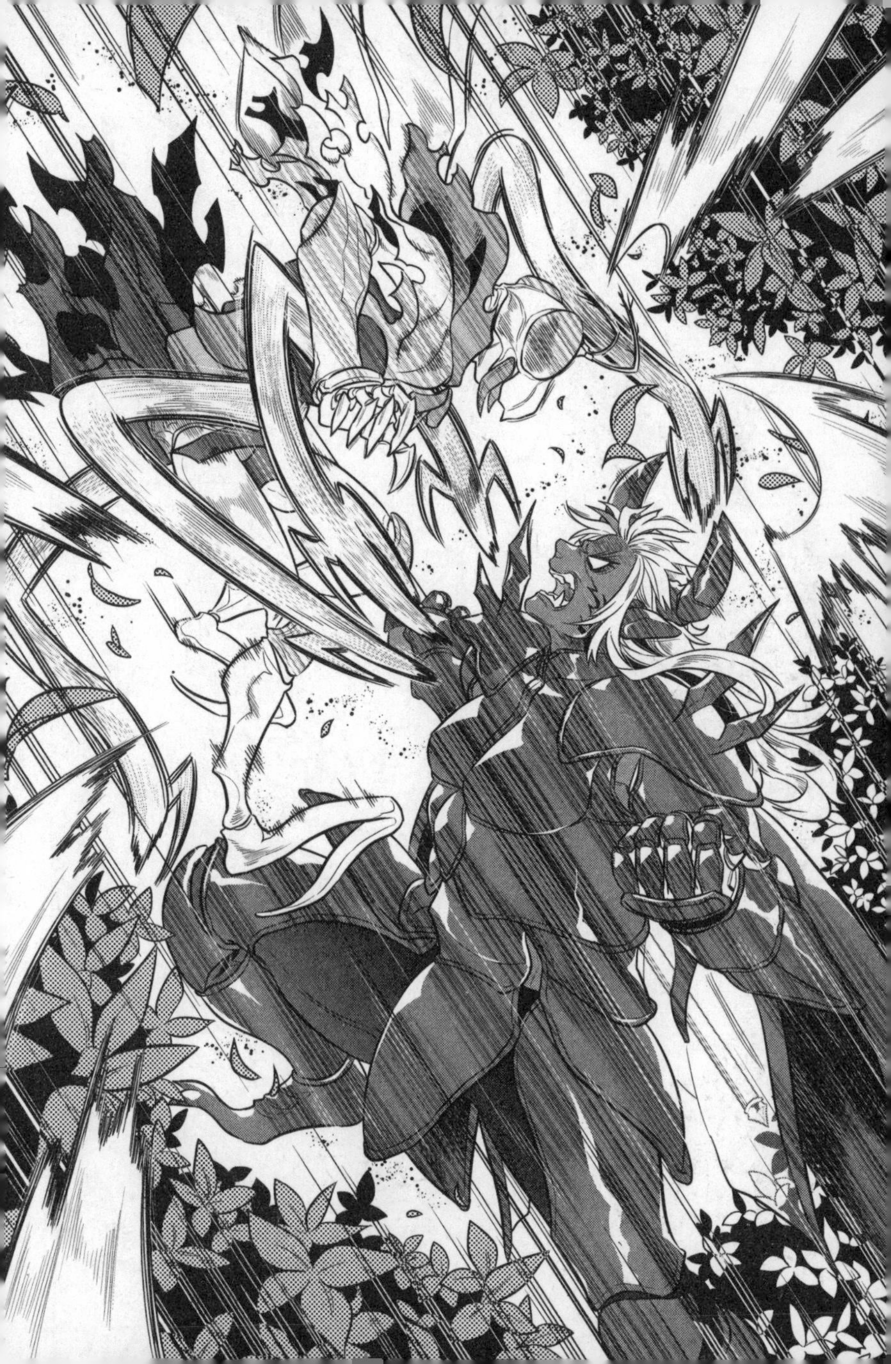

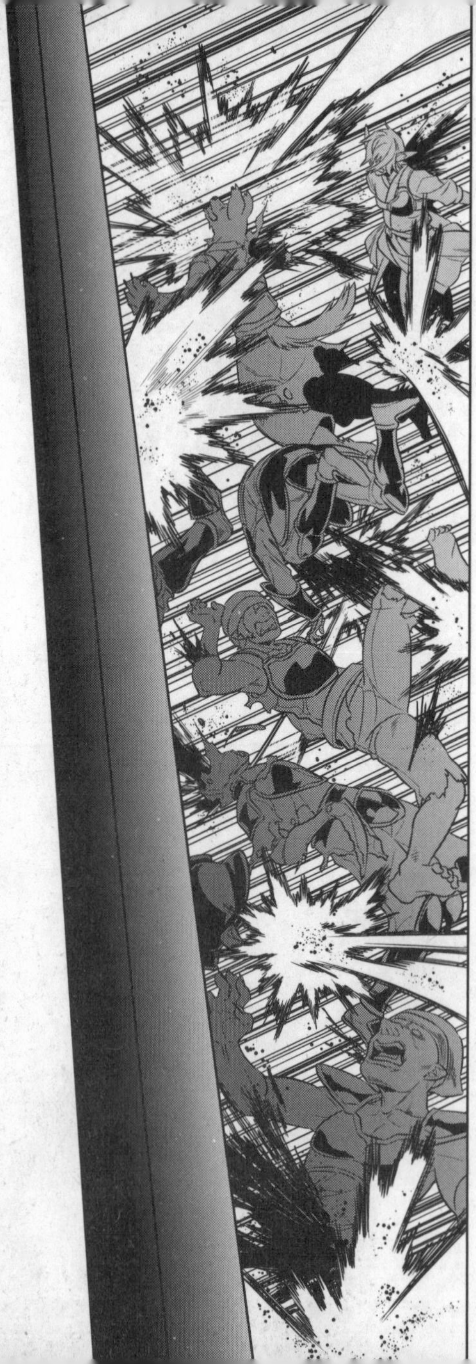

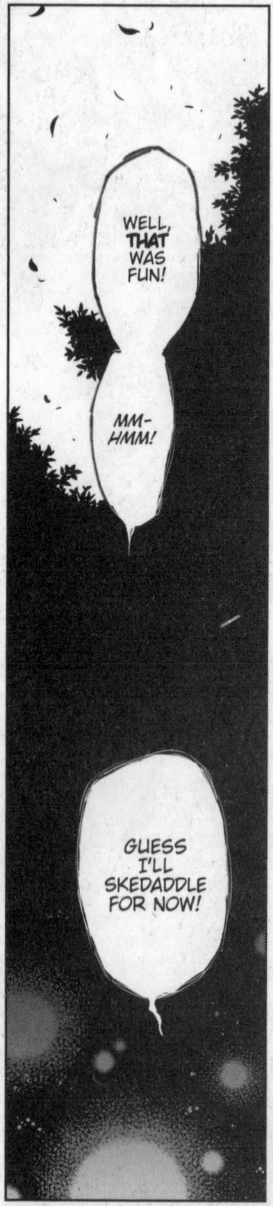
WELL, THAT WAS FUN!
MM-HMM!
GUESS I'LL SKEDADDLE FOR NOW!

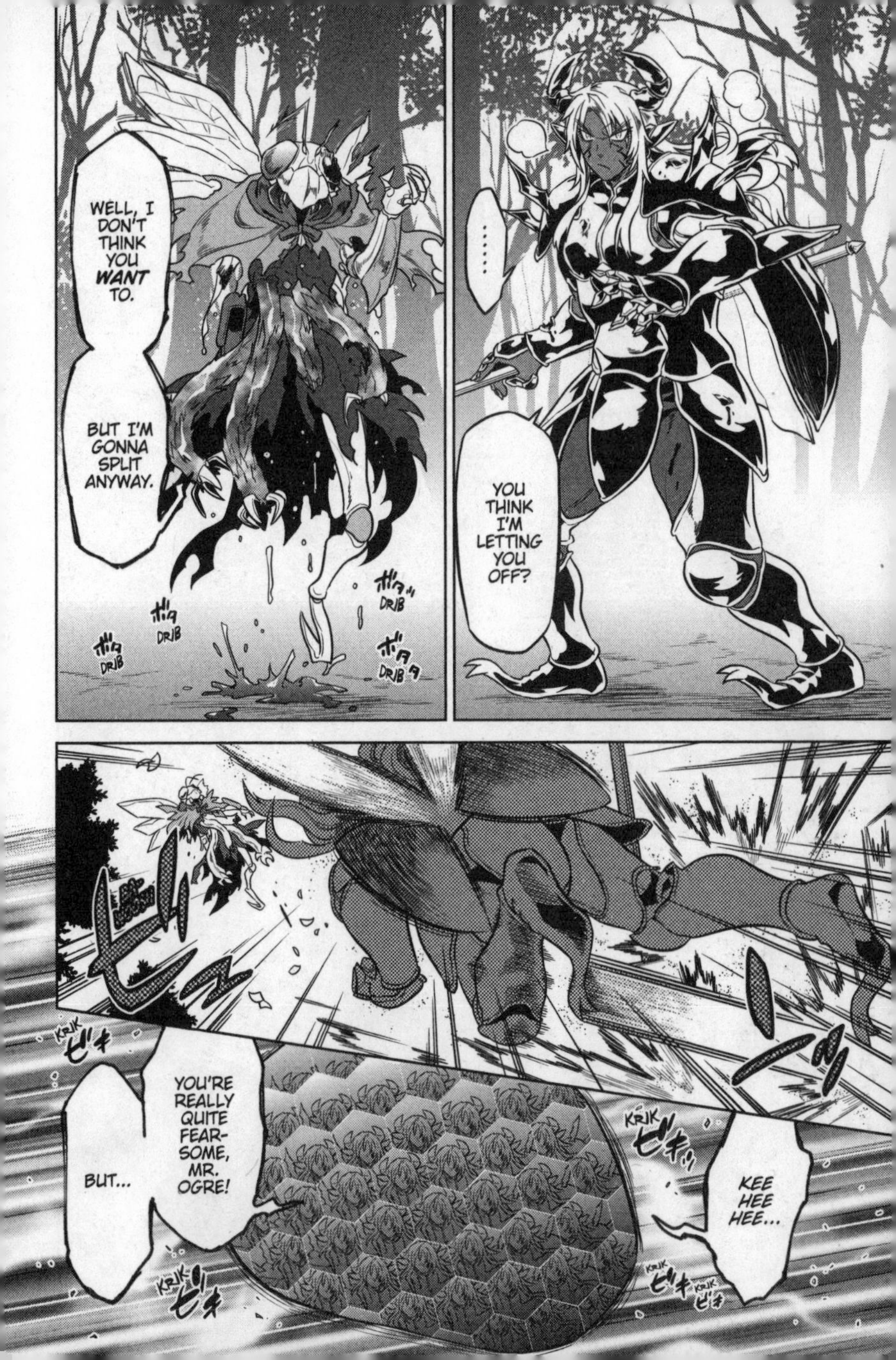
......
YOU THINK I'M LETTING YOU OFF?
WELL, I DON'T THINK YOU WANT TO.
BUT I'M GONNA SPLIT ANYWAY.
DRIB
DRIB
DRIB
DRIB
KRIK
KEE HEE HEE...
YOU'RE REALLY QUITE FEAR-SOME, MR. OGRE!
BUT...
KRIK
KRIK
KRIK
KRIK

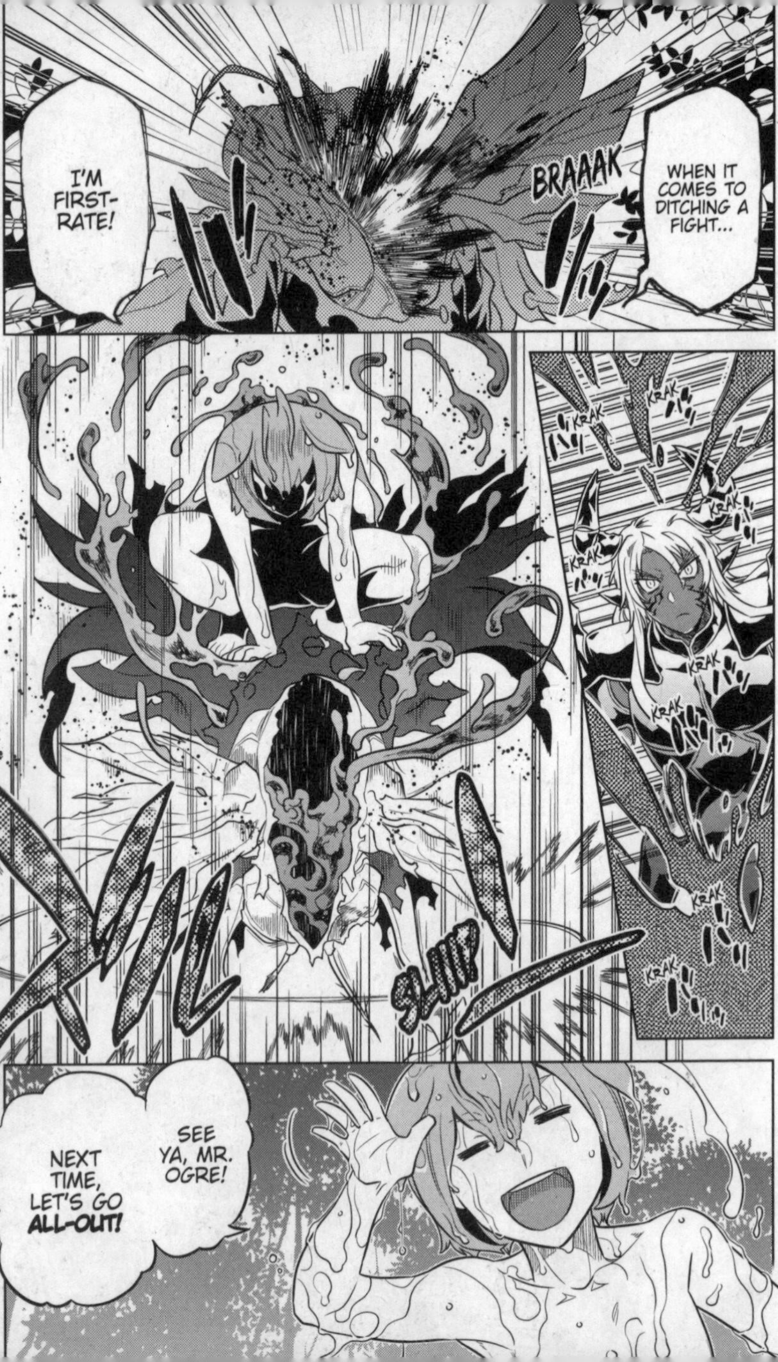
WHEN IT COMES TO DITCHING A FIGHT...
BRAAAK
I'M FIRST-RATE!
KRAK
KRAK
KRAK
KRAK
KRAK
KRAK
KRAK
KRAK
SLIIIP
SEE YA, MR. OGRE!
NEXT TIME, LET'S GO **ALL-OUT!**

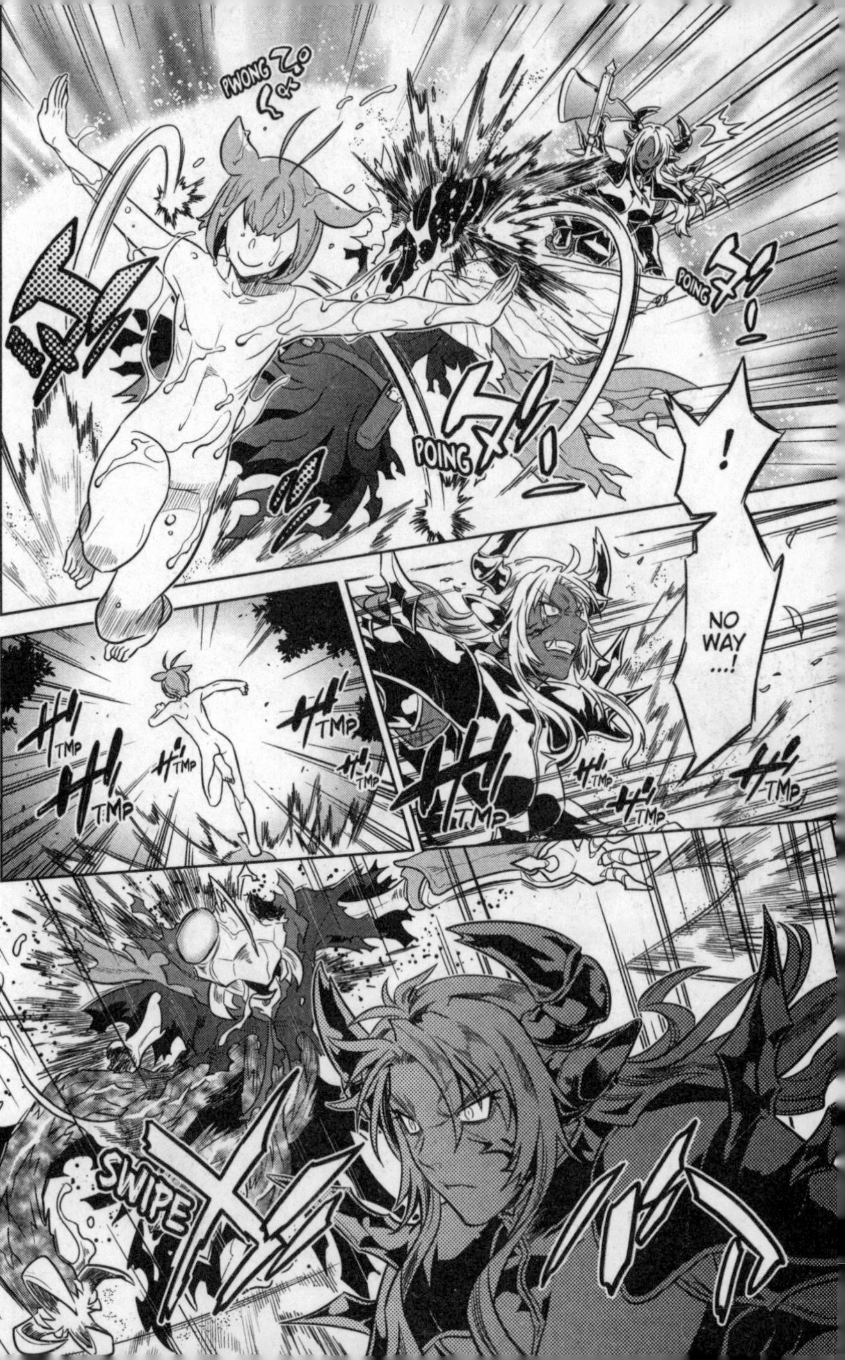
POING
!
POING
PWONG
NO WAY ...!
TMP
TMP
TMP
TMP
TMP
TMP
TMP
TMP
TMP
SWIPE

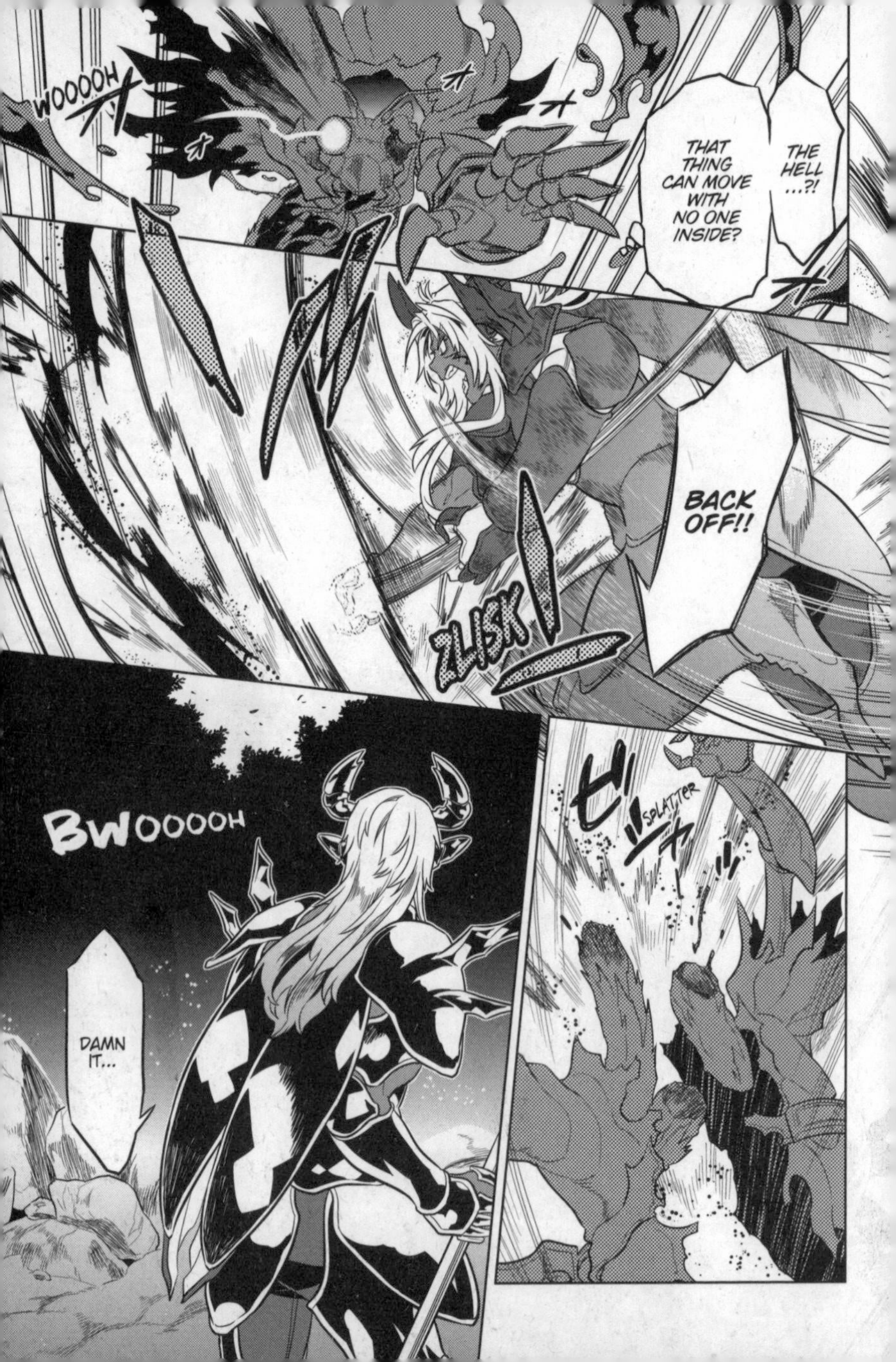
THE HELL ...?!
THAT THING CAN MOVE WITH NO ONE INSIDE?
WOOOOH
BACK OFF!!
ZLISK
SPLATTER
BWOOOOH
DAMN IT...

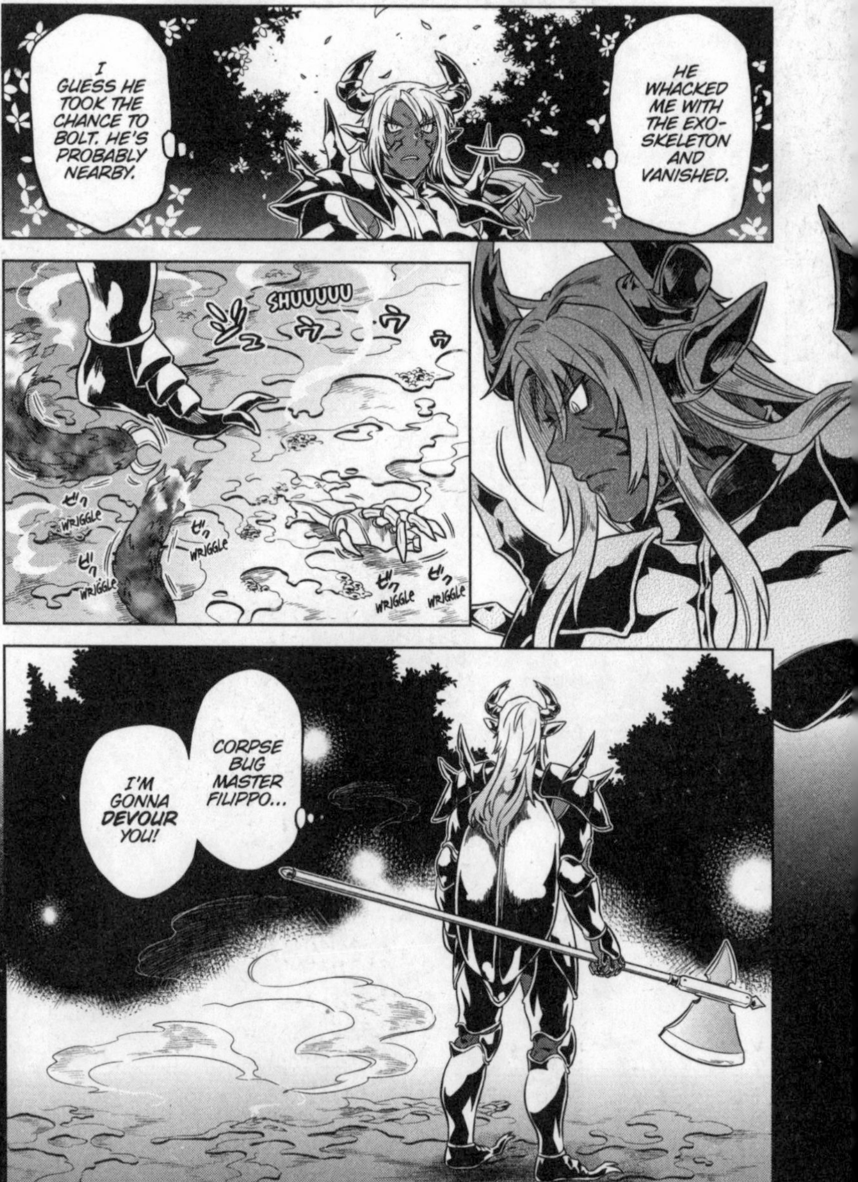
HE WHACKED ME WITH THE EXO-SKELETON AND VANISHED.
I GUESS HE TOOK THE CHANCE TO BOLT. HE'S PROBABLY NEARBY.
SHUUUUU
WRIGGLE
WRIGGLE
WRIGGLE
WRIGGLE
WRIGGLE
CORPSE BUG MASTER FILIPPO...
I'M GONNA DEVOUR YOU!

▶ CONTINUE

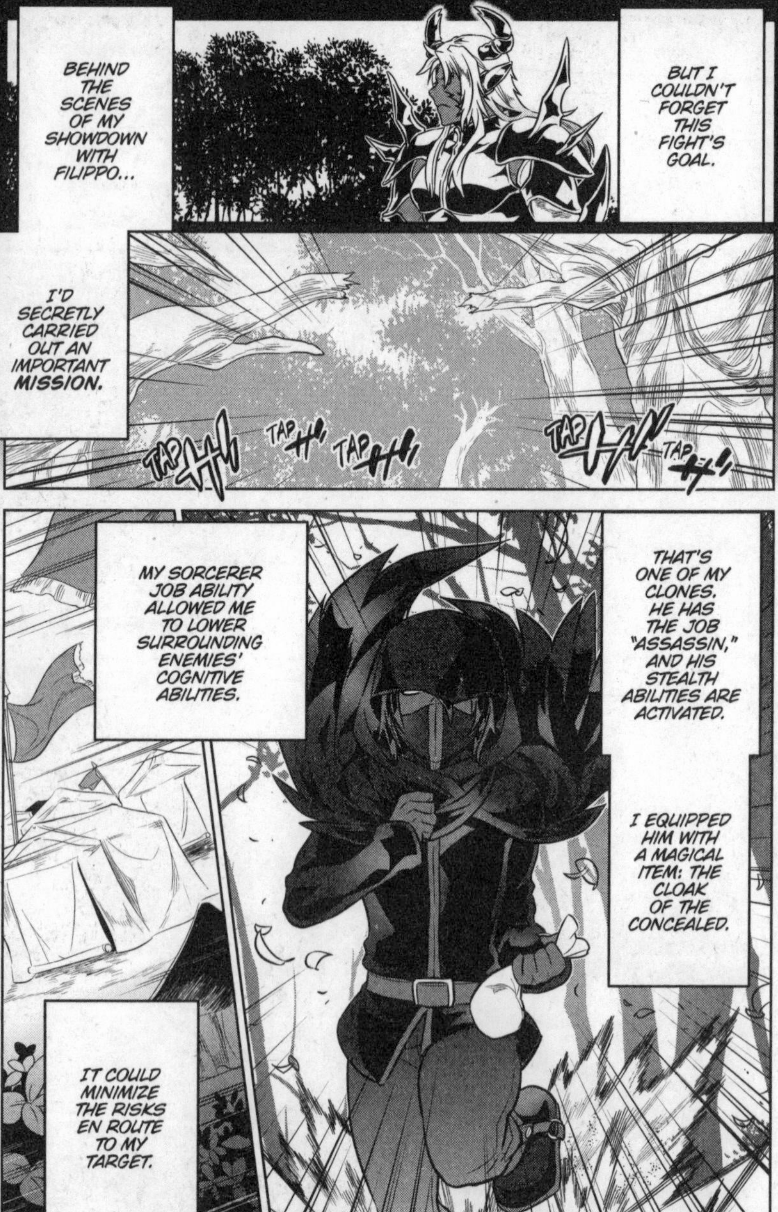
BUT I COULDN'T FORGET THIS FIGHT'S GOAL.
BEHIND THE SCENES OF MY SHOWDOWN WITH FILIPPO...
TAP TAP TAP TAP TAP
I'D SECRETLY CARRIED OUT AN IMPORTANT **MISSION.**
THAT'S ONE OF MY CLONES. HE HAS THE JOB "ASSASSIN," AND HIS STEALTH ABILITIES ARE ACTIVATED.
MY SORCERER JOB ABILITY ALLOWED ME TO LOWER SURROUNDING ENEMIES' COGNITIVE ABILITIES.
I EQUIPPED HIM WITH A MAGICAL ITEM: THE CLOAK OF THE CONCEALED.
IT COULD MINIMIZE THE RISKS EN ROUTE TO MY TARGET.

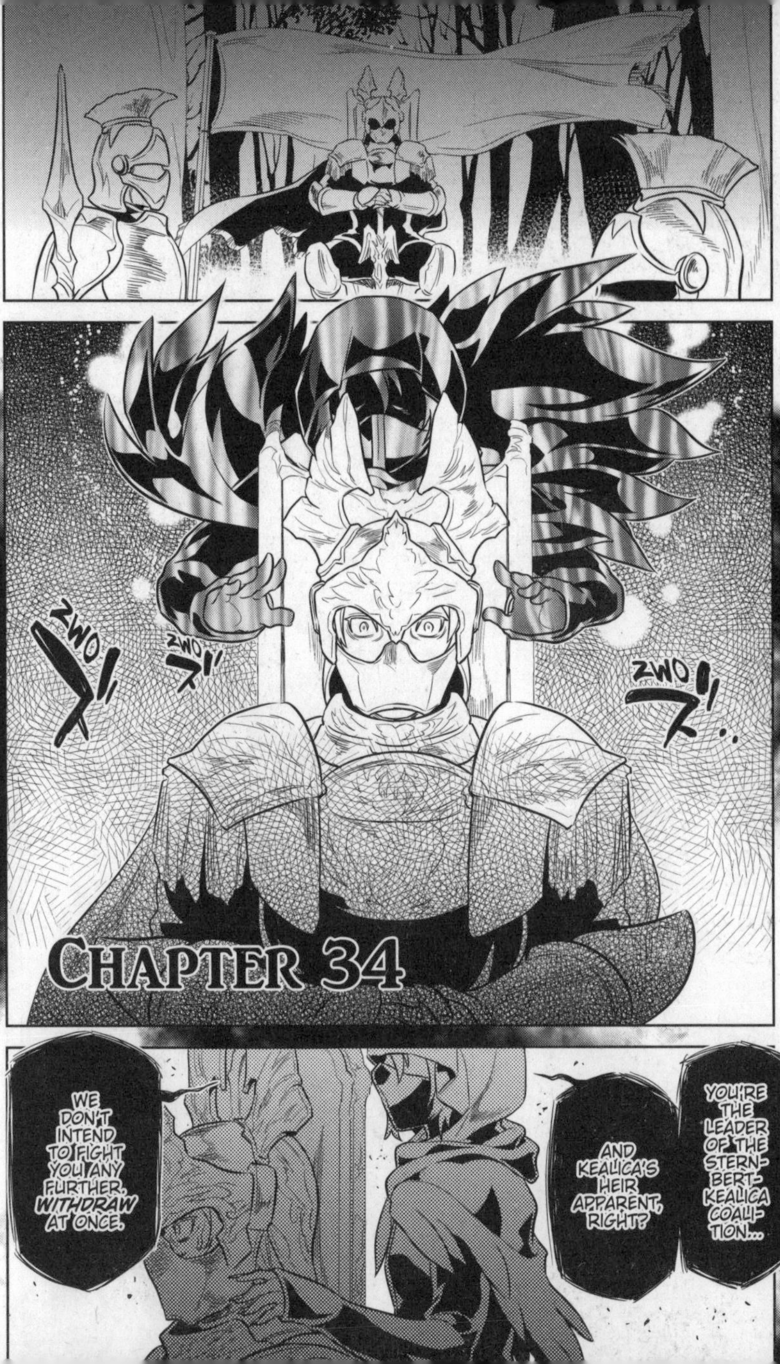

ZWO..
ZWO
ZWO
CHAPTER 34
YOU'RE THE LEADER OF THE STERN-BERT-KEALICA COALITION...
AND KEALICA'S HEIR APPARENT, RIGHT?
WE DON'T INTEND TO FIGHT YOU ANY FURTHER. *WITHDRAW* AT ONCE.

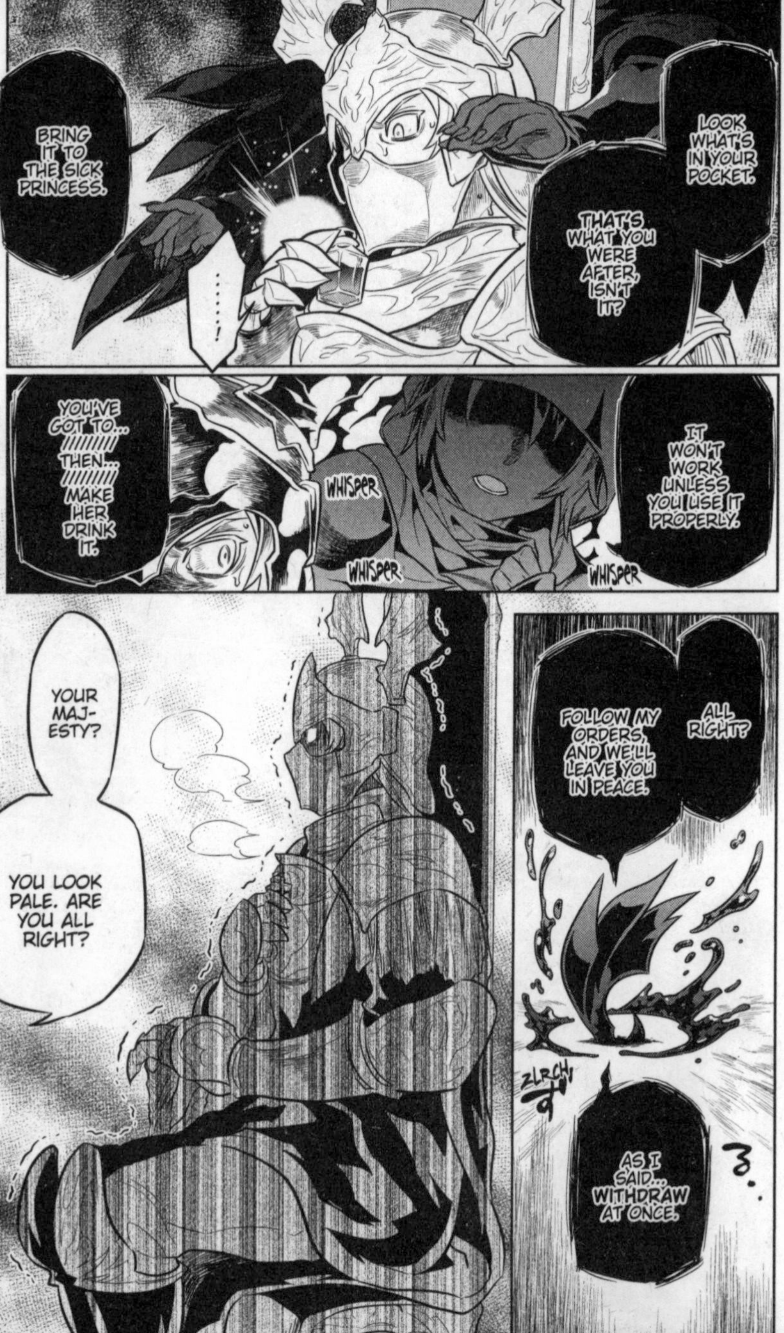
LOOK WHAT'S IN YOUR POCKET.
THAT'S WHAT YOU WERE AFTER, ISN'T IT?
BRING IT TO THE SICK PRINCESS.
......!
IT WON'T WORK UNLESS YOU USE IT PROPERLY.
WHISPER
WHISPER
YOU'VE GOT TO... ////// THEN... ////// MAKE HER DRINK IT.
WHISPER
ALL RIGHT?
FOLLOW MY ORDERS, AND WE'LL LEAVE YOU IN PEACE.
ZLRCH!
AS I SAID... WITHDRAW AT ONCE.
YOUR MAJ-ESTY?
YOU LOOK PALE. ARE YOU ALL RIGHT?

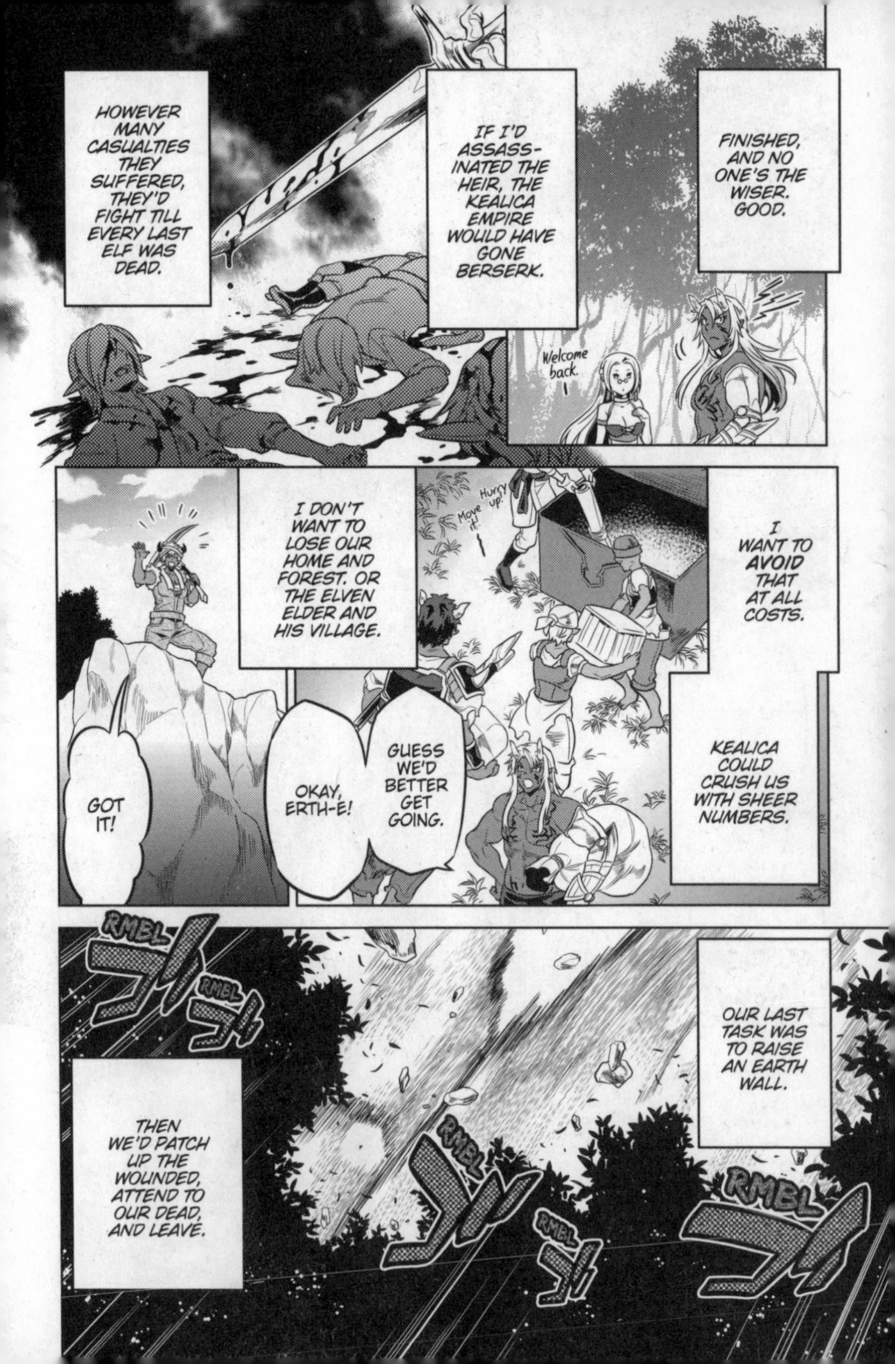
FINISHED, AND NO ONE'S THE WISER. GOOD.
Welcome back.
IF I'D ASSASS-INATED THE HEIR, THE KEALICA EMPIRE WOULD HAVE GONE BERSERK.
HOWEVER MANY CASUALTIES THEY SUFFERED, THEY'D FIGHT TILL EVERY LAST ELF WAS DEAD.
I WANT TO AVOID THAT AT ALL COSTS.
KEALICA COULD CRUSH US WITH SHEER NUMBERS.
I DON'T WANT TO LOSE OUR HOME AND FOREST. OR THE ELVEN ELDER AND HIS VILLAGE.
Hurry up!
Move it!
GUESS WE'D BETTER GET GOING.
OKAY, ERTH-E!
GOT IT!
OUR LAST TASK WAS TO RAISE AN EARTH WALL.
RMBL
RMBL
THEN WE'D PATCH UP THE WOUNDED, ATTEND TO OUR DEAD, AND LEAVE.
RMBL
RMBL
RMBL

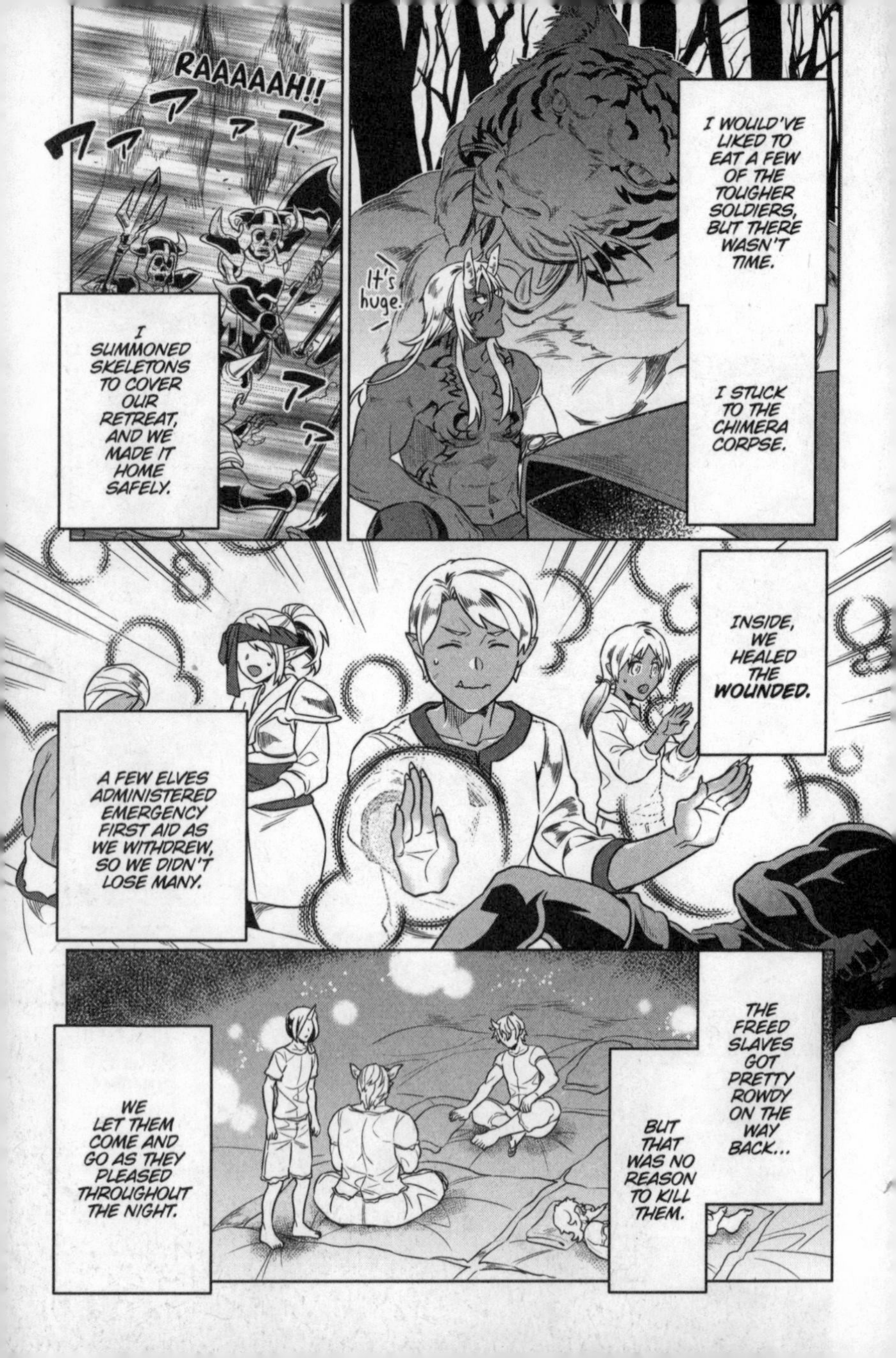
I WOULD'VE LIKED TO EAT A FEW OF THE TOUGHER SOLDIERS, BUT THERE WASN'T TIME.
It's huge.
I STUCK TO THE CHIMERA CORPSE.
RAAAAAH!!
I SUMMONED SKELETONS TO COVER OUR RETREAT, AND WE MADE IT HOME SAFELY.
INSIDE, WE HEALED THE WOUNDED.
A FEW ELVES ADMINISTERED EMERGENCY FIRST AID AS WE WITHDREW, SO WE DIDN'T LOSE MANY.
THE FREED SLAVES GOT PRETTY ROWDY ON THE WAY BACK...
BUT THAT WAS NO REASON TO KILL THEM.
WE LET THEM COME AND GO AS THEY PLEASED THROUGHOUT THE NIGHT.

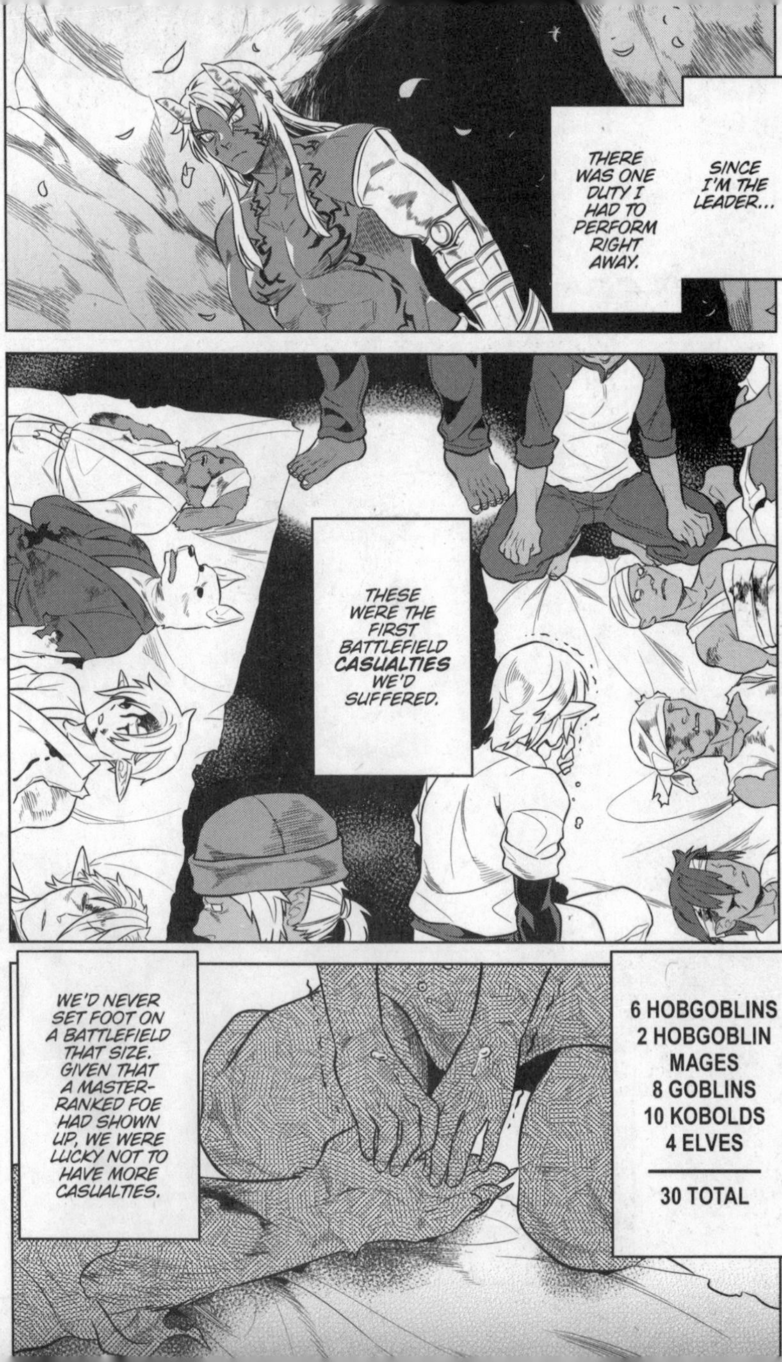
SINCE I'M THE LEADER...
THERE WAS ONE DUTY I HAD TO PERFORM RIGHT AWAY.
THESE WERE THE FIRST BATTLEFIELD CASUALTIES WE'D SUFFERED.
6 HOBGOBLINS
2 HOBGOBLIN MAGES
8 GOBLINS
10 KOBOLDS
4 ELVES
30 TOTAL
WE'D NEVER SET FOOT ON A BATTLEFIELD THAT SIZE. GIVEN THAT A MASTER-RANKED FOE HAD SHOWN UP, WE WERE LUCKY NOT TO HAVE MORE CASUALTIES.

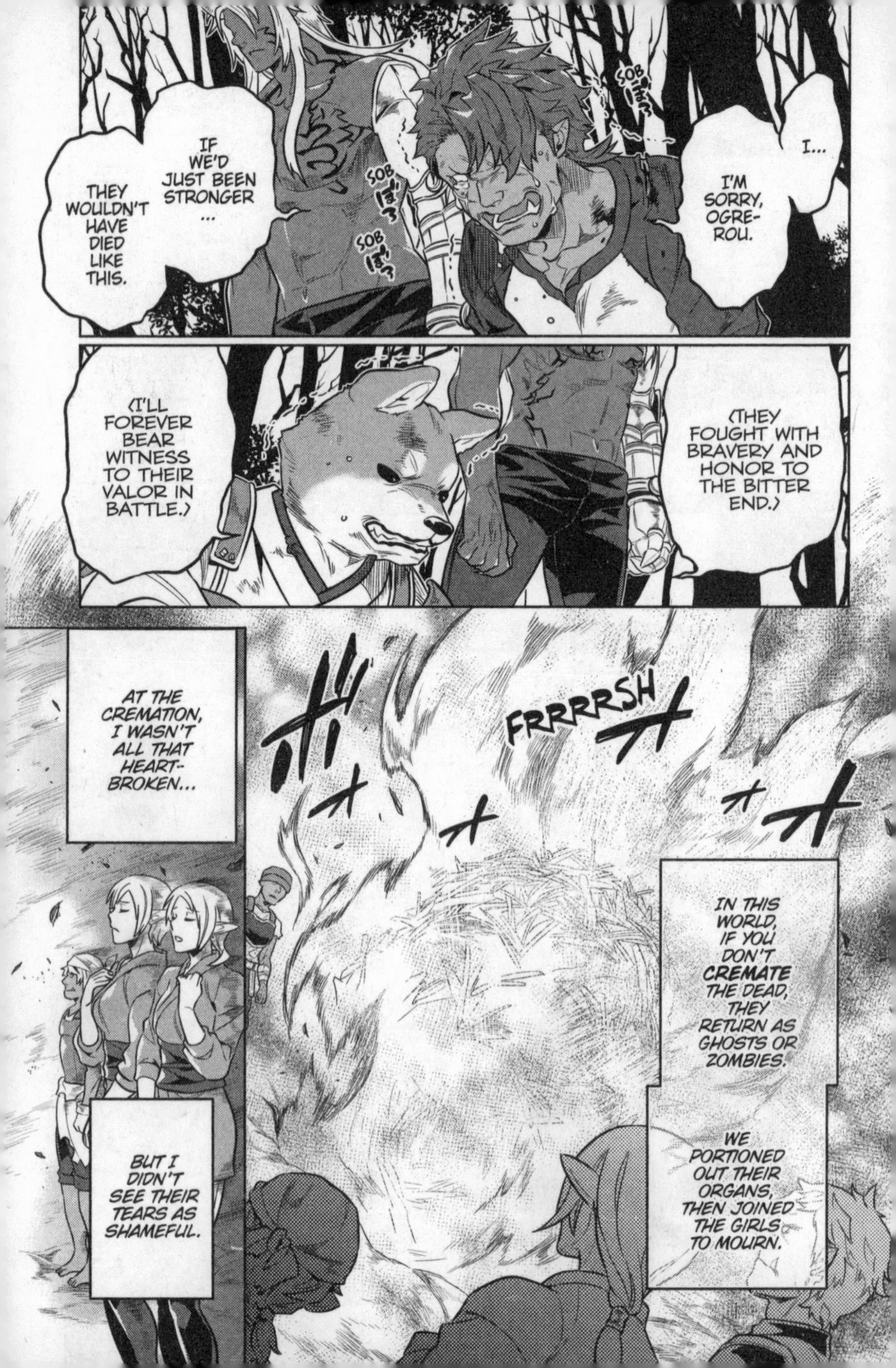
I...
I'M SORRY, OGRE-ROU.
SOB
SOB
SOB
IF WE'D JUST BEEN STRONGER...
THEY WOULDN'T HAVE DIED LIKE THIS.
〈THEY FOUGHT WITH BRAVERY AND HONOR TO THE BITTER END.〉
〈I'LL FOREVER BEAR WITNESS TO THEIR VALOR IN BATTLE.〉
FRRRRSH
IN THIS WORLD, IF YOU DON'T CREMATE THE DEAD, THEY RETURN AS GHOSTS OR ZOMBIES.
WE PORTIONED OUT THEIR ORGANS, THEN JOINED THE GIRLS TO MOURN.
AT THE CREMATION, I WASN'T ALL THAT HEART-BROKEN...
BUT I DIDN'T SEE THEIR TEARS AS SHAMEFUL.

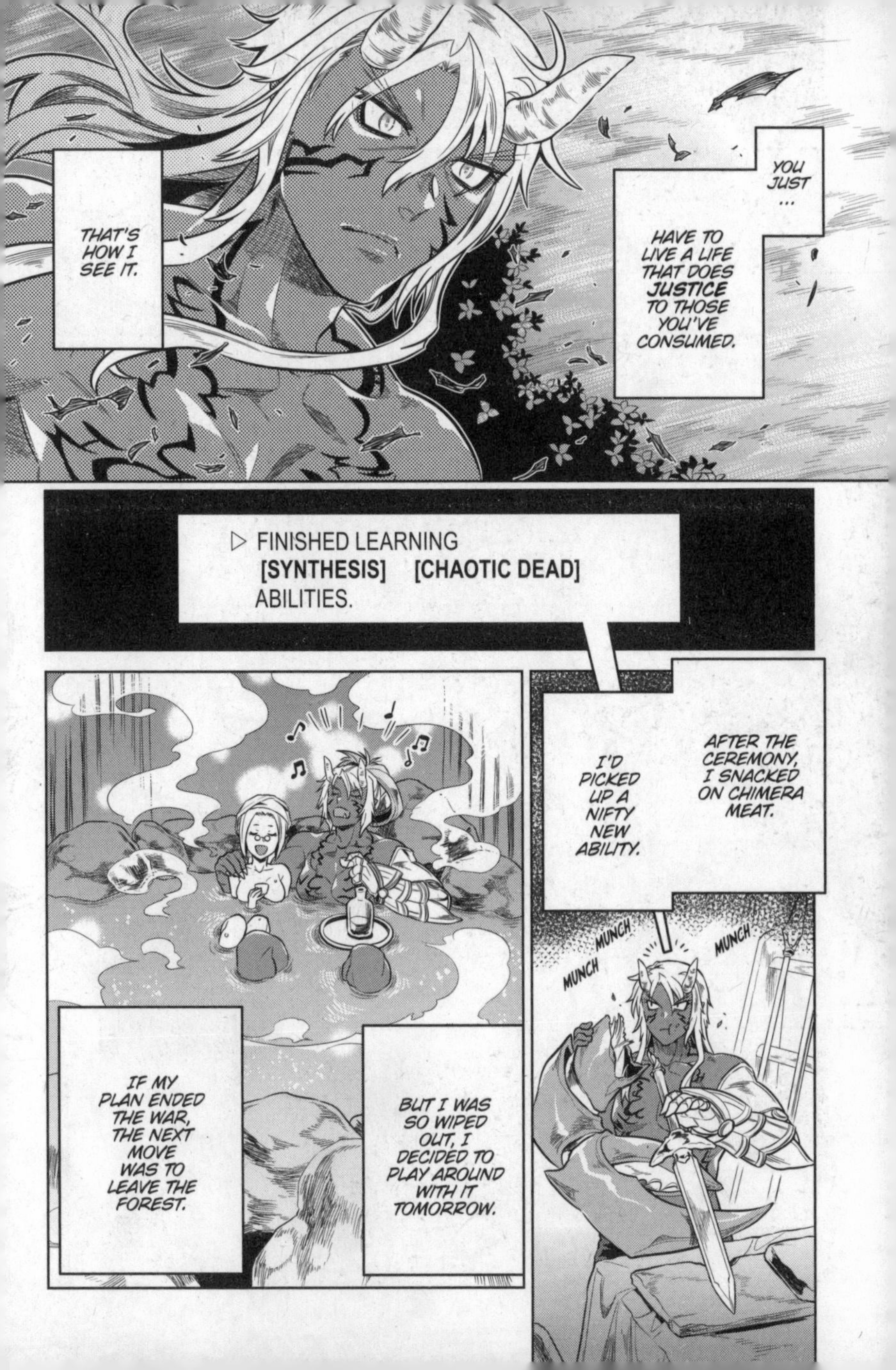
YOU JUST ...
HAVE TO LIVE A LIFE THAT DOES JUSTICE TO THOSE YOU'VE CONSUMED.
THAT'S HOW I SEE IT.
▷ FINISHED LEARNING [SYNTHESIS] [CHAOTIC DEAD] ABILITIES.
AFTER THE CEREMONY, I SNACKED ON CHIMERA MEAT.
I'D PICKED UP A NIFTY NEW ABILITY.
MUNCH
MUNCH
MUNCH
IF MY PLAN ENDED THE WAR, THE NEXT MOVE WAS TO LEAVE THE FOREST.
BUT I WAS SO WIPED OUT, I DECIDED TO PLAY AROUND WITH IT TOMORROW.

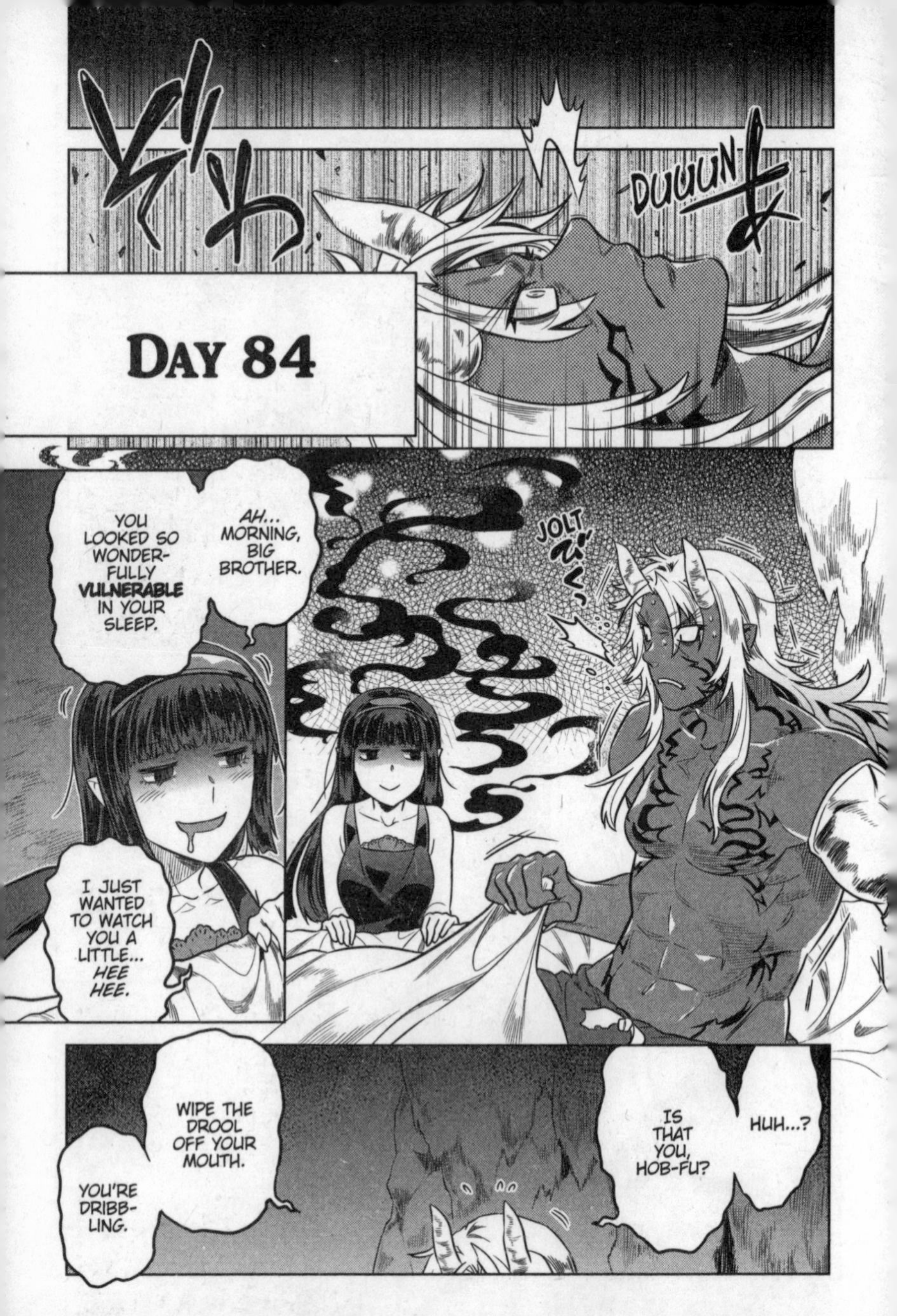
DUUUN
DAY 84
JOLT
AH... MORNING, BIG BROTHER.
YOU LOOKED SO WONDER-FULLY **VULNERABLE** IN YOUR SLEEP.
I JUST WANTED TO WATCH YOU A LITTLE... *HEE HEE.*
HUH...?
IS THAT YOU, HOB-FU?
WIPE THE DROOL OFF YOUR MOUTH.
YOU'RE DRIBB-LING.

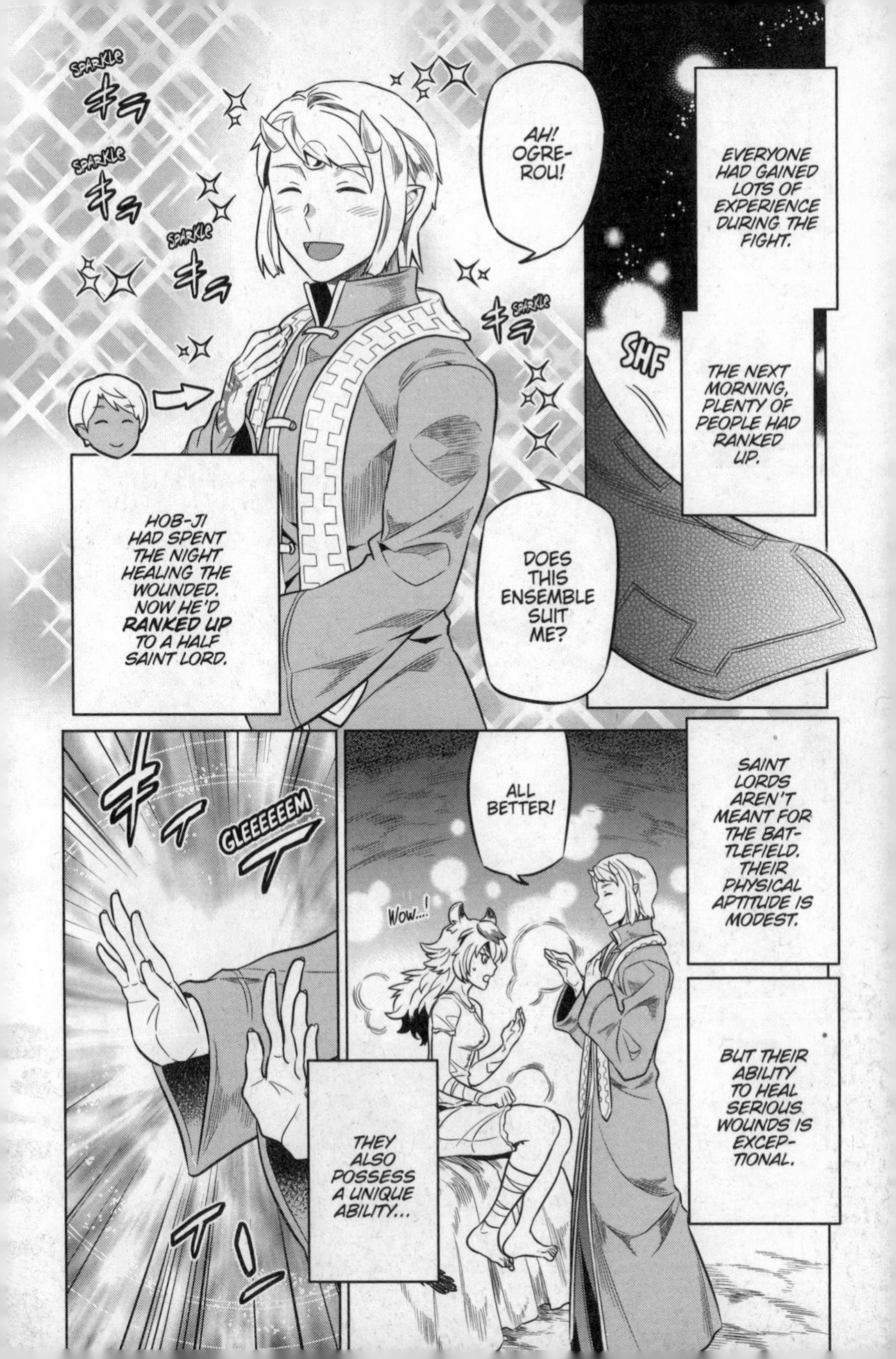

EVERYONE HAD GAINED LOTS OF EXPERIENCE DURING THE FIGHT.
THE NEXT MORNING, PLENTY OF PEOPLE HAD RANKED UP.
SHF
AH! OGRE-ROU!
SPARKLE
キラ
SPARKLE
キラ
SPARKLE
キラ
SPARKLE
キラ
DOES THIS ENSEMBLE SUIT ME?
HOB-JI HAD SPENT THE NIGHT HEALING THE WOUNDED. NOW HE'D **RANKED UP** TO A HALF SAINT LORD.
SAINT LORDS AREN'T MEANT FOR THE BAT-TLEFIELD. THEIR PHYSICAL APTITUDE IS MODEST.
BUT THEIR ABILITY TO HEAL SERIOUS WOUNDS IS EXCEP-TIONAL.
ALL BETTER!
WOW...!
GLEEEEEEM
THEY ALSO POSSESS A UNIQUE ABILITY...

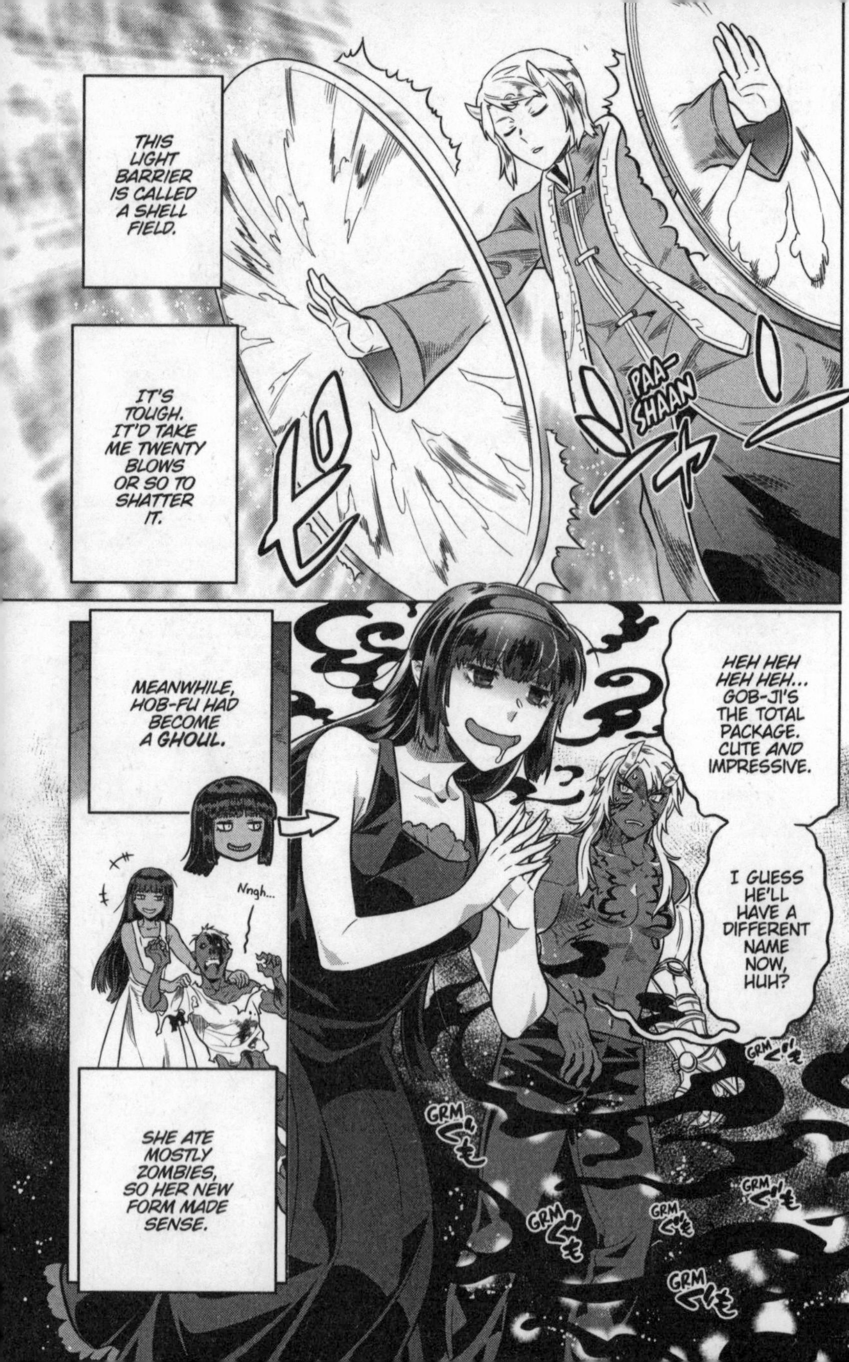
THIS LIGHT BARRIER IS CALLED A SHELL FIELD.
PAA-SHAAN
IT'S TOUGH. IT'D TAKE ME TWENTY BLOWS OR SO TO SHATTER IT.
HEH HEH HEH HEH... GOB-JI'S THE TOTAL PACKAGE. CUTE AND IMPRESSIVE.
MEANWHILE, HOB-FU HAD BECOME A GHOUL.
I GUESS HE'LL HAVE A DIFFERENT NAME NOW, HUH?
Nngh...
GRM
GRM
SHE ATE MOSTLY ZOMBIES, SO HER NEW FORM MADE SENSE.
GRM
GRM
GRM
GRM

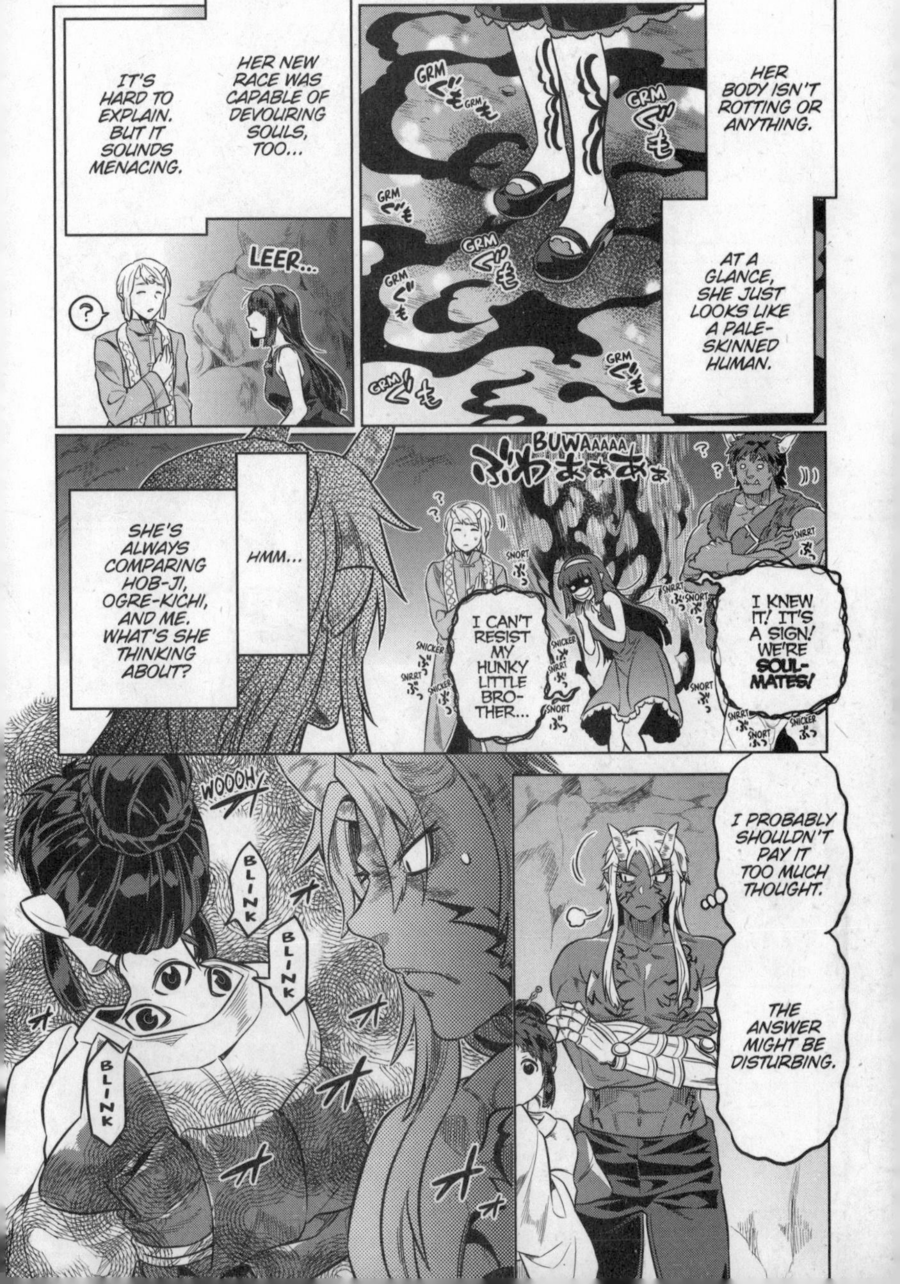
HER BODY ISN'T ROTTING OR ANYTHING.
GRM ぐも
AT A GLANCE, SHE JUST LOOKS LIKE A PALE-SKINNED HUMAN.
HER NEW RACE WAS CAPABLE OF DEVOURING SOULS, TOO...
IT'S HARD TO EXPLAIN. BUT IT SOUNDS MENACING.
LEER...
?
BUWAAAAA ぶわぁぁぁぁ
I KNEW IT! IT'S A SIGN! WE'RE SOUL-MATES!
SNORT ぷっ
SNICKER ぷっ
I CAN'T RESIST MY HUNKY LITTLE BRO-THER...
HMM...
SHE'S ALWAYS COMPARING HOB-JI, OGRE-KICHI, AND ME. WHAT'S SHE THINKING ABOUT?
I PROBABLY SHOULDN'T PAY IT TOO MUCH THOUGHT.
THE ANSWER MIGHT BE DISTURBING.
WOOOH
BLINK
BLINK
BLINK

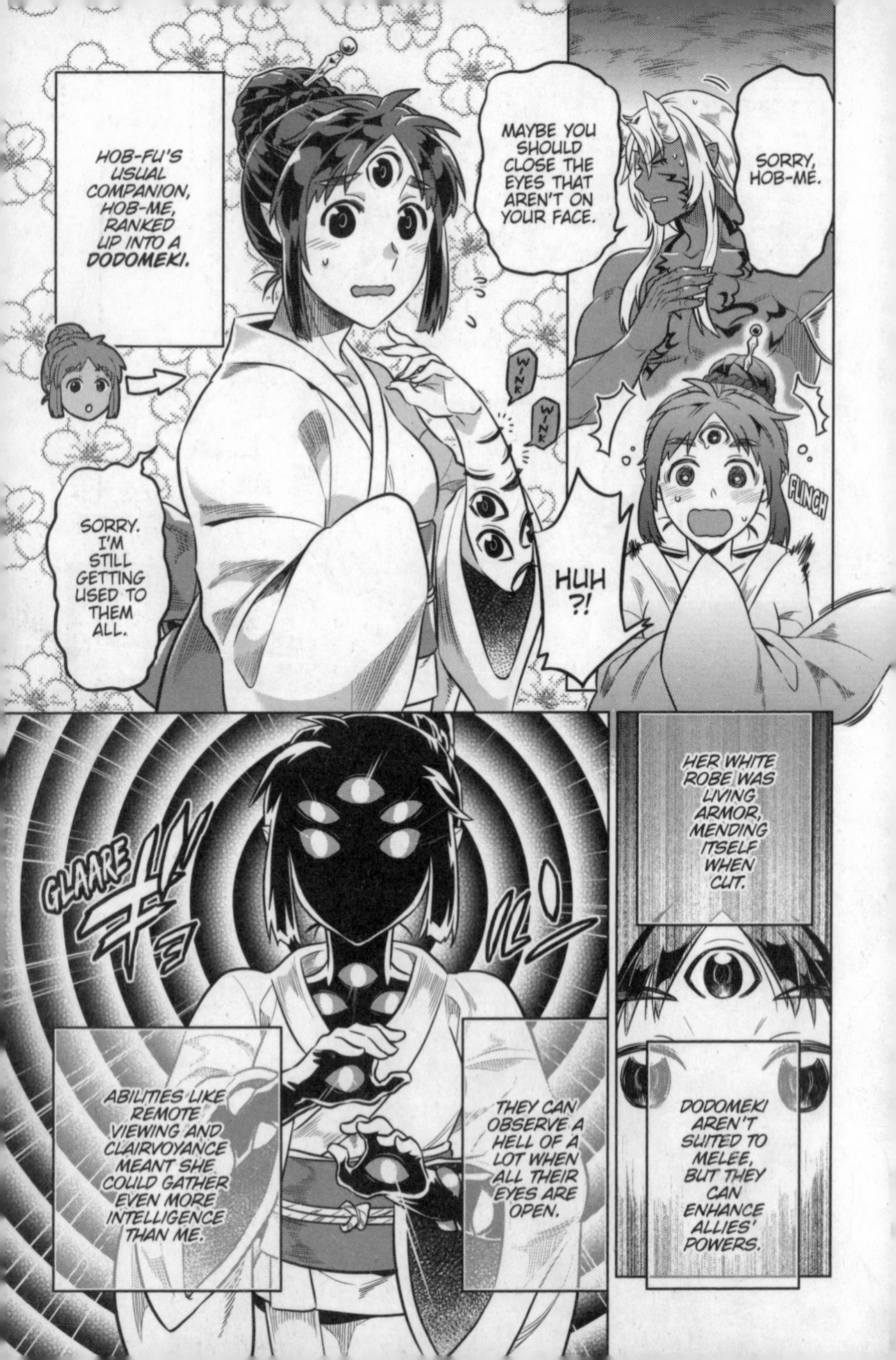
SORRY, HOB-ME.
MAYBE YOU SHOULD CLOSE THE EYES THAT AREN'T ON YOUR FACE.
FLINCH
HUH ?!
HOB-FU'S USUAL COMPANION, HOB-ME, RANKED UP INTO A DODOMEKI.
WINK
WINK
SORRY. I'M STILL GETTING USED TO THEM ALL.
HER WHITE ROBE WAS LIVING ARMOR, MENDING ITSELF WHEN CUT.
DODOMEKI AREN'T SUITED TO MELEE, BUT THEY CAN ENHANCE ALLIES' POWERS.
GLAARE
THEY CAN OBSERVE A HELL OF A LOT WHEN ALL THEIR EYES ARE OPEN.
ABILITIES LIKE REMOTE VIEWING AND CLAIRVOYANCE MEANT SHE COULD GATHER EVEN MORE INTELLIGENCE THAN ME.

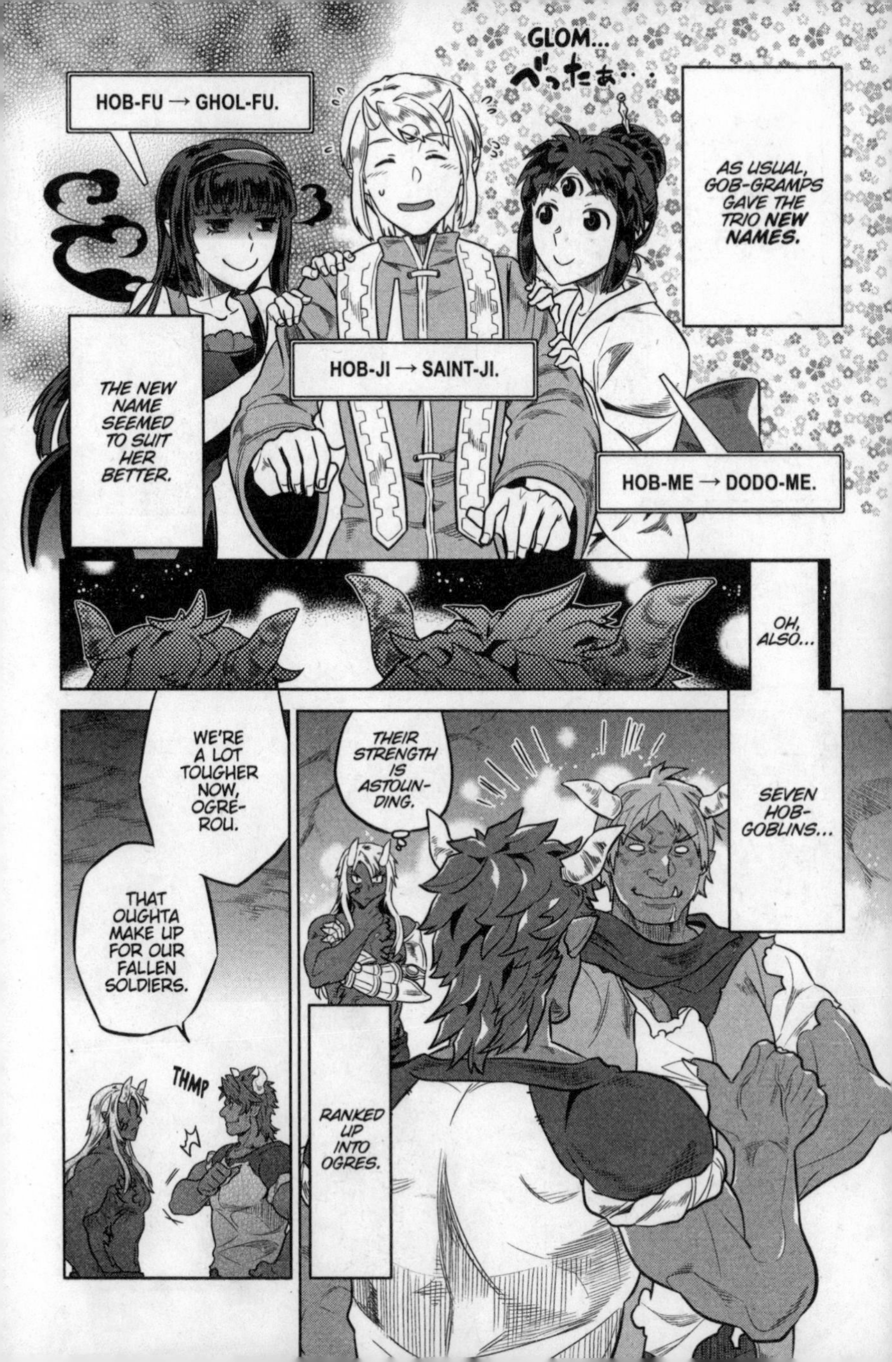
GLOM...
べったぁ…
AS USUAL, GOB-GRAMPS GAVE THE TRIO NEW NAMES.
HOB-FU → GHOL-FU.
HOB-JI → SAINT-JI.
HOB-ME → DODO-ME.
THE NEW NAME SEEMED TO SUIT HER BETTER.
OH, ALSO...
SEVEN HOB-GOBLINS...
RANKED UP INTO OGRES.
THEIR STRENGTH IS ASTOUNDING.
WE'RE A LOT TOUGHER NOW, OGRE-ROU.
THAT OUGHTA MAKE UP FOR OUR FALLEN SOLDIERS.
THMP

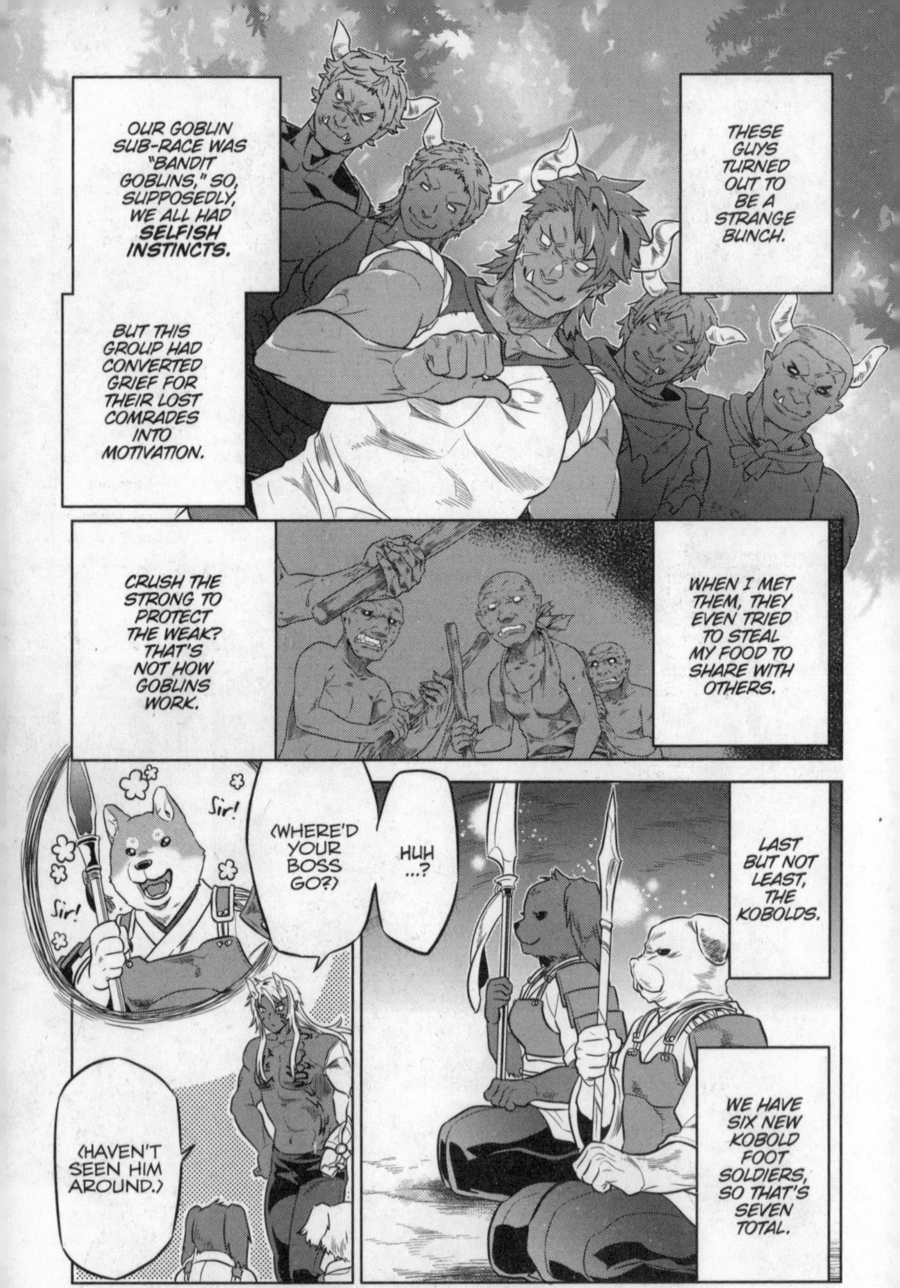
THESE GUYS TURNED OUT TO BE A STRANGE BUNCH.
OUR GOBLIN SUB-RACE WAS "BANDIT GOBLINS," SO, SUPPOSEDLY, WE ALL HAD **SELFISH INSTINCTS.**
BUT THIS GROUP HAD CONVERTED GRIEF FOR THEIR LOST COMRADES INTO MOTIVATION.
WHEN I MET THEM, THEY EVEN TRIED TO STEAL MY FOOD TO SHARE WITH OTHERS.
CRUSH THE STRONG TO PROTECT THE WEAK? THAT'S NOT HOW GOBLINS WORK.
LAST BUT NOT LEAST, THE KOBOLDS.
WE HAVE SIX NEW KOBOLD FOOT SOLDIERS, SO THAT'S SEVEN TOTAL.
HUH ...?
(WHERE'D YOUR BOSS GO?)
Sir!
Sir!
(HAVEN'T SEEN HIM AROUND.)

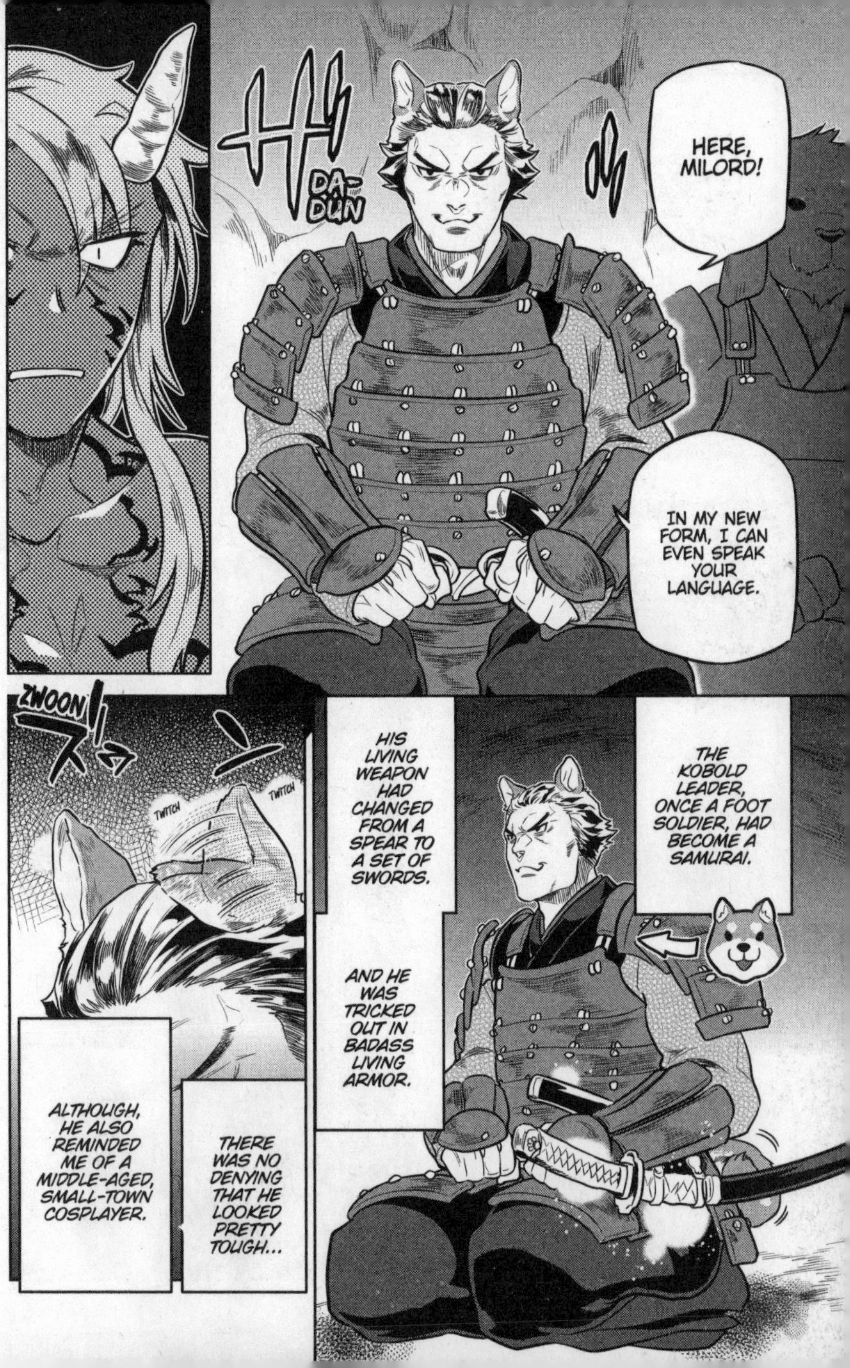
DA-DUN
HERE, MILORD!
IN MY NEW FORM, I CAN EVEN SPEAK YOUR LANGUAGE.
THE KOBOLD LEADER, ONCE A FOOT SOLDIER, HAD BECOME A SAMURAI.
HIS LIVING WEAPON HAD CHANGED FROM A SPEAR TO A SET OF SWORDS.
AND HE WAS TRICKED OUT IN BADASS LIVING ARMOR.
ZWOON
TWITCH
TWITCH
THERE WAS NO DENYING THAT HE LOOKED PRETTY TOUGH...
ALTHOUGH, HE ALSO REMINDED ME OF A MIDDLE-AGED, SMALL-TOWN COSPLAYER.

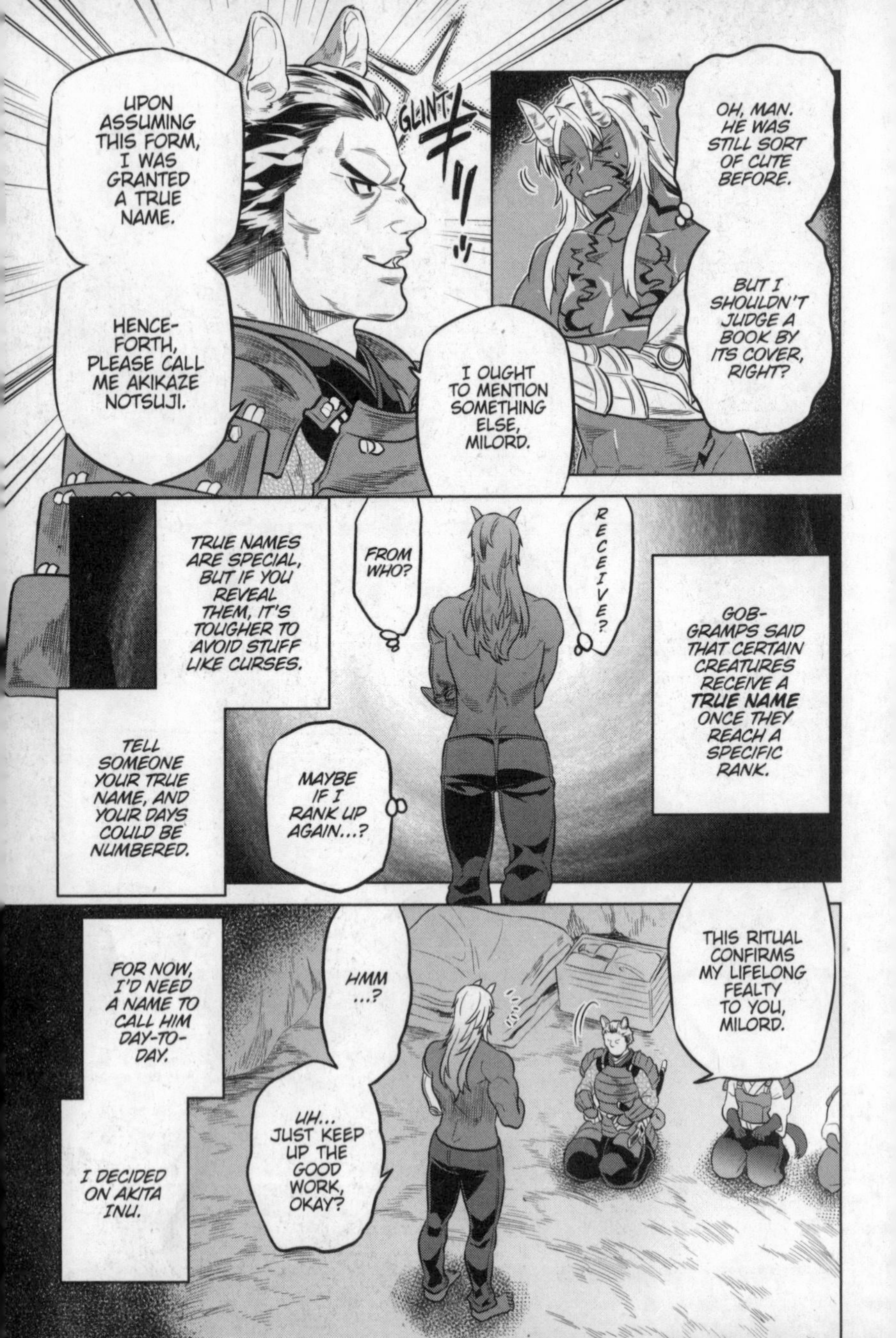
OH, MAN. HE WAS STILL SORT OF CUTE BEFORE.
BUT I SHOULDN'T JUDGE A BOOK BY ITS COVER, RIGHT?
I OUGHT TO MENTION SOMETHING ELSE, MILORD.
UPON ASSUMING THIS FORM, I WAS GRANTED A TRUE NAME.
GLINT
HENCE-FORTH, PLEASE CALL ME AKIKAZE NOTSUJI.
GOB-GRAMPS SAID THAT CERTAIN CREATURES RECEIVE A TRUE NAME ONCE THEY REACH A SPECIFIC RANK.
RECEIVE?
FROM WHO?
MAYBE IF I RANK UP AGAIN...?
TRUE NAMES ARE SPECIAL, BUT IF YOU REVEAL THEM, IT'S TOUGHER TO AVOID STUFF LIKE CURSES.
TELL SOMEONE YOUR TRUE NAME, AND YOUR DAYS COULD BE NUMBERED.
THIS RITUAL CONFIRMS MY LIFELONG FEALTY TO YOU, MILORD.
HMM ...?
UH... JUST KEEP UP THE GOOD WORK, OKAY?
FOR NOW, I'D NEED A NAME TO CALL HIM DAY-TO-DAY.
I DECIDED ON AKITA INU.

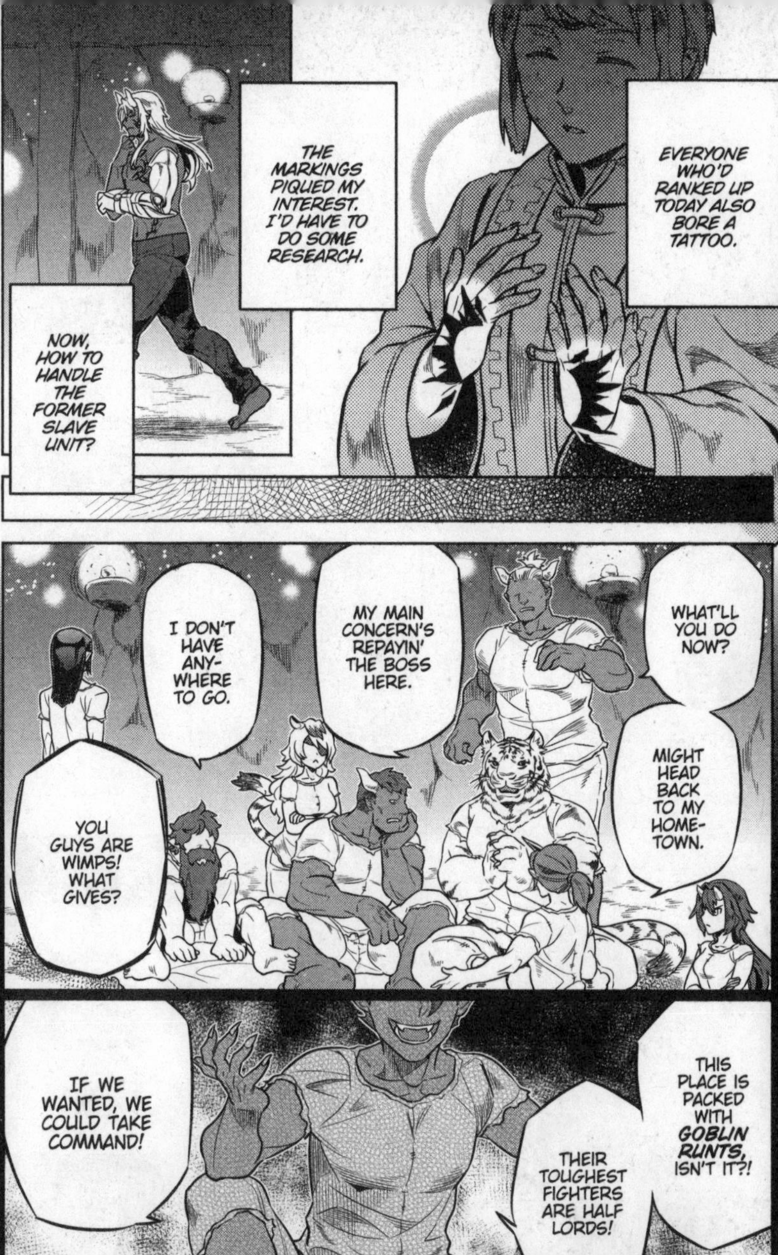
EVERYONE WHO'D RANKED UP TODAY ALSO BORE A TATTOO.
THE MARKINGS PIQUED MY INTEREST. I'D HAVE TO DO SOME RESEARCH.
NOW, HOW TO HANDLE THE FORMER SLAVE UNIT?
WHAT'LL YOU DO NOW?
MIGHT HEAD BACK TO MY HOME-TOWN.
MY MAIN CONCERN'S REPAYIN' THE BOSS HERE.
I DON'T HAVE ANY-WHERE TO GO.
YOU GUYS ARE WIMPS! WHAT GIVES?
THIS PLACE IS PACKED WITH **GOBLIN RUNTS,** ISN'T IT?!
THEIR TOUGHEST FIGHTERS ARE HALF LORDS!
IF WE WANTED, WE COULD TAKE COMMAND!

▶ CONTINUE

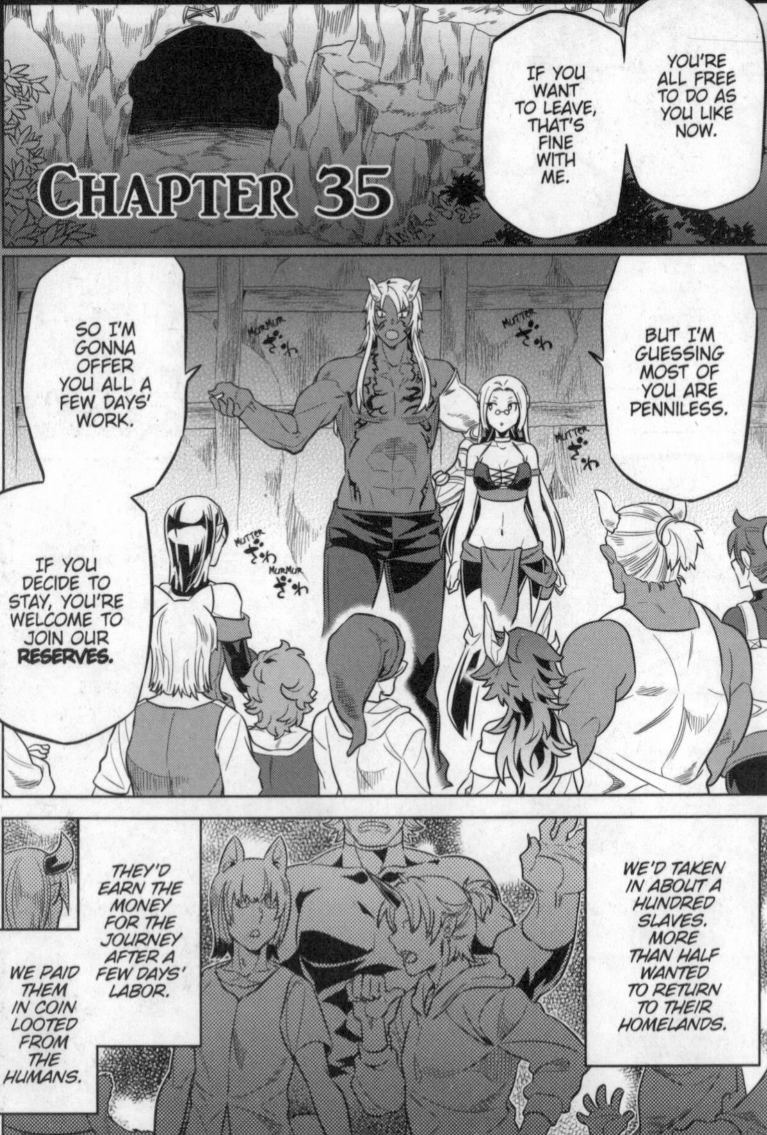
CHAPTER 35
YOU'RE ALL FREE TO DO AS YOU LIKE NOW.
IF YOU WANT TO LEAVE, THAT'S FINE WITH ME.
BUT I'M GUESSING MOST OF YOU ARE PENNILESS.
MUTTER ざわ
MUTTER ざわ
MURMUR ざわ
SO I'M GONNA OFFER YOU ALL A FEW DAYS' WORK.
MUTTER ざわ
MURMUR ざわ
IF YOU DECIDE TO STAY, YOU'RE WELCOME TO JOIN OUR **RESERVES.**
WE'D TAKEN IN ABOUT A HUNDRED SLAVES. MORE THAN HALF WANTED TO RETURN TO THEIR HOMELANDS.
THEY'D EARN THE MONEY FOR THE JOURNEY AFTER A FEW DAYS' LABOR.
WE PAID THEM IN COIN LOOTED FROM THE HUMANS.

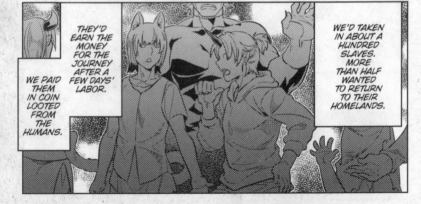

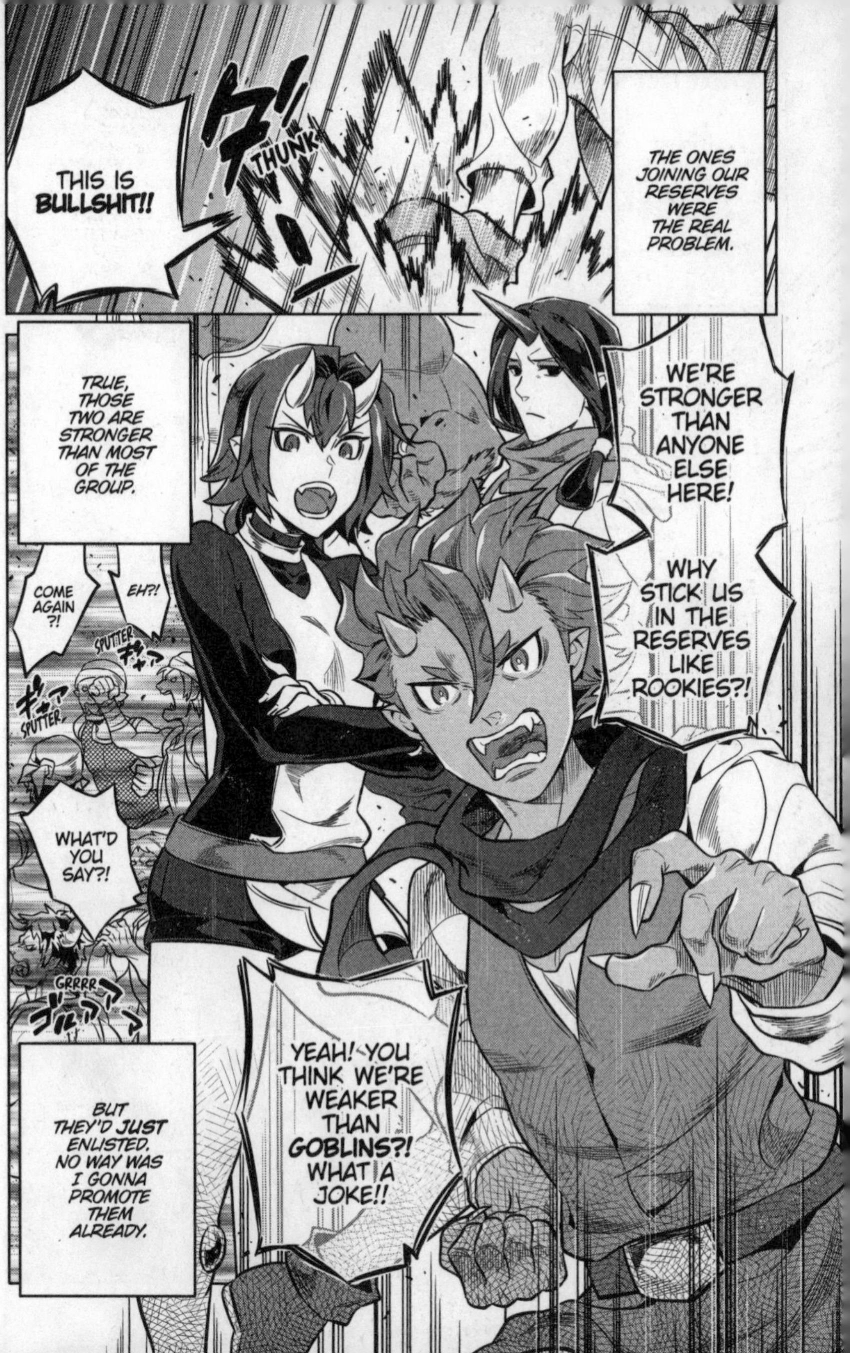
THE ONES JOINING OUR RESERVES WERE THE REAL PROBLEM.
THUNK
THIS IS BULLSHIT!!
WE'RE STRONGER THAN ANYONE ELSE HERE!
TRUE, THOSE TWO ARE STRONGER THAN MOST OF THE GROUP.
WHY STICK US IN THE RESERVES LIKE ROOKIES?!
EH?!
COME AGAIN?!
SPUTTER
SPUTTER
WHAT'D YOU SAY?!
GRRRR
YEAH! YOU THINK WE'RE WEAKER THAN GOBLINS?! WHAT A JOKE!!
BUT THEY'D JUST ENLISTED. NO WAY WAS I GONNA PROMOTE THEM ALREADY.

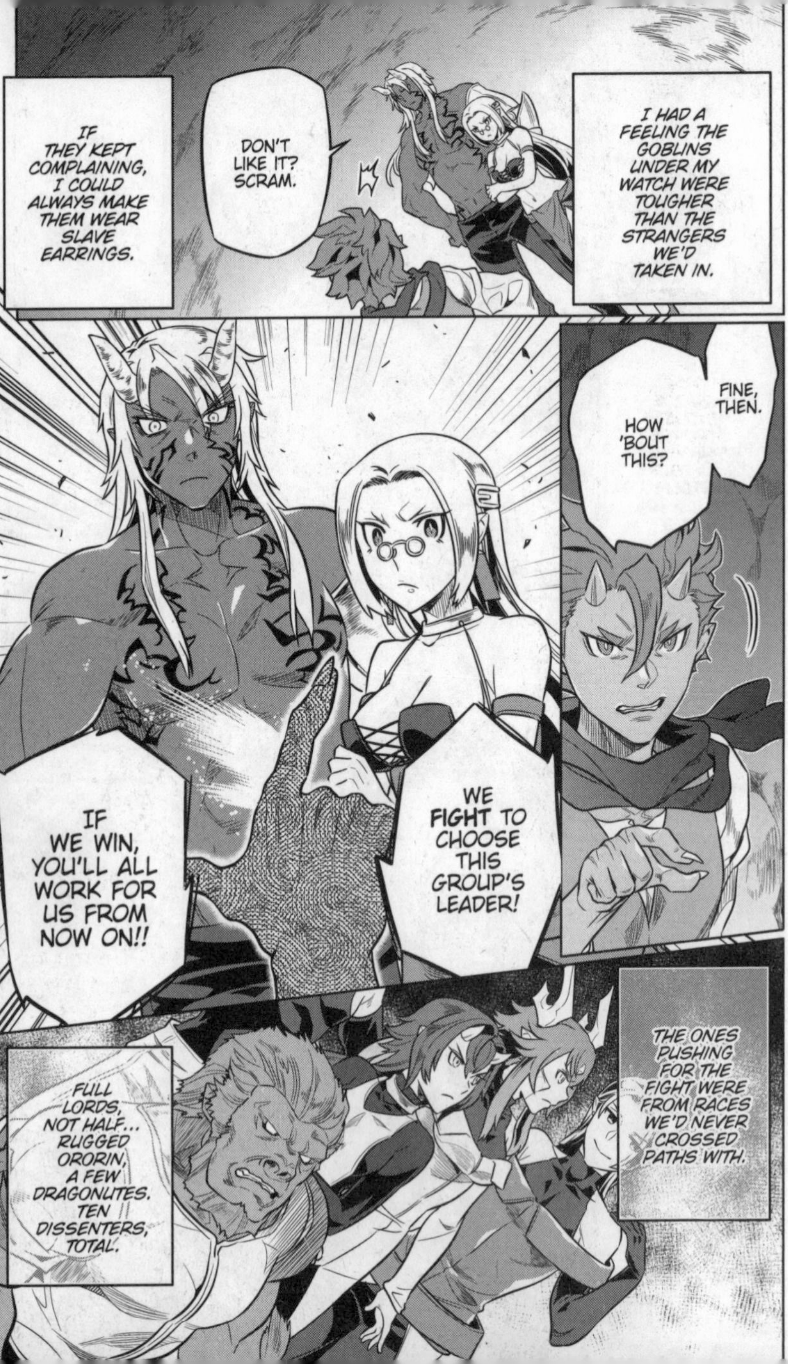
I HAD A FEELING THE GOBLINS UNDER MY WATCH WERE TOUGHER THAN THE STRANGERS WE'D TAKEN IN.
DON'T LIKE IT? SCRAM.
IF THEY KEPT COMPLAINING, I COULD ALWAYS MAKE THEM WEAR SLAVE EARRINGS.
FINE, THEN.
HOW 'BOUT THIS?
WE FIGHT TO CHOOSE THIS GROUP'S LEADER!
IF WE WIN, YOU'LL ALL WORK FOR US FROM NOW ON!!
THE ONES PUSHING FOR THE FIGHT WERE FROM RACES WE'D NEVER CROSSED PATHS WITH.
FULL LORDS, NOT HALF... RUGGED ORORIN, A FEW DRAGONUTES. TEN DISSENTERS, TOTAL.

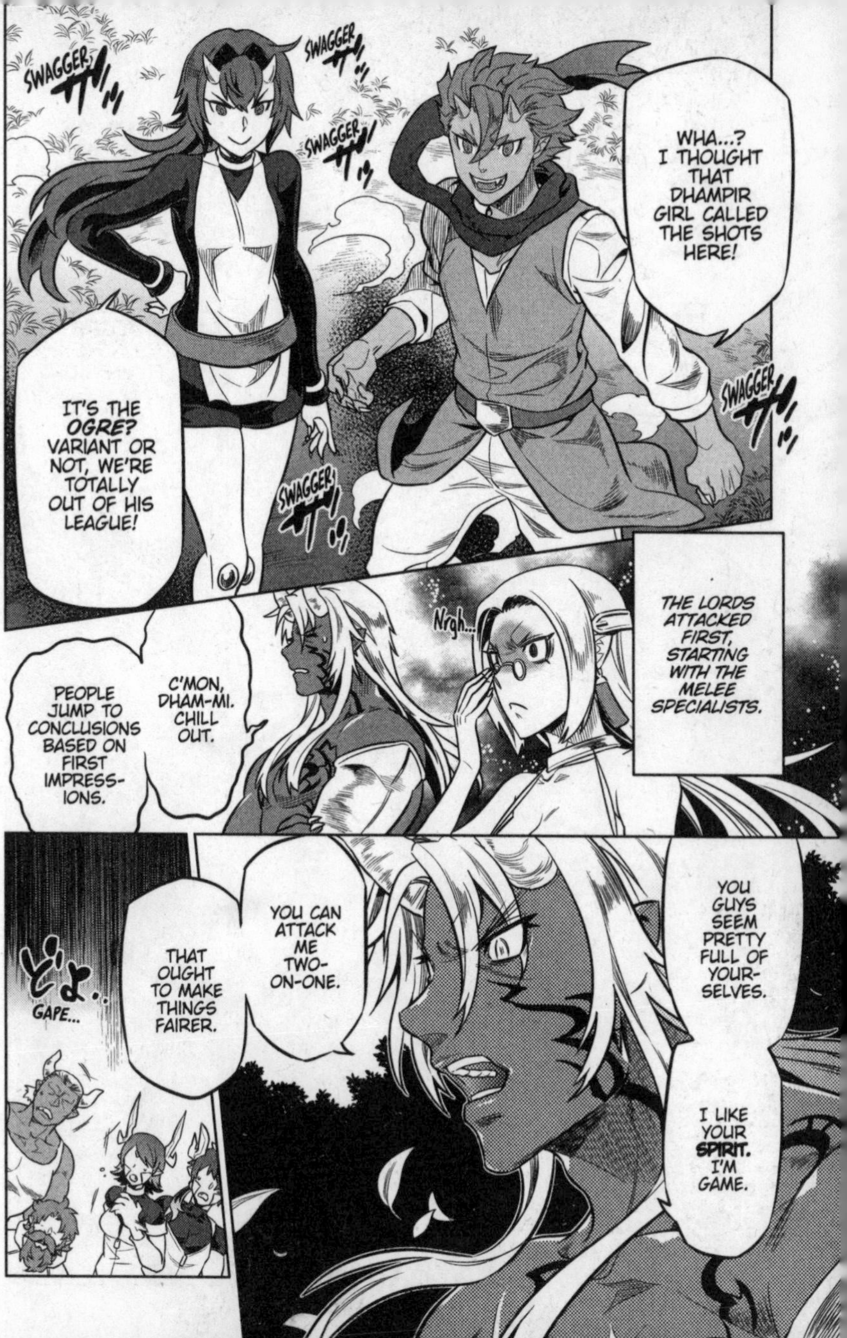

SWAGGER
SWAGGER
SWAGGER
WHA...? I THOUGHT THAT DHAMPIR GIRL CALLED THE SHOTS HERE!
SWAGGER
SWAGGER
IT'S THE OGRE? VARIANT OR NOT, WE'RE TOTALLY OUT OF HIS LEAGUE!
THE LORDS ATTACKED FIRST, STARTING WITH THE MELEE SPECIALISTS.
Nrgh...
C'MON, DHAM-MI. CHILL OUT.
PEOPLE JUMP TO CONCLUSIONS BASED ON FIRST IMPRESSIONS.
YOU GUYS SEEM PRETTY FULL OF YOUR-SELVES.
I LIKE YOUR SPIRIT. I'M GAME.
YOU CAN ATTACK ME TWO-ON-ONE.
THAT OUGHT TO MAKE THINGS FAIRER.
どよ..
GAPE...

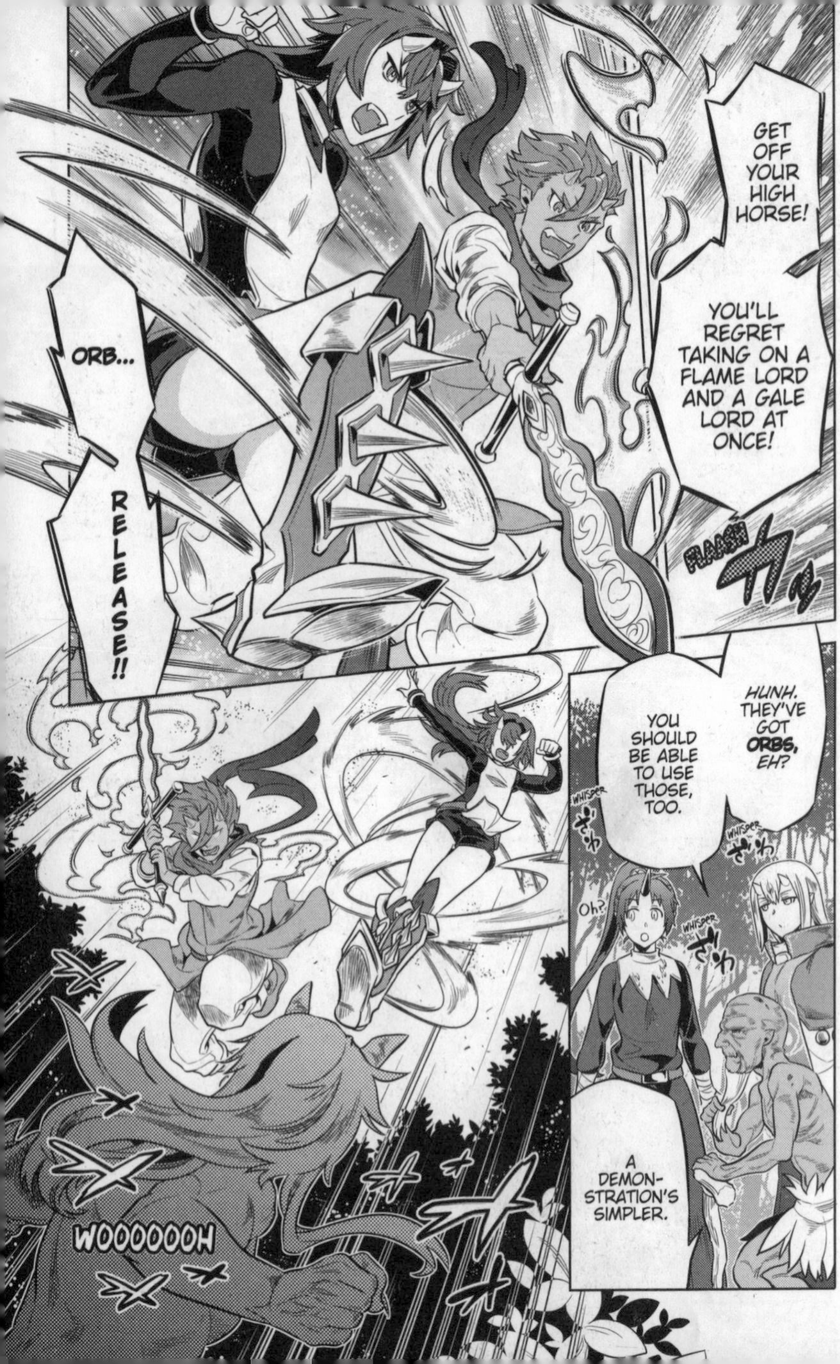
GET OFF YOUR HIGH HORSE!
YOU'LL REGRET TAKING ON A FLAME LORD AND A GALE LORD AT ONCE!
FLAASH
ORB...
RELEASE!!
HUNH. THEY'VE GOT ORBS, EH?
YOU SHOULD BE ABLE TO USE THOSE, TOO.
WHISPER
WHISPER
WHISPER
Oh?
A DEMON-STRATION'S SIMPLER.
WOOOOOOH

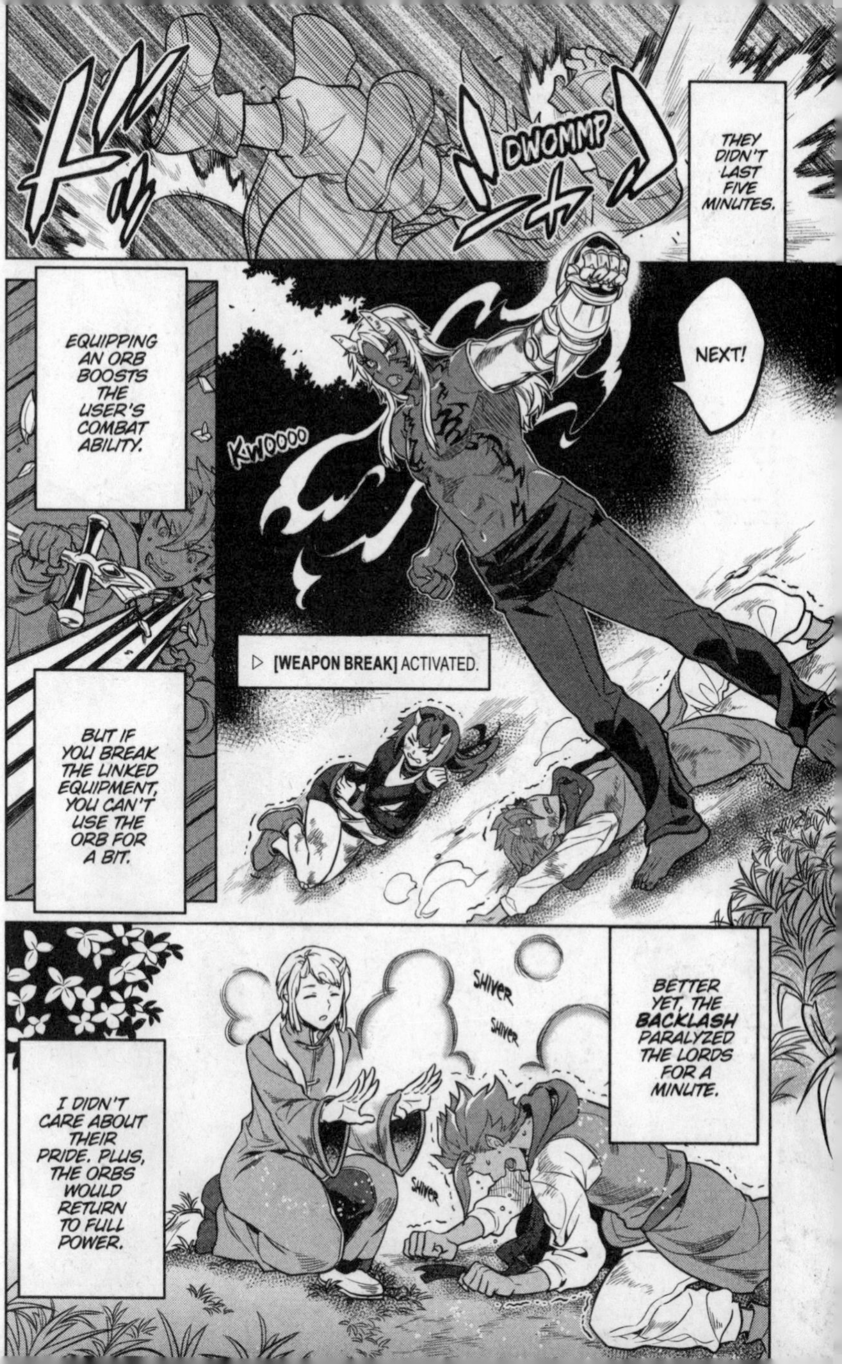
THEY DIDN'T LAST FIVE MINUTES.
DWOMMP
NEXT!
KWOOOO
▷ [WEAPON BREAK] ACTIVATED.
EQUIPPING AN ORB BOOSTS THE USER'S COMBAT ABILITY.
BUT IF YOU BREAK THE LINKED EQUIPMENT, YOU CAN'T USE THE ORB FOR A BIT.
BETTER YET, THE BACKLASH PARALYZED THE LORDS FOR A MINUTE.
SHIVER
SHIVER
SHIVER
I DIDN'T CARE ABOUT THEIR PRIDE. PLUS, THE ORBS WOULD RETURN TO FULL POWER.

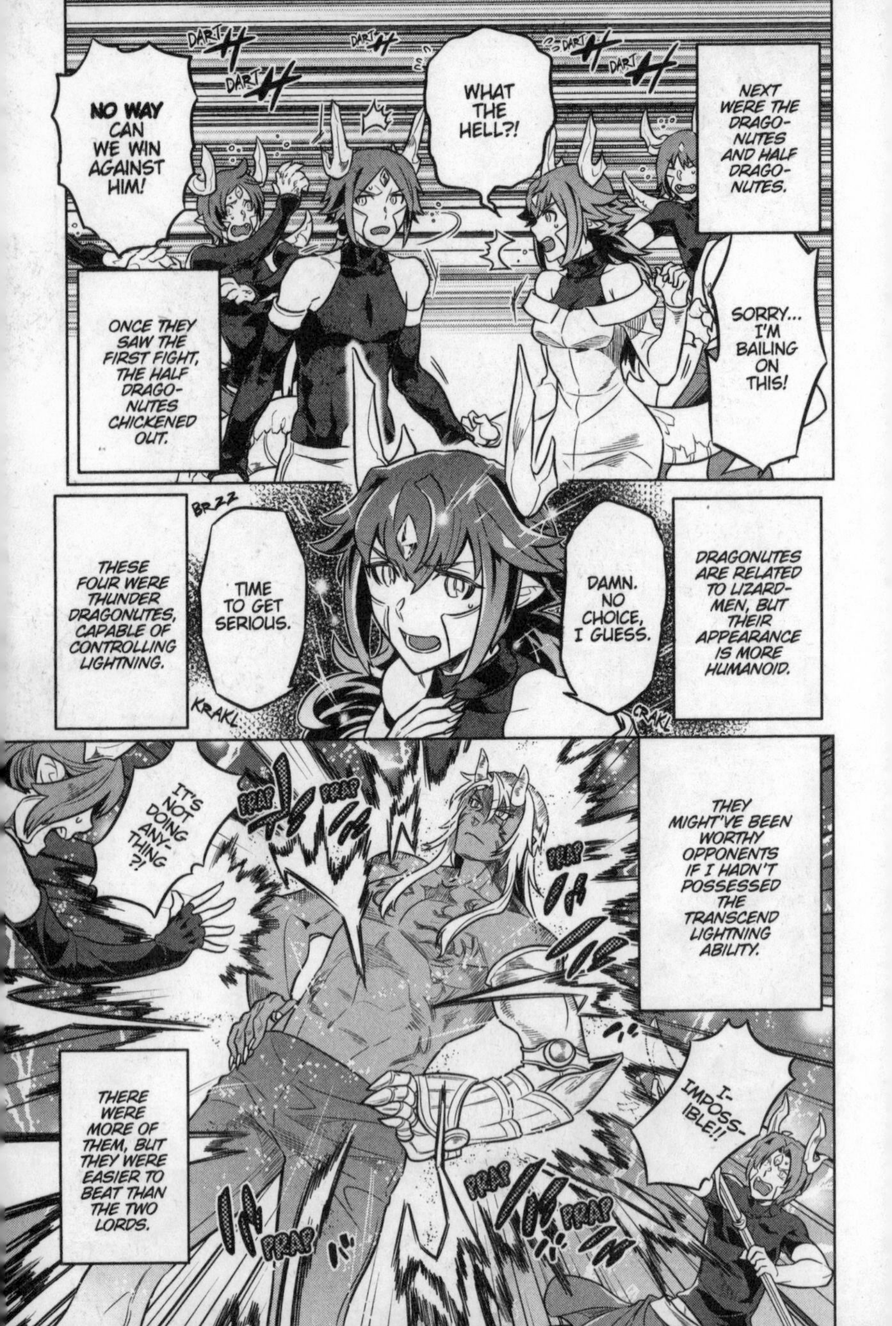

NEXT WERE THE DRAGONUTES AND HALF DRAGONUTES.
DART
DART
WHAT THE HELL?!
DART
DART
DART
NO WAY CAN WE WIN AGAINST HIM!
SORRY... I'M BAILING ON THIS!
ONCE THEY SAW THE FIRST FIGHT, THE HALF DRAGONUTES CHICKENED OUT.
DRAGONUTES ARE RELATED TO LIZARDMEN, BUT THEIR APPEARANCE IS MORE HUMANOID.
DAMN. NO CHOICE, I GUESS.
CRAKL
BRZZ
TIME TO GET SERIOUS.
KRAKL
THESE FOUR WERE THUNDER DRAGONUTES, CAPABLE OF CONTROLLING LIGHTNING.
THEY MIGHT'VE BEEN WORTHY OPPONENTS IF I HADN'T POSSESSED THE TRANSCEND LIGHTNING ABILITY.
FRAP
FRAP
FRAP
IT'S NOT DOING ANYTHING?!
I-IMPOSSIBLE!!
FRAP
FRAP
FRAP
THERE WERE MORE OF THEM, BUT THEY WERE EASIER TO BEAT THAN THE TWO LORDS.

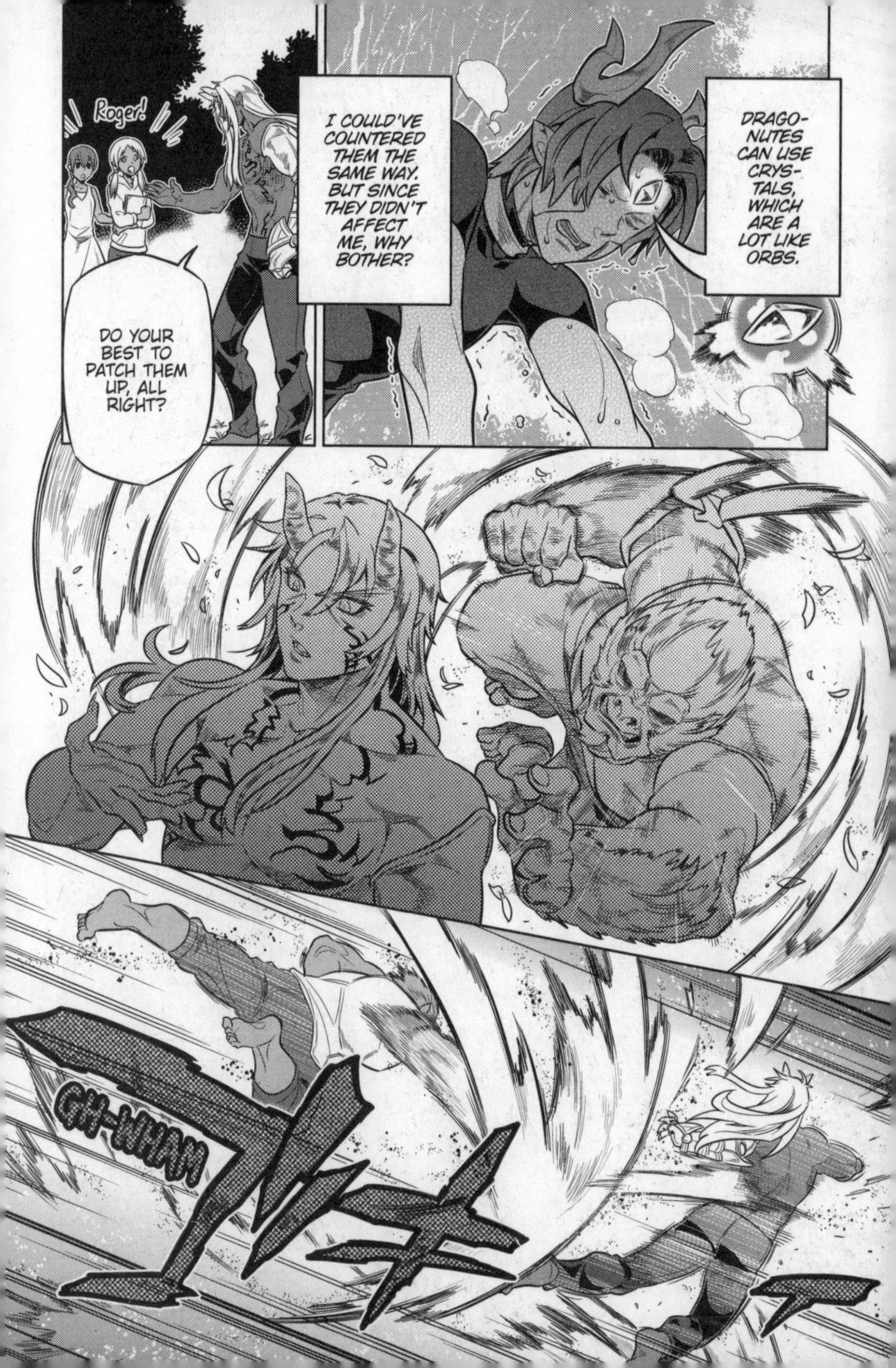
DRAGONUTES CAN USE CRYSTALS, WHICH ARE A LOT LIKE ORBS.
I COULD'VE COUNTERED THEM THE SAME WAY. BUT SINCE THEY DIDN'T AFFECT ME, WHY BOTHER?
Roger!
DO YOUR BEST TO PATCH THEM UP, ALL RIGHT?
GH-WHAM

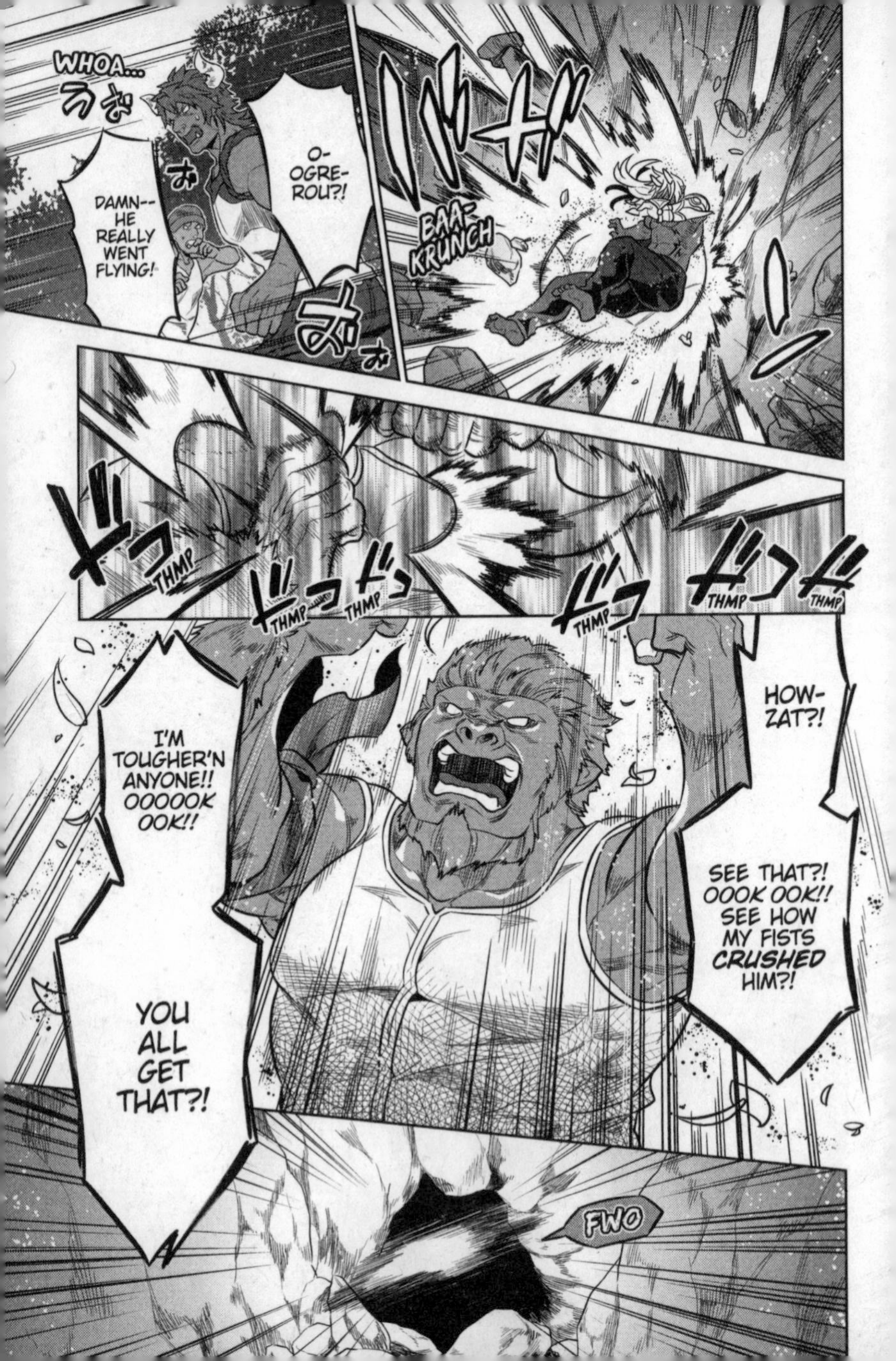
BAA-KRUNCH
WHOA...
O-OGRE-ROU?!
DAMN-- HE REALLY WENT FLYING!
THMP
THMP
THMP
THMP
THMP
THMP
HOW-ZAT?!
SEE THAT?! OOOK OOK!! SEE HOW MY FISTS **CRUSHED** HIM?!
I'M TOUGHER'N ANYONE!! OOOOOK OOK!!
YOU ALL GET THAT?!
FWO

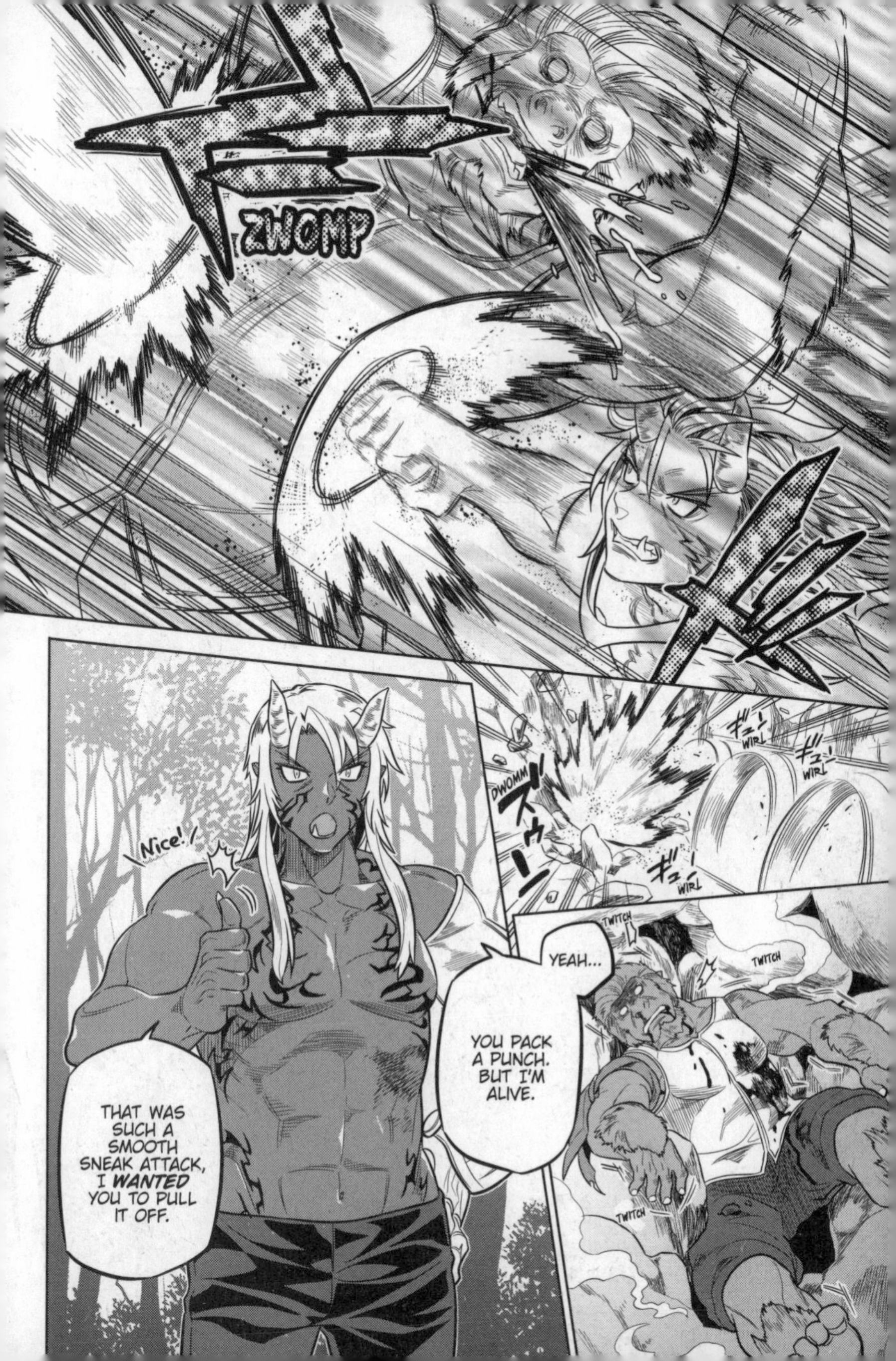
ZWOMP
DWOMM
ズウーン
ギュ WIRL
ギュ WIRL
ギュ WIRL
TWITCH
TWITCH
TWITCH
YEAH...
YOU PACK A PUNCH. BUT I'M ALIVE.
Nice!
THAT WAS SUCH A SMOOTH SNEAK ATTACK, I **WANTED** YOU TO PULL IT OFF.

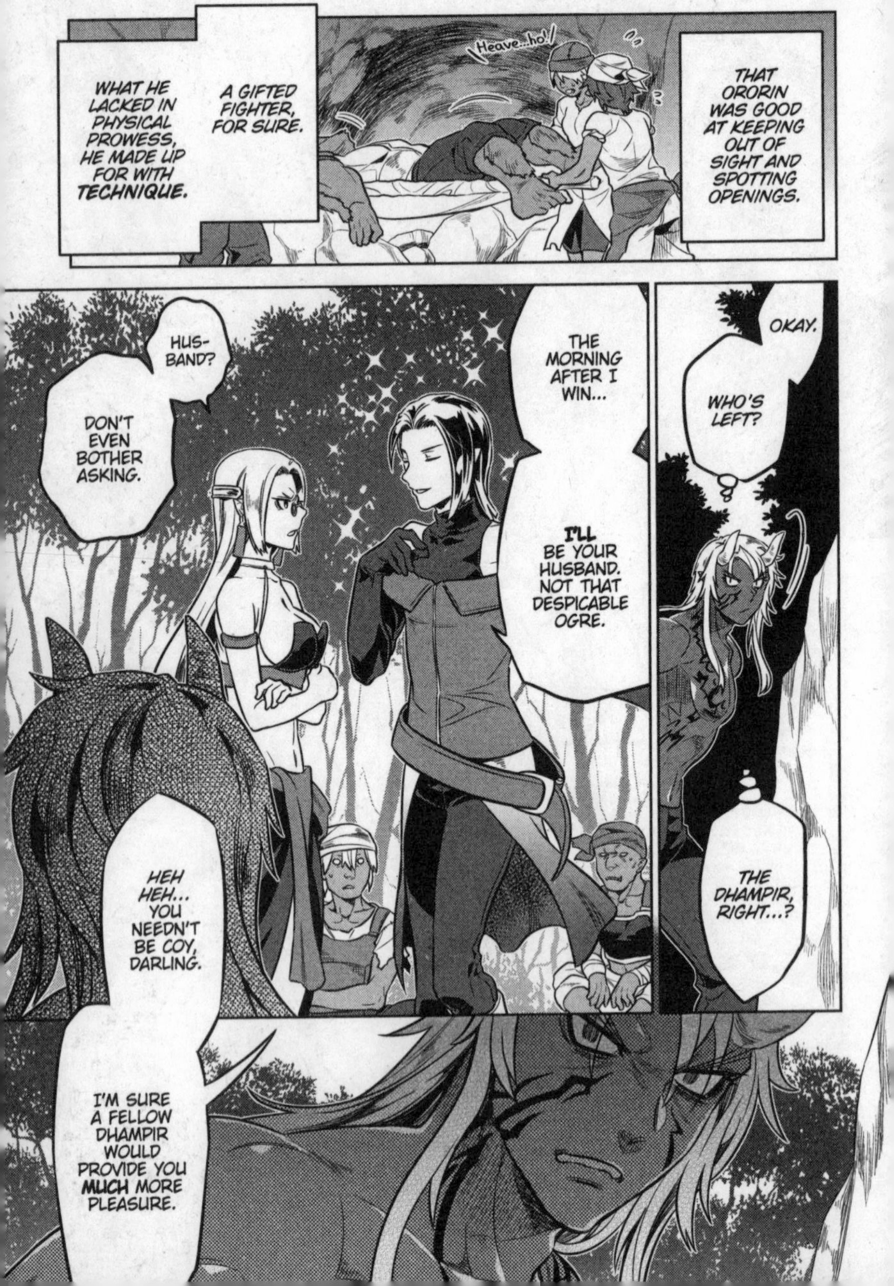
THAT ORORIN WAS GOOD AT KEEPING OUT OF SIGHT AND SPOTTING OPENINGS.
Heave...ho!
A GIFTED FIGHTER, FOR SURE.
WHAT HE LACKED IN PHYSICAL PROWESS, HE MADE UP FOR WITH TECHNIQUE.
OKAY.
WHO'S LEFT?
THE DHAMPIR, RIGHT...?
THE MORNING AFTER I WIN...
I'LL BE YOUR HUSBAND. NOT THAT DESPICABLE OGRE.
HUS-BAND?
DON'T EVEN BOTHER ASKING.
HEH HEH... YOU NEEDN'T BE COY, DARLING.
I'M SURE A FELLOW DHAMPIR WOULD PROVIDE YOU MUCH MORE PLEASURE.

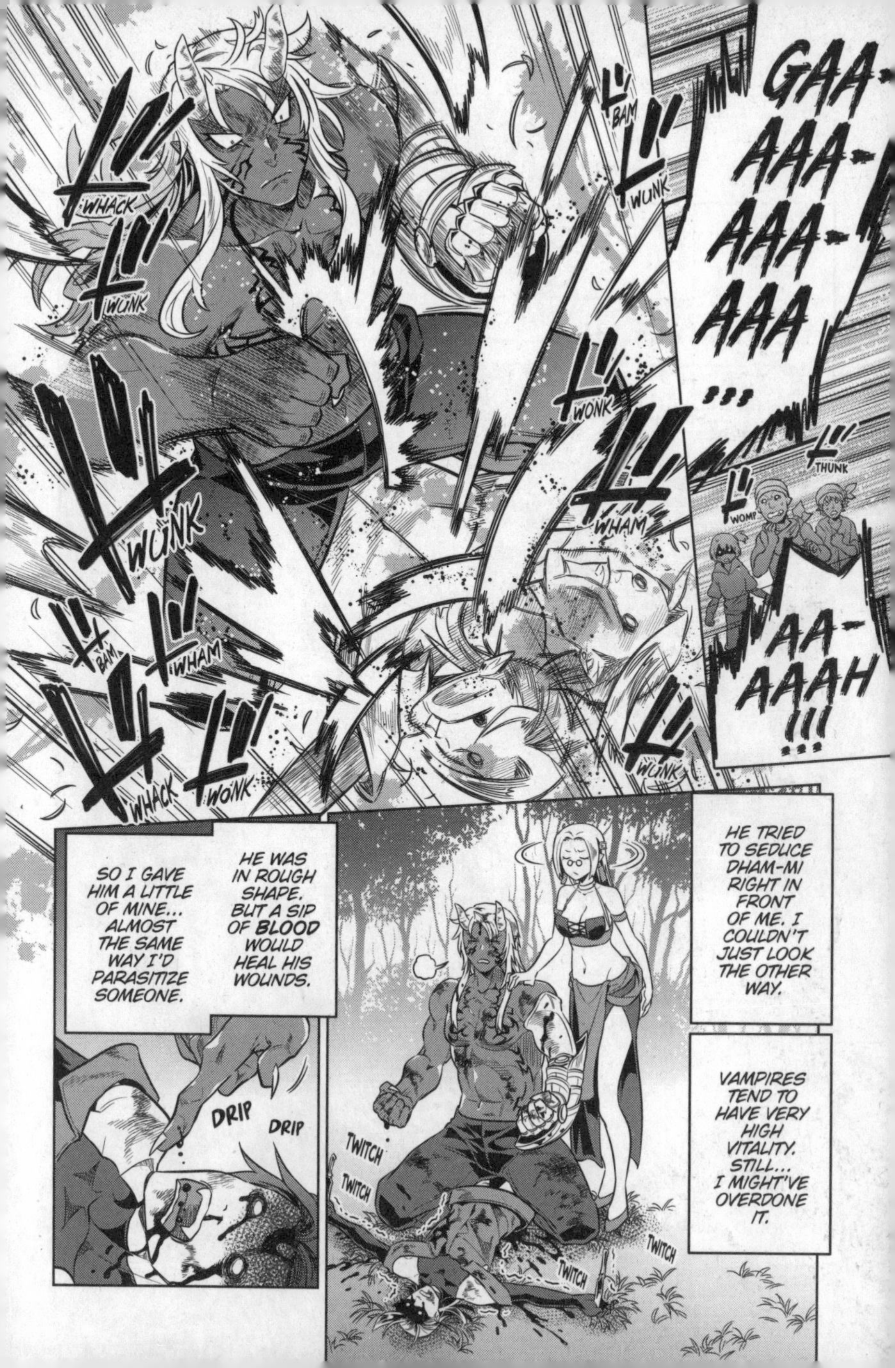
GAA-AAA-AAA-AAA...!
THUNK
WOMP
AA-AAAH!!!
BAM
WUNK
WONK
WHAM
WUNK
WHACK
WUNK
WUNK
BAM
WHAM
WHACK
WONK
HE TRIED TO SEDUCE DHAM-MI RIGHT IN FRONT OF ME. I COULDN'T JUST LOOK THE OTHER WAY.
VAMPIRES TEND TO HAVE VERY HIGH VITALITY. STILL... I MIGHT'VE OVERDONE IT.
TWITCH
TWITCH
TWITCH
TWITCH
HE WAS IN ROUGH SHAPE. BUT A SIP OF BLOOD WOULD HEAL HIS WOUNDS.
SO I GAVE HIM A LITTLE OF MINE... ALMOST THE SAME WAY I'D PARASITIZE SOMEONE.
DRIP
DRIP

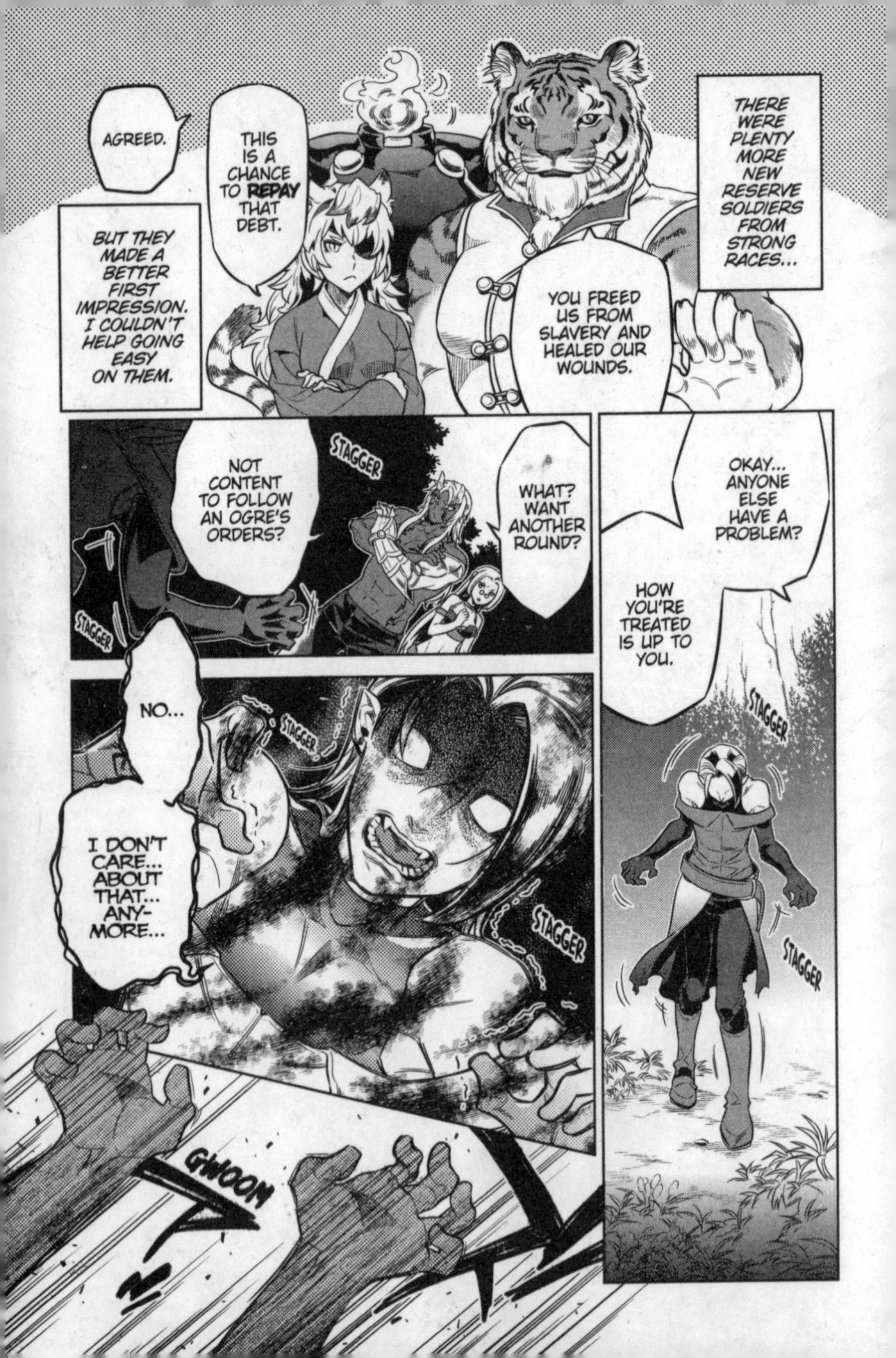
THERE WERE PLENTY MORE NEW RESERVE SOLDIERS FROM STRONG RACES...
YOU FREED US FROM SLAVERY AND HEALED OUR WOUNDS.
THIS IS A CHANCE TO REPAY THAT DEBT.
AGREED.
BUT THEY MADE A BETTER FIRST IMPRESSION. I COULDN'T HELP GOING EASY ON THEM.
OKAY... ANYONE ELSE HAVE A PROBLEM?
HOW YOU'RE TREATED IS UP TO YOU.
STAGGER
STAGGER
WHAT? WANT ANOTHER ROUND?
NOT CONTENT TO FOLLOW AN OGRE'S ORDERS?
STAGGER
STAGGER
NO...
STAGGER
I DON'T CARE... ABOUT THAT... ANY-MORE...
STAGGER
GWOOM

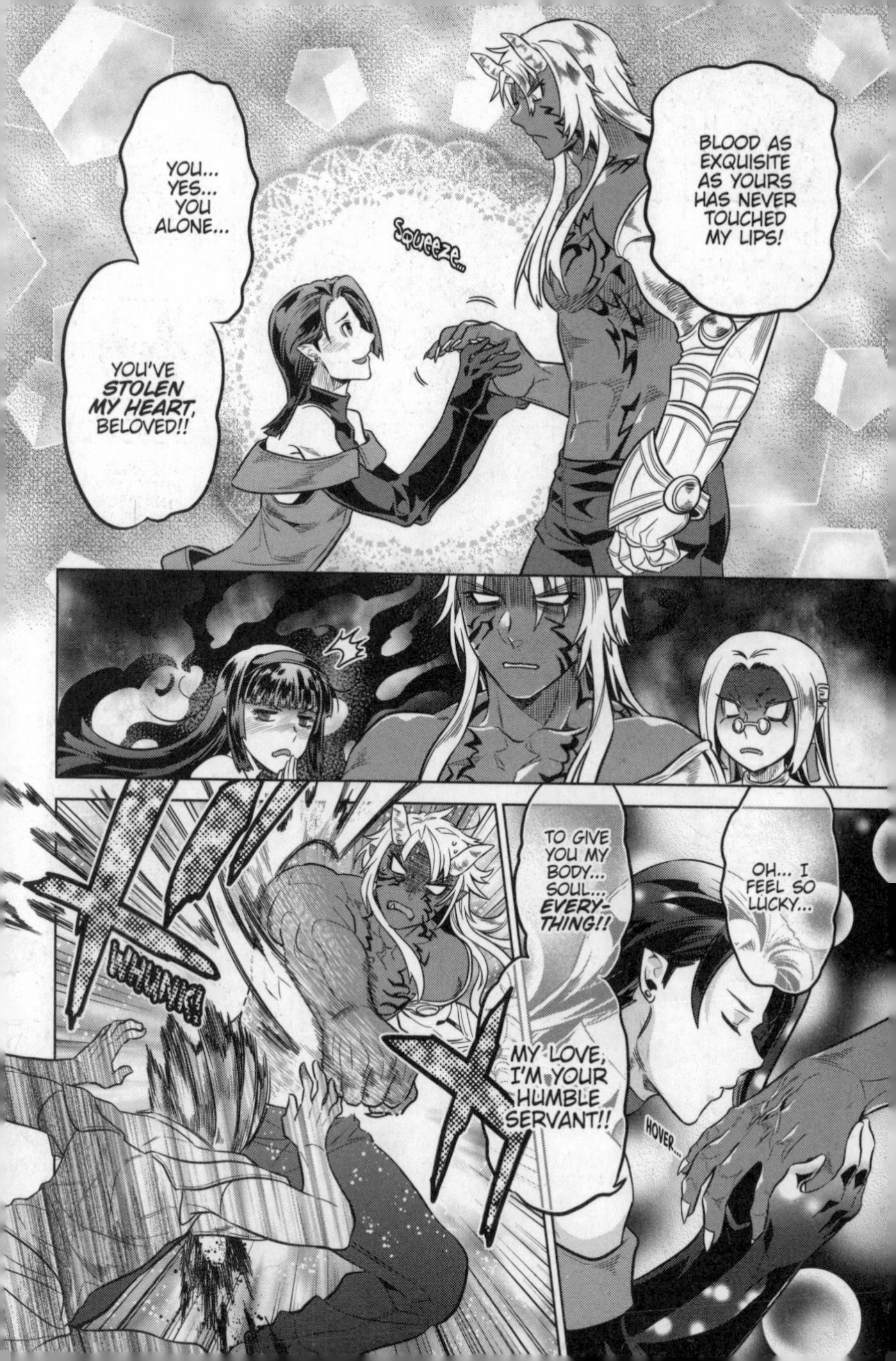
BLOOD AS EXQUISITE AS YOURS HAS NEVER TOUCHED MY LIPS!
Squeeze...
YOU... YES... YOU ALONE...
YOU'VE **STOLEN MY HEART,** BELOVED!!
OH... I FEEL SO LUCKY...
TO GIVE YOU MY BODY... SOUL... **EVERY-THING!!**
MY LOVE, I'M YOUR HUMBLE SERVANT!!
HOVER...
WHUNK!

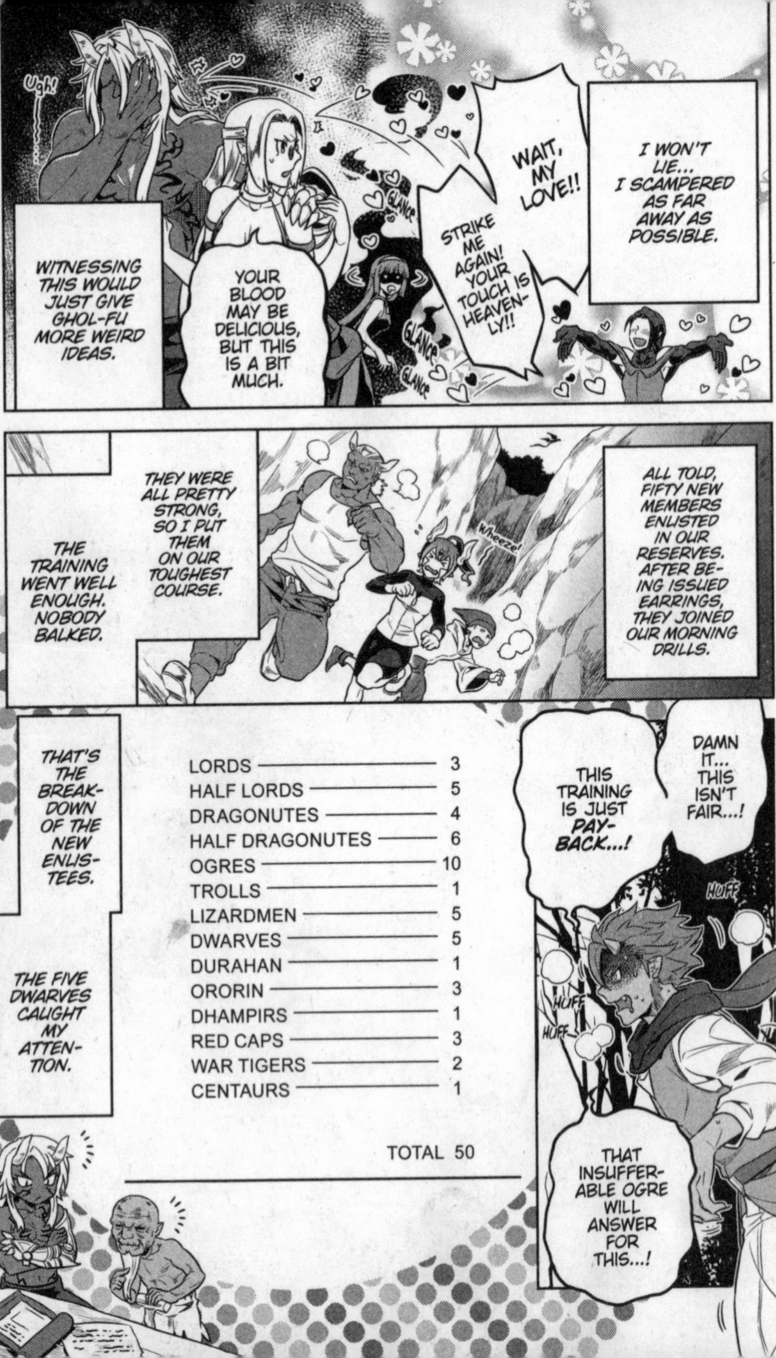
I WON'T LIE... I SCAMPERED AS FAR AWAY AS POSSIBLE.
WAIT, MY LOVE!!
STRIKE ME AGAIN! YOUR TOUCH IS HEAVEN-LY!!
GLANCE
GLANCE
GLANCE
GLANCE
YOUR BLOOD MAY BE DELICIOUS, BUT THIS IS A BIT MUCH.
WITNESSING THIS WOULD JUST GIVE GHOL-FU MORE WEIRD IDEAS.
Ugh!
ALL TOLD, FIFTY NEW MEMBERS ENLISTED IN OUR RESERVES. AFTER BE-ING ISSUED EARRINGS, THEY JOINED OUR MORNING DRILLS.
Wheeze!
THEY WERE ALL PRETTY STRONG, SO I PUT THEM ON OUR TOUGHEST COURSE.
THE TRAINING WENT WELL ENOUGH. NOBODY BALKED.
DAMN IT... THIS ISN'T FAIR...!
THIS TRAINING IS JUST PAY-BACK...!
HUFF
HUFF
HUFF
THAT INSUFFER-ABLE OGRE WILL ANSWER FOR THIS...!
THAT'S THE BREAK-DOWN OF THE NEW ENLIS-TEES.
LORDS 3
HALF LORDS 5
DRAGONUTES 4
HALF DRAGONUTES 6
OGRES 10
TROLLS 1
LIZARDMEN 5
DWARVES 5
DURAHAN 1
ORORIN 3
DHAMPIRS 1
RED CAPS 3
WAR TIGERS 2
CENTAURS 1
TOTAL 50
THE FIVE DWARVES CAUGHT MY ATTEN-TION.

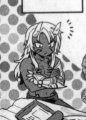

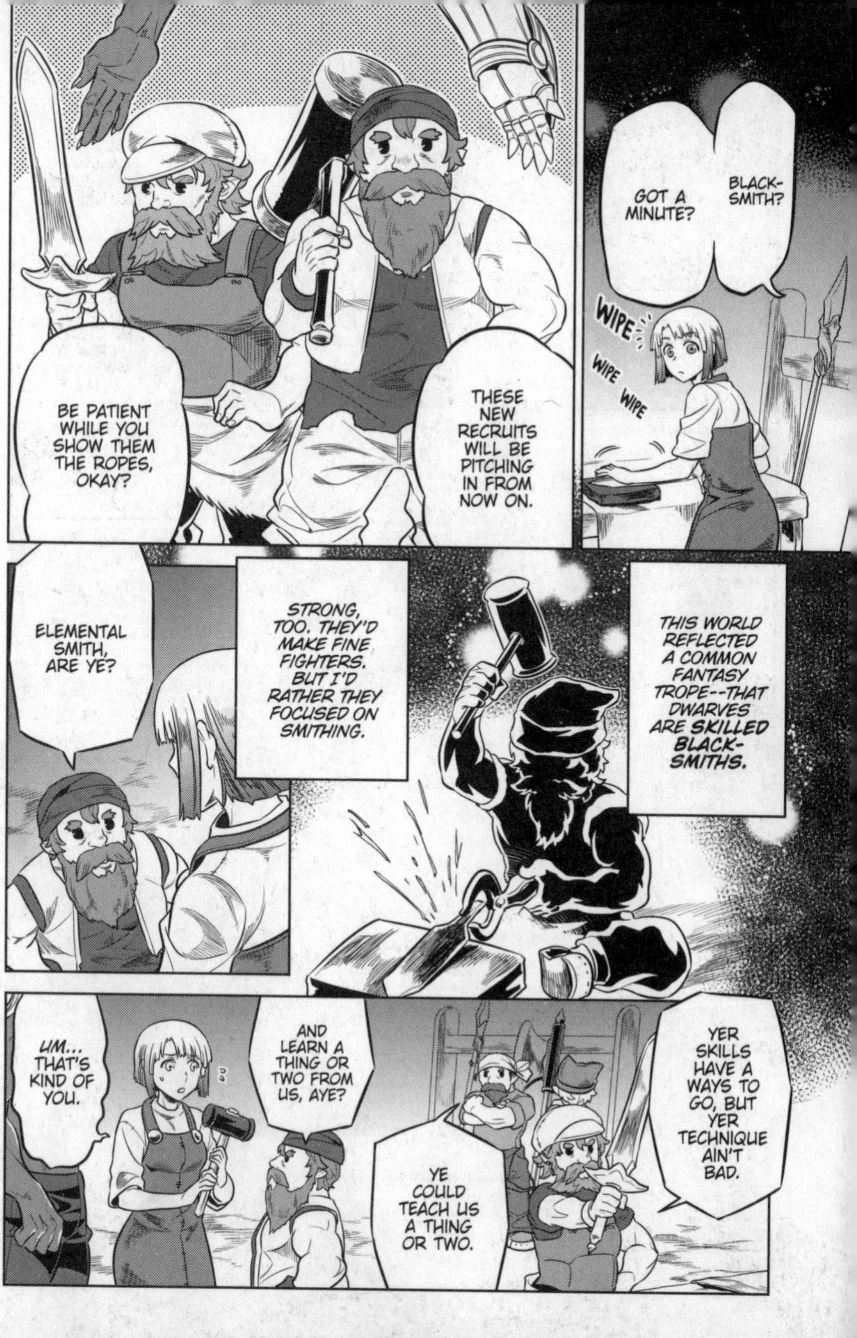

BLACK-SMITH?
GOT A MINUTE?
WIPE
WIPE
WIPE
THESE NEW RECRUITS WILL BE PITCHING IN FROM NOW ON.
BE PATIENT WHILE YOU SHOW THEM THE ROPES, OKAY?
THIS WORLD REFLECTED A COMMON FANTASY TROPE--THAT DWARVES ARE SKILLED BLACK-SMITHS.
STRONG, TOO. THEY'D MAKE FINE FIGHTERS. BUT I'D RATHER THEY FOCUSED ON SMITHING.
ELEMENTAL SMITH, ARE YE?
YER SKILLS HAVE A WAYS TO GO, BUT YER TECHNIQUE AIN'T BAD.
YE COULD TEACH US A THING OR TWO.
AND LEARN A THING OR TWO FROM US, AYE?
UM... THAT'S KIND OF YOU.

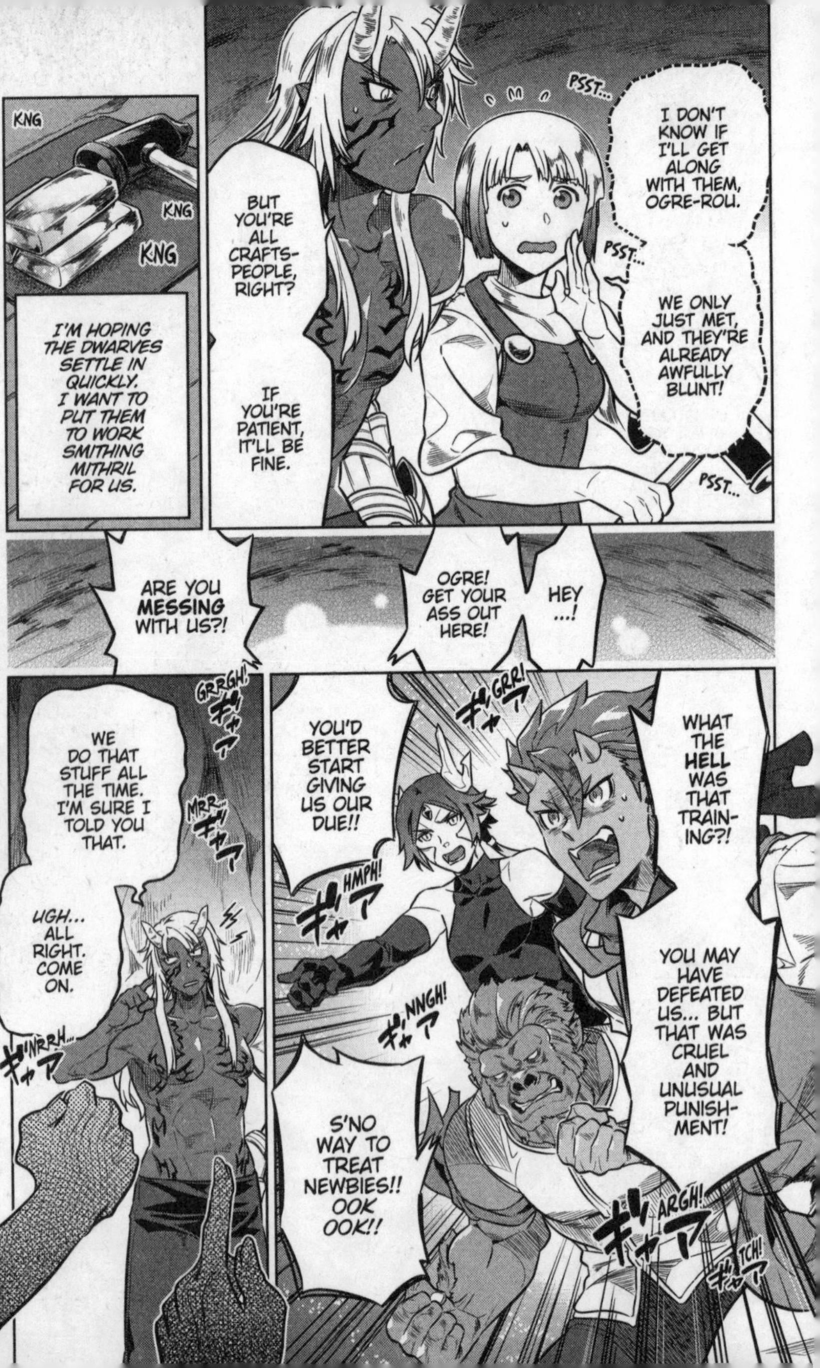
PSST...
I DON'T KNOW IF I'LL GET ALONG WITH THEM, OGRE-ROU.
PSST...
WE ONLY JUST MET, AND THEY'RE ALREADY AWFULLY BLUNT!
PSST...
BUT YOU'RE ALL CRAFTS-PEOPLE, RIGHT?
IF YOU'RE PATIENT, IT'LL BE FINE.
KNG
KNG
KNG
I'M HOPING THE DWARVES SETTLE IN QUICKLY. I WANT TO PUT THEM TO WORK SMITHING MITHRIL FOR US.
HEY ...!
OGRE! GET YOUR ASS OUT HERE!
ARE YOU **MESSING** WITH US?!
WHAT THE **HELL** WAS THAT TRAIN-ING?!
GRR!
YOU'D BETTER START GIVING US OUR DUE!!
HMPH!
YOU MAY HAVE DEFEATED US... BUT THAT WAS CRUEL AND UNUSUAL PUNISH-MENT!
NNGH!
S'NO WAY TO TREAT NEWBIES!! OOK OOK!!
ARGH!
TCH!
GRRGH!
WE DO THAT STUFF ALL THE TIME. I'M SURE I TOLD YOU THAT.
MRR...
UGH... ALL RIGHT. COME ON.
NRRH...

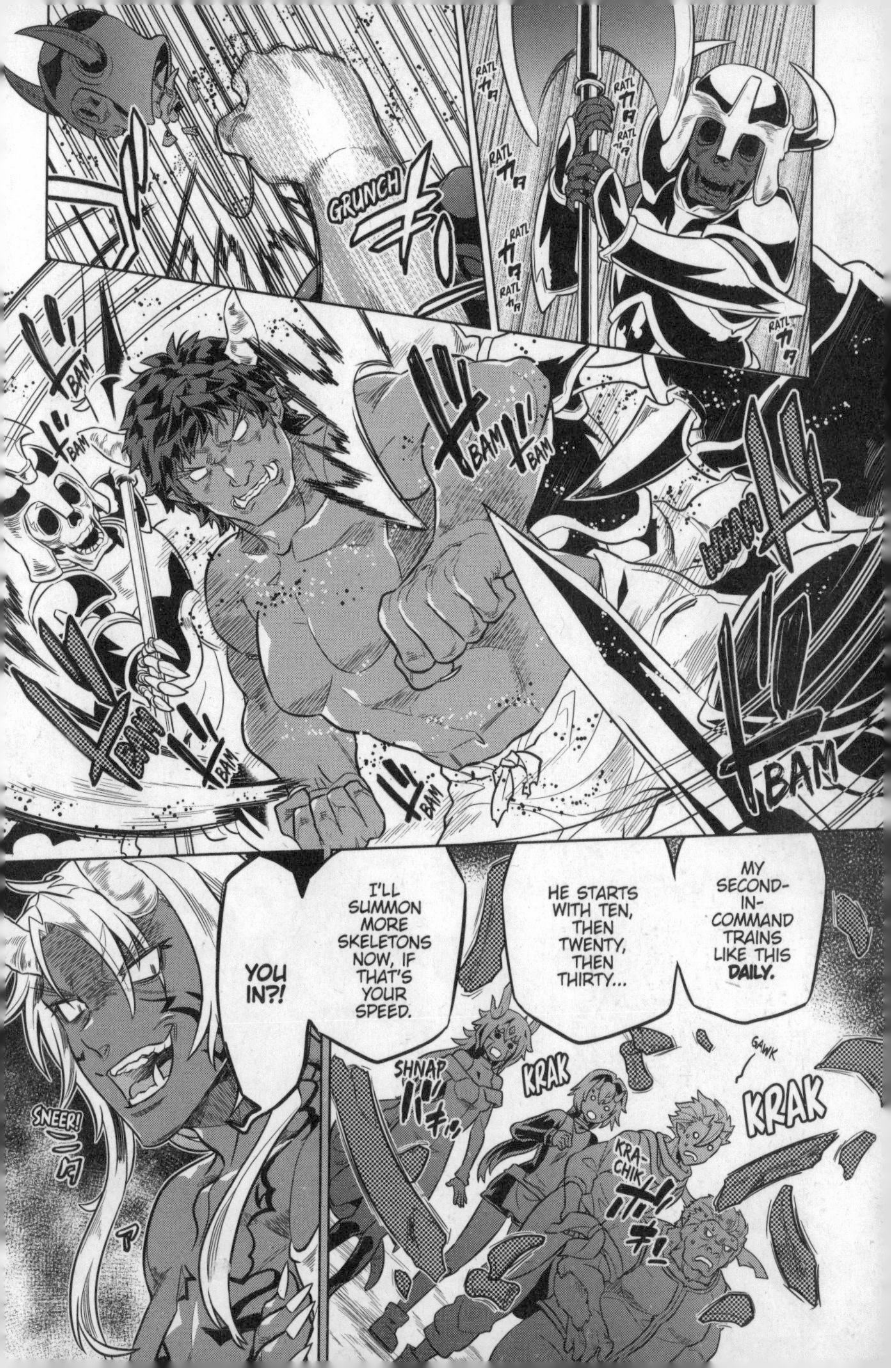

RATL
RATL
RATL
RATL
RATL
RATL
RATL
GRUNCH
WHAM
BAM
BAM
BAM
BAM
BAM
BAM
BAM
MY SECOND-IN-COMMAND TRAINS LIKE THIS DAILY.
HE STARTS WITH TEN, THEN TWENTY, THEN THIRTY...
I'LL SUMMON MORE SKELETONS NOW, IF THAT'S YOUR SPEED.
YOU IN?!
GAWK
KRAK
KRA-CHIK
KRAK
SHNAP
SNEER!

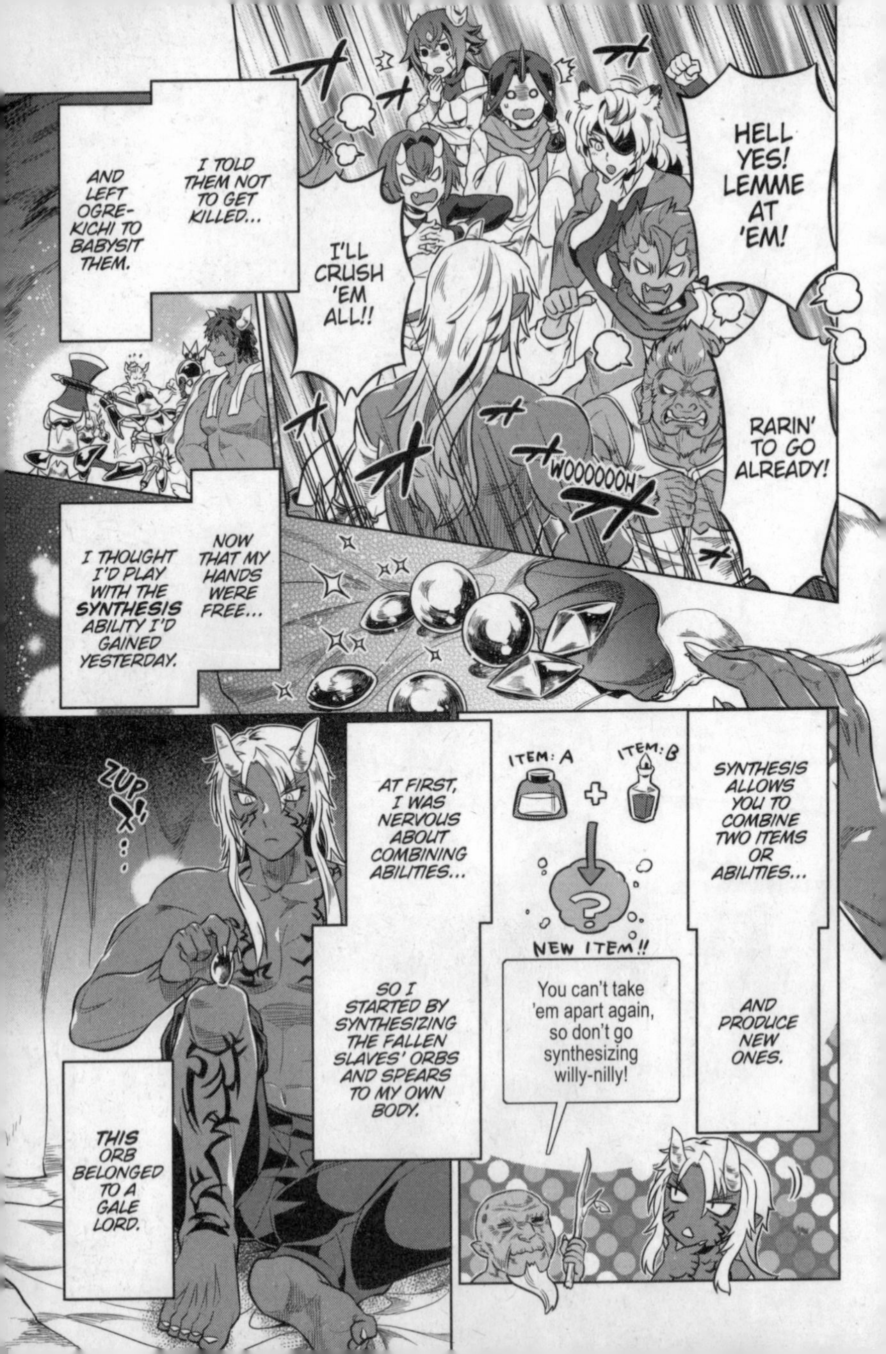
HELL YES! LEMME AT 'EM!
I'LL CRUSH 'EM ALL!!
RARIN' TO GO ALREADY!
WOOOOOOH
I TOLD THEM NOT TO GET KILLED...
AND LEFT OGRE-KICHI TO BABYSIT THEM.
NOW THAT MY HANDS WERE FREE...
I THOUGHT I'D PLAY WITH THE SYNTHESIS ABILITY I'D GAINED YESTERDAY.
SYNTHESIS ALLOWS YOU TO COMBINE TWO ITEMS OR ABILITIES...
ITEM: A
ITEM: B
NEW ITEM!!
AND PRODUCE NEW ONES.
You can't take 'em apart again, so don't go synthesizing willy-nilly!
AT FIRST, I WAS NERVOUS ABOUT COMBINING ABILITIES...
SO I STARTED BY SYNTHESIZING THE FALLEN SLAVES' ORBS AND SPEARS TO MY OWN BODY.
ZUP
THIS ORB BELONGED TO A GALE LORD.

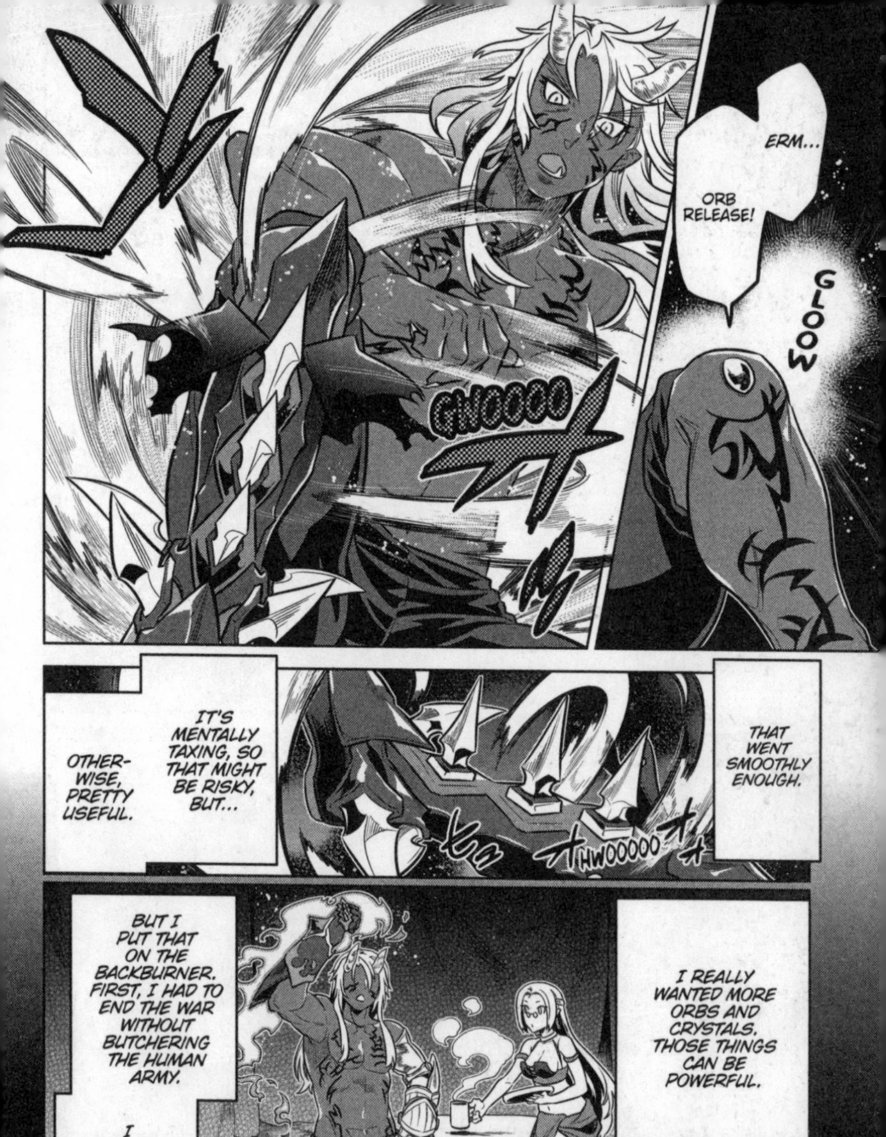
ERM...
ORB RELEASE!
GLOOW
GWOOOO
THAT WENT SMOOTHLY ENOUGH.
IT'S MENTALLY TAXING, SO THAT MIGHT BE RISKY, BUT...
OTHER-WISE, PRETTY USEFUL.
HWOOOOO
I REALLY WANTED MORE ORBS AND CRYSTALS. THOSE THINGS CAN BE POWERFUL.
BUT I PUT THAT ON THE BACKBURNER. FIRST, I HAD TO END THE WAR WITHOUT BUTCHERING THE HUMAN ARMY.
I EXPERI-MENTED WITH THE ORBS AND CRYSTALS UNTIL THE WEE HOURS.

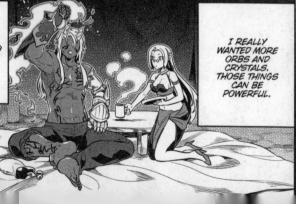

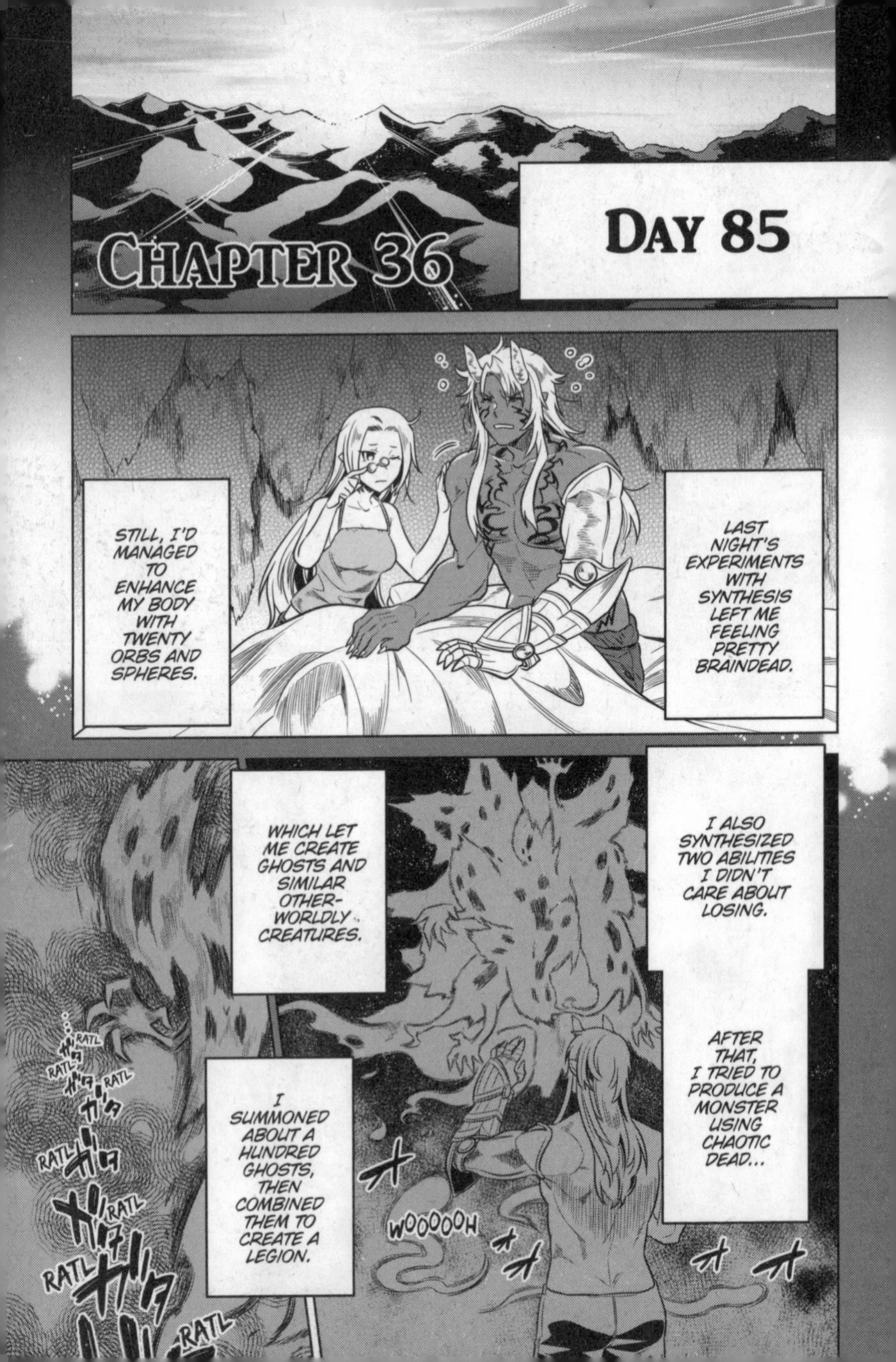
CHAPTER 36
DAY 85
LAST NIGHT'S EXPERIMENTS WITH SYNTHESIS LEFT ME FEELING PRETTY BRAINDEAD.
STILL, I'D MANAGED TO ENHANCE MY BODY WITH TWENTY ORBS AND SPHERES.
I ALSO SYNTHESIZED TWO ABILITIES I DIDN'T CARE ABOUT LOSING.
WHICH LET ME CREATE GHOSTS AND SIMILAR OTHER-WORLDLY CREATURES.
I SUMMONED ABOUT A HUNDRED GHOSTS, THEN COMBINED THEM TO CREATE A LEGION.
AFTER THAT, I TRIED TO PRODUCE A MONSTER USING CHAOTIC DEAD...
RATL
RATL
RATL
RATL
RATL
RATL
RATL
WOOOOOH

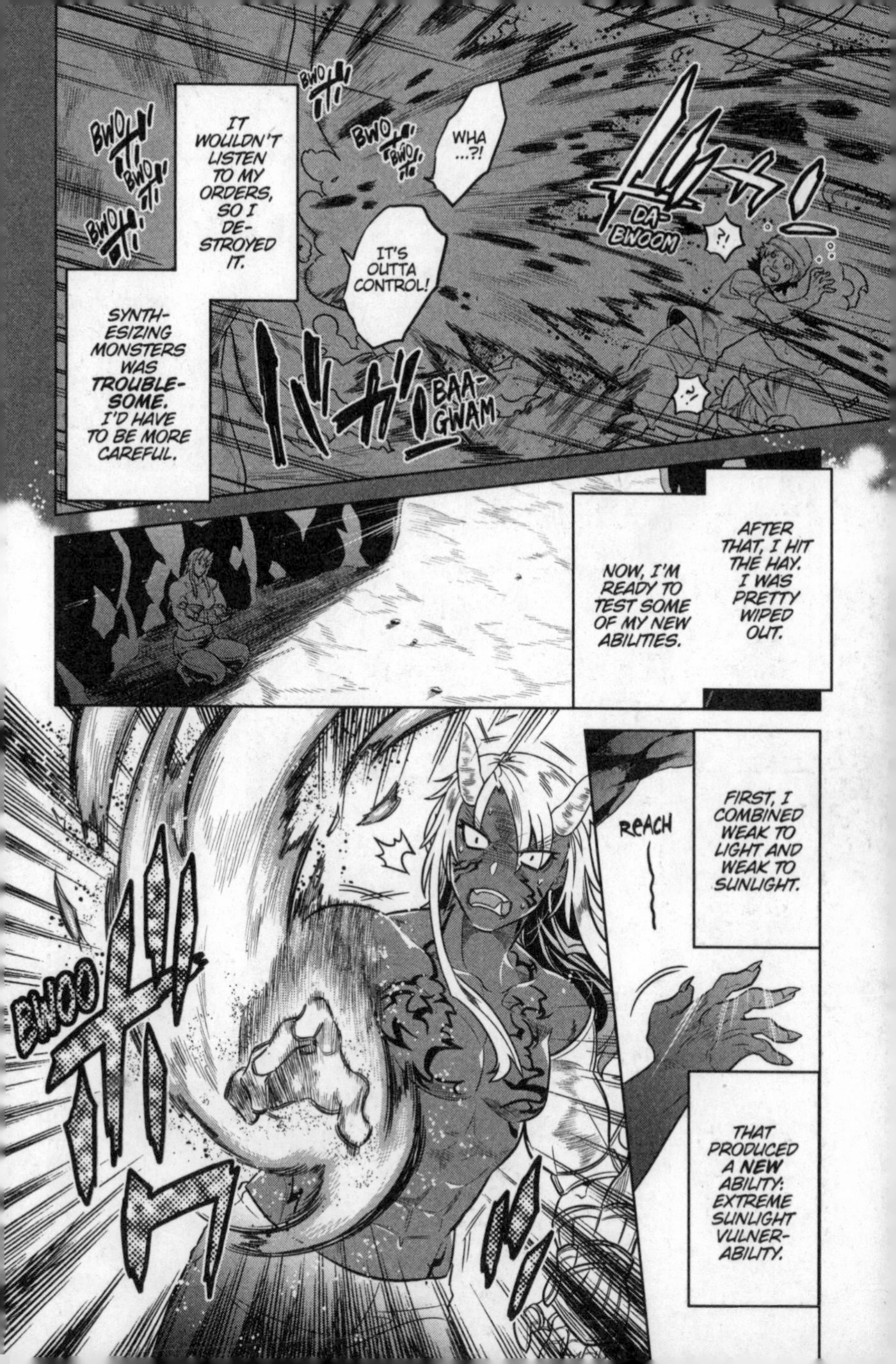
DA-BWOOM
?!
WHA ...?!
BWO
BWO
BWO
IT'S OUTTA CONTROL!
?!
BAA-GWAM
BWO
BWO
BWO
IT WOULDN'T LISTEN TO MY ORDERS, SO I DE-STROYED IT.
SYNTH-ESIZING MONSTERS WAS TROUBLE-SOME. I'D HAVE TO BE MORE CAREFUL.
AFTER THAT, I HIT THE HAY. I WAS PRETTY WIPED OUT.
NOW, I'M READY TO TEST SOME OF MY NEW ABILITIES.
FIRST, I COMBINED WEAK TO LIGHT AND WEAK TO SUNLIGHT.
REACH
THAT PRODUCED A NEW ABILITY: EXTREME SUNLIGHT VULNER-ABILITY.
BWOO

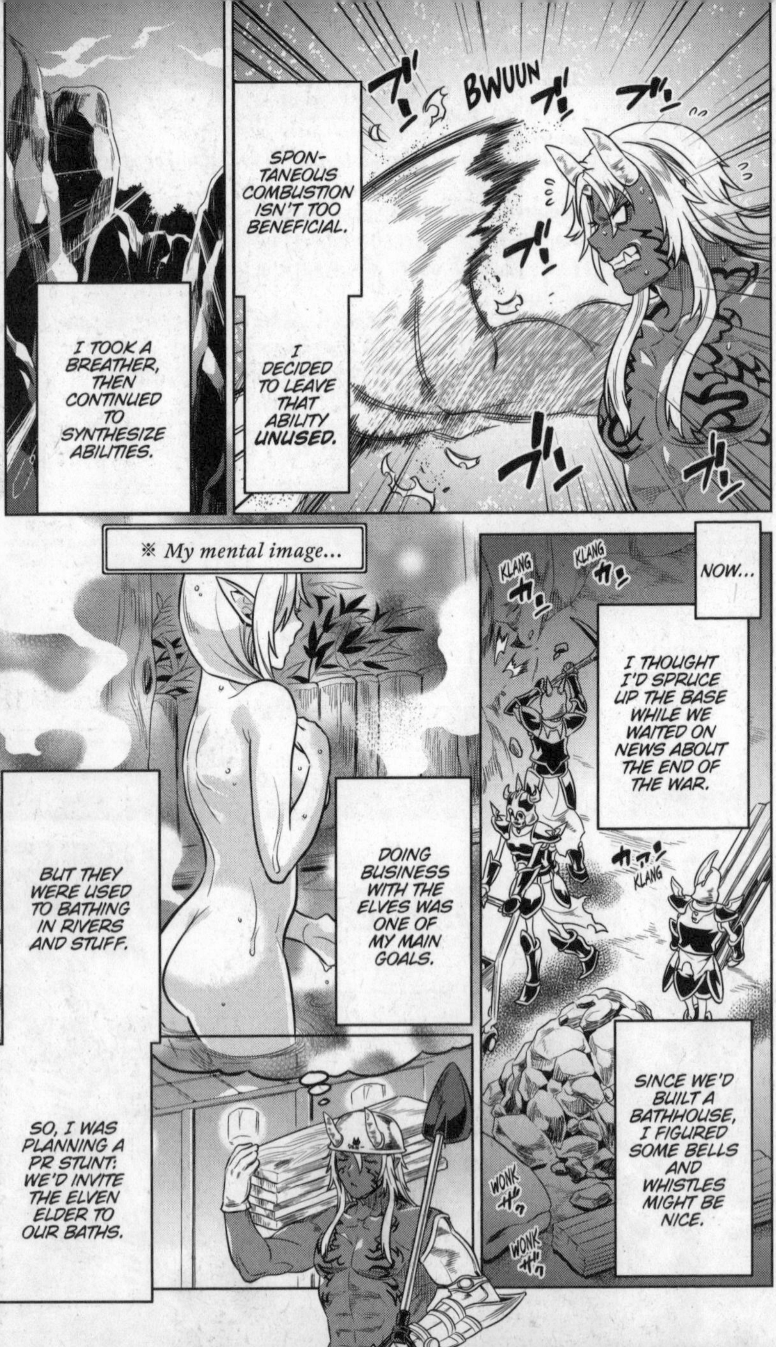
SPON-TANEOUS COMBUSTION ISN'T TOO BENEFICIAL.
BWUUN
I DECIDED TO LEAVE THAT ABILITY UNUSED.
I TOOK A BREATHER, THEN CONTINUED TO SYNTHESIZE ABILITIES.
NOW...
KLANG
KLANG
I THOUGHT I'D SPRUCE UP THE BASE WHILE WE WAITED ON NEWS ABOUT THE END OF THE WAR.
KLANG
SINCE WE'D BUILT A BATHHOUSE, I FIGURED SOME BELLS AND WHISTLES MIGHT BE NICE.
WONK
WONK
※ My mental image...
DOING BUSINESS WITH THE ELVES WAS ONE OF MY MAIN GOALS.
BUT THEY WERE USED TO BATHING IN RIVERS AND STUFF.
SO, I WAS PLANNING A PR STUNT: WE'D INVITE THE ELVEN ELDER TO OUR BATHS.

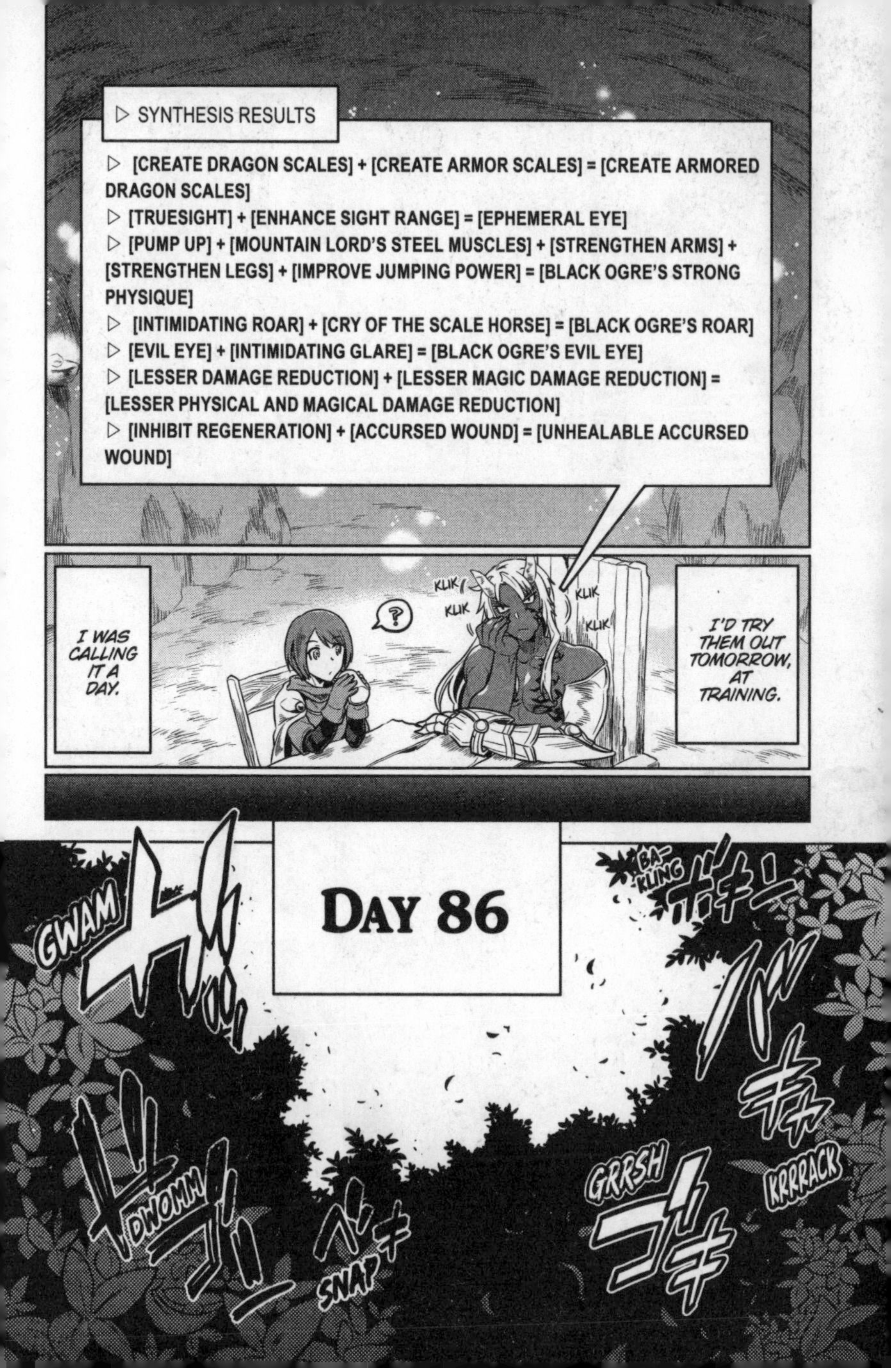
▷ SYNTHESIS RESULTS
▷ [CREATE DRAGON SCALES] + [CREATE ARMOR SCALES] = [CREATE ARMORED DRAGON SCALES]
▷ [TRUESIGHT] + [ENHANCE SIGHT RANGE] = [EPHEMERAL EYE]
▷ [PUMP UP] + [MOUNTAIN LORD'S STEEL MUSCLES] + [STRENGTHEN ARMS] + [STRENGTHEN LEGS] + [IMPROVE JUMPING POWER] = [BLACK OGRE'S STRONG PHYSIQUE]
▷ [INTIMIDATING ROAR] + [CRY OF THE SCALE HORSE] = [BLACK OGRE'S ROAR]
▷ [EVIL EYE] + [INTIMIDATING GLARE] = [BLACK OGRE'S EVIL EYE]
▷ [LESSER DAMAGE REDUCTION] + [LESSER MAGIC DAMAGE REDUCTION] = [LESSER PHYSICAL AND MAGICAL DAMAGE REDUCTION]
▷ [INHIBIT REGENERATION] + [ACCURSED WOUND] = [UNHEALABLE ACCURSED WOUND]
I'D TRY THEM OUT TOMORROW, AT TRAINING.
KLIK KLIK
KLIK KLIK
?
I WAS CALLING IT A DAY.
BA-KLING
DAY 86
GWAM
KRRRACK
GRRSH
SNAP
DWOMM

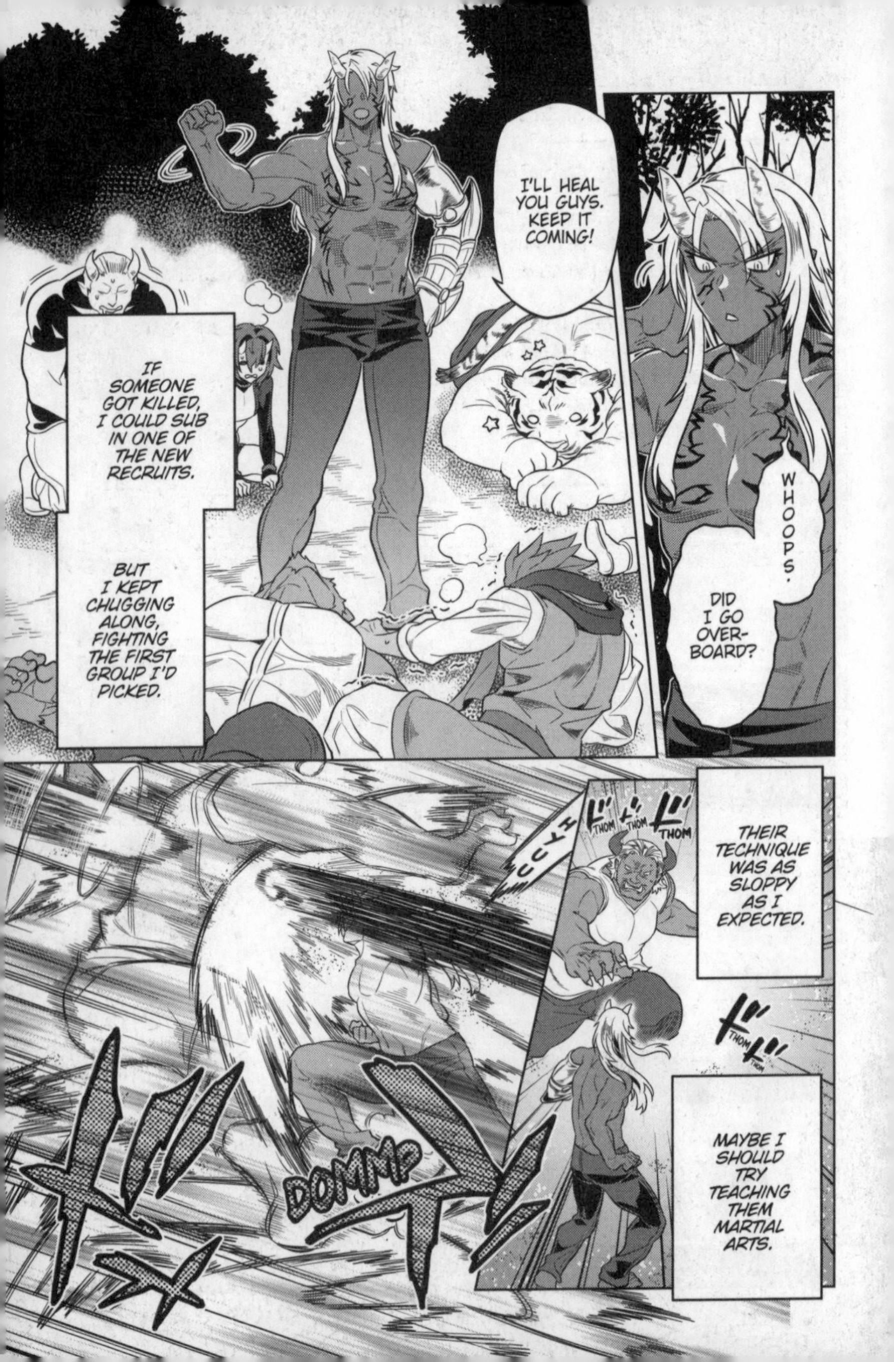
WHOOPS.
DID I GO OVER-BOARD?
I'LL HEAL YOU GUYS. KEEP IT COMING!
IF SOMEONE GOT KILLED, I COULD SUB IN ONE OF THE NEW RECRUITS.
BUT I KEPT CHUGGING ALONG, FIGHTING THE FIRST GROUP I'D PICKED.
THEIR TECHNIQUE WAS AS SLOPPY AS I EXPECTED.
THOM THOM THOM
THOM THOM
MAYBE I SHOULD TRY TEACHING THEM MARTIAL ARTS.
HYUUU
DOMMP

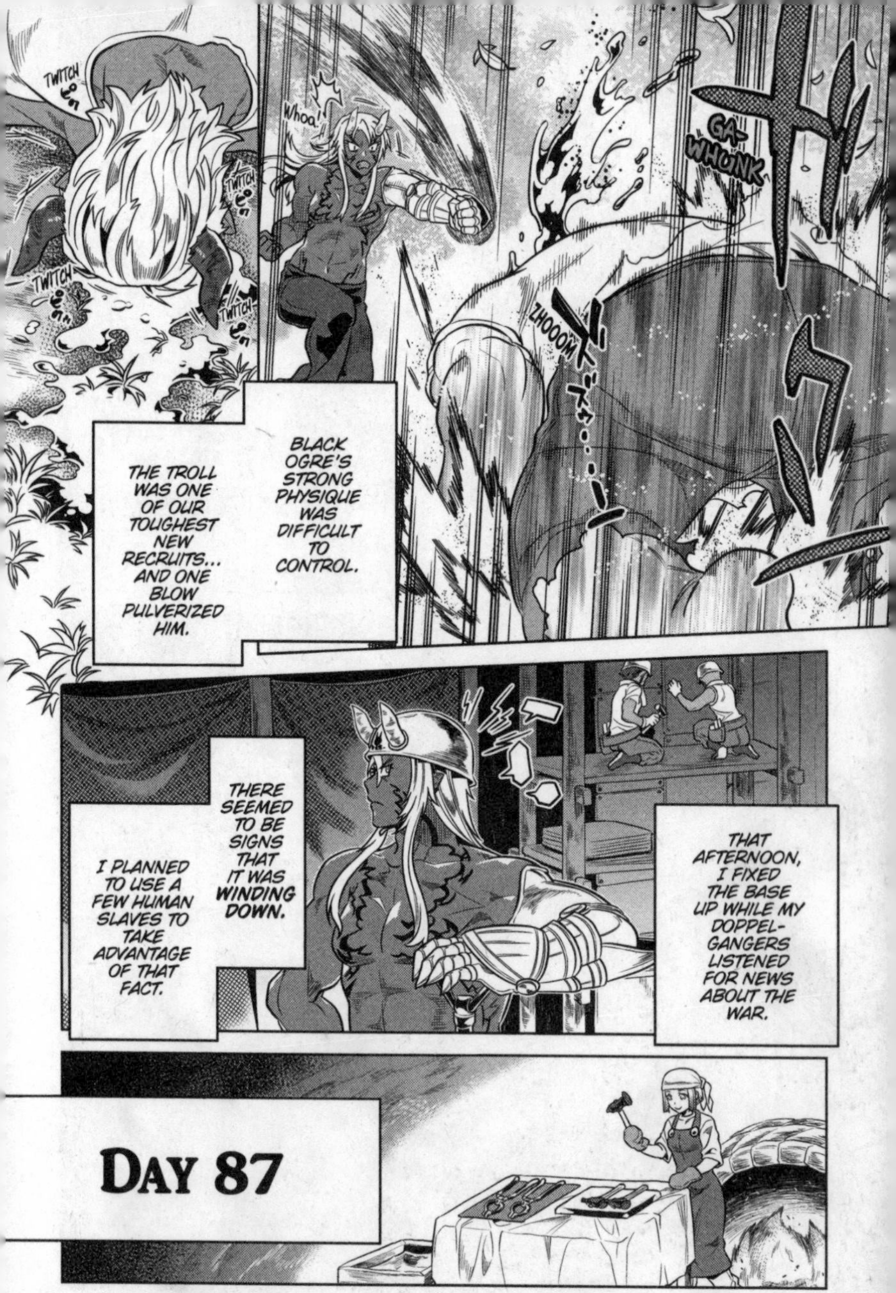
GA-WHUNK
Whoa!
ZHOOOM
BLACK OGRE'S STRONG PHYSIQUE WAS DIFFICULT TO CONTROL.
THE TROLL WAS ONE OF OUR TOUGHEST NEW RECRUITS... AND ONE BLOW PULVERIZED HIM.
TWITCH
TWITCH
TWITCH
TWITCH
THAT AFTERNOON, I FIXED THE BASE UP WHILE MY DOPPEL-GANGERS LISTENED FOR NEWS ABOUT THE WAR.
THERE SEEMED TO BE SIGNS THAT IT WAS WINDING DOWN.
I PLANNED TO USE A FEW HUMAN SLAVES TO TAKE ADVANTAGE OF THAT FACT.
DAY 87

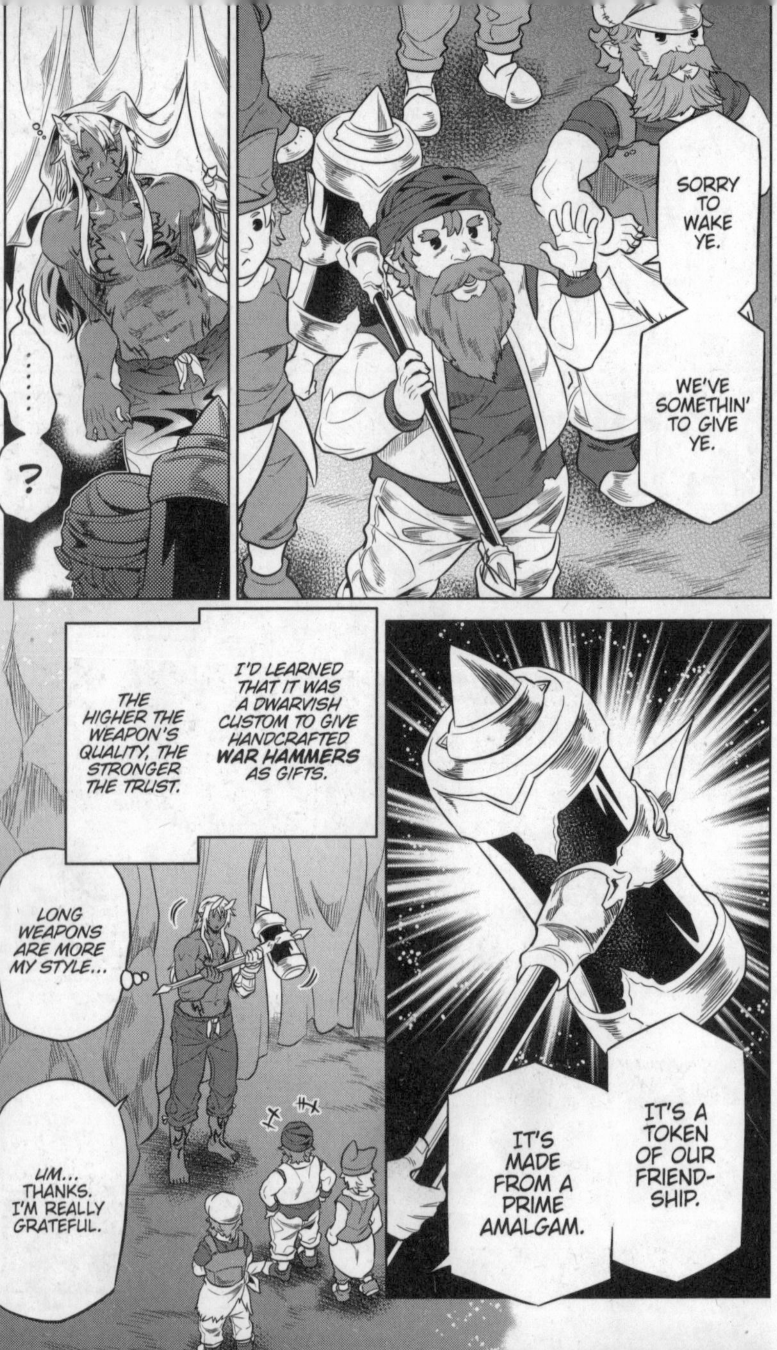
SORRY TO WAKE YE.
WE'VE SOMETHIN' TO GIVE YE.
......
?
IT'S A TOKEN OF OUR FRIEND-SHIP.
IT'S MADE FROM A PRIME AMALGAM.
I'D LEARNED THAT IT WAS A DWARVISH CUSTOM TO GIVE HANDCRAFTED **WAR HAMMERS** AS GIFTS.
THE HIGHER THE WEAPON'S QUALITY, THE STRONGER THE TRUST.
LONG WEAPONS ARE MORE MY STYLE...
UM... THANKS. I'M REALLY GRATEFUL.

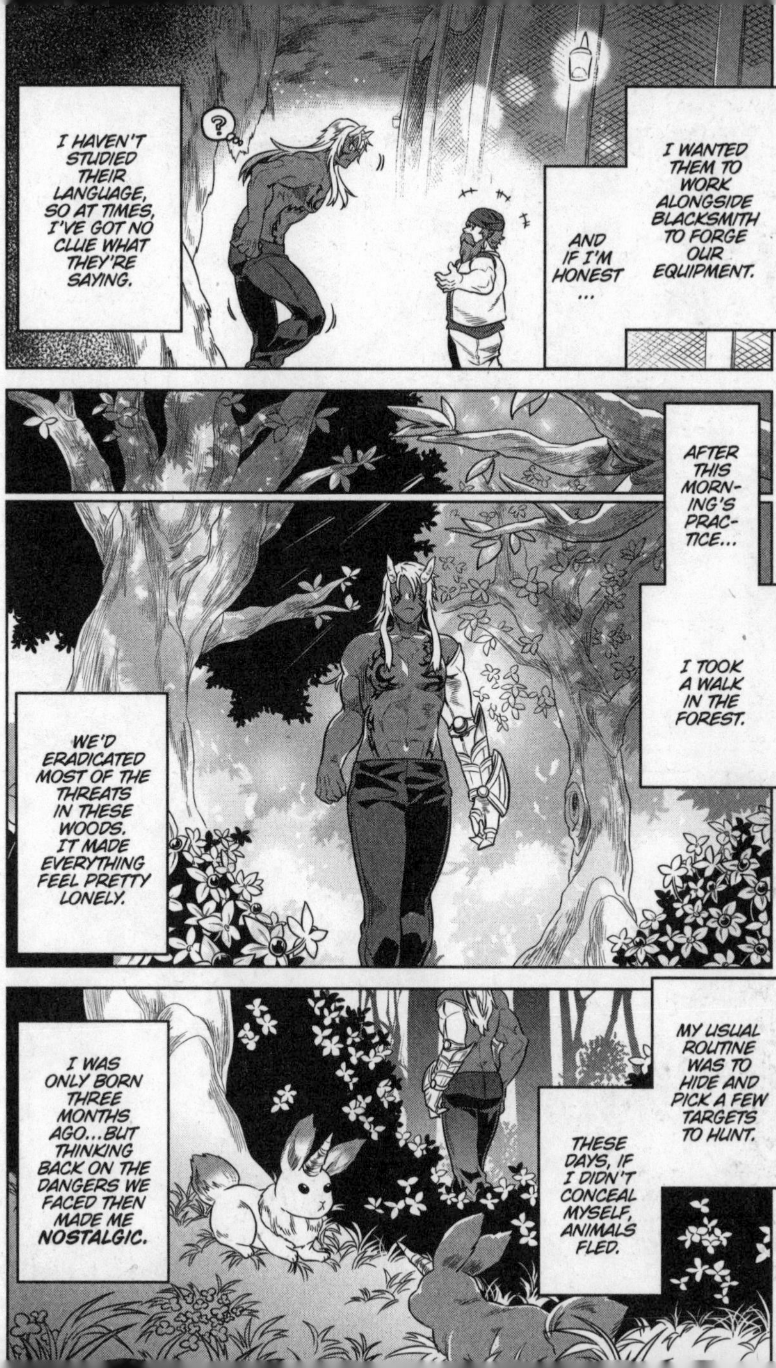
I WANTED THEM TO WORK ALONGSIDE BLACKSMITH TO FORGE OUR EQUIPMENT.
AND IF I'M HONEST ...
I HAVEN'T STUDIED THEIR LANGUAGE, SO AT TIMES, I'VE GOT NO CLUE WHAT THEY'RE SAYING.
?
AFTER THIS MORNING'S PRACTICE...
I TOOK A WALK IN THE FOREST.
WE'D ERADICATED MOST OF THE THREATS IN THESE WOODS. IT MADE EVERYTHING FEEL PRETTY LONELY.
MY USUAL ROUTINE WAS TO HIDE AND PICK A FEW TARGETS TO HUNT.
THESE DAYS, IF I DIDN'T CONCEAL MYSELF, ANIMALS FLED.
I WAS ONLY BORN THREE MONTHS AGO...BUT THINKING BACK ON THE DANGERS WE FACED THEN MADE ME NOSTALGIC.

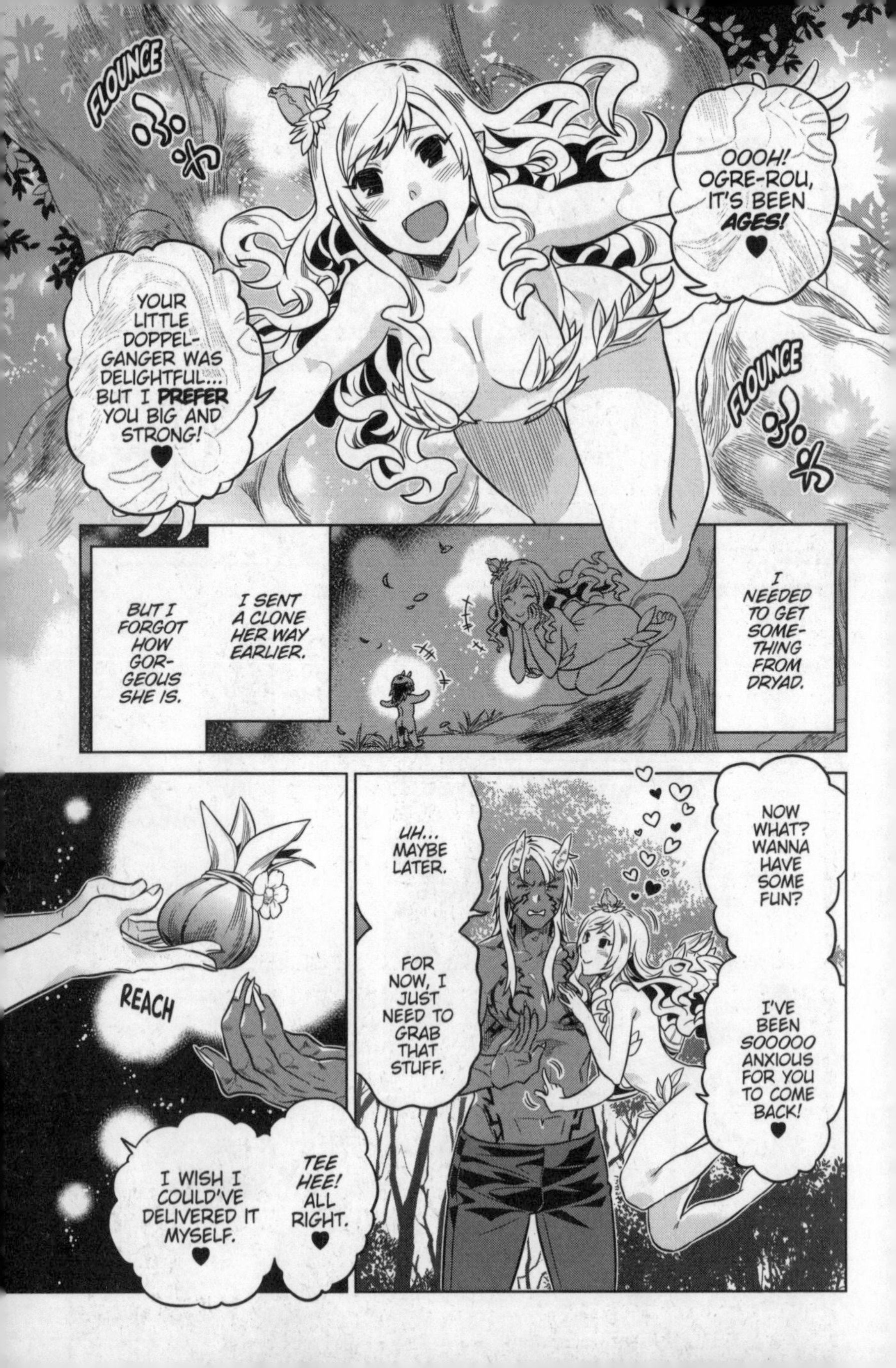
OOOH! OGRE-ROU, IT'S BEEN **AGES!** ♥
FLOUNCE
YOUR LITTLE DOPPEL-GANGER WAS DELIGHTFUL... BUT I **PREFER** YOU BIG AND STRONG! ♥
FLOUNCE
I NEEDED TO GET SOME-THING FROM DRYAD.
I SENT A CLONE HER WAY EARLIER.
BUT I FORGOT HOW GOR-GEOUS SHE IS.
NOW WHAT? WANNA HAVE SOME FUN?
UH... MAYBE LATER.
I'VE BEEN SOOOOO ANXIOUS FOR YOU TO COME BACK! ♥
FOR NOW, I JUST NEED TO GRAB THAT STUFF.
REACH
TEE HEE! ALL RIGHT. ♥
I WISH I COULD'VE DELIVERED IT MYSELF. ♥

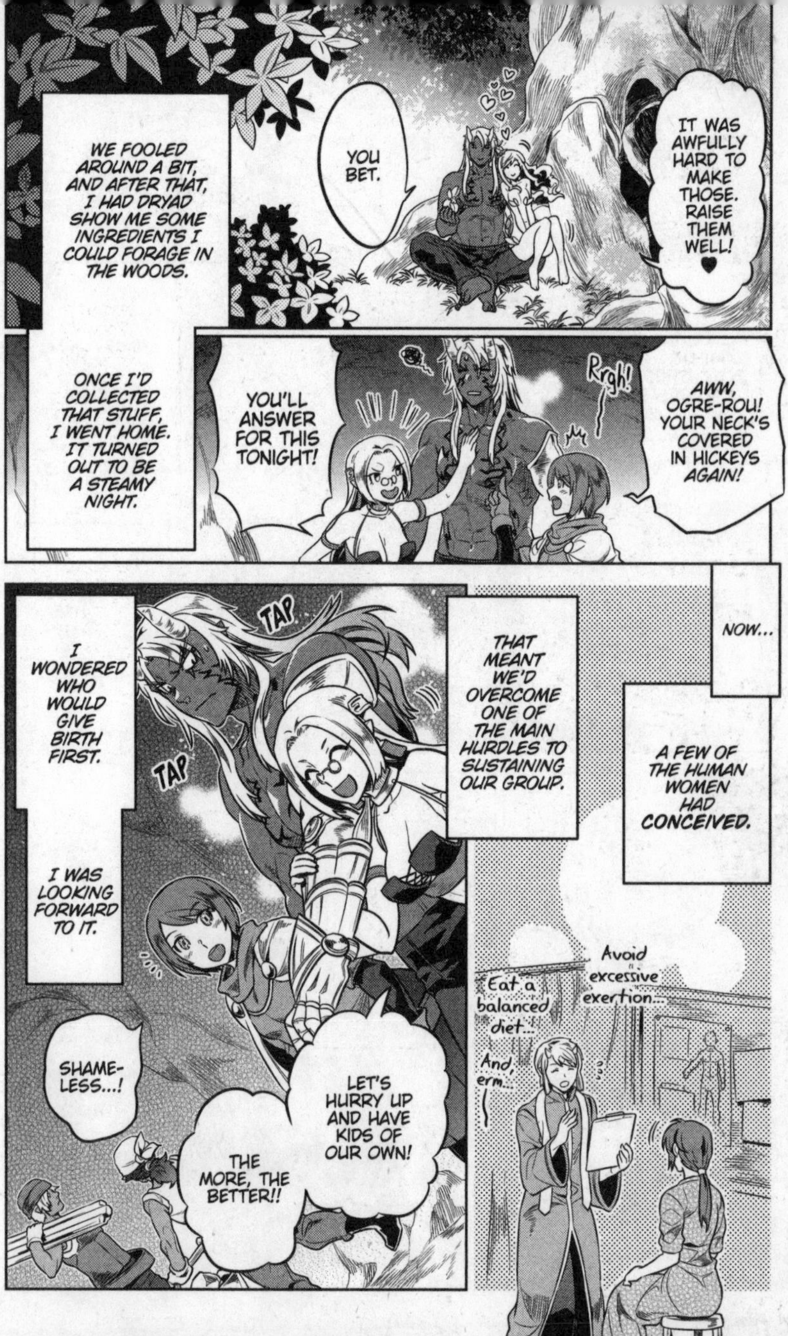
IT WAS AWFULLY HARD TO MAKE THOSE. RAISE THEM WELL! ♥
YOU BET.
WE FOOLED AROUND A BIT, AND AFTER THAT, I HAD DRYAD SHOW ME SOME INGREDIENTS I COULD FORAGE IN THE WOODS.
AWW, OGRE-ROU! YOUR NECK'S COVERED IN HICKEYS AGAIN!
Rrgh!
YOU'LL ANSWER FOR THIS TONIGHT!
ONCE I'D COLLECTED THAT STUFF, I WENT HOME. IT TURNED OUT TO BE A STEAMY NIGHT.
NOW...
A FEW OF THE HUMAN WOMEN HAD CONCEIVED.
Avoid excessive exertion...
Eat a balanced diet...
And, erm...
THAT MEANT WE'D OVERCOME ONE OF THE MAIN HURDLES TO SUSTAINING OUR GROUP.
TAP
I WONDERED WHO WOULD GIVE BIRTH FIRST.
TAP
I WAS LOOKING FORWARD TO IT.
LET'S HURRY UP AND HAVE KIDS OF OUR OWN!
THE MORE, THE BETTER!!
SHAME-LESS...!

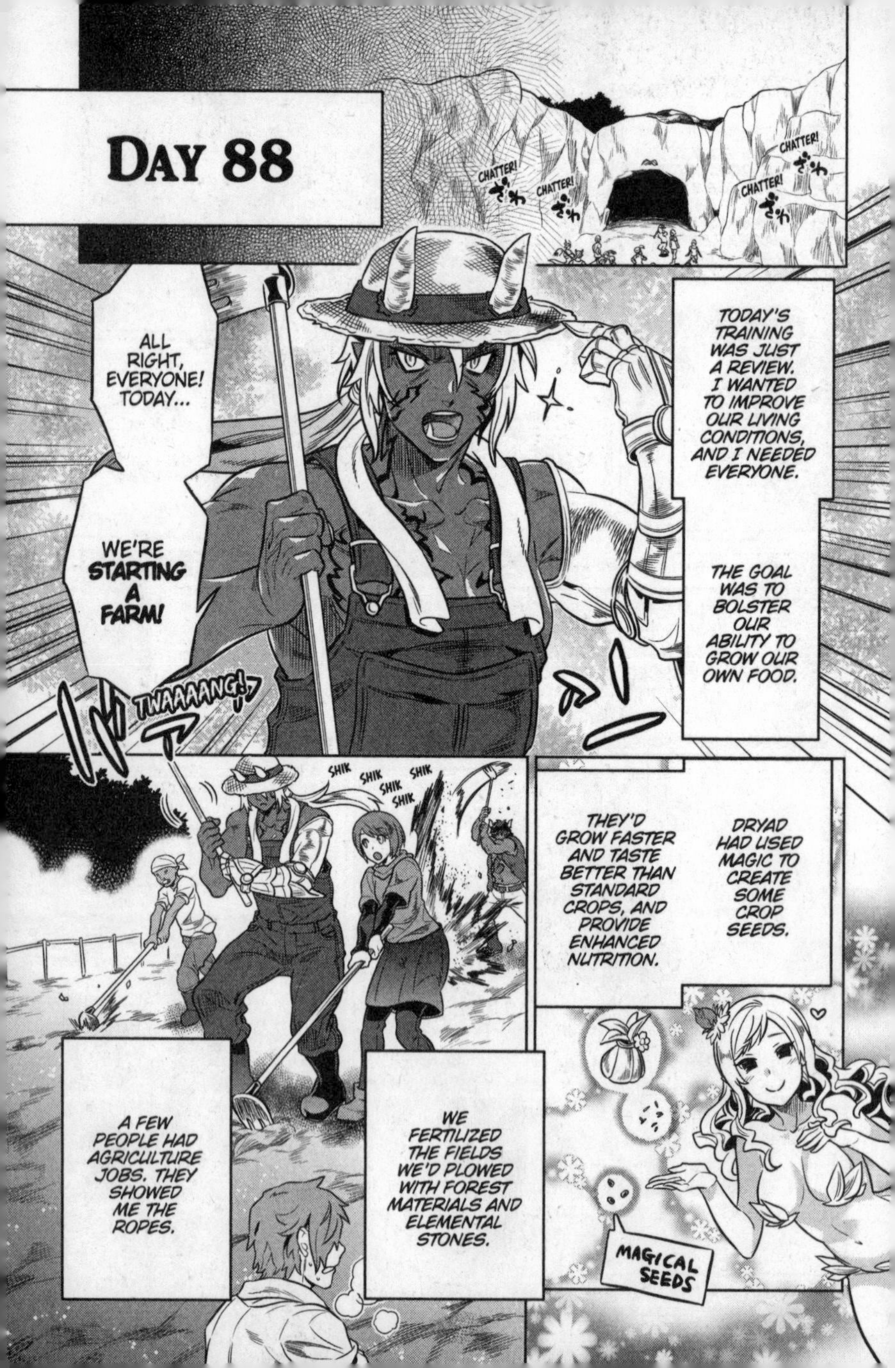
CHATTER!
CHATTER!
CHATTER!
CHATTER!
DAY 88
TODAY'S TRAINING WAS JUST A REVIEW. I WANTED TO IMPROVE OUR LIVING CONDITIONS, AND I NEEDED EVERYONE.
THE GOAL WAS TO BOLSTER OUR ABILITY TO GROW OUR OWN FOOD.
ALL RIGHT, EVERYONE! TODAY...
WE'RE STARTING A FARM!
TWAAAANG!
DRYAD HAD USED MAGIC TO CREATE SOME CROP SEEDS.
THEY'D GROW FASTER AND TASTE BETTER THAN STANDARD CROPS, AND PROVIDE ENHANCED NUTRITION.
MAGICAL SEEDS
SHIK SHIK SHIK SHIK SHIK
WE FERTILIZED THE FIELDS WE'D PLOWED WITH FOREST MATERIALS AND ELEMENTAL STONES.
A FEW PEOPLE HAD AGRICULTURE JOBS. THEY SHOWED ME THE ROPES.

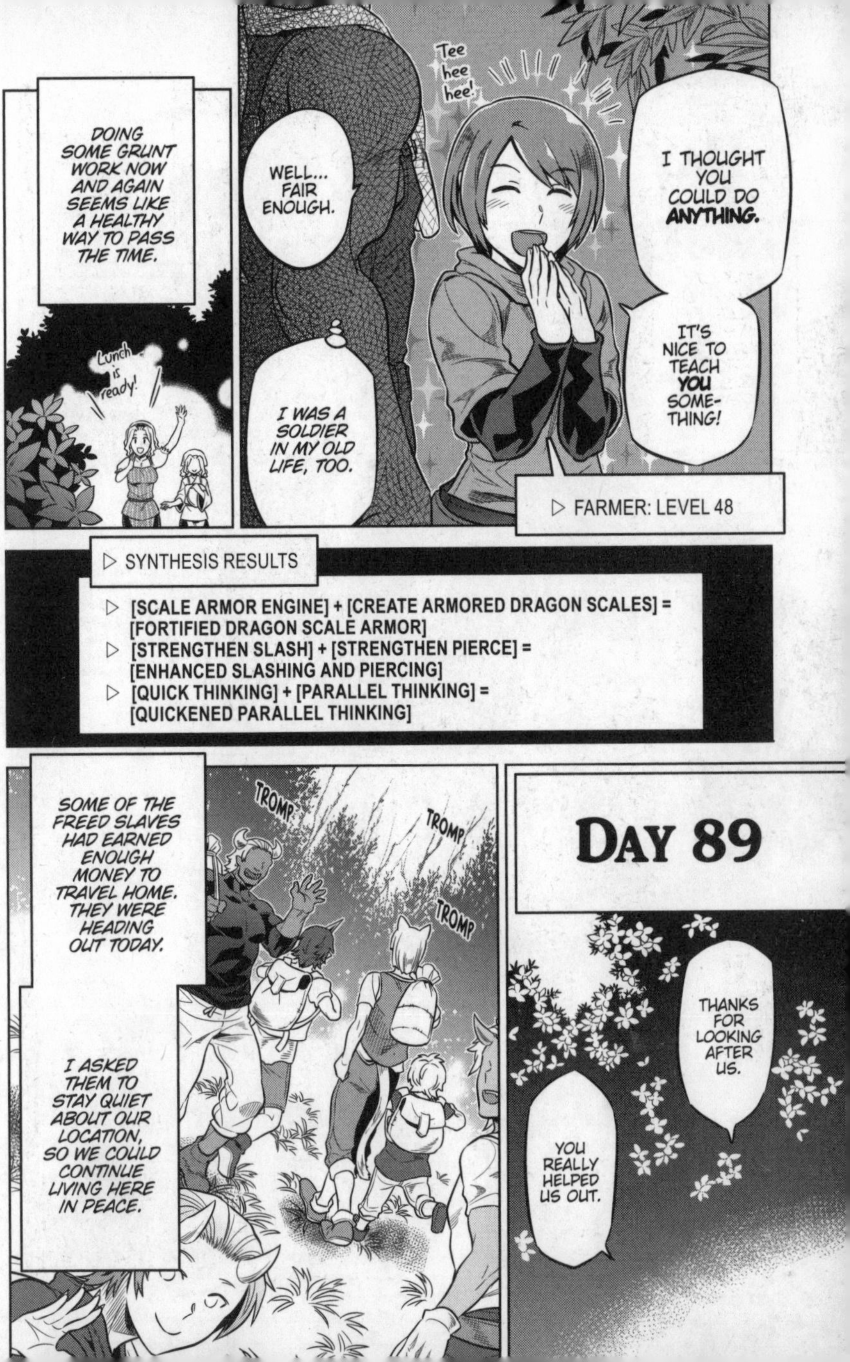
Tee hee hee!
I THOUGHT YOU COULD DO ANYTHING.
IT'S NICE TO TEACH YOU SOMETHING!
▷ FARMER: LEVEL 48
WELL... FAIR ENOUGH.
I WAS A SOLDIER IN MY OLD LIFE, TOO.
DOING SOME GRUNT WORK NOW AND AGAIN SEEMS LIKE A HEALTHY WAY TO PASS THE TIME.
Lunch is ready!
▷ SYNTHESIS RESULTS
▷ [SCALE ARMOR ENGINE] + [CREATE ARMORED DRAGON SCALES] = [FORTIFIED DRAGON SCALE ARMOR]
▷ [STRENGTHEN SLASH] + [STRENGTHEN PIERCE] = [ENHANCED SLASHING AND PIERCING]
▷ [QUICK THINKING] + [PARALLEL THINKING] = [QUICKENED PARALLEL THINKING]
DAY 89
THANKS FOR LOOKING AFTER US.
YOU REALLY HELPED US OUT.
SOME OF THE FREED SLAVES HAD EARNED ENOUGH MONEY TO TRAVEL HOME. THEY WERE HEADING OUT TODAY.
TROMP
TROMP
TROMP
I ASKED THEM TO STAY QUIET ABOUT OUR LOCATION, SO WE COULD CONTINUE LIVING HERE IN PEACE.

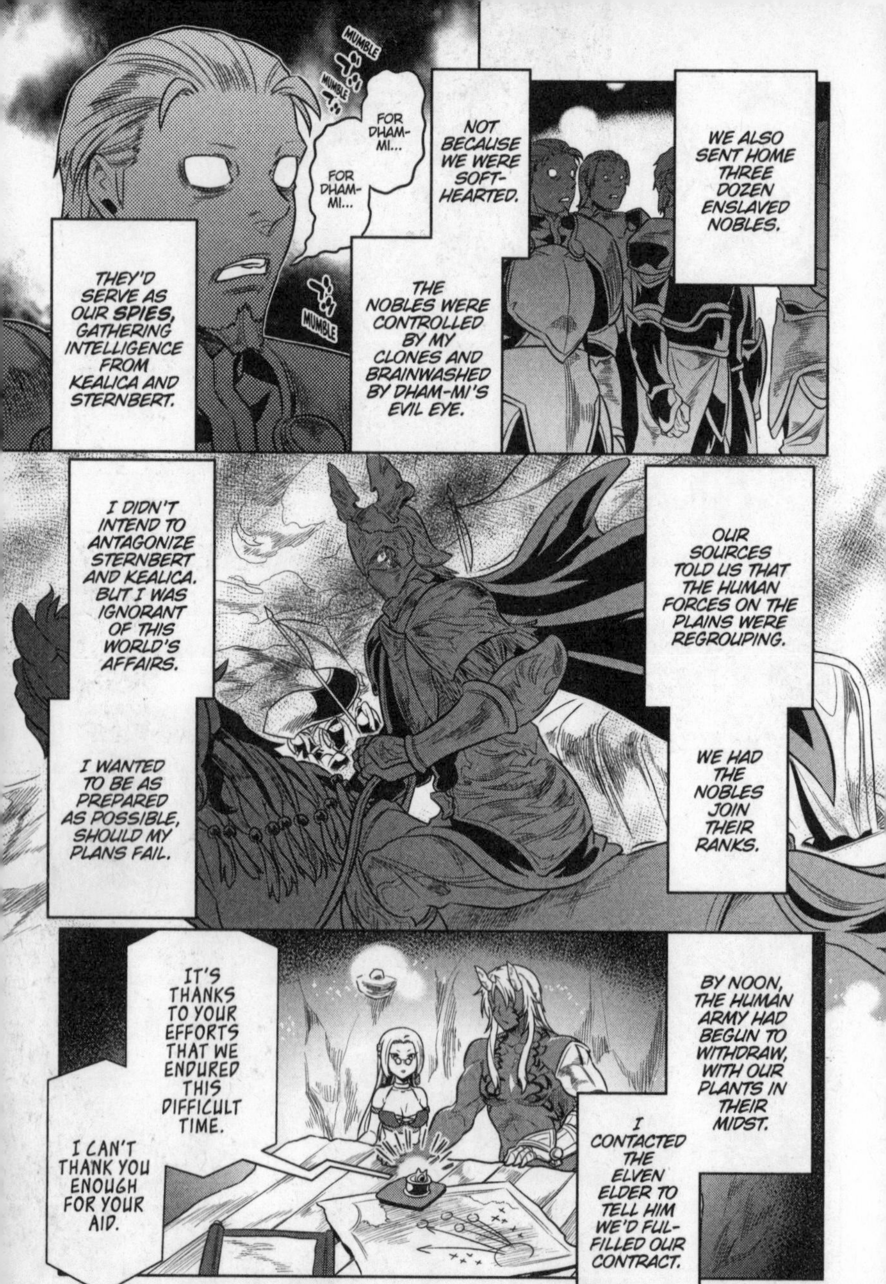
WE ALSO SENT HOME THREE DOZEN ENSLAVED NOBLES.
NOT BECAUSE WE WERE SOFT-HEARTED.
THE NOBLES WERE CONTROLLED BY MY CLONES AND BRAINWASHED BY DHAM-MI'S EVIL EYE.
MUMBLE
MUMBLE
FOR DHAM-MI...
FOR DHAM-MI...
THEY'D SERVE AS OUR SPIES, GATHERING INTELLIGENCE FROM KEALICA AND STERNBERT.
MUMBLE
OUR SOURCES TOLD US THAT THE HUMAN FORCES ON THE PLAINS WERE REGROUPING.
WE HAD THE NOBLES JOIN THEIR RANKS.
I DIDN'T INTEND TO ANTAGONIZE STERNBERT AND KEALICA. BUT I WAS IGNORANT OF THIS WORLD'S AFFAIRS.
I WANTED TO BE AS PREPARED AS POSSIBLE, SHOULD MY PLANS FAIL.
BY NOON, THE HUMAN ARMY HAD BEGUN TO WITHDRAW, WITH OUR PLANTS IN THEIR MIDST.
I CONTACTED THE ELVEN ELDER TO TELL HIM WE'D FUL-FILLED OUR CONTRACT.
IT'S THANKS TO YOUR EFFORTS THAT WE ENDURED THIS DIFFICULT TIME.
I CAN'T THANK YOU ENOUGH FOR YOUR AID.

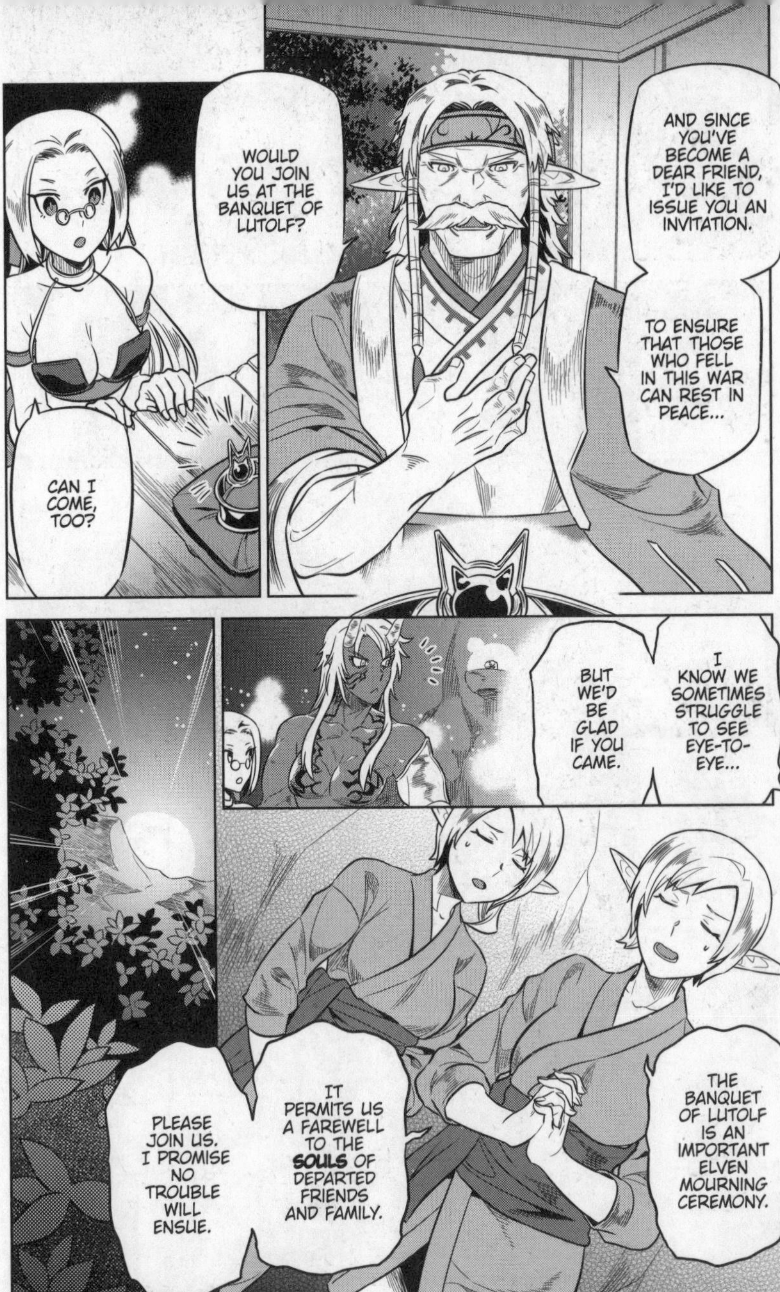
AND SINCE YOU'VE BECOME A DEAR FRIEND, I'D LIKE TO ISSUE YOU AN INVITATION.
TO ENSURE THAT THOSE WHO FELL IN THIS WAR CAN REST IN PEACE...
WOULD YOU JOIN US AT THE BANQUET OF LUTOLF?
CAN I COME, TOO?
I KNOW WE SOMETIMES STRUGGLE TO SEE EYE-TO-EYE...
BUT WE'D BE GLAD IF YOU CAME.
THE BANQUET OF LUTOLF IS AN IMPORTANT ELVEN MOURNING CEREMONY.
IT PERMITS US A FAREWELL TO THE **SOULS** OF DEPARTED FRIENDS AND FAMILY.
PLEASE JOIN US. I PROMISE NO TROUBLE WILL ENSUE.

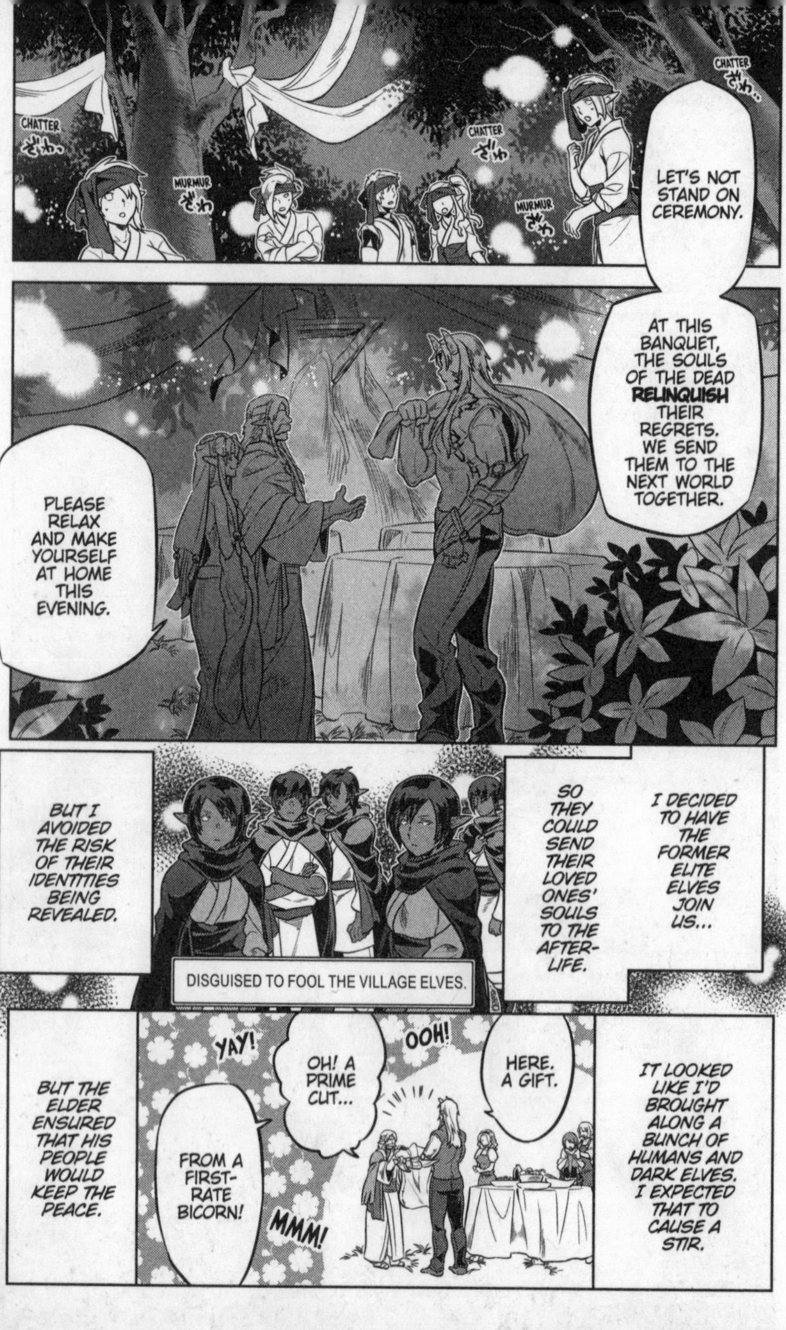
CHATTER ざわ..
LET'S NOT STAND ON CEREMONY.
CHATTER ざわ
MURMUR ざわ
MURMUR ざわ
CHATTER ざわ
AT THIS BANQUET, THE SOULS OF THE DEAD RELINQUISH THEIR REGRETS. WE SEND THEM TO THE NEXT WORLD TOGETHER.
PLEASE RELAX AND MAKE YOURSELF AT HOME THIS EVENING.
I DECIDED TO HAVE THE FORMER ELITE ELVES JOIN US...
SO THEY COULD SEND THEIR LOVED ONES' SOULS TO THE AFTER-LIFE.
DISGUISED TO FOOL THE VILLAGE ELVES.
BUT I AVOIDED THE RISK OF THEIR IDENTITIES BEING REVEALED.
IT LOOKED LIKE I'D BROUGHT ALONG A BUNCH OF HUMANS AND DARK ELVES. I EXPECTED THAT TO CAUSE A STIR.
HERE. A GIFT.
OOH!
OH! A PRIME CUT...
YAY!
FROM A FIRST-RATE BICORN!
MMM!
BUT THE ELDER ENSURED THAT HIS PEOPLE WOULD KEEP THE PEACE.

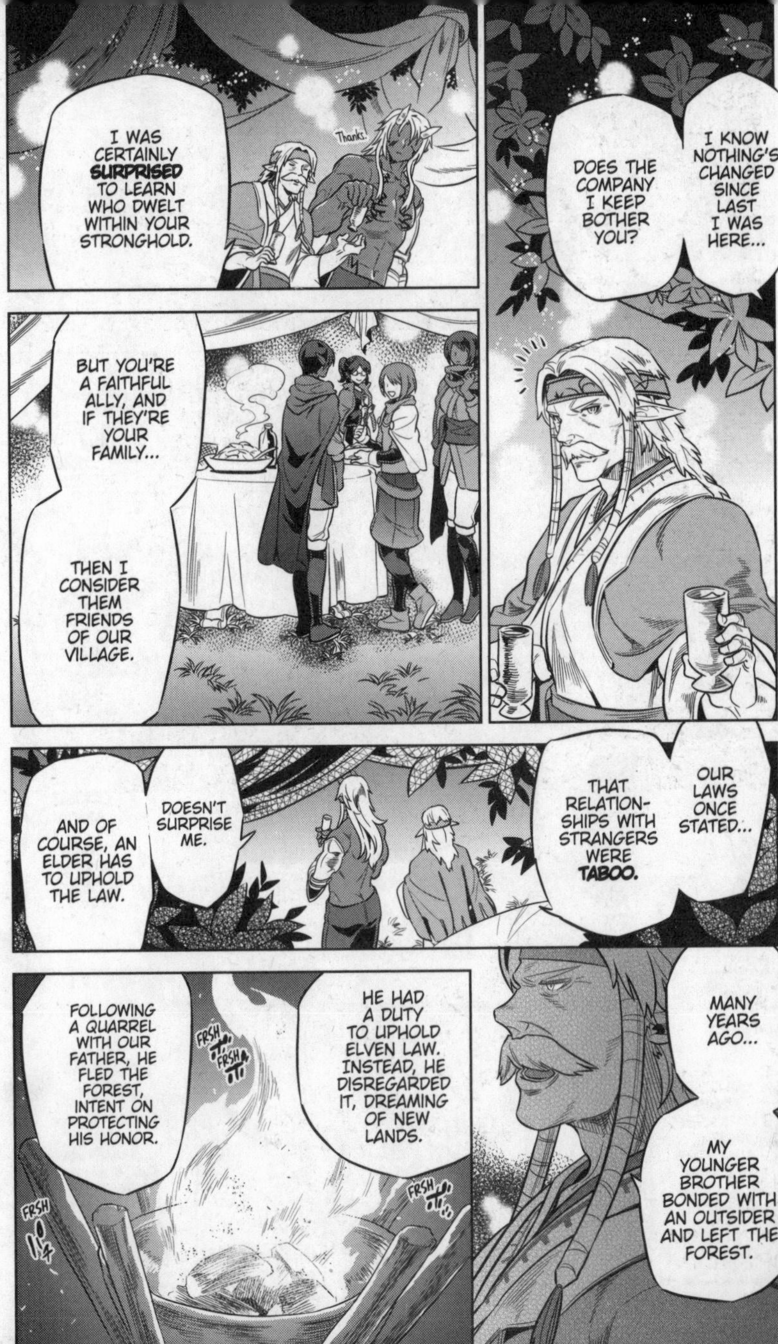
I KNOW NOTHING'S CHANGED SINCE LAST I WAS HERE...
DOES THE COMPANY I KEEP BOTHER YOU?
Thanks.
I WAS CERTAINLY **SURPRISED** TO LEARN WHO DWELT WITHIN YOUR STRONGHOLD.
BUT YOU'RE A FAITHFUL ALLY, AND IF THEY'RE YOUR FAMILY...
THEN I CONSIDER THEM FRIENDS OF OUR VILLAGE.
OUR LAWS ONCE STATED...
THAT RELATIONSHIPS WITH STRANGERS WERE **TABOO.**
DOESN'T SURPRISE ME.
AND OF COURSE, AN ELDER HAS TO UPHOLD THE LAW.
MANY YEARS AGO...
MY YOUNGER BROTHER BONDED WITH AN OUTSIDER AND LEFT THE FOREST.
HE HAD A DUTY TO UPHOLD ELVEN LAW. INSTEAD, HE DISREGARDED IT, DREAMING OF NEW LANDS.
FRSH
FOLLOWING A QUARREL WITH OUR FATHER, HE FLED THE FOREST, INTENT ON PROTECTING HIS HONOR.
FRSH
FRSH
FRSH

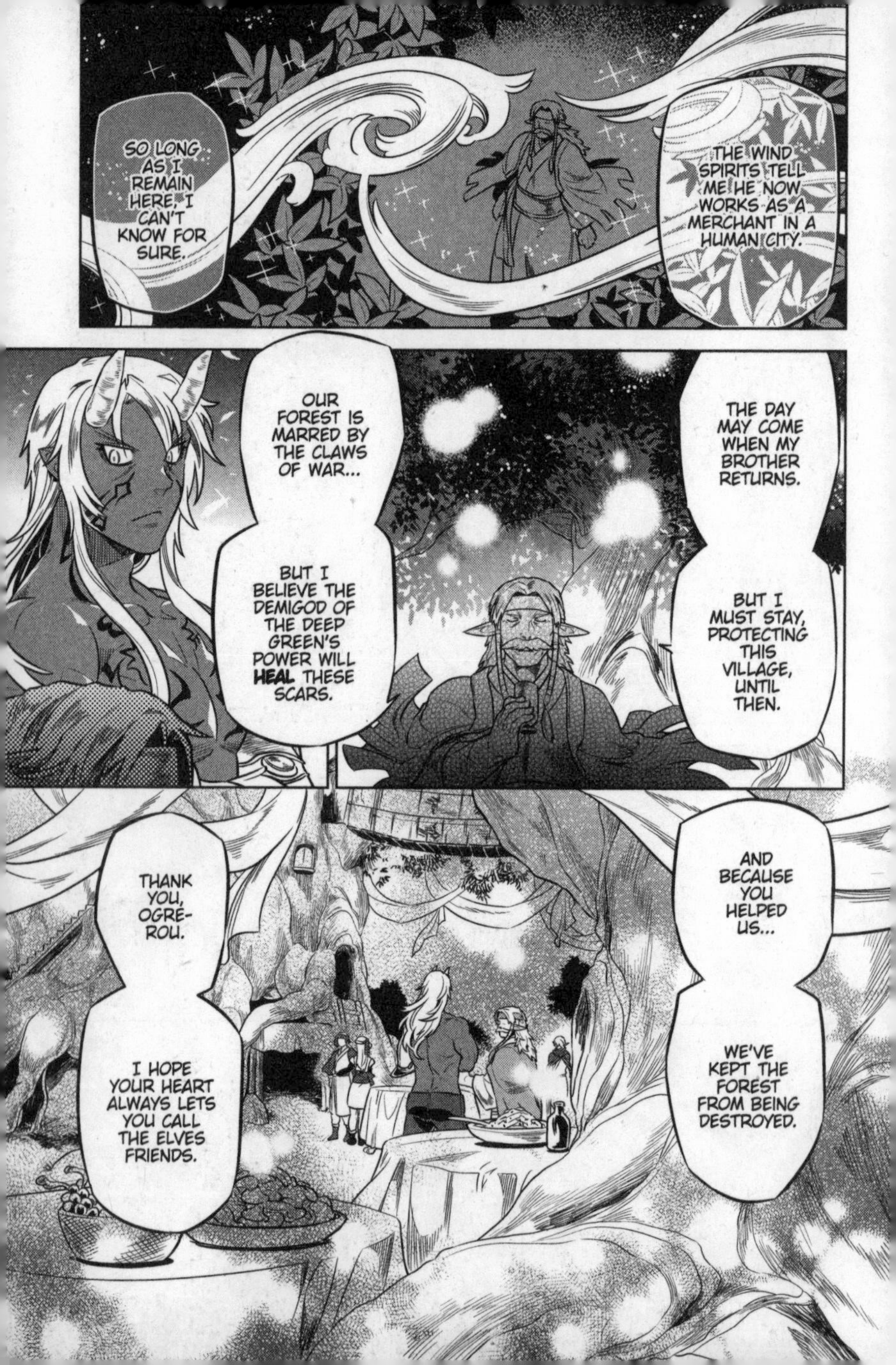
THE WIND SPIRITS TELL ME HE NOW WORKS AS A MERCHANT IN A HUMAN CITY.
SO LONG AS I REMAIN HERE, I CAN'T KNOW FOR SURE.
THE DAY MAY COME WHEN MY BROTHER RETURNS.
BUT I MUST STAY, PROTECTING THIS VILLAGE, UNTIL THEN.
OUR FOREST IS MARRED BY THE CLAWS OF WAR...
BUT I BELIEVE THE DEMIGOD OF THE DEEP GREEN'S POWER WILL **HEAL** THESE SCARS.
AND BECAUSE YOU HELPED US...
WE'VE KEPT THE FOREST FROM BEING DESTROYED.
THANK YOU, OGRE-ROU.
I HOPE YOUR HEART ALWAYS LETS YOU CALL THE ELVES FRIENDS.

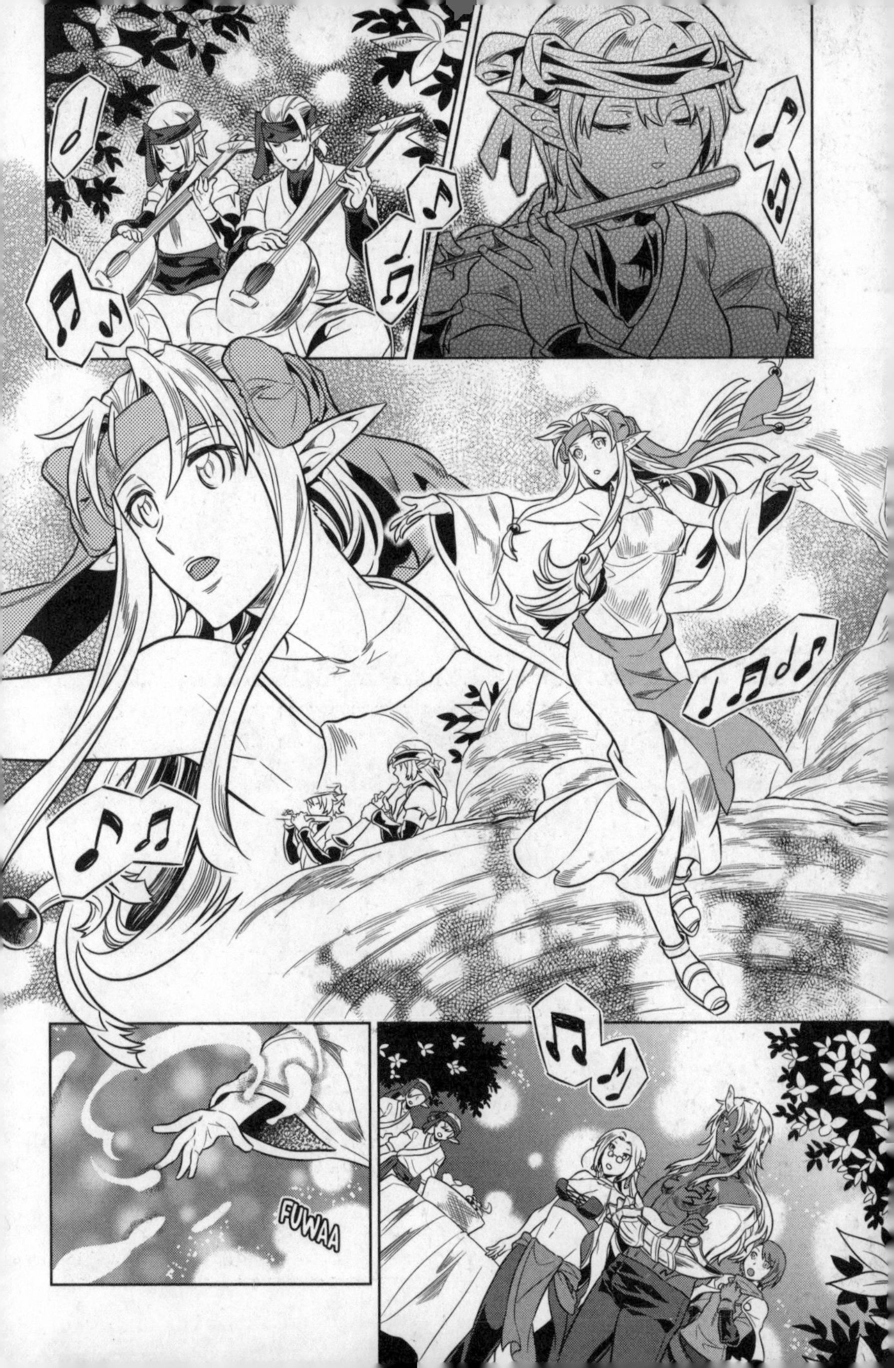
FUWAA

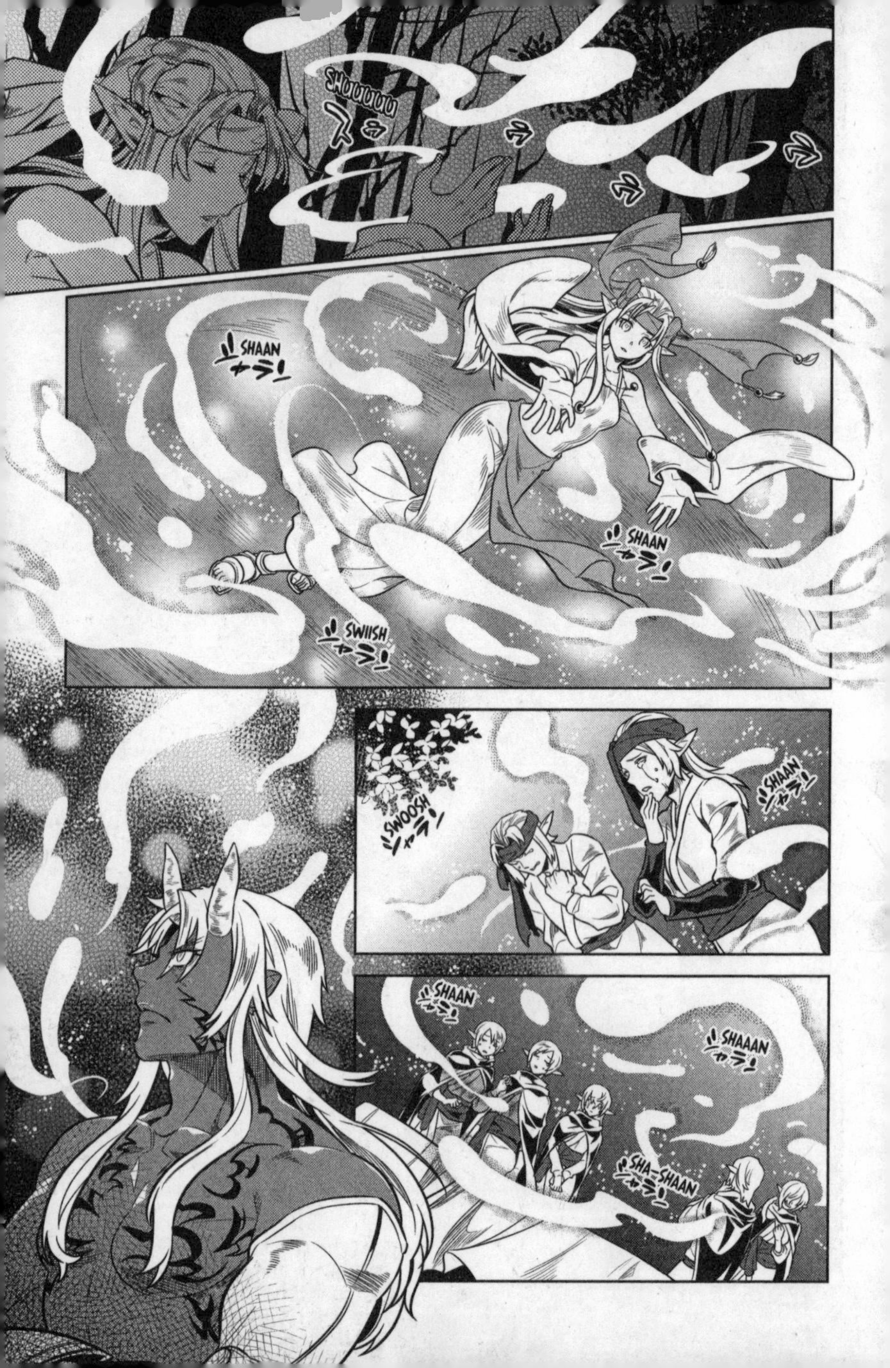

SHOOOOOO
SHAAN
SHAAN
SWIISH
SHAAN
SWOOSH
SHAAAN
SHAAN
SHA-SHAAN

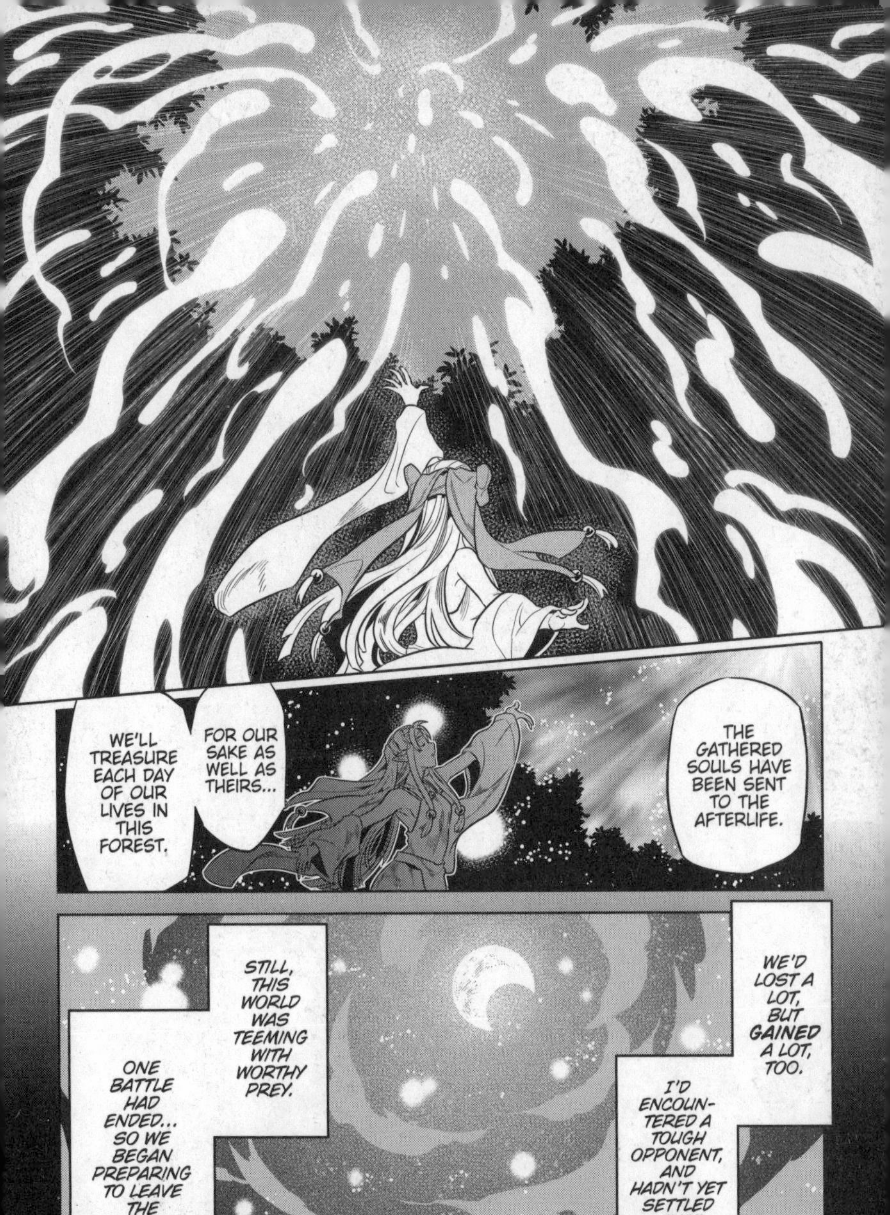
THE GATHERED SOULS HAVE BEEN SENT TO THE AFTERLIFE.
FOR OUR SAKE AS WELL AS THEIRS...
WE'LL TREASURE EACH DAY OF OUR LIVES IN THIS FOREST.
WE'D LOST A LOT, BUT GAINED A LOT, TOO.
I'D ENCOUN-TERED A TOUGH OPPONENT, AND HADN'T YET SETTLED THAT SCORE.
STILL, THIS WORLD WAS TEEMING WITH WORTHY PREY.
ONE BATTLE HAD ENDED... SO WE BEGAN PREPARING TO LEAVE THE FOREST.

▷ CONTINUE

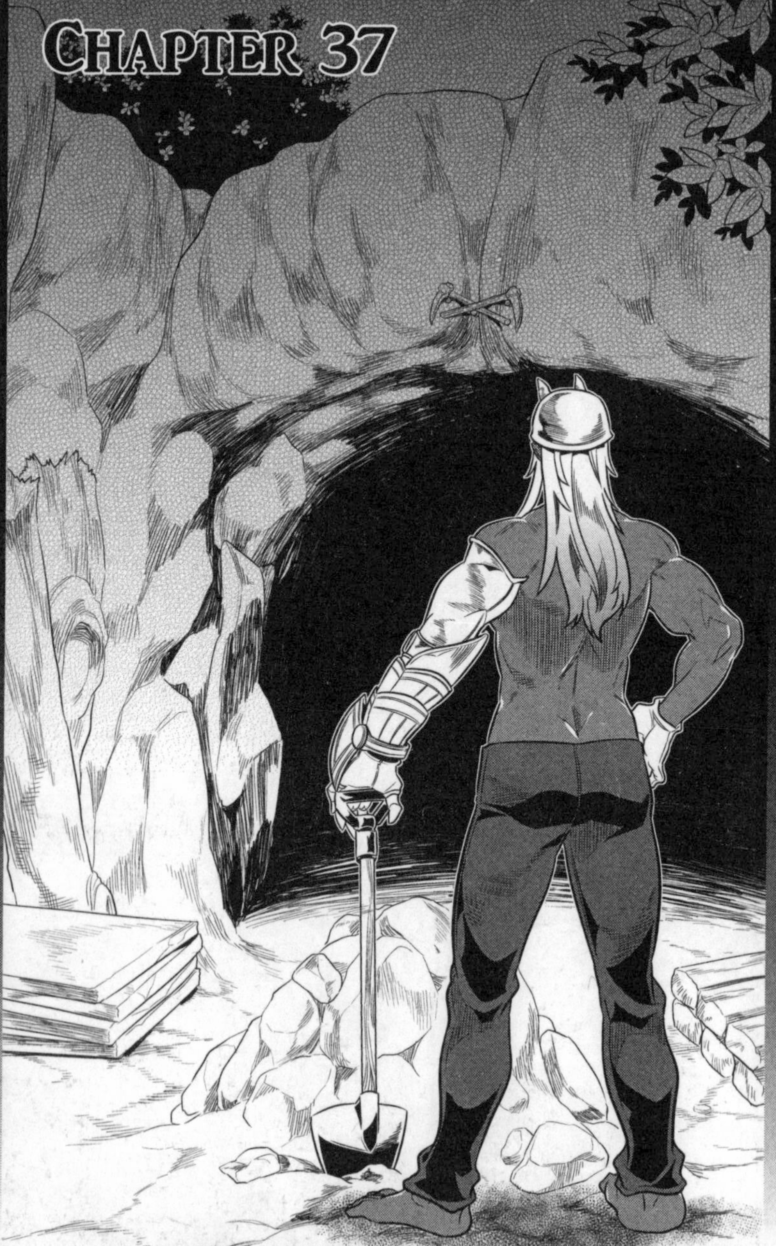
CHAPTER 37

DAY 90

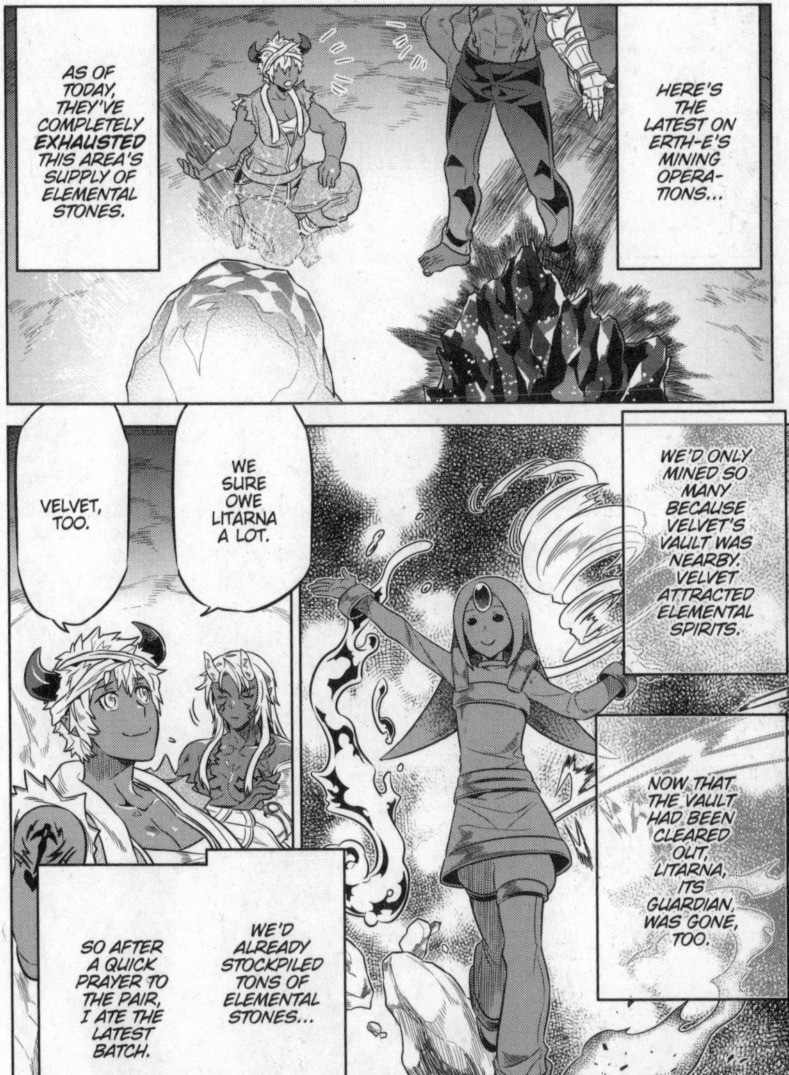
HERE'S THE LATEST ON ERTH-E'S MINING OPERATIONS...
AS OF TODAY, THEY'VE COMPLETELY **EXHAUSTED** THIS AREA'S SUPPLY OF ELEMENTAL STONES.
WE'D ONLY MINED SO MANY BECAUSE VELVET'S VAULT WAS NEARBY. VELVET ATTRACTED ELEMENTAL SPIRITS.
NOW THAT THE VAULT HAD BEEN CLEARED OUT, LITARNA, ITS GUARDIAN, WAS GONE, TOO.
WE SURE OWE LITARNA A LOT.
VELVET, TOO.
WE'D ALREADY STOCKPILED TONS OF ELEMENTAL STONES...
SO AFTER A QUICK PRAYER TO THE PAIR, I ATE THE LATEST BATCH.

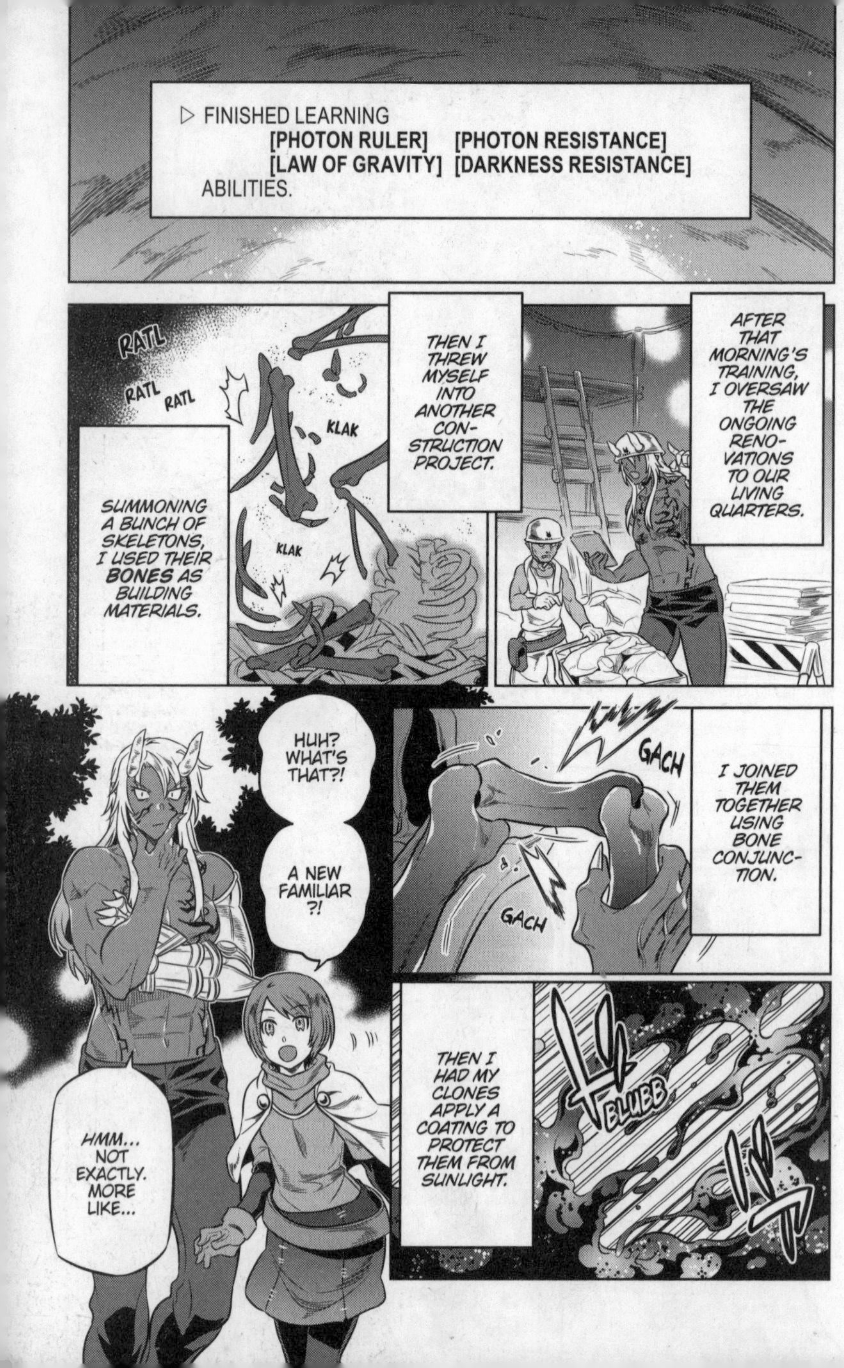
▷ FINISHED LEARNING
[PHOTON RULER] [PHOTON RESISTANCE]
[LAW OF GRAVITY] [DARKNESS RESISTANCE]
ABILITIES.
AFTER THAT MORNING'S TRAINING, I OVERSAW THE ONGOING RENOVATIONS TO OUR LIVING QUARTERS.
THEN I THREW MYSELF INTO ANOTHER CON-STRUCTION PROJECT.
RATL
RATL
RATL
KLAK
KLAK
SUMMONING A BUNCH OF SKELETONS, I USED THEIR **BONES** AS BUILDING MATERIALS.
GACH
I JOINED THEM TOGETHER USING BONE CONJUNC-TION.
GACH
BLUBB
THEN I HAD MY CLONES APPLY A COATING TO PROTECT THEM FROM SUNLIGHT.
HUH? WHAT'S THAT?!
A NEW FAMILIAR?!
HMM... NOT EXACTLY. MORE LIKE...

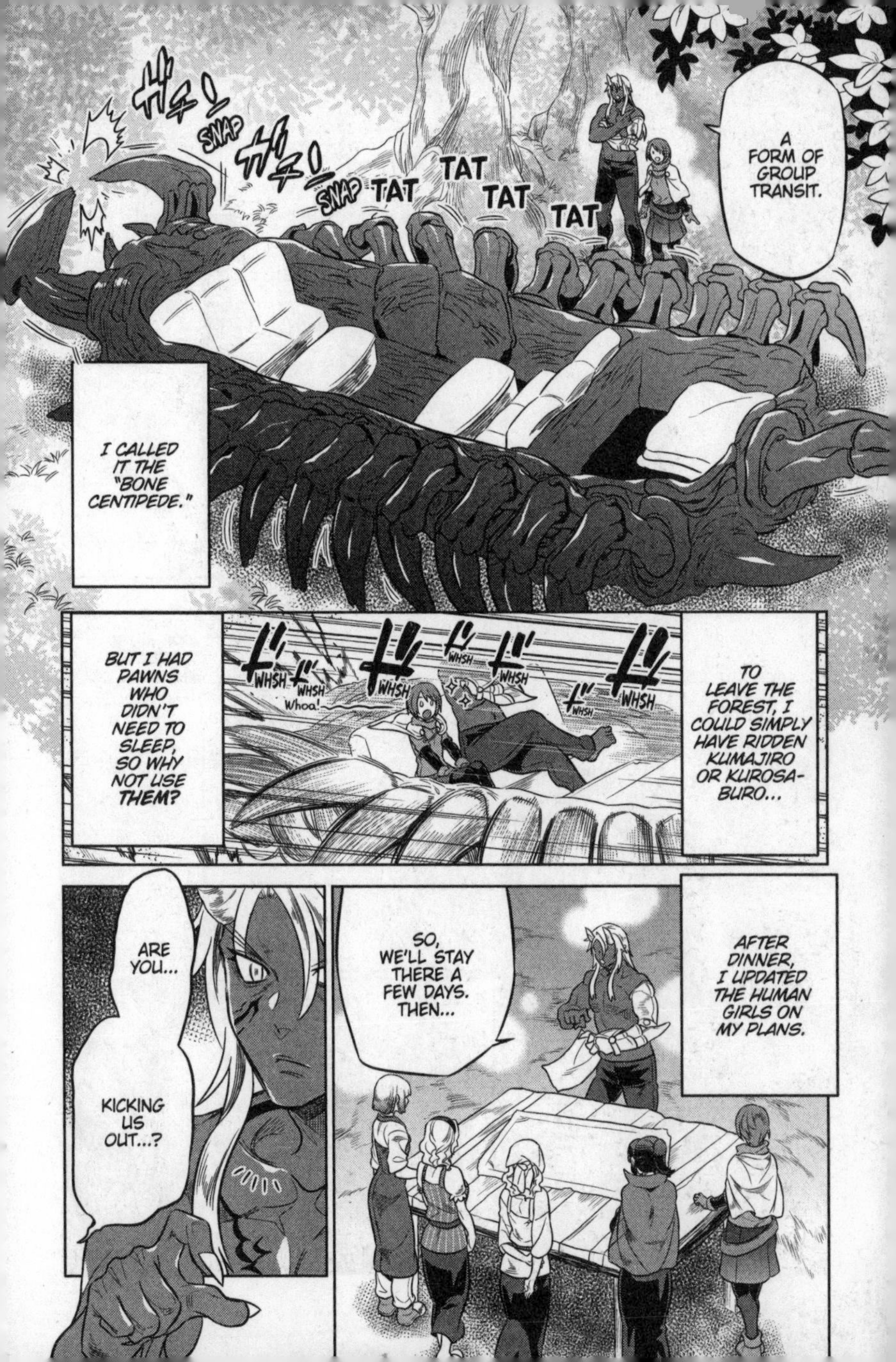
A FORM OF GROUP TRANSIT.
SNAP
SNAP
TAT TAT TAT TAT
I CALLED IT THE "BONE CENTIPEDE."
TO LEAVE THE FOREST, I COULD SIMPLY HAVE RIDDEN KUMAJIRO OR KUROSA-BURO...
WHSH WHSH WHSH WHSH WHSH WHSH WHSH
Whoa!
BUT I HAD PAWNS WHO DIDN'T NEED TO SLEEP, SO WHY NOT USE THEM?
AFTER DINNER, I UPDATED THE HUMAN GIRLS ON MY PLANS.
SO, WE'LL STAY THERE A FEW DAYS. THEN...
ARE YOU...
KICKING US OUT...?

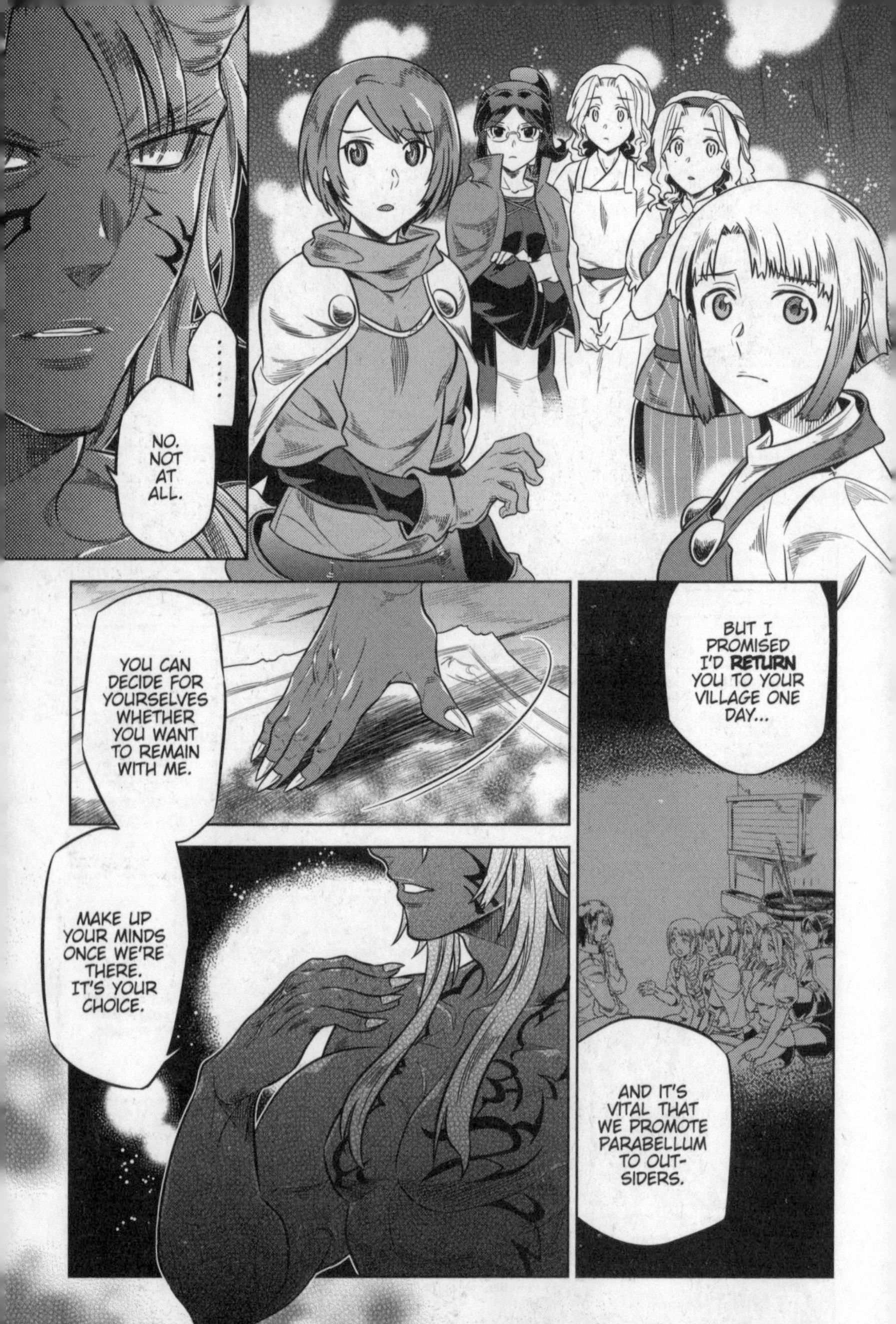
......
NO. NOT AT ALL.
BUT I PROMISED I'D **RETURN** YOU TO YOUR VILLAGE ONE DAY...
AND IT'S VITAL THAT WE PROMOTE PARABELLUM TO OUT-SIDERS.
YOU CAN DECIDE FOR YOURSELVES WHETHER YOU WANT TO REMAIN WITH ME.
MAKE UP YOUR MINDS ONCE WE'RE THERE. IT'S YOUR CHOICE.

DAY 91

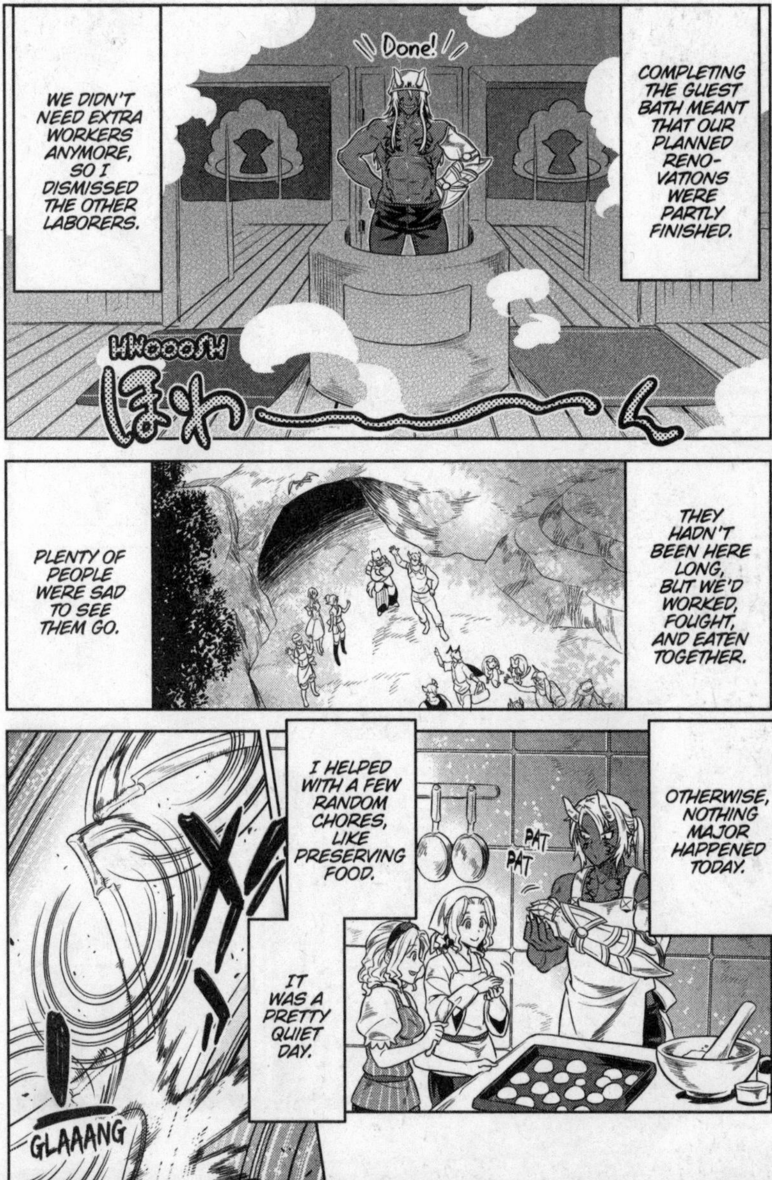
COMPLETING THE GUEST BATH MEANT THAT OUR PLANNED RENO-VATIONS WERE PARTLY FINISHED.
Done!
WE DIDN'T NEED EXTRA WORKERS ANYMORE, SO I DISMISSED THE OTHER LABORERS.
HWOOOSH
ほわ〜〜〜ん
THEY HADN'T BEEN HERE LONG, BUT WE'D WORKED, FOUGHT, AND EATEN TOGETHER.
PLENTY OF PEOPLE WERE SAD TO SEE THEM GO.
OTHERWISE, NOTHING MAJOR HAPPENED TODAY.
PAT PAT
I HELPED WITH A FEW RANDOM CHORES, LIKE PRESERVING FOOD.
IT WAS A PRETTY QUIET DAY.
GLAAANG

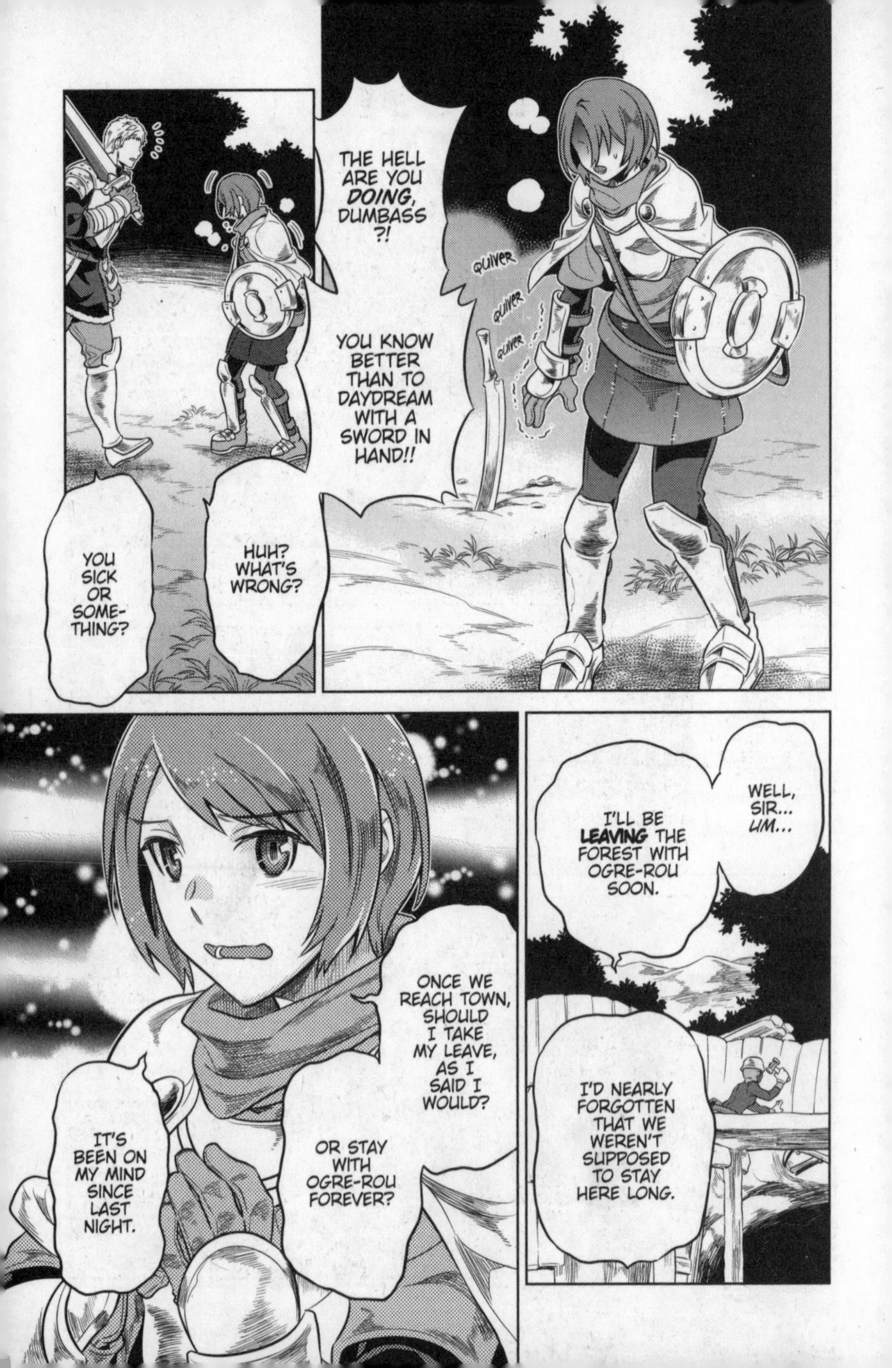
QUIVER
QUIVER
QUIVER
THE HELL ARE YOU DOING, DUMBASS?!
YOU KNOW BETTER THAN TO DAYDREAM WITH A SWORD IN HAND!!
HUH? WHAT'S WRONG?
YOU SICK OR SOME-THING?
WELL, SIR... UM...
I'LL BE LEAVING THE FOREST WITH OGRE-ROU SOON.
I'D NEARLY FORGOTTEN THAT WE WEREN'T SUPPOSED TO STAY HERE LONG.
ONCE WE REACH TOWN, SHOULD I TAKE MY LEAVE, AS I SAID I WOULD?
OR STAY WITH OGRE-ROU FOREVER?
IT'S BEEN ON MY MIND SINCE LAST NIGHT.

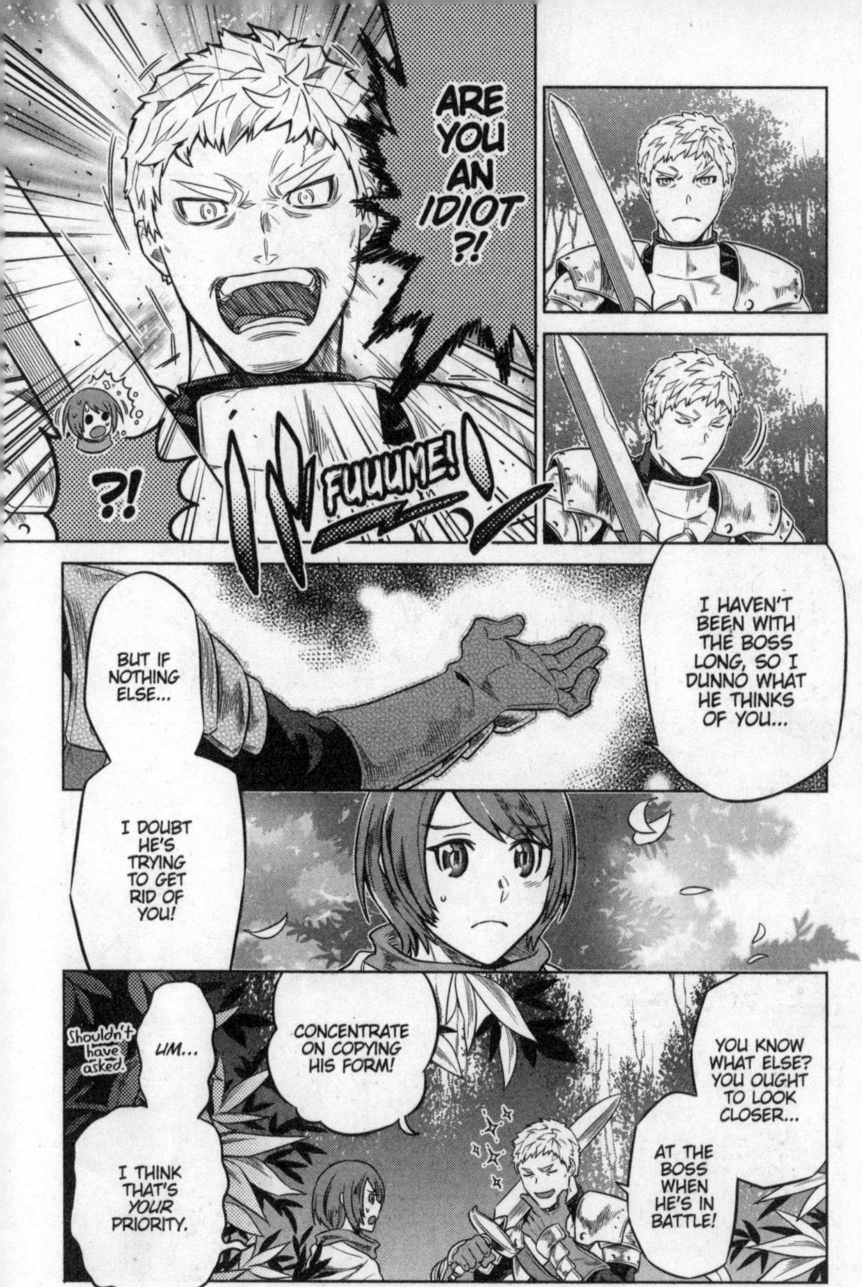
ARE YOU AN IDIOT ?!
FUUUME!
?!
I HAVEN'T BEEN WITH THE BOSS LONG, SO I DUNNO WHAT HE THINKS OF YOU...
BUT IF NOTHING ELSE...
I DOUBT HE'S TRYING TO GET RID OF YOU!
YOU KNOW WHAT ELSE? YOU OUGHT TO LOOK CLOSER...
AT THE BOSS WHEN HE'S IN BATTLE!
CONCENTRATE ON COPYING HIS FORM!
UM...
Shouldn't have asked.
I THINK THAT'S YOUR PRIORITY.

DAY 92

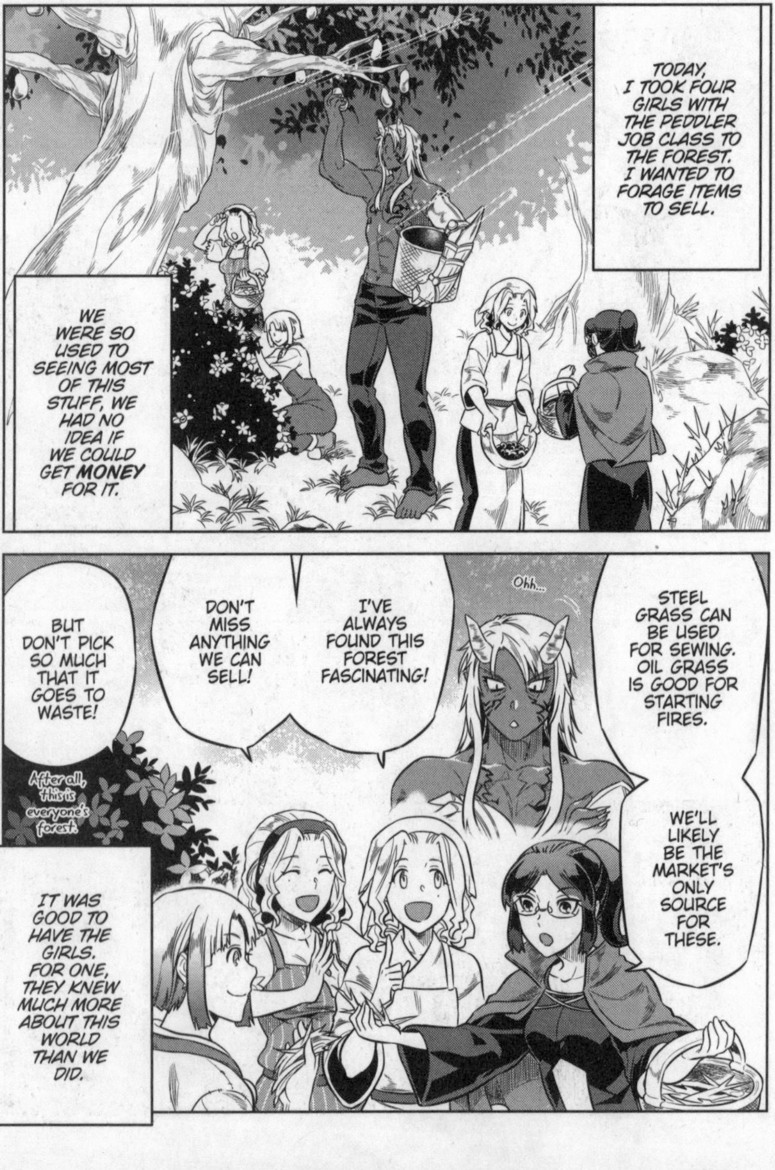
TODAY, I TOOK FOUR GIRLS WITH THE PEDDLER JOB CLASS TO THE FOREST. I WANTED TO FORAGE ITEMS TO SELL.
WE WERE SO USED TO SEEING MOST OF THIS STUFF, WE HAD NO IDEA IF WE COULD GET **MONEY** FOR IT.
STEEL GRASS CAN BE USED FOR SEWING. OIL GRASS IS GOOD FOR STARTING FIRES.
Ohh...
I'VE ALWAYS FOUND THIS FOREST FASCINATING!
DON'T MISS ANYTHING WE CAN SELL!
BUT DON'T PICK SO MUCH THAT IT GOES TO WASTE!
After all, this is everyone's forest.
WE'LL LIKELY BE THE MARKET'S ONLY SOURCE FOR THESE.
IT WAS GOOD TO HAVE THE GIRLS. FOR ONE, THEY KNEW MUCH MORE ABOUT THIS WORLD THAN WE DID.

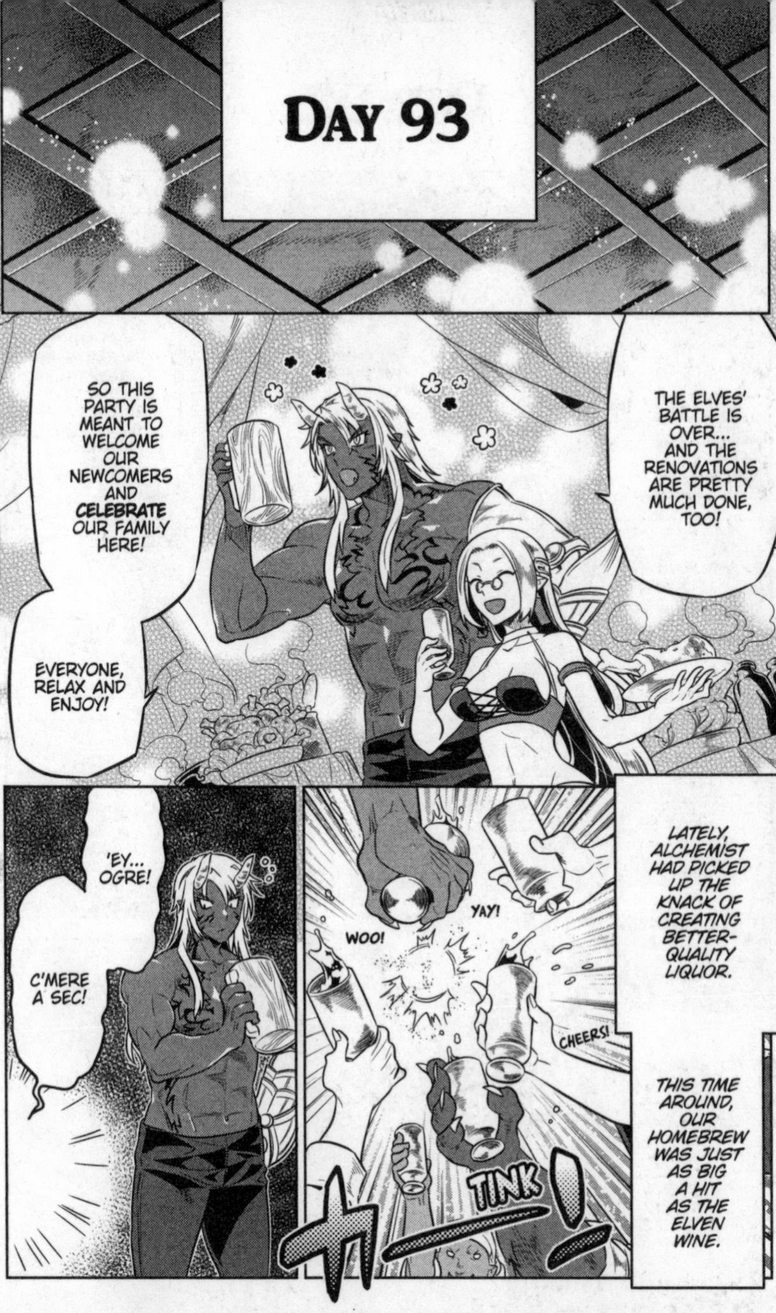
DAY 93
THE ELVES' BATTLE IS OVER... AND THE RENOVATIONS ARE PRETTY MUCH DONE, TOO!
SO THIS PARTY IS MEANT TO WELCOME OUR NEWCOMERS AND **CELEBRATE** OUR FAMILY HERE!
EVERYONE, RELAX AND ENJOY!
LATELY, ALCHEMIST HAD PICKED UP THE KNACK OF CREATING BETTER-QUALITY LIQUOR.
THIS TIME AROUND, OUR HOMEBREW WAS JUST AS BIG A HIT AS THE ELVEN WINE.
YAY!
WOO!
CHEERS!
TINK
'EY... OGRE!
C'MERE A SEC!

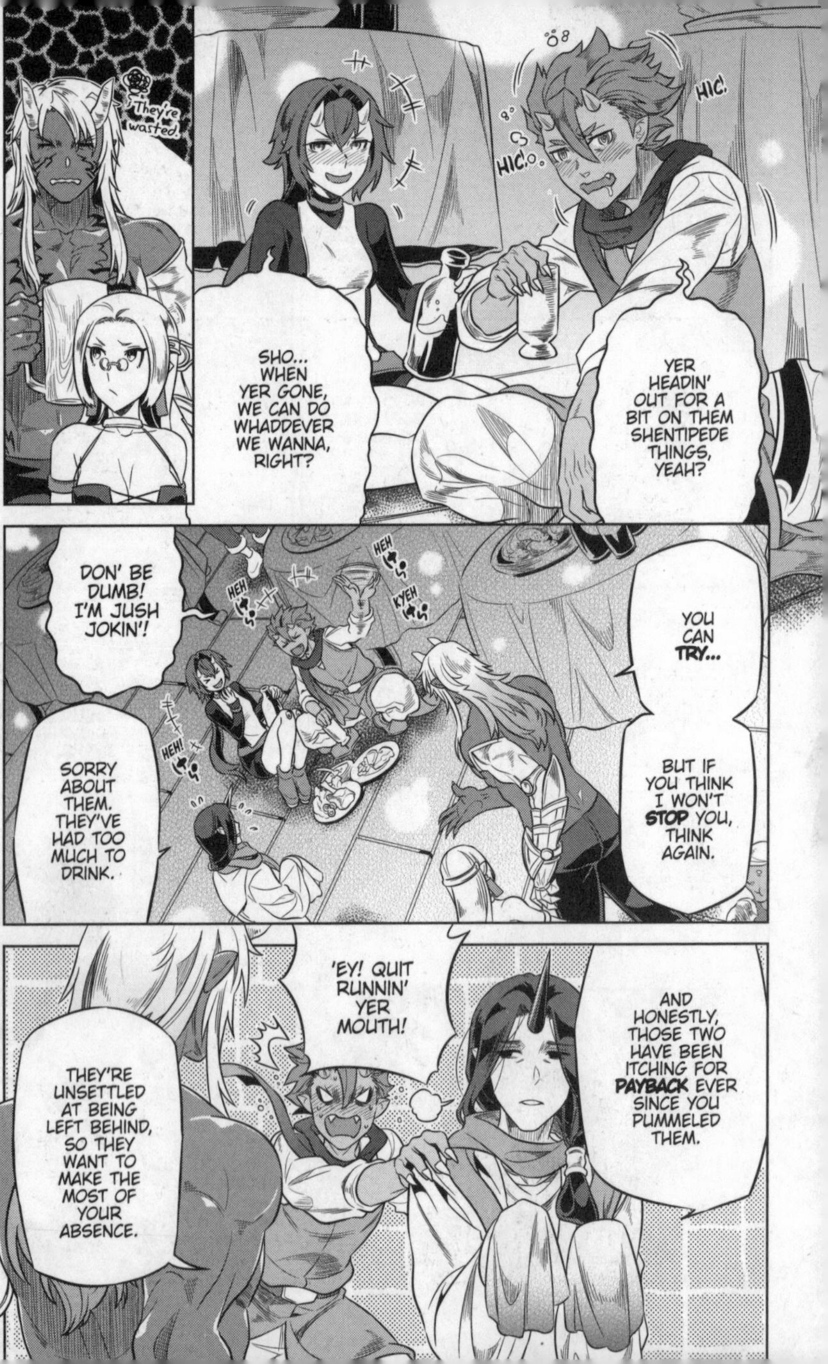
HIC!
HIC!
YER HEADIN' OUT FOR A BIT ON THEM SHENTIPEDE THINGS, YEAH?
SHO... WHEN YER GONE, WE CAN DO WHADDEVER WE WANNA, RIGHT?
They're wasted.
YOU CAN TRY...
BUT IF YOU THINK I WON'T STOP YOU, THINK AGAIN.
KYEH
HEH
HEH
DON' BE DUMB! I'M JUSH JOKIN'!
HEH!
SORRY ABOUT THEM. THEY'VE HAD TOO MUCH TO DRINK.
AND HONESTLY, THOSE TWO HAVE BEEN ITCHING FOR PAYBACK EVER SINCE YOU PUMMELED THEM.
'EY! QUIT RUNNIN' YER MOUTH!
THEY'RE UNSETTLED AT BEING LEFT BEHIND, SO THEY WANT TO MAKE THE MOST OF YOUR ABSENCE.

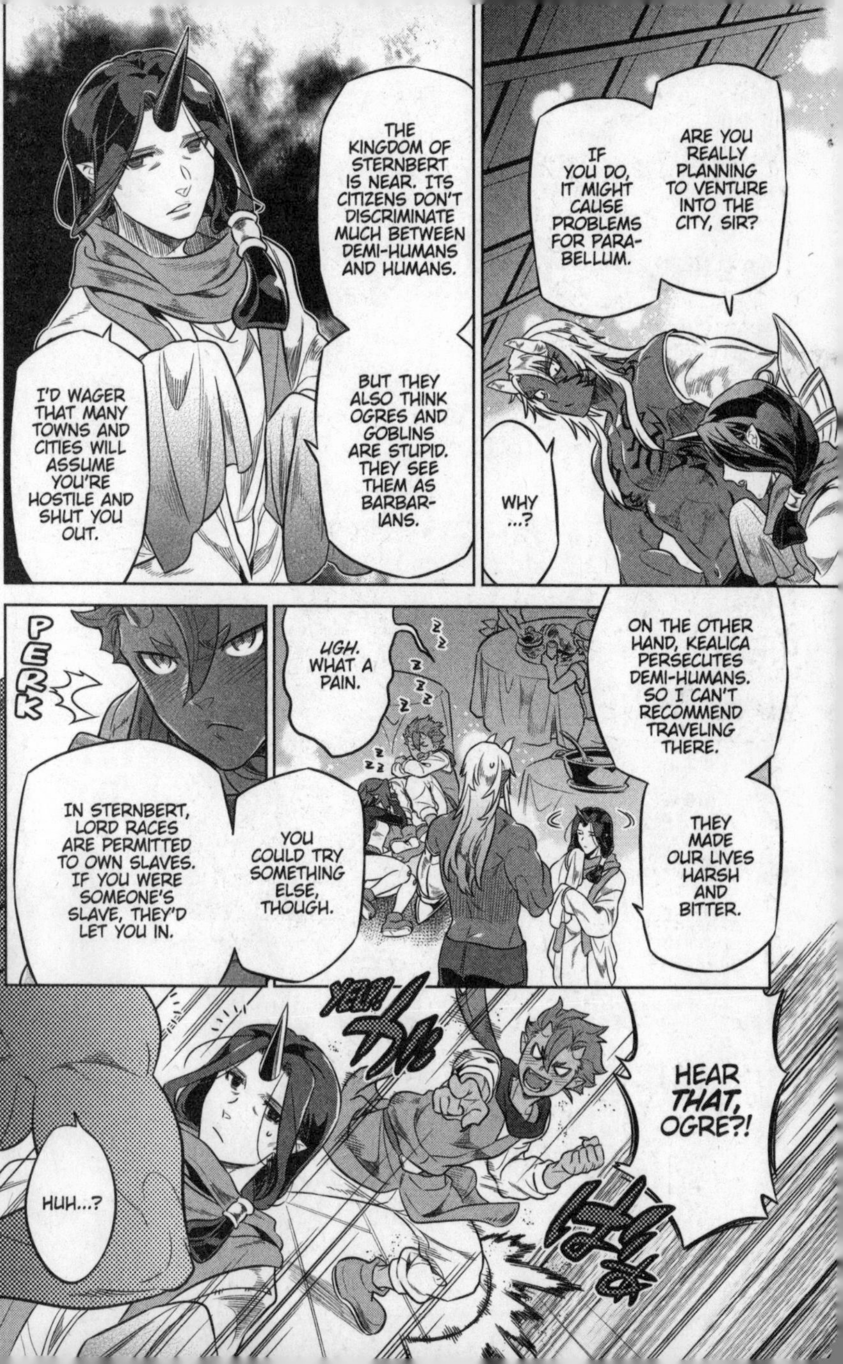
ARE YOU REALLY PLANNING TO VENTURE INTO THE CITY, SIR?
IF YOU DO, IT MIGHT CAUSE PROBLEMS FOR PARA-BELLUM.
WHY ...?
THE KINGDOM OF STERNBERT IS NEAR. ITS CITIZENS DON'T DISCRIMINATE MUCH BETWEEN DEMI-HUMANS AND HUMANS.
BUT THEY ALSO THINK OGRES AND GOBLINS ARE STUPID. THEY SEE THEM AS BARBAR-IANS.
I'D WAGER THAT MANY TOWNS AND CITIES WILL ASSUME YOU'RE HOSTILE AND SHUT YOU OUT.
ON THE OTHER HAND, KEALICA PERSECUTES DEMI-HUMANS. SO I CAN'T RECOMMEND TRAVELING THERE.
THEY MADE OUR LIVES HARSH AND BITTER.
UGH. WHAT A PAIN.
PERK
YOU COULD TRY SOMETHING ELSE, THOUGH.
IN STERNBERT, LORD RACES ARE PERMITTED TO OWN SLAVES. IF YOU WERE SOMEONE'S SLAVE, THEY'D LET YOU IN.
HEAR THAT, OGRE?!
YEAH!
HUH...?

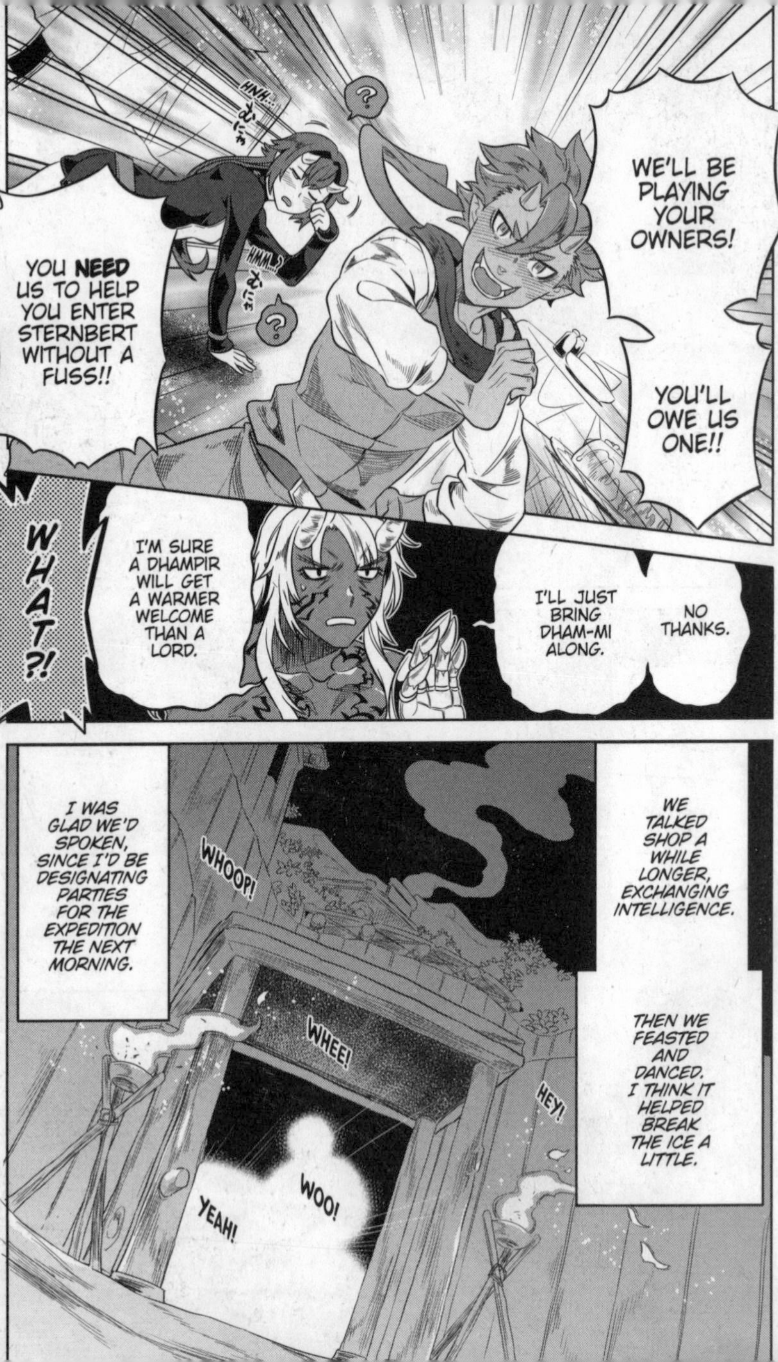
WE'LL BE PLAYING YOUR OWNERS!
YOU'LL OWE US ONE!!
HNH...
?
HMM...?
?
YOU **NEED** US TO HELP YOU ENTER STERNBERT WITHOUT A FUSS!!
NO THANKS.
I'LL JUST BRING DHAM-MI ALONG.
I'M SURE A DHAMPIR WILL GET A WARMER WELCOME THAN A LORD.
WHAT?!
WE TALKED SHOP A WHILE LONGER, EXCHANGING INTELLIGENCE.
THEN WE FEASTED AND DANCED. I THINK IT HELPED BREAK THE ICE A LITTLE.
HEY!
WHEE!
WHOOP!
I WAS GLAD WE'D SPOKEN, SINCE I'D BE DESIGNATING PARTIES FOR THE EXPEDITION THE NEXT MORNING.
WOO!
YEAH!

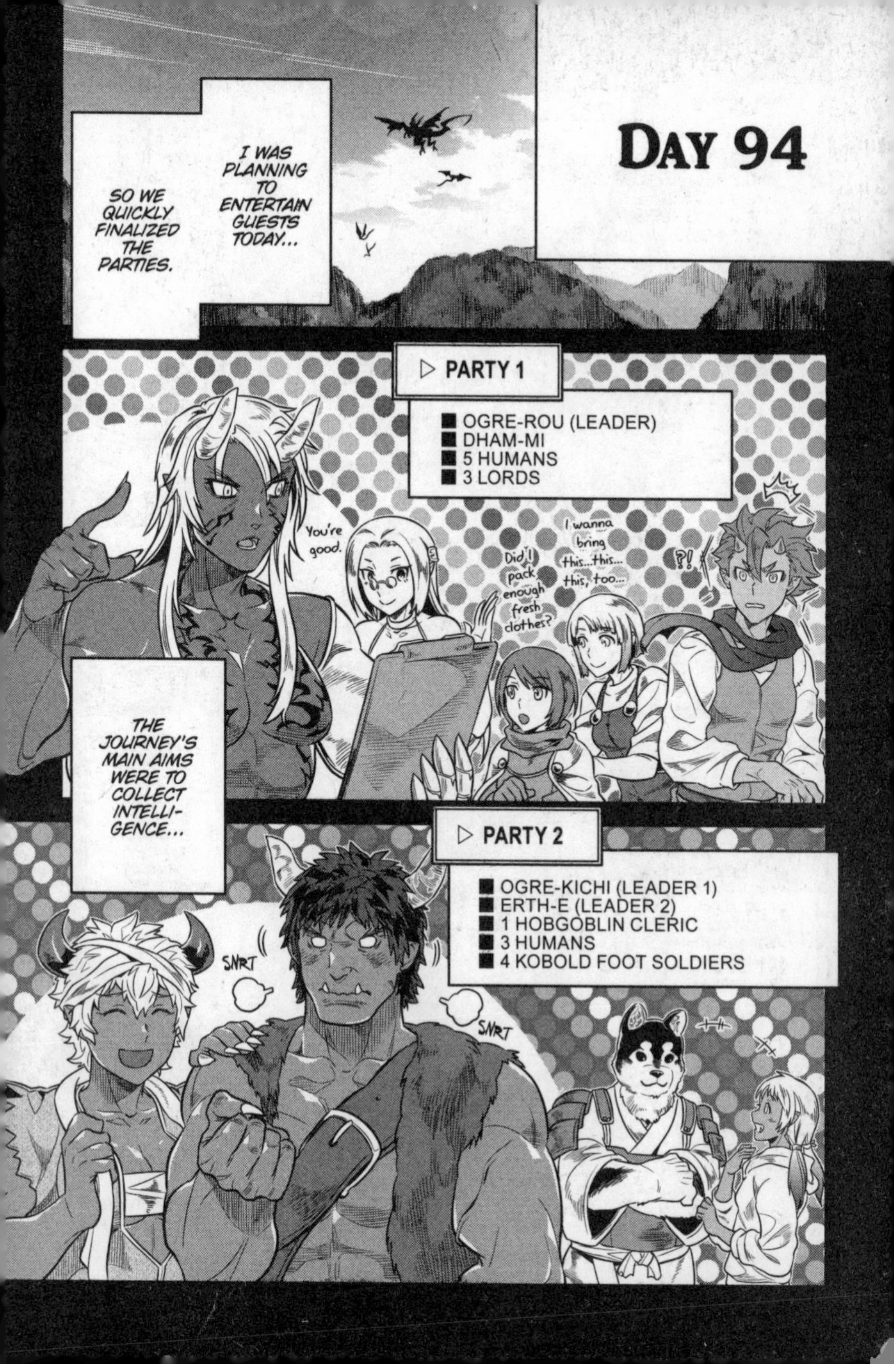
DAY 94
I WAS PLANNING TO ENTERTAIN GUESTS TODAY...
SO WE QUICKLY FINALIZED THE PARTIES.
▷ PARTY 1
■ OGRE-ROU (LEADER)
■ DHAM-MI
■ 5 HUMANS
■ 3 LORDS
?!
I wanna bring this... this... this, too...
Did I pack enough fresh clothes?
You're good.
THE JOURNEY'S MAIN AIMS WERE TO COLLECT INTELLI-GENCE...
▷ PARTY 2
■ OGRE-KICHI (LEADER 1)
■ ERTH-E (LEADER 2)
■ 1 HOBGOBLIN CLERIC
■ 3 HUMANS
■ 4 KOBOLD FOOT SOLDIERS
SNRT
SNRT

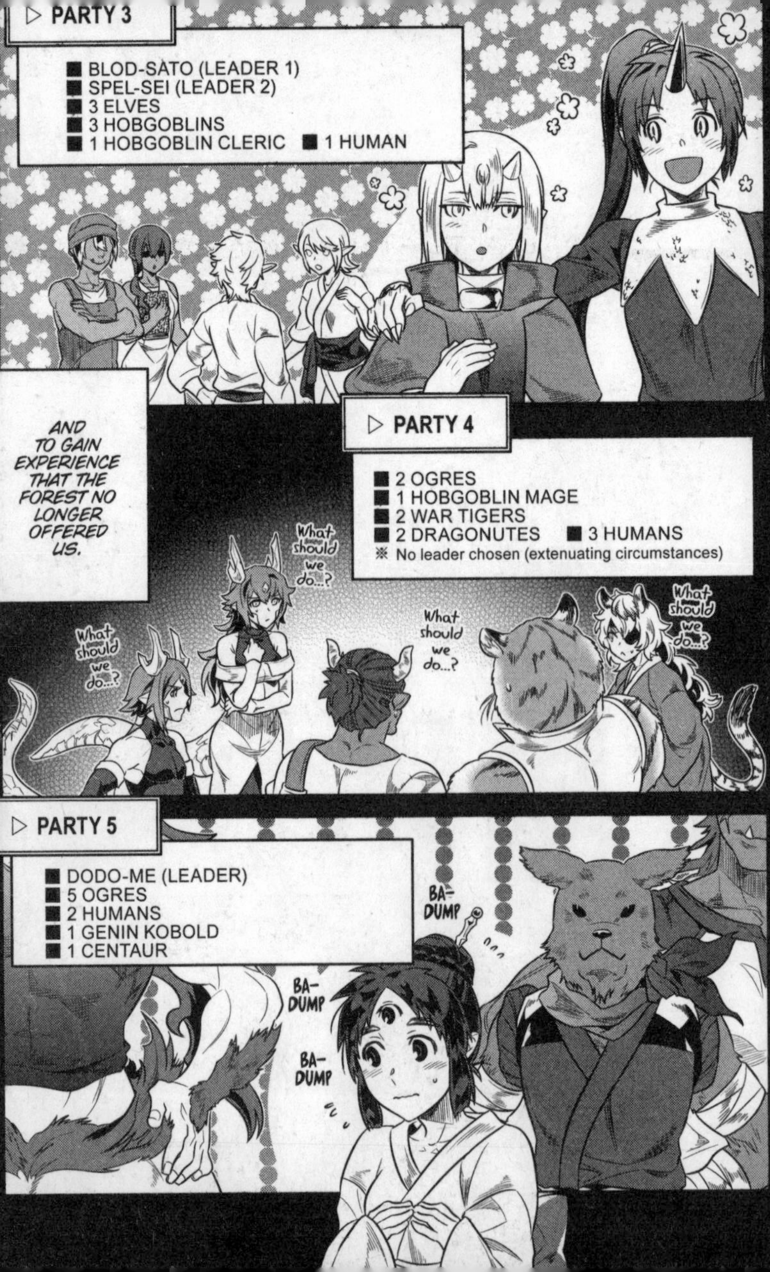

▷ PARTY 3
■ BLOD-SATO (LEADER 1)
■ SPEL-SEI (LEADER 2)
■ 3 ELVES
■ 3 HOBGOBLINS
■ 1 HOBGOBLIN CLERIC ■ 1 HUMAN
AND TO GAIN EXPERIENCE THAT THE FOREST NO LONGER OFFERED US.
▷ PARTY 4
■ 2 OGRES
■ 1 HOBGOBLIN MAGE
■ 2 WAR TIGERS
■ 2 DRAGONUTES ■ 3 HUMANS
※ No leader chosen (extenuating circumstances)
What should we do...?
What should we do...?
What should we do...?
What should we do...?
▷ PARTY 5
■ DODO-ME (LEADER)
■ 5 OGRES
■ 2 HUMANS
■ 1 GENIN KOBOLD
■ 1 CENTAUR
BA-DUMP
BA-DUMP
BA-DUMP

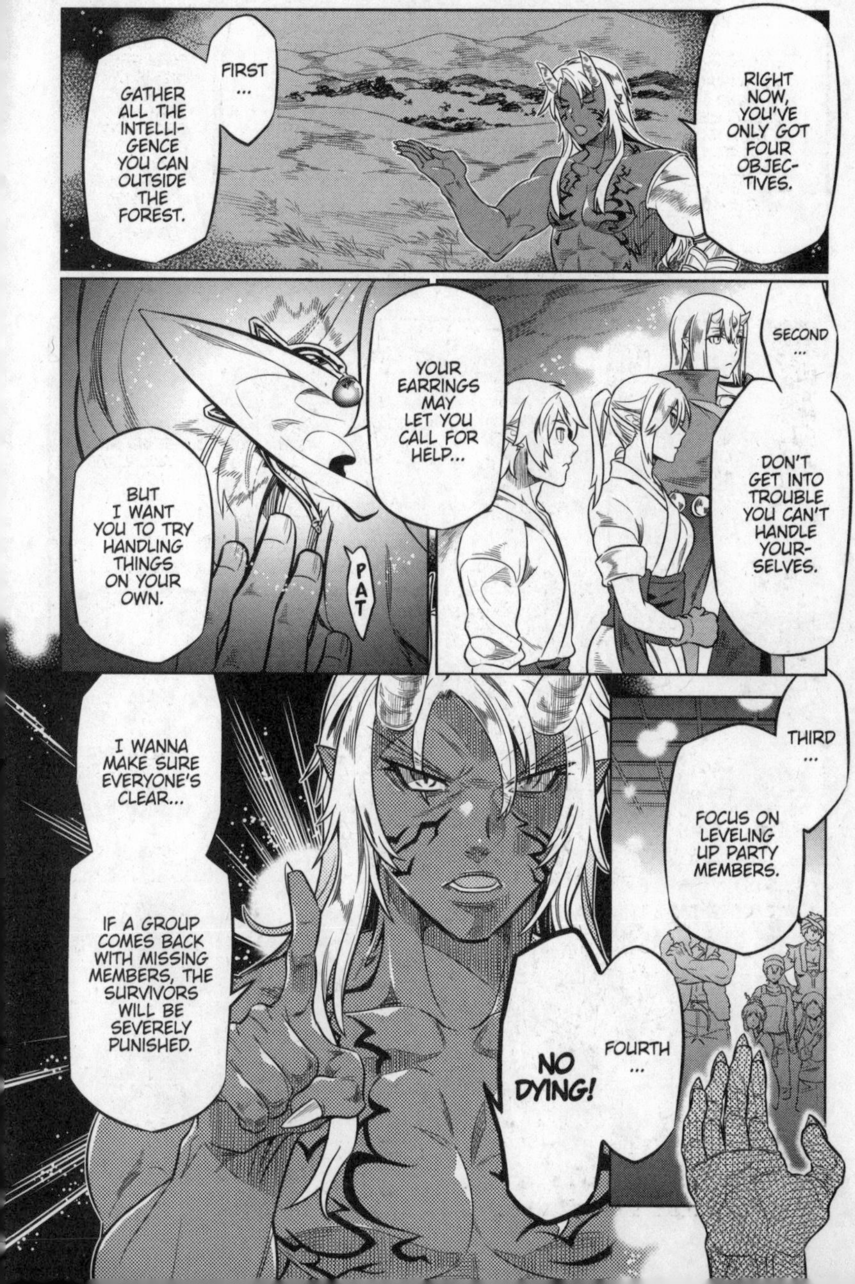
RIGHT NOW, YOU'VE ONLY GOT FOUR OBJECTIVES.
FIRST ...
GATHER ALL THE INTELLIGENCE YOU CAN OUTSIDE THE FOREST.
SECOND ...
DON'T GET INTO TROUBLE YOU CAN'T HANDLE YOURSELVES.
YOUR EARRINGS MAY LET YOU CALL FOR HELP...
PAT
BUT I WANT YOU TO TRY HANDLING THINGS ON YOUR OWN.
THIRD ...
FOCUS ON LEVELING UP PARTY MEMBERS.
FOURTH ...
NO DYING!
I WANNA MAKE SURE EVERYONE'S CLEAR...
IF A GROUP COMES BACK WITH MISSING MEMBERS, THE SURVIVORS WILL BE SEVERELY PUNISHED.

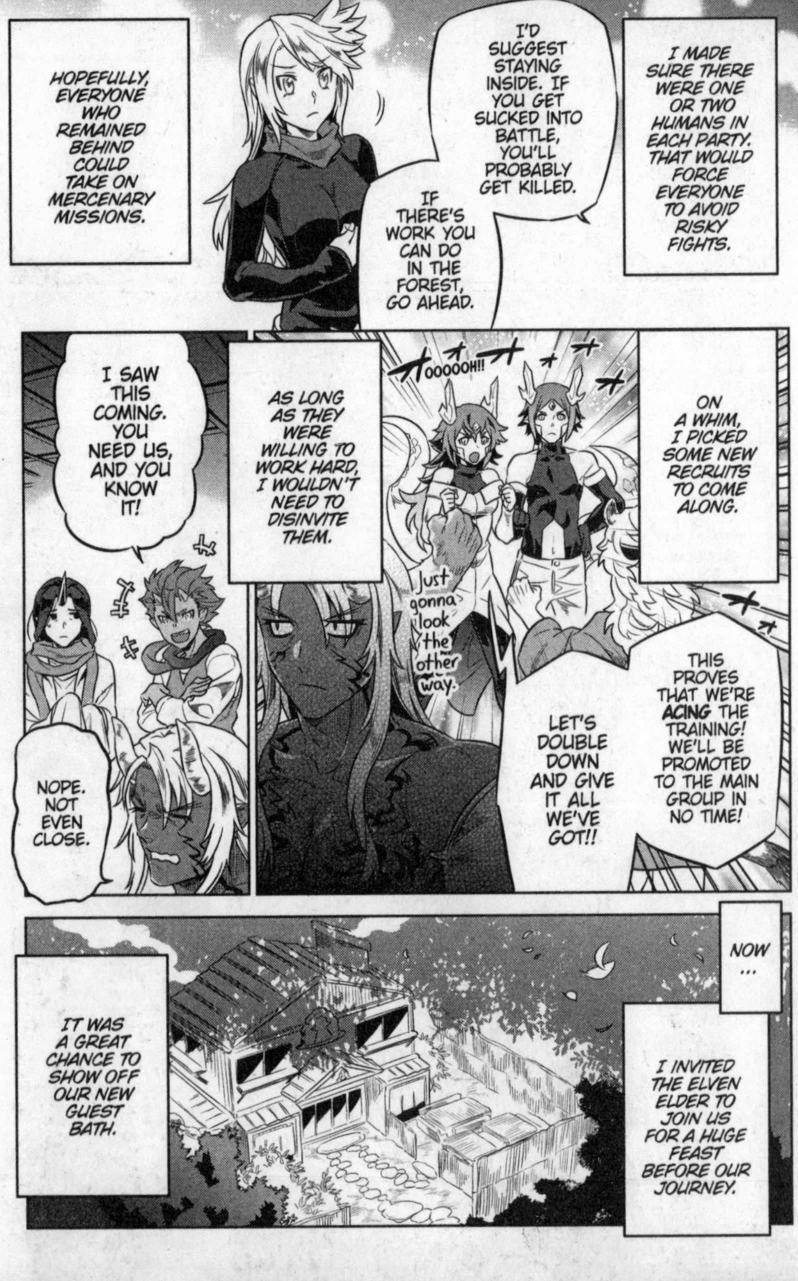

I MADE SURE THERE WERE ONE OR TWO HUMANS IN EACH PARTY. THAT WOULD FORCE EVERYONE TO AVOID RISKY FIGHTS.
I'D SUGGEST STAYING INSIDE. IF YOU GET SUCKED INTO BATTLE, YOU'LL PROBABLY GET KILLED.
IF THERE'S WORK YOU CAN DO IN THE FOREST, GO AHEAD.
HOPEFULLY, EVERYONE WHO REMAINED BEHIND COULD TAKE ON MERCENARY MISSIONS.
ON A WHIM, I PICKED SOME NEW RECRUITS TO COME ALONG.
OOOOOOH!!
THIS PROVES THAT WE'RE ACING THE TRAINING! WE'LL BE PROMOTED TO THE MAIN GROUP IN NO TIME!
LET'S DOUBLE DOWN AND GIVE IT ALL WE'VE GOT!!
Just gonna look the other way.
AS LONG AS THEY WERE WILLING TO WORK HARD, I WOULDN'T NEED TO DISINVITE THEM.
I SAW THIS COMING. YOU NEED US, AND YOU KNOW IT!
NOPE. NOT EVEN CLOSE.
NOW ...
I INVITED THE ELVEN ELDER TO JOIN US FOR A HUGE FEAST BEFORE OUR JOURNEY.
IT WAS A GREAT CHANCE TO SHOW OFF OUR NEW GUEST BATH.

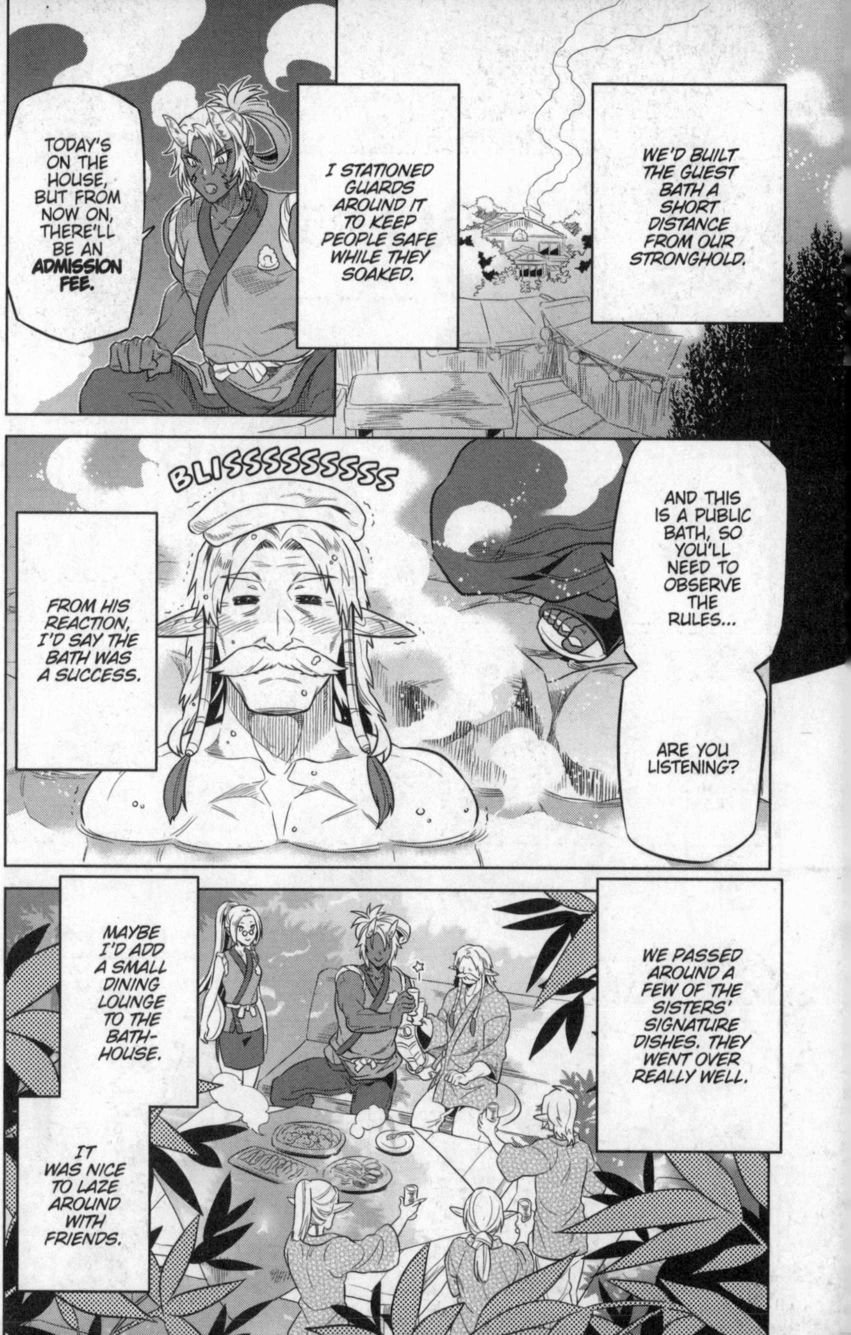
WE'D BUILT THE GUEST BATH A SHORT DISTANCE FROM OUR STRONGHOLD.
I STATIONED GUARDS AROUND IT TO KEEP PEOPLE SAFE WHILE THEY SOAKED.
TODAY'S ON THE HOUSE, BUT FROM NOW ON, THERE'LL BE AN **ADMISSION FEE.**
AND THIS IS A PUBLIC BATH, SO YOU'LL NEED TO OBSERVE THE RULES... ARE YOU LISTENING?
BLISSSSSSSSSS
FROM HIS REACTION, I'D SAY THE BATH WAS A SUCCESS.
WE PASSED AROUND A FEW OF THE SISTERS' SIGNATURE DISHES. THEY WENT OVER REALLY WELL.
MAYBE I'D ADD A SMALL DINING LOUNGE TO THE BATH-HOUSE.
IT WAS NICE TO LAZE AROUND WITH FRIENDS.

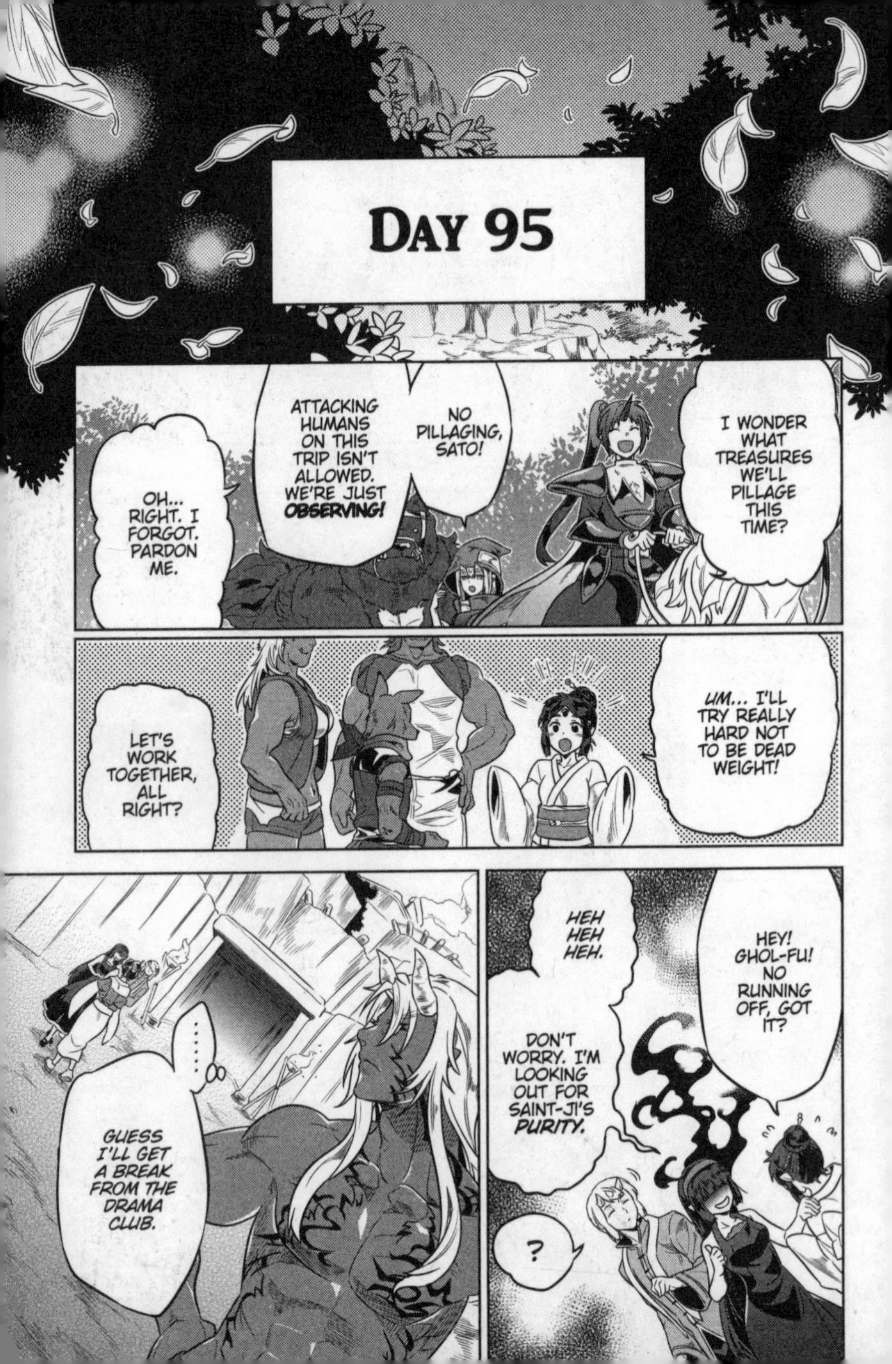
DAY 95
I WONDER WHAT TREASURES WE'LL PILLAGE THIS TIME?
NO PILLAGING, SATO!
ATTACKING HUMANS ON THIS TRIP ISN'T ALLOWED. WE'RE JUST **OBSERVING!**
OH... RIGHT. I FORGOT. PARDON ME.
UM... I'LL TRY REALLY HARD NOT TO BE DEAD WEIGHT!
LET'S WORK TOGETHER, ALL RIGHT?
HEY! GHOL-FU! NO RUNNING OFF, GOT IT?
HEH HEH HEH.
DON'T WORRY. I'M LOOKING OUT FOR SAINT-JI'S *PURITY.*
?
......
GUESS I'LL GET A BREAK FROM THE DRAMA CLUB.

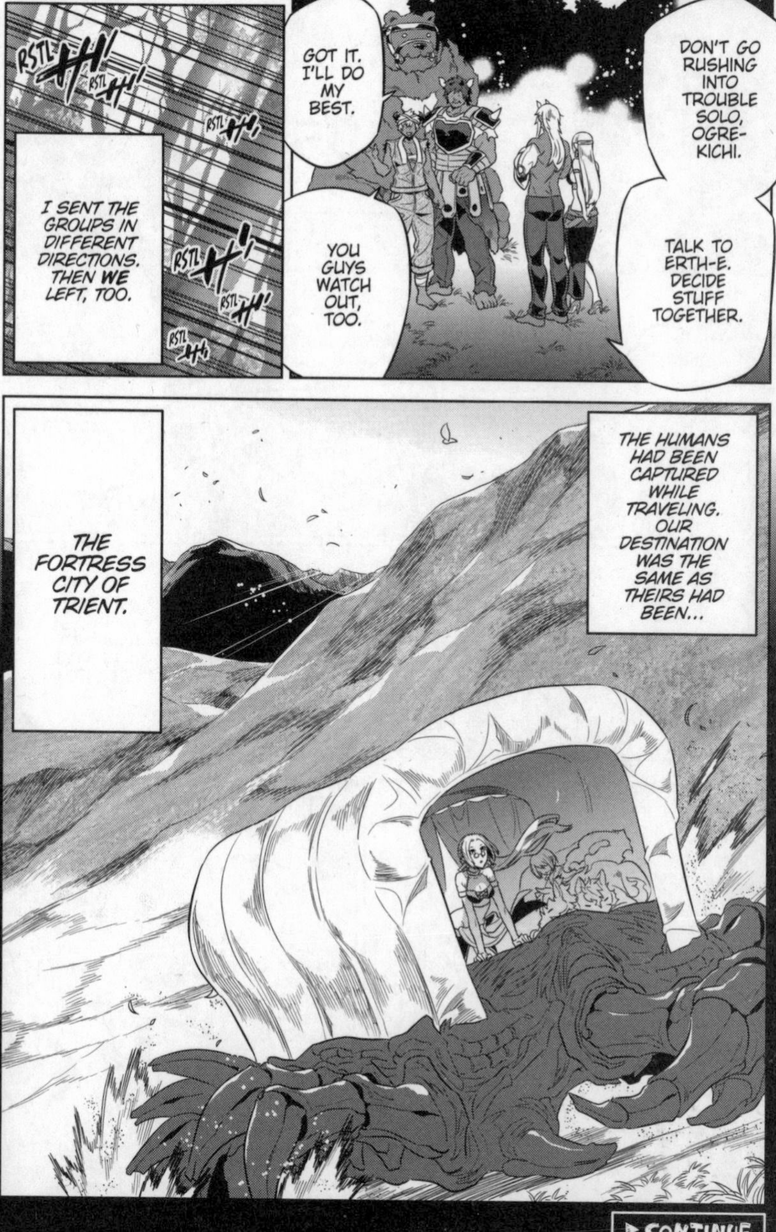
DON'T GO RUSHING INTO TROUBLE SOLO, OGRE-KICHI.
GOT IT. I'LL DO MY BEST.
TALK TO ERTH-E. DECIDE STUFF TOGETHER.
YOU GUYS WATCH OUT, TOO.
RSTL
RSTL
RSTL
I SENT THE GROUPS IN DIFFERENT DIRECTIONS. THEN WE LEFT, TOO.
RSTL
RSTL
RSTL
THE HUMANS HAD BEEN CAPTURED WHILE TRAVELING. OUR DESTINATION WAS THE SAME AS THEIRS HAD BEEN...
THE FORTRESS CITY OF TRIENT.

▶ CONTINUE

Re:Monster

4

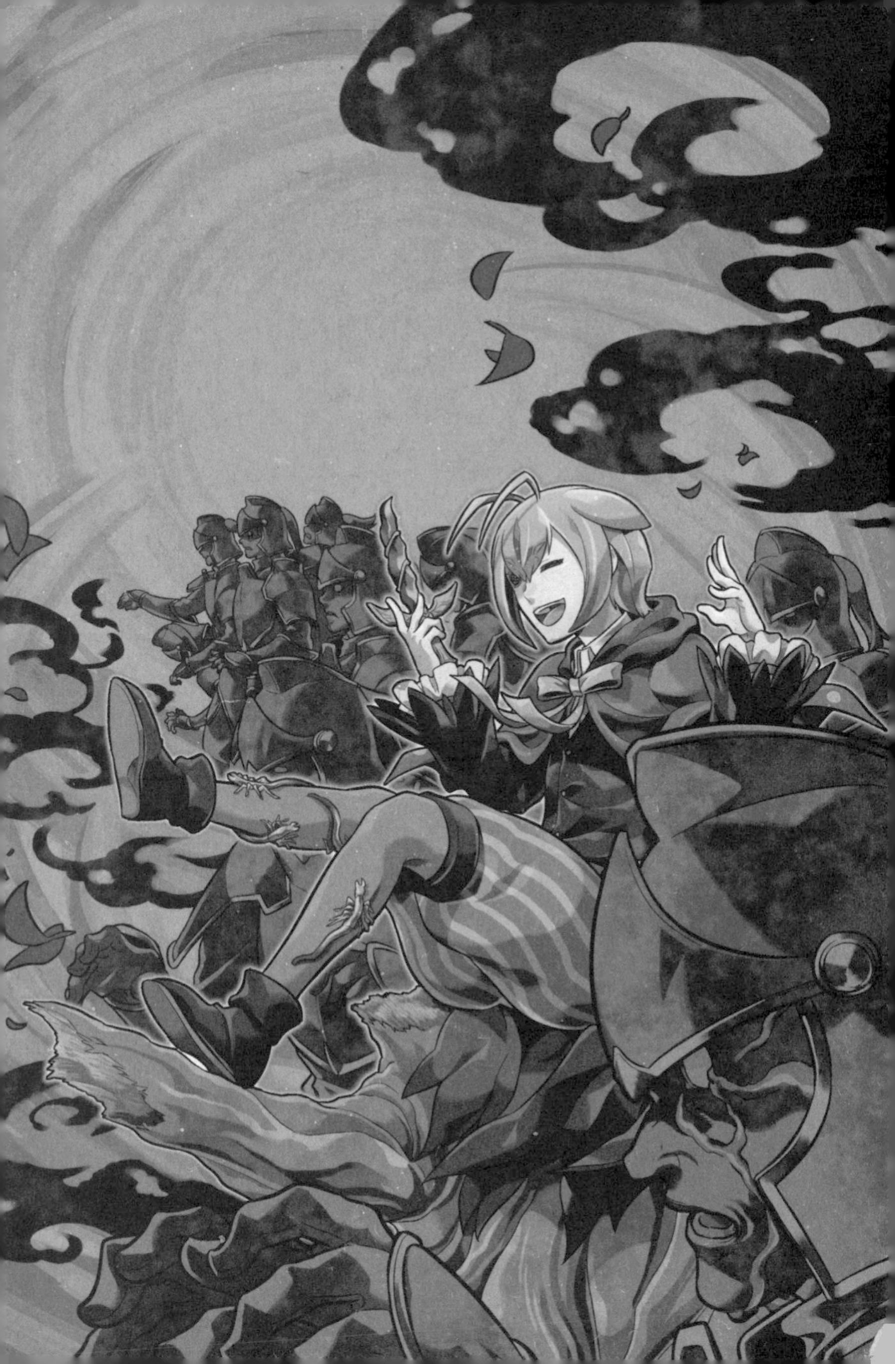

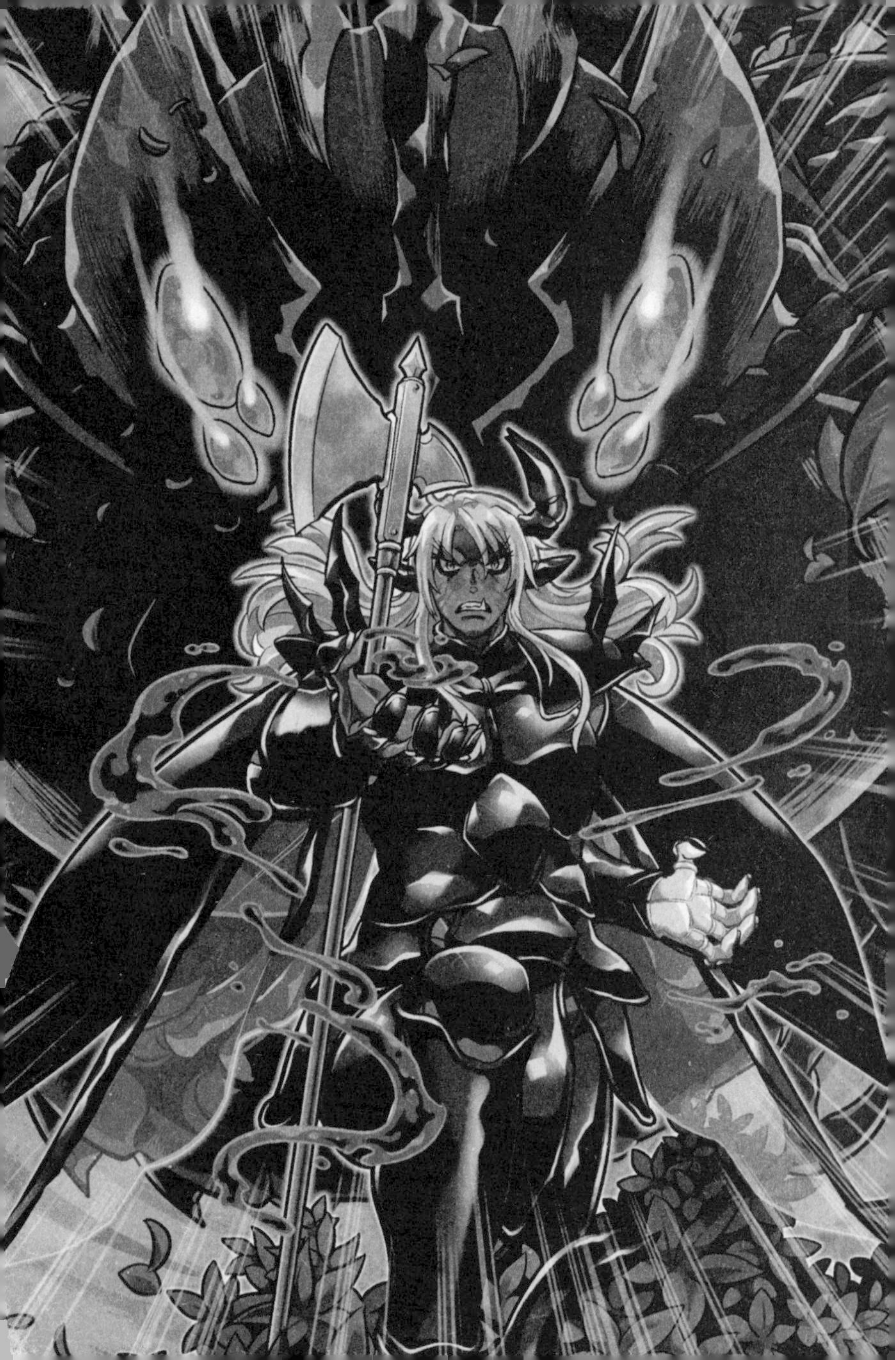

Re:Monster